HARVARD STUDIES IN ENGLISH
VOLUME XX

ENGLAND'S ELIZA

BY

ELKIN CALHOUN WILSON

Qui voudra figurer, d'vn ouurage parfect,
La beauté, la Vertu, l'Ornement, et les graces,
De Nature des Dieux, de l'vniuers, des Graces,
Accoure contempler la grand'ELIZABETH

HYMNE. *A tres-haute tres-puissante tres vertueuse et tres-magna-nime princesse, Elizabeth royne d'Angleterre, France, et Irelande. &c. Presentee a sa maiesté par . . . Georges de la Motthe, Gentil-homme Francoys.* 1586

Bodleian Library MS. Fr.e.1, fol. 7

ENGLAND'S ELIZA

BY

ELKIN CALHOUN WILSON

FRANK CASS & CO. LTD.
1966

Published in Great Britain by
FRANK CASS AND COMPANY LIMITED
10 Woburn Walk
London W. C. 1

C - 6191758-3

Printed in U.S.A.

To
MY MOTHER
AND THE MEMORY OF
MY FATHER

PREFACE

ENGLAND'S ELIZA is a study of the idealization of Queen Elizabeth in the poetry of her age. I have aligned various types of laudatory verse to show the nature of the idealization and its place in Elizabethan literature. The verse could not be exhaustive, but it is representative. My comment seeks to show that the concept of England's Eliza grew inevitably from the spirit of the age in happy conjunction with the unique character and achievement of its queen. It was not practicable to move beyond 1603 and see the tradition of Good Queen Bess arise. England's Eliza, however, appears as a vital symbol for imaginations which were nourished by medieval devotion, chivalric love, revived pagan idealism, new religious zeal, and profound patriotism.

I wish to thank Harvard University and the Folger Shakespeare Library for furthering my studies: a Dexter Travelling Fellowship in 1933 first made available for me the resources of English libraries, and a research fellowship in the Folger for 1936–1937 enabled me to finish my work amid ideal surroundings. Officers and attendants in the Harvard College Library have constantly aided me; those in the Bodleian Library and the British Museum have been very liberal of their time and service. The late Sir Leicester Harmsworth generously opened to me his library at Bexhill-on-Sea. I am also indebted to the University Library, Cambridge, the National Library of Wales, the Lambeth Palace Library, the Henry E. Huntington Library and Art Gallery, the Newberry Library, the Library of Congress, and the libraries of Cornell, Yale, and Northwestern universities.

My illustrations, as the list of them will reveal, have been made possible by kind permissions for reproduction which have come from the Bodleian Library, the Director of the Library of Harvard University, Col. F. J. B. Wingfield Digby, the Trustees of the British Museum, and the Lord Chamberlain's Office.

When I have reproduced titles directly from the original volumes, I have respected spelling and punctuation, reduced running capitals, and ignored italics. London is the place of publication of all books cited unless some other place is named.

Professor H. E. Rollins has, all along, befriended my book immeasurably, and my gratitude is great and abiding. For several years Professor G. L. Kittredge guided my studies with the kindness and wisdom that make him revered everywhere. Professor Robert Hillyer has my warm thanks for aid and encouragement. Dr. J. Q. Adams, Dr. G. E. Dawson, Miss Jenkins Smith — all of the Folger staff have been as kind and helpful as their library is rich and beautiful. My debt to many scholars, some of them generous friends, is suggested in the notes. But I should like to thank immediately for their various kindnesses: Professors Marjorie Hope Nicolson, J. S. P. Tatlock, J. B. Munn, J. W. Spargo, V. B. Heltzel, W. H. Irving, J. D. A. Ogilvy, A. W. Milden, D. H. Bishop, and Lane Cooper; also Miss Teener Hall, Mr. Evan D. Jones, Mr. and Mrs. F. L. Kent, Dr. Pierce Butler, and Dr. G. B. Harrison. As for my wife — only omnipotent Eliza could reward her.

E. C. W.

ITHACA, NEW YORK
November 21, 1938

CONTENTS

ILLUSTRATIONS

ENGLAND'S ELIZA

We intermeddle not with her description as she was a Sovereigne Prince, too high for our pen, and performed by others already, though not by any done so fully, but that still room is left for the endeavours of Posterity to adde thereunto. We consider her onely as she was a worthy Lady, her private virtues rendring her to the imitation, and her publick to the admiration of all. — "The Life of Queen Elizabeth," in Thomas Fuller's *The Holy State*, 1642

CHAPTER I

Judith in the Broadsides

THE SUBJECTS of Queen Elizabeth had imaginations which were half medieval. Their fathers had been long accustomed to traditional symbols for social, political, and religious ideals. Before those old symbols passed away the children warmed them into new and useful life. If apprehended with sympathy, their use of a hallowed inheritance keeps a singular beauty for men who have other gods nearer to the mind's desire, if not always, perhaps, to the heart's.

Queen Elizabeth came to symbolize for her people all they most loved. Her beauty, her talents, her wit and brilliance, and her virginity were distinctions magnified by success as a ruler for forty-four crucial years. Her character focused surviving medieval spirituality and courtly love, revived pagan myth, new religious ardor, and profound patriotism. The change from the actual queen and woman into the perfect sovereign and lady, Gloriana and Belphœbe, was indeed a fugitive dream in essence. I shall seek to show that the dream, however, is embalmed and treasured up in the books of the age with significance for anyone who would understand its poetry better.

I shall exhibit first the portrait of Queen Elizabeth that survives in the humble broadside ballads of her reign. Of almost no poetic worth in themselves, the broadsides do give a direct insight into the minds and hearts of her people. They show the concept of Gloriana taking form, to be expressed eventually by cultivated poets. Of course such artists applied refined colors to this vulgar press sketch of

Gloriana; but the secure base for their fine oils, often imported, was the humble drawing of the ballad-mongers.

The earliest appearance of Queen Elizabeth that I have discovered in the broadside ballads is that in *A Godly Psalme, of Marye Queene*, by Richard Beeard, 1553. Stanza 41 in this celebration of Mary Tudor runs:

> Lord saue our Queene moast graciouse
> From euel and from feare:
> The Lady eke Elizabeth,
> Her godly sister deare.[1]

So early do the ballads strike a dominant note in their song — Elizabeth as a "godly" lady to be God's special care.

Mary died a tragic figure. Her Spanish marriage had antagonized her people, as the ballads against it showed; she had lost Calais; and Protestant flames had only been fanned by her sadly misguided efforts to impose Catholicism on the realm. When her "sister deare" ascended the throne a shout of welcome rang throughout England, and the ballad-mongers did not fail to echo it. *A Songe betwene the Quene's Majestie and Englande* by William Birch voices this loving welcome with a simple charm. England and "Bessy" appear in dialogue:

> E. Come over the born Bessy,
> Come over the born Bessy,
> Swete Bessey come over to me;
> And I will thé take,
> And my dere Lady make
> Before all other that ever I see.
>
> B. My thinke I hear a voice,
> At whom I do rejoyce,
> And aunswer thé now I shall: —
> Tel me, I say,

---

[1] *Fugitive Tracts*, first series, 1493–1600, ed. W. C. Hazlitt, 1875, no. 18.

What art thou that biddes me com away,
And so earnestly doost me call?

E.   I am thy lover faire,
    Hath chose thé to mine heir,
And my name is mery Englande;
    Therefore, come away,
    And make no more delaye,
Swete Bessie! give me thy hande.

B.   Here is my hand,
    My dere lover Englande,
I am thine both with mind and hart,
    For ever to endure,
    Thou maiest be sure,
Untill death us two do part.

E.   Lady, this long space
    Have I loved thy grace,
More then I durste well saye;
    Hoping, at the last,
    When all stormes were past,
For to see this joyfull daye.

The lovers bemoan their long separation and "Bessy's" tribulations before she reached the throne; but she will forgive the enemies that wronged her because they suspected that she "was not of their religion." She will forgive

    Al such as do live,
If they wil hereafter amend;
    And for those that are gone,
    God forgeve them every one,
And his mercy on them extend!

.   .   .   .   .   .

E.   Oh, swete virgin pure!
    Longe may ye endure
To reigne over us in this lande:

For your workes do accord,
Ye are the handmaid of the Lord,
For he hath blessed you with his hand.[2]

At the outset of Elizabeth's long reign there is this testimony in the ballads to the understanding between queen
and people. Favorite notes are sounded: God has brought
her to the throne in spite of all foes; His daughter will
graciously forgive them; she is a "swete virgin pure," the
blessed "handmaid of the Lord." This simple song of devotion which greeted "Bessy" never wholly died out.
And for it she kept always a sensitive ear, however far she
wandered in political labyrinths.

Already Elizabeth's good is identified with the success
of the Protestant faith. The ardent embrace that the early
ballads give her is probably both the expression of a people
weary of the bloodshed and turmoil of Mary's reign and
the maneuver of its Protestant leaders to win the allegiance
of a circumspect politician. Their embrace will prove a
diplomatic embarrassment at times, but at the beginning
of her reign Elizabeth knows its value in establishing her
security.

[2] *The Harleian Miscellany*, ed. William Oldys and Thomas Park, X (1813),
260–262. See a curious piece of seven stanzas, called *Queen Elizabeth's Rejoycing*,
in which the queen expresses her joy on coming to the crown (*Ballads from Manuscripts*, ed. F. J. Furnivall and W. R. Morfill, II [1873], 112–113). The fourth
stanza of the *Songe* associates itself with two dramatic episodes in the queen's
reign. In 1559 the Lower House urged the wisdom of marriage. Elizabeth drew
off her coronation ring and declared: "*yea, to satisfie you, I have already ioyned
my selfe in marriage to an husband, namely, the Kingdome of* England. *And behold
(said she, which I marvaile ye have forgotten,) the pledge of this my wedlocke and
marriage with my Kingdome,* . . . And doe not (*saith she*) upbraid me with miserable lacke of *children: for every one of you, and as many as are Englishmen, are
children, and kinsmen to me: Of whom if God deprive me not, (which God forbid) I
cannot without iniury be accompted barraine*" (William Camden, *Annals, or, the
historie of the most renowned and Victorious Princesse Elizabeth*, 3d ed., 1635,
p. 16). When that ring was filed off her finger a short time before her death because "it was so growne into the flesh, that it could not be drawne off," it "was
taken as a sad presage, as if it portended that that marriage with her Kingdome
contracted by the Ring, would be dissolved" (p. 584).

Thomas Brice voices this Protestant enthusiasm for the new queen in 1559 in a history of Protestant martyrs month by month from 1555 to that blessed November 17 when "GOD sent us our ELIZABETH." [3] Each stanza of his clumsy doggerel concludes with "We wished for our ELIZABETH," or its equivalent, after a series of *when*'s that chronicle Protestant sacrifices. Further testifying to Protestant enthusiasm for the queen in 1559 is John Awdelay's *The wonders of England.* It is a brief review of English history since 1553, when God, as punishment for the sins of the land, took away good King Edward. The people and Elizabeth herself suffered sorely in darkness and persecution under Mary until God relented and sent the savior "by God nowe Quene."

> With that the skies their hue did change,
> And light out-shone in darkenes steede;
> Up, said this God with voice not strange,
> Elizabeth, thys realme nowe guyde!
> My wyll in thee doo not thou hyde,
> And vermine darke let not abyde
> In thys thy land!
> Straightway the people out dyd cry, —
> Praysed be God and God saue thee,
> Quene of England! [4]

At this time [5] the spirit moved Richard Mulcaster to send Elizabeth *A newe Ballade* warning her against the hostile designs of the Catholic party. In it he recites the history of her "progenitours," especially as they had been tricked by an unscrupulous clergy; Henry VIII cleaned house only for the "wicked priestes" to deceive "King Edward, which

---

[3] *An English Garner,* ed. Edward Arber, Birmingham, IV (1882), 154–169.

[4] *A Collection of Seventy-Nine Black-Letter Ballads and Broadsides,* pub. Joseph Lilly, 1870, p. 97. In placing this ballad I follow H. E. Rollins, *A History of the English Black-Letter Broadside Ballad,* an unpublished Harvard University thesis, 1917, p. 150.

[5] Rollins, p. 91.

was a good and vertuous child," and completely bring in
again the "Romyshe lore" under Mary. The first and last
stanzas will suggest the spirit of the whole:

O dere Lady Elysabeth, which art our right and vertous Quene,
   God hath endued the w^t mercy and fayth, as by thy workes it
     may be sene,
Wherefore, good Quene, I counsayle thee, Lady, Lady,
   For to beware of the spiritualtie, most dere Lady.

     .   .   .   .

Then God sent vs your noble Grace, as in dede it was highe tyme,
   Whiche dothe all Popery cleane deface, and set vs forth God's
     trewe deuine, —
For whome we are all bound to praye, Lady, Lady,
   Longe life to raigne bothe night and day, moste dere Ladye.[6]

More venturesome is the somewhat equivocal compliment
in *Other thus it is, or thus it shoulde bee.*[7] The description
of a perfect state of things in stanza after stanza ends always with a qualifying refrain, "Other thus it is, or thus it
shoulde bee." So are the defects of contemporary society
suggested. The ballad is something of a warning to the
people and to the queen in the early years before her government had proved itself to the greater part of the popu-
lation, which was ready to join the political party that
fortune prospered. It concludes with a prayer that looks
forward to achievement with God's aid more than back
upon it.

   Sometimes the balladist sings of Elizabeth the lady, but
even then she tends to turn into God's royal handmaid.
Representative no doubt of much early celebration of which
one can only get tantalizing echoes, is the title of a lost
ballad, *In the prayse of worthy ladyes here in by name and
espesyally o^r quene Elysabeth so worthy of fame*, entered by

   [6] Lilly, pp. 30–32.
   [7] Pages 247–250.

"Tho. Hackett" in 1561–62.[8] Perhaps *A Strife betwene Appelles and Pigmalion*, entered in 1565–66,[9] affords a fair idea of how the "worthiest lady" was praised in even these early years. In it Bernard Garter feigns a contest between the two artists for superiority. Pigmalion forms a statue of a woman of such surpassing beauty that Dame Nature takes it away, gives it life, and restores it to earth as Queen Elizabeth.

> Lorde! yf Appelles now did know,
>   Or yf Pigmalion once should heare,
> Of this their worke the worthie show,
>   Since Nature gaue it life to beare;
> No doubt at all her worthie prayse
> Those selie Grekes from death wold rayse.
>
> Then those that daylie see her grace,
>   Whose vertue passeth euerie wight, —
> Her comelie corps, her christall face, —
>   They ought to pray, both day and night,
> That God may graunt most happie state
> Vnto that Princesse and her mate.[10]

Yet it is Elizabeth the queen who most inspires the balladist. One of the few ballads of poetic distinction is about her. A "'pycture of quene Elyzabeth' was entered to Gyles Godhed on the books of the Stationers' Company, 1562–3."[11] Below this picture were the following verses:

> Loe here the pearle,
>   Whom God and man doth loue:
> Loe here on earth
>   The onely starre of light:

---

[8] H. E. Rollins, *An Analytical Index to the Ballad-Entries (1557–1709) in the Registers of the Company of Stationers of London*, Chapel Hill, N. C., 1924, no. 1245. Numbers hereafter refer to this *Index*.

[9] No. 91, where the piece I quote is identified with *A songe of Appelles with an other Dytty*, entered to Alex. Lacy in this year.

[10] Lilly, p. 153.

[11] Page 281.

Loe here the queene,
　　Whom no mishap can moue
To chaunge her mynde
　　From vertues chief delight!
Loe here the heart
　　That so hath honord God,
That, for her loue,
　　We feele not of his rod:
Pray for her health,
　　Such as good subiectes bee:
Oh Princely Dame,
　　There is none like to thee! [12]

In this humble broadside the popular view of Elizabeth is expressed with an appealing sincerity that should give pause to the critic who would dismiss praise of the queen as mere lip-service exacted by an inordinately vain woman. So early in the reign does the queen emerge as a legendary figure in verse written for the English common folk.

Prayers for Elizabeth, formal and incidental, are constant in the celebration of her in the broadsides. They show a people always anxious to have God's care for their queen. The conventional custom of praying for the sovereign will not finally account for their number and for their sincerity. Many such prayers which I cannot tarry to illustrate [13] are paralleled in the quotations I do present.

[12] Pages 36–37. The original broadside is in the British Museum (Huth 50.[28.]).

[13] See, before 1569 and roughly chronological, broadside prayers and allusions in a *Catalogue of a Collection of Printed Broadsides in the Possession of the Society of Antiquaries of London*, ed. Robert Lemon, 1866, p. 18; *Ballads and Broadsides Chiefly of the Elizabethan Period*, ed. H. L. Collmann, Oxford, 1912, p. 23; Lilly, p. 172; Collmann, pp. 26, 255; Lilly, p. 104; and *Old English Ballads 1553–1625*, ed. H. E. Rollins, Cambridge, 1920, p. 284.

I should like to emphasize the importance of the countless prayers, formal and incidental, for Elizabeth as God's chosen queen by citing a few of them in various books printed during the reign. Notable prayers appear in the following volumes: Anthony Anderson, *An Approved Medicine against the deserued Plague*, 1593, sigs. B2–B3; *Orations, of Arsanes agaynst Philip the trecherous kyng of*

As has been seen, Elizabeth's triumph over all foes in reaching the throne impressed Englishmen during the early years of her reign. Now, with an equilibrium in her government established, she meets a test of its security in the

---

Macedone, [1560?], sigs. A2ᵛ–A3; Stephen Bateman, *The Doome Warning all Men to the Judgemente*, 1581, sig. Ee8; Edward Dering, *Godlie Priuate Praiers, for Householders to meditate vppon, and to saye in theyr Families*, 1580, sigs. E6ᵛ–E8ᵛ; John Field, *Godly Prayers and Meditations*, 1601, sigs. H7–I3ᵛ; William Lightfoot, *The Complaint of England*, 1587, sigs. I2–I2ᵛ; *A fourme of common prayer . . . necessarie for the present tyme and state*, [1572], sig. B2ᵛ; *A fourme of Prayer, necessary for the time and state*, 1588, sigs. C3ᵛ–C4; *An Order for Prayer and Thankes-giuing (necessary to be vsed in these dangerous times) for the safetie and preseruation of her Maiesty and this realme*, 1594, sigs. C4–C4ᵛ; I. or J. S., *The Pitiful estate of the Time present*, 1564, sigs. D6ᵛ–D7; Salvianus, *A second and third blast of retrait from plaies and Theaters*, 1580, sigs. I5ᵛ–I6; *The Sinner's Sacrifice. Certeine prayers and godly meditatyons very nedefull for euery Christen*, 1601, sigs. U2–U2ᵛ, U7ᵛ–U8; Christopher Stile, *Psalmes of Inuocation vnto God, To preserue her Maiestie and the people of this lande, from the power of our enemies*, 1588, (notable references throughout); Thomas Stoughton, *A generall treatise against poperie*, Cambridge, 1598, sigs. M7–M7ᵛ (cf. sigs. I2ᵛ–I3ᵛ); R. A., *The hauen of hope: Containing godlie Praiers and meditations for diuers purposes*, 1585, sigs. L7–M4; Thomas Acheley, *The key of knowledge Contayning sundry godly Prayers and Meditations*, 1571, sigs. G3ᵛ–H1, Z6ᵛ–Z7ᵛ; A. B., *The Fame of the faithful, to trye the truthe in controuersie*, 1578, sigs. R2–R3ᵛ; *A beautifull Baybush to shrowd vs from the sharpe showers of sinne*, 1589, sigs. L7–L7ᵛ, U6ᵛ–U7; Thomas Becon, *The pomaunder of Prayer*, [1560?], sigs. H5–H5ᵛ; Henry Bedel, *A Sermon exhortyng to pitie the poore*, 1572, sig. E4; John Davies, *A priuate mans potion, for the health of England*, 1591, sigs. E4–G1 (cf. ardent praise of the queen throughout the book); Roger Edwardes, *A boke of very Godly Psalmes and prayers*, 1570, sigs. G4–G6ᵛ; *Certayne godly exercises meditacions and prayers*, [1560?], sigs. H6ᵛ–H7; John Norden, *A pensiue mans practise Very profitable for all personnes, wherein are conteyned very deuout and necessary prayers for sundry godlie purposes*, 1584, sigs. A5ᵛ–A6ᵛ; *A true and plaine declaration of the horrible Treasons, practised by William Parry the Traitor, against the Queenes Maiestie*, [1585], sigs. H1–H3; Philip Stubbes, *A perfect Pathway to Felicitie, Conteining godly Meditations*, 1592, sigs. G6ᵛ–G8ᵛ; Thomas Tymme, *The Poore Mans Pater noster, with a prepar-atiue to praier*, 1598, sigs. P3ᵛ–P5ᵛ; Edward Hutchins, *Sampsons iavvbone against the Spiritual Philistine Containing sundry Godly and Christian praiers*, 1601, sigs. H1–H2ᵛ, H6ᵛ–H10; Alexander Nowell, *Catechismus paruus pueris primùm Latinè qui ediscatur, proponendus in Scholis*, 1573, sig. B7; R. W., *A Castle for the Soule, Conteining many godly Prayers, and diuine Meditations*, 1578, sigs. M2–M2ᵛ, P2–P3; Francis Seager, *The Schoöle of Vertue, and booke of good nurture, teaching children and youth their duties. . . . Also certaine Praiers and Graces*, 1582, sigs. C7, D3, D4ᵛ, D6, D7; *A godly Garden out of the which most comfortable*

Northern Rebellion of 1569. In *Almightie God I pray his Holy Spirite to send, The iust mannes hart stedfast to stay, and wicked liues to mend* there is the following prayer:

G od saue our noble queene, Lorde, graunt this, we requyre;
E mong vs here long shee may raigne, and cut short papes desyre;
S end out thy wrath, O Lorde, confound with open shame
T hose which in hart vnto her grace long lyfe doe not proclaime!
O ut pull those hatefull harts, which in spight rage and boyle

A gainst thy truth, her grace, good men; O Lorde, thou canst
   them foyle.[14]

Enemies are feared. *A Complaynt agaynst the wicked enemies of Christ in that they haue so tyrannusly handled the poore Chrystians* (entered on September 4, 1564) bemoans those who sought

> Both to destroy our realme
> and Elisabeth our Quene

during her perilous days before 1559; but it insists that

---

herbs may be gathered for the health of the wounded conscience of all penitent sinners, 1574, sigs. H2–H2^v, Z4^v; and Urbanus Regius, *An Homely or Sermon of Good and Euill Angels: . . . Translated into English by Ri: Robinson,* 1593, sigs. E4–E6^v (an ardent prayer by the translator for "our honorable Hester, diuine Debora, ioyfull Iudeth, and deerely beloued Daniell"). See, too, the so-called "Queen Elizabeth's Prayer Book" — *A booke of Christian Prayers, collected out of the aunciēt writers, and best learned in our tyme, vvorthy to be read with an earnest mynde of all Christians, in these daungerous and troublesome dayes, that God for Christes sake will yet still be mercyfull vnto vs* — first printed by John Day in 1578. It and later editions have at the outset engravings of Elizabeth kneeling in prayer. She is frequently mentioned in its prayers for various occasions; and there are at least two notable prayers for her (sigs. L3^v–M1, Mm3^v–Mm4).

[14] Lilly, pp. 168–169. In the *Index* (no. 801) the ballad here quoted is identified as probably *An exhorte and eke I pray that God his spirite will sende &c,* entered in 1566–67. To be noted is no. 4 of the *Index, An a b c with a prayer,* entered in 1564–65. "Perhaps this was an early version of A right Godly and Christiane a. b. c. Shewinge the dewty of every degre, ending with a prayer in three stanzas for Queen Elizabeth instead of for James I as do 299 and 989, which are apparently later editions of this same ballad."

Such ympes of Sathans kynde
do stand and florysh styll,
Whiche do suppresse all truth
and do maynteine al yll.[15]

A few years later those "ympes of Sathans kynde" rose in
rebellion against Elizabeth's rule, which had become increasingly associated with the ascendancy of Protestantism. Great alarm was felt at court and among the people
when news came of the Rebellion in the North in 1569; the
successful crushing of it by the end of the year evoked
Protestant thanks aplenty, echoed in many ballads.[16]
Probably rushed from the press soon after news of the up-
rising reached London was a prayer for divine protection,
*A godly ditty or prayer to be song vnto God for the preserua-
tion of his Church, our Queene and Realme, against all
Traytours, Rebels, and papisticall enemies.* The first of two
introductory stanzas in this piece by John Awdelay is:

Preserue thy seruaunt, Lord,
　　Elizabeth, our Queene;
Be thou her shield and sword, —
　　Now let thy power be seene.
That this, our queene annoynted,
　　May vanquish al her foes;
And, as by thee appoynted,
　　Let her lay sword on those.[17]

Loyal subjects are called to the support of this "queene
annoynted" in *Sapartons Alarum to all such as do beare the*

---

[15] Collmann, p. 46.

[16] I am concerned chiefly with extant ballads inspired by the Rebellion as
they reveal attitudes toward the queen. Many titles of lost pieces suggest treatments very similar to those I illustrate. Such titles are numerous in the *Index*:
nos. 1495, 1660, 1664, 1941, 2040, 2176, 2243, 2286, 2406, and 2900. One must
remember always that only a part, though probably a representative part, of the
ephemeral broadsides survive.

[17] Lilly, p. 121. No doubt following swiftly on news of the defeat of the rebels
was the journalistic ballad, *Joyfull Newes for true Subiectes, to God and the Crowne,
The Rebelles are cooled, their Bragges be put downe* (pp. 231–235).

name of true souldiers, in England or elswheare. The last
stanza prays for the queen:

> So thus my leaue I take; —
> O souldier, now farewell:
> No more to do now will I make,
> But God preserue Queene EL.[18]

Patriotic William Elderton called Englishmen to the
queen's aid in a curious broadside, *A Ballad intituled,
Prepare ye to the plowe*. After the introductory couplet,
"The queene holdes the plow, to continew good feede;
Trustie subiectes, be readie to helpe, if she neede," there
is much moralizing, and finally a prayer:

> God saue her Grace that holds the plow,
>   To sowe this trusty treasure;
> Though many a one be stubborn now,
>   And harrow it but at leasure:
> God graunt that he that harrowed Hell
>   In guardon still may haue her,
> And send you grace that thinke not well
>   Of God, that so doth saue hir.[19]

Elderton's odd figure suggests the rustic idealization of the
queen by the people who lived closest to the English soil
she was felt to be preserving. In a similar style Elderton
wrote *A Ballad intituled, A newe Well a daye, As playne,
maister papist, as Donstable waye* [20] (also entered in 1569–
70). And when the Duke of Norfolk was beheaded in 1572
for his part in the Rebellion, Elderton subordinated a personal sympathy for the duke to loyalty to his queen in
A Balad intituled the Dekaye of the Duke.[21]

---

[18] Page 120. In the *Index* (no. 59) it is noted that *All Mars his men Drawe
nere*, entered in 1568–69, is the first line of this ballad in Lilly; so I accept that
date for *Sapartons Alarum*.

[19] Lilly, pp. 174–178. The date is after the *Index*, no. 2178.

[20] Lilly, pp. 1–5. The date is after the *Index*, no. 1911.

[21] *Harleian Miscellany*, X, 270–271.

The numerous ballads that appear after this suppressed rebellion paint in violent colors the victory of a Protestant queen over papists and traitors. High satisfaction with the averted danger surges in *A Ballad reioysinge the sodaine fall, Of Rebels that thought to deuower vs all.*[22] Being "trew to the Crowne" is essentially the burden of *A ballat intituled Northomberland newes, Wherin you maye see what Rebelles do vse.*[23] John Phillip identifies rebellion with opposition to God and his prince and the "Peace of Englande." The "discord in the North" was "against the Trueth and Queene." The queen is merciful, but she refuses to stay her wrath forever; she and England are one. The concluding prayer for "our Ryall Rose" is notable in this *A Balad intituled, A cold Pye for the Papists, Wherein is contayned: The Trust of true Subiectes for suppressyng of Sedicious Papistrie and Rebellion: to the maintenance of the Gospell, and the publique Peace of Englande.*[24] Her majesty's store of mercy soon leads William Seres to laud all her virtues in *An Aunswere to the Proclamation of the Rebels in the North*:

> But this I would ye should me tell:
>   when she came to hir throne,
> What was she then, of age or wit?
>   giue aunswere euery one.
> Was not hir age so competent,
>   and eke hir head so wise,
> As none that heard, or did hir knowe,
>   could more in hir deuise?
> Yea, you your selues (I dare well say)
>   at that same present houre,

---

[22] Lilly, pp. 266–270. The date is after the *Index*, no. 2557.
[23] Collmann, pp. 114–116.
[24] Page 211. Cf. the prayer that ends John Barker's *The Plagues of Northomberland* (Lilly, p. 59).

> Of all the Princes farre or néere
>   tooke hir to be the flowre.

.   .   .   .   .   .

> Was euer lande so gouerned
>   sith conquest heretofore,
> As this hath bene in all respectes
>   this xj yeares and more?
> What peace, what rest, what quietnesse,
>   what welth, what helth hath reynde,
> What iustice hath bene ministred,
>   to all that haue complainde.
> Was euer Prince so mercifull
>   as this most noble Queene? [25]

Treachery to Elizabeth as the Lord's anointed even recalls
Judas's betrayal. Yet clearly a deep love of native land
and the queen who personifies it animates this fierce prejudice against Englishmen who added rebellion to their
Catholicism.

The lost ballad, *A godly meditation in myter for the preservation of the quenes maiestie for peace* (entered in 1569–70),[26]
must have exalted the queen fervently. Edmund Elviden
celebrated this new year with *A Neweyeres gift to the Rebellious persons in the North partes of England* in which the
queen's mercy is lauded, and rebels are warned to repent:

> A gratious Lady is your Queene,
>   A Princes louyng ryght,
> In mynde as meke as pitifull,
>   And neuer wrought you spyght.[27]

The new year brought a move from Rome that was
provocative of added zeal among the balladists: Pius V
excommunicated Elizabeth. Thomas Bette in *A newe*

---

[25] *Fugitive Tracts*, first series, no. 22.
[26] *Index*, no. 1002.
[27] *Fugitive Tracts*, first series, no. 23.

Ballade, intituled, Agaynst Rebellious and false rumours
(printed in 1570) fears England, after eleven years of
peace, will "be plagued right sone" for her sins.[28] In the
wake of the bull of excommunication came some of the
anticipated plagues. Religious and political trouble culminated in sensational plots against the queen. The putting down of the Rebellion had inspired *A Lamentation
from Rome, how the Pope, doth bewayle, That the Rebelles in
England can not preuayle* in which one learns that "God in
heauen hath made a vowe, to kepe all his," and will "ayd
with right his beloued prince" when the pope rages.[29]
After John Felton on May 15, 1570, nailed the bull issued
by Pius V before the Bishop of London's palace, the pope
was more than ever dramatized by the balladists. When
Felton was hanged, drawn, and quartered, the broadsides
gloated in their mixture of bigotry and patriotism. In a
rough piece called *The braineles blessing of the Bull* (entered in 1570-71) the pope is denounced in some barbarous
personifications:

> Stand backe, good dogs, the bul he leapes and flinges,
> He bleates and bleathes as he a-baightyng were,
> And fomes at mouth, lyke boare with bristled heare;
>
> .   .   .   .
>
> Go home, mad bull, to Rome, and pardon soules
> That pyne away in purgatorie paynes, —
> Go triumph there, where credit most remaines.[30]

By contrast with the master of such a "bull" Elizabeth
must have seemed to many simple imaginations the Lord's
anointed indeed.

Felton's execution is dramatized in several ballads. In

---

[28] Lilly, pp. 239–243.
[29] Collmann, p. 221.
[30] Lilly, pp. 224–225. The date is after the *Index*, no. 227.

The end and Confession of Iohn Felton who suffred in Paules Churcheyeard in London, the .viii. of August, for high Treason. 1570, a description of the execution gives way to an ardent prayer for God's queen.[31] *A letter to Rome, to declare to yᵉ Pope, Iohn Felton his freend is hangd in a rope: And farther, a right his grace to enforme, He dyed a Papist, and seemd not to turne* is a satirical ballad by Stephen Peele (entered in 1570-71). It makes one suspect that Felton was more loyal to his faith than concerned with blessing the princess who had him executed. The balladist cries out:

> Let him be shryned then
>   Accordyng to his merits due,
> As you haue others doen
>   That proue vnto their Prince vntrue.[32]

Peele is journalist enough to feature a broadside in which, after the pope's harangue, the queen appears as victorious over God's enemies. In *The Pope in his fury doth answer returne, To a letter yᵉ which to Rome is late come* (entered in 1570-71) there is a violent answer to *A Letter to Rome*; the pope admits that

> Their queene hath chast the rebels all
> That loued to bow their knees to Ball,
> And hanged their quarters on the wall
>   As meat for crowes and pyes.

But he declares that those "deuyls"

> That to their prince haue ben vnkynde,
> Be sure, with mee they shall be shrynde
>   As they deserued haue.[33]

---

[31] Collmann, p. 147.

[32] Page 204. Thomas Knell's *A piththy note to Papists all and some that ioy in Feltons Martirdome*, [1570] (Lambeth Palace Library, xxx.8.17[3]), is an extended poem in broadside style in which there is rejoicing for the preservation of God's queen.   [33] Lilly, pp. 34-35.

Other individual traitors were abused in broadsides that
show essentially the same queen — a merciful mother,
directed by the true God, and necessarily just to a brood
of "vipers" who would turn against her. *A discription of
Nortons falcehod of Yorke shyre, and of his fatall farewel* has
the following lines:

> And bountie of our curteous Queene
> > Too long hath spared her foe.
> But God, whose grace inspires her harte,
> > Wyll not abyde the spight
> Of Rebels rage, who rampe to reach
> > From her, her title quight.
> Although shee flowe in pitifull zeale,
> > And loueth to sucke no blood:
> Yet God a caueat wyll her lend
> > T'appease those Vipers moode.
>
>   .   .   .   .   .   .
>
> Who sekes surmising to dis[pose]
> > A Ruler sent by God:
> Is subiect sure, deuoide of grace
> > The cause of his owne rod.
>
>   .   .   .   .   .   .
>
> > Yea, bastards sure they bee,
> Who our good mother Queene of [loue]
> > Withstand rebelliouslie.[34]

The queen is again identified with the true religion in *An
admonition to Doctor Story beeing condemned of high Treason, sent to him before his death, but because it came to late to
his hands: it is now put in print t[hat it may] be a warning to
all other papists whereby they may repent and [call to God for]
mercy, cleue to his holy woord and liue ac[cording to the] Doctrine of the same* (entered in 1570–71):

[34] Collmann, pp. 150–152.

Consider what great benefits, we haue of her good grace,
Shee dooth maintain Gods holy woord, to shine in euery place.
How godly hath she ruled vs, by wise councels aduice:
Of such a precious iewel you, papists knowe not the price.
She seeketh to doo harme to none, but to doo all men good:
Yea, to her foes y^t sought her death, she hath not sought their
    blood
Til now of late they did rebel, high treason to conspire:
Then was it time to cut them off, and hang them somewhat hier.
To end, God saue her maiestye, from bloody papists vain:
And Lord send her olde Nestors yeeres, w^t vs to liue and reigne.[35]

Patriotic and religious prejudices continue to center upon the queen. The Rebellion reverberates in the mind of the balladist, and prayers for her conclude many curious pieces.[36] An allegorical ballad, *The cruel assault of Gods Fort*, insists that God has defended the English "Fort," that

    [He] sent this Fort (which is hys Loue)
    A godly captaine to keepe it well.
      Which when in Fort she did appere,
    And flag of truce spred in her hand:
    Aloud she cried, cease nowe your yre,
    And yelde to me right heyre of England.
      Then scattred were the Papists host,
    Their flags of fire to ground did fall.
    Their flaming brandes which oft they tost,
    Were clene out quentch at our Quenes call.

    .   .   .   .

    So God wil spare vs our Quene long,
    So God will make our land encrease:

---

[35] Collmann, p. 99.

[36] See *A free admonition without any fees, To warne the Papistes to beware of three trees* (Collmann, pp. 10–12), printed in 1571, and *A Balade of a Preist that loste his nose, For sayinge of masse, as I suppose* (Lilly, pp. 141–144). I have found no date for the latter piece, but it seems not out of place here.

So God wyl builde our fort so strong,
That no enmies dare to it prease.

To this say al right Christen men,
God saue our Quene. Amen. Amen.[37]

Almost any trouble anywhere was capital for the moralist
bent upon preaching loyalty to England and Elizabeth.
She appears at the end of *A very Lamentable and woful discours of the fierce fluds, whiche lately flowed in Bedford shire,
in Lincoln shire, and in many other places, with the great
losses of sheep and other Cattel. The v. of October. Anno
Domini. 1570,*[38] and *A Warning to London by the Fall of
Antwerp.*[39] Traitors to England and the queen are as
monstrously shaped as was the inspiration of I. P.'s (John
Pitts?) [40] *An exhortacion or warnynge to all men, for amend-
ment of lyfe* with its prose prelude, *A meruaylous straunge
deformed Swyne* (entered in 1570–71). It ends with the
expected prayer for her.[41] Of course during these years
there were other views of the queen than those that I have
been illustrating; on the Scottish border minstrels sang with
somewhat different sympathies; [42] but the dominant view
in the London broadsides is very well focused in *A Dialogue betweene a Christian and Consolation*, written, it would
seem, in direct answer to *A Dialogue betwene a Catholike
and Consolation* by one who did not fully appreciate "the
onely Phœnix of her kinde."

[37] Collmann, pp. 8–9. "It may have been licensed 1571–76, or not at all"
(p. 9). In the *Index* (no. 430) it is noted that the piece is a moralization of *The
Cruell assaulte of Cupydes forte*, entered in 1565–66.
[38] Collmann, p. 268.
[39] *Old Ballads, from Early Printed Copies*, ed. J. P. Collier, Percy Society,
1840, p. 91. Collier (p. 89) places the ballad soon after 1576.
[40] No. 1795.
[41] Lilly, pp. 189–190.
[42] Two such ballads, not in the style of the London broadsides, are *The Rising
in the North* and *Northumberland Betrayed by Douglas* (*Percy's Reliques of Ancient
English Poetry*, ed. H. B. Wheatley, I [1876], 266–294).

CHRISTIAN SPEAKETH FIRST.

Is chaste Susanna in the Iudges handes?

.   .   .   .

CONSOLATION.

No, Susans foes the Lord will cut in twaine.[43]

Before continuing to present broadsides that celebrate the queen directly, usually in association with some momentous national event, I should direct a side glance at some scattered allusions to the queen and lady not so far noted.[44] Such incidental tributes show how deeply placed the queen was in the popular consciousness, and the common love and esteem in which she was held.

Each year brought events that aligned Elizabeth's government more and more with opposition to Catholicism. In 1572, St. Bartholomew's Day, for example, brought new forces to bear on the delicate Scottish question. It led the Scotch government to draw still closer to Elizabeth. In *The tragical end and death of Lord Iames Regent of Scotland, lately set forth in Scottish, and printed at Edinburgh. 1570. And now partly turned into English* (printed in London in 1570) Robert Sempill had remembered Elizabeth in his

---

[43] *Ballads from Manuscripts*, II, 187. Although this piece was evoked by the Campion episode, the attitude which it illustrates obtains in these earlier years.

[44] Such allusions appear in *A Dolefull Ditty, or Sorowfull Sonet, of the Lord Darly, Nevew to the Noble and Worthy King, King Henry the Eyght (Harleian Miscellany*, X, 265); *An Epitaphe declaryng the lyfe and end of D. Edmund Boner &c.* (Collmann, p. 41); *An Epitaphe vpon the worthy and Honorable Lady, the Lady Knowles* (p. 199); *A proper new Balad in praise of my Ladie Marques, whose Death is bewailed* (Lilly, p. 15); *A pleasant Poesie, or sweete Nosegay of fragrant smellyng Flowers gathered in the Garden of heauenly Pleasure, the holy and blessed Bible* (p. 8) in which Elizabeth is placed with all the great "flowers" of Biblical story from Moses on; *A proper new balade expressyng the fames, Concerning a warning to al London dames* (Collmann, pp. 207–208); *A fearefull and terrible Example of Gods iuste iudgement executed vpon a lewde Fellow (Broadside Black-letter Ballads*, ed. J. P. Collier, 1868, p. 47); and *A new yeres Gyft, intituled, A playne Pathway to perfect rest* (Collmann, p. 279).

prayers for his "yong King." [45] Now, after seeking to establish a parallel between the murder of Darnley and the massacre, Sempill angles for the aid of "wyse Quene Elizabeth" in *Ane new Ballet set out be ane fugitiue Scottisman that fled out of Paris at this lait Murther* (printed in 1572):

> The Lord saue Elizabeth, thair ane gude woman,
>   That cauldly and bauldly debait will our quarrell
> With men and with money, baith armour and graith,
> As scho hes befoir tyme defendit this Faith.
>
> .   .   .   .
>
> The Lord send vs quyetnes, and keip our ȝoung king,
> The Quene of Inglands Maiestie, and lang mot thai ring.[46]

Elizabeth, perplexed by the problem of Scotland, could yet hear sweet praise even in doleful good night ballads. *An Epitaph vpon the death of the honorable, syr Edward Saunders Knight, Lorde cheefe Baron of the Exchequer, who dyed the .19. of Nouember. 1576*, reads toward its end:

> O peerlesse pearle, O Diamond deer, O Queene of Queenes farwell,
>   Your royall Maiestie god preserue, in England long to dwell.
> Farwell the *Phoenix* of the woorld, farwell my soueraigne Queene,
> Farwell most noble vertuous prince, *Mineruas* mate I weene.
>
> .   .   .   .
>
> My hart my mind my loue I leaue, vnto my prince behinde.
> Farwell you nobles of this land, farwell you Iudges graue,
>   Farwell my felowes freends and mates, your Queene I say God saue.[47]

Accession Day in 1578 was occasion for thanksgiving to God and praise of the queen He had saved from all trait-

[45] Collmann, p. 243.   [46] Lilly, p. 41.
[47] Collmann, p. 175. Cf. similar praise in the pamphlets, *Certayne versis writtene by Thomas Brooke Gētleman in the tyme of his imprysōment the daye before his deathe*, Norwich, 1570 (Bodleian Arch. Bodl. D. c. 48); and *The manner of the death and execution of Arnold Cosbie*, 1591 (Bodleian 4.° C.16.Art.BS).

ors; but its songs echo now only in the titles of lost ballads.[48] Yet probably typical of the lost pieces was *A prayer and also a thankesgiuing vnto God, for his great mercy in giuing and preseruing our Noble Queene Elizabeth to liue and reigne ouer vs, to his honour and glory and our comfort in Christ Iesus: to be sung the xvii day of November 1577*:

> O holy, holy, holy Lord!
> shalbe our dayly song
> for thy good giftes bestowed on vs
> this ninetene yeres now long;
> And for our Queen Elizabeth,
> which so long time hath been,
> through thy good prouidence, O Lord!
> our good & gracious Queen.
>
> . . . .
>
> Wee magnifie thee euery one,
> and wil do while wee lyue,
> for thy great mercy shewde on vs
> for this gift thou didst giue;
> Elizabeth our noble Queene,
> which on this day tooke place
> in royall seat this Realme to guide,
> Lord, blesse and keepe her grace!
>
> From foreine foes, O Lord! her keepe,
> and enemies at home.[49]

Such thankfulness probably seemed doubly right to the populace after an accident on July 17, 1579. William El-

---

[48] Such titles are: *A viewe to All Traytors to warne them from yeir wycked dealinge and howe God shall prosper their prynce to their great Confusion* (no. 2816); *A psalme or songe of praise and thankes gyvinge to be songe on the xvijth Day of november for the Quenes Maiesty* (no. 2218); *A songe for yche subiect that in England beares breathe to praise God and saie God save Quene Elizabeth* (no. 2481); *A songe of reioycinge wherein maie be seene howe muche little England is bound to our quene* (no. 2487); and *An Antheme or songe beginninge Lord save and blesse with good encrease the Churche our quene and realm in peac* (no. 88).

[49] *Broadside Black-letter Ballads*, pp. 17-19.

derton capitalized the episode with *A newe Ballade, declaryng the daungerous Shootyng of the Gunne at the Courte.* "Our noble Queene Elizabeth, tooke barge for her delight" with the French ambassador on the Thames. But soon a bullet accidentally fired from Thomas Appletree's gun passed very near her and struck a boatman. She was of course marvelously composed and brave. Poor Appletree was about to be hanged as a "forein foe" when Elizabeth, no doubt with her eye on the political effect of all her movements, pardoned him. The ballad gives a "front-page" portrait of the heroine of the hour:

Herself in sight and presence by, when that the bullet came,
She sawe him hurt, she sawe him fall, yet shrunck not at the
    same;
Neither made she any fearfull shewe to seme to be dismaied,
Nor seemed to the embassadour of any thyng afraied.
            Weepe, weepe, &c.

But havyng suche a mightie mynde, as passeth tongue to tell,
She stept unto the wounded man, and bad hym take it well:
His gushyng blood could not abashe her noble courage then,
But she was readier to give helpe, then all the noble men.
            Weepe, weepe, &c.

.   .   .   .

With blubring teares it is no bote to tell the weepyng eyes
That were full woe of suche a shot, where all our saftie lyes:

.   .   .   .

The Queene that sawe this sacrifice a ready wretch to dye,
Whose pittie pleadith pardon still, put forthe her princely eye —

and pardoned the offender! The captain of her guard properly impressed the people with the queen's noble conduct:

And tolde againe, if that mishap had happened on her grace
The staie of true religion, how perlous were the case:

Which might have turnde to bloody warres, of strange and forein
    foes,
Alas! how had wee been acurste, our comfort so to lose.
              Weepe, weepe, &c.

Then of the mercie of her grace, her subjects lives to save,
By whom these xx yeres in peace, suche quiet lives wee have:
The teares fell doune on every side, and aloude the people crie,
The Almightie long preserve her grace to governe prosprouslie.
              Weepe, weepe, &c.

The laste of all he saied againe, marke yet this piteous Queene,
For all this vile unhappie facte, so leudely doen and seene,
Retournes to her inured course, of mercie to forgive,
That this accursed shall not dye, but pardons hym to live.
              Weepe, weepe, &c.

And then to heare the people shoute, and see them clapt their
    hands,
Who would have torne his fleshe before, being in hangman's
    hands,
To see the goodnesse of her grace, to suche greate pitie bent,
It made the stoniest harte of all, astonied to lament.
              Weepe, weepe, &c.[50]

Elderton concludes with the expected prayer for Elizabeth's preservation. After one has made all allowance for
his journalism and the queen's political tact there remains
an important picture of queen and people in this broadside.

The merciful lady of this ballad is the heroine of Lodowick Lloyd's *A Dittie to the tune of Welshe Sydãnen, made
to the Queenes maj.* (entered in 1579):

Flee stately Juno Samos fro, from Delos straight Diana go;
Minerva Athens must forsake, Sydanen Queen your seat must
    take:
        Sidanen conquers kinges with quill;
        Sidanen governs states at will;

[50] *Harleian Miscellany*, X, 272–274.

Sidanen feares her foes with pen;
With peas Sidanen conquers men.

Almost all celebrated ladies of ancient history or myth and
of the Scriptures make way for her.

On seas doth Neptune serve her beck; on earth doth Eolus tend
    her check
In field doth Mars her fame defend, in skies doth Jove her state
    comende.
        The Sone, the mone, the starres confesse
        Sidanen must the skies possesse;
        Earth, water, fire, and also aire
        With Eccho, sownde Sidanen faire.

In woodes the Dryades dawnce for ioye; on hilles the Oriades
    skippes so coye
In fieldes the Fawnes and Satyrs plaie; on fludds the Nayades
    thus do saie;
        Sidanen fedd on Pallas papp,
        Sidanen lulde in Junos lapp;
        Sidanen taught in Vestas towre;
        Sidanen nurst in Venus bowre.

With godds Pandora is her name: with men Pamphila is the
    same,
Eche where she is Pausophia stalld, in Bryttain she Sidanen
    cauld:
        From Brutus stemme, from Dardan line,
        Sidanen is a Phenix fine;
        From Cambers soile, from Hector's seed,
        Sidanen princely doth exceed.[51]

One should remember that about this same year a great
poet makes fine verses of very similar materials; this broad-

[51] *The British Bibliographer*, ed. Sir Egerton Brydges, I (1810), 338–339.
Identified (no. 249) with *A ballat of brittishe Sidanen applied by a courtier to ye
praise of ye Quene*, entered in 1579. This *Dittie* of Elizabeth as Sidanen (i.e.,
"the silken one" or "the one clad in silk") and a similar piece by Meredithe
Hanmer appear in the National Library of Wales MS. 3040 B (= Mostyn MS.
132), pp. 110–114.

side portrait is in oils surprisingly similar to those Spenser uses in the April eclogue. The difference between Lloyd's verses and Spenser's lovely stanzas comes from the hands that painted more than from the paints used.

A lost ballad, *Ye Receyvinge of the Quenes maiestie into Norwiche* (entered in 1579),[52] proves that the progresses of this paragon of queens were reported for the pleasure of the London crowd. In *A new Yorkshyre Song Intituled: Yorke, Yorke, for my monie* (entered on November 16, 1582)[53] an envious city longs for a royal visit:

> God graunt that (once) her Maiestie
> Would come her Cittie of Yorke to see,
> For the comfort great of that Countree,
>   as well as she doth to London.
> Nothing shal be thought to deare
> To see her Highnes person there,
> With such obedient loue and feare
>   as euer she had in London.[54]

Another broadside view of the queen is suggested by a short piece entitled *Vpon Sir Francis Drakes returne from his Voyage about y*^e* world & the Queenes meeting him.*[55] When Drake sailed back to England in 1580, he was welcomed on board his ship by his queen and knighted. This ballad affords a glimpse of "Cynthia, the Ladie of the Sea" — of Elizabeth as she came to personify England in the minds of the seamen of her age. One finds, too, that the celebration of the queen as she stimulated remnants of chivalric idealism in her noblemen echoed now in the humble broadsides; a lost ballad, *The challenge of the Justes*, was entered in January, 1581.[56] But the broadside portrait

---

[52] No. 2249.
[53] No. 3050.
[54] *The Roxburghe Ballads*, ed. William Chappell, I (1871), 9.
[55] *Ballads from Manuscripts*, II, 100–101.
[56] No. 279.

of the queen in spectacular progress, as the patroness of
English voyagers, or as a magnet for such chivalric exaltation of the lady as lingered on in her England is pale beside
that painting of her already illustrated — God's chosen
queen miraculously shielded from treacherous papists.

In 1580 the "belman" rightly prayed for Elizabeth in
The belman's good morrow,[57] for the early eighties were very
fruitful in plots against her. The bull of 1570 had stiffened
Elizabeth's government in its attitude toward English
Catholics, but it had not so destroyed their loyalty to the
crown that serious persecution of them resulted. However,
Allen's Jesuit mission of 1580 forced more strenuous policies. Fortunately, it is not necessary for me to decide just
how far Campion, Parsons, and their associates were traitors in full truth; they were so considered when identified
by the popular mind with the attempt to overthrow Elizabeth's government. Rampant loyalty to the queen led
most of the balladists to consider Campion and others who
met his fate as the devil's own, and to exult over them
when they were executed in the name of God's true princess. Catholic balladists in a pathetic dilemma portray the
queen as sadly misinformed about the real nature of Catholics. In a broadside *Vpon the death of M. Edmund Campion, one of the Societie of the holy name of Jesus*, Campion
is martyrized and Elizabeth appears as wronged by in-
formers:

> My soueraigne Liege, behold your subiects end —
> your secret foes do misenforme your grace: —
> who in your cause their holy liues would spend
> as traytors dye, a rare and monstrous case! [58]

Similar is *The complaynt of a Catholike for the death of M.
Edmund Campion* which martyrizes Campion, yet ends

[57] *The Shirburn Ballads 1585–1616*, ed. Andrew Clark, Oxford, 1907, p. 185.
The date is after the *Index*, no. 183.
[58] *Ballads from Manuscripts*, II, 168.

with a sincere prayer for the misinformed queen.[59] But
the zealous Protestant balladist retorted directly with
*Verses in the Libell, made in prayse of the death of Maister
Campion, one of the societie of the holie name of Jesus; heere
chaunged to the reproofe of him and the other Traitours*:

> Her Maiestie to be depriu'd of lyfe,
>   A forraine power to enter in our Land;
> Secrete rebellion must at home be rife,
>   Seducing Preests receiu'd that charge in hand;
>   All this was cloaked with Religious showe,
>   But Justice tried, and found it was not so.
>
> ·   ·   ·   ·   ·   ·   ·   ·   ·   ·   ·
>
> My gratious Princesse, see your Subiects mone,
>   Such secret foes among them should be found,
> Who serue your Grace in duety euery one,
>   though treason seek to make their harts vnsound.[60]

About this time William Elderton wrote *A new Ballad
declaring the great Treason conspired against the young King
of Scots, and how one Andrew Browne an Englishman, which
was the Kings Chamberlaine, prevented the same.* He warned
the enemy that Elizabeth would not tamely see her godson
misused.[61] But plots at home — Throckmorton, Parry,
and Somerville — soon afforded all the news the ballads
could capitalize; and many pieces damning the traitors and
rejoicing in the preservation of the queen followed. Typical, probably, is a broadside that presents God as frustrat-
ing Elizabeth's enemies even as He preserved Israel fleeing
from Pharaoh. In *Englands Lamentation For the late Trea-*

---

[59] II, 179.

[60] II, 181–182. See the conventional prayer in *The Complaint of a Christian,
remembring the vnnaturall treasons of Edmund Campion and his Confederates* (II,
190) and in *A Triumph for true Subiects, and a Terrour vnto al Traitours: By the
example of the late death of Edmund Campion, Ralphe Sherwin, and Thomas Bryan*
(*Old English Ballads*, p. 68).

[61] *Harleian Miscellany*, X, 267. The date is after the *Index*, no. 525.

sons conspired against the Queenes Maiestie by Frances
Throgmorton: who was executed at Tyborne, on the 10 day of
July, Anno 1584, England herself cries out:

> With brinishe teares, with sobbing sighes,
>   I, Englande, plunge in paine,
> To see and heare such secret sectes
>   amongst my people raine.

> .   .   .   .

> And where the Lord of Lords hath set,
>   his handmaide pure and cleene,
> Annoynting her my rightfull Prince,
>   to raigne a royall Queene:
> Indued with wisedome from above,
>   and storde with knowledge great,
> That flying Fame through all the world
>   her praises doth repeate.

> .   .   .   .

> Haue you not peace and plentie store,
>   which other realmes do want?
> Haue you not worldly pleasures more,
>   whereof there is no skant?
> Haue I not fostered you with foode,
>   which Nature yeelds not loth?
> Haue I not fed you dayntily
>   with milke and hony both?

> .   .   .   .

> And haue not I a carefull Prince,
>   the prop of all our stay,
> Which loueth me, which cares for you,
>   and prayes for vs eche day? [62]

This broadside shows how England and Elizabeth become
identified in the mind of the people, and the continued
view of her as having God's particular care. Indicative of

[62] *Broadside Black-letter Ballads,* pp. 21-23.

the rejoicing for Elizabeth's deliverance from traitors is
the title of a lost ballad, *A psalme to be songe as a thankse-
gyvinge on the xvijth of November 1584. for the Queenes happie Reigne &c.*[63] *A famous dittie of the joyful receauing of
the Queens moste excellent maiestie by the worthy citizens of
London, the xij. day of Nouember, 1584, at her graces comming to Saint James* shows Elizabeth made a legendary
queen by her people.

> The people flocked there amain,
>   The multitude was great to see;
> Their joyful harts were glad, and fain
>   To view her princely maiesty,
> Who at the length came riding by,
> Within her chariot openly;
> Euen with a noble princely train
> Of lords and ladies of great fame.
>
> Her maiesty was glad to see
>   Her subiects in so good a case,
> Which then fell humbly on their knee,
>   Desiring God to saue her grace.
> And like a noble prince that day
>   For them in like sorte did she pray;
> And curteously she answered still,
> I thank you all for your good will.
>
> .　　.　　.　　.　　.　　.　　.　　.
>
> Then plesantly she passed on,
>   Til she vnto Saint James came,
> And alwaies, as she went along,
>   The people cri'd with might and main, —
> O Lord, preserue your noble grace,
> And all your secret foes deface!
> God blesse and keep our noble queen,
> Whose like on earth was neuer seen!

---

[63] No. 2219.

What traitors hart can be so hard
   To hurt or harme that princely flower?
What wretch from grace is so debard,
   That can against her seem to lower,
Which is the onely star of light,
That doth amaze all princes sight, —
A moste renowned virgin queen,
Whose like on earth was neuer seen?

The daughter of a noble king,
   Descending of a royall race,
Whose fame through all the world doth ring,
   Whose vertues shines in euery place: —
The diamond of delight and ioy,
Which guides her cuntry from anoy;
A moste renowned virgin queen,
Whose like on earth was neuer seen.

The peerles pearle of princes all,
   So ful of pitty, peace, and loue,
Whose mercy is not proued small,
   When foule offendors doo her mooue.
A phenix of moste noble minde,
Vnto her subiects good and kinde;
A moste renowned virgin queen,
Whose like on earth was neuer seen.

The seruant of the mighty God,
   Which dooth preserue her day and night,
For whome we feel not of his rod,
   Although the pope hath doon his spite.
The cheef maintainer of his Woord,
Wherein consists our heauenly food; —
O Lord, preserue our noble queen,
Whose like on earth was neuer seen!

   .   .   .   .

In many dangers hath she been,
   But God was euermore her guide;

He wil not see our gratious queen
   To suffer harme through traitors pride;
But euery one which sought her fall,
The Lord did stil confound them all,
And such as thought her life to spill
Themselues moste desperately did kil.[64]

The last two stanzas of this notable broadside condemn traitors "against th' annointed of the Lord," and pray earnestly for the long preservation of the queen "whose like on earth was neuer seen." The idealization in such broadside verses is born of a deep identification of the person of the sovereign with the national life itself. If one reads for "queen," "the life of England," the sincerity of the symbolism becomes clear; and if the unique qualities of the queen and lady are remembered such idealization is further accounted for. In this piece, too, there are epithets that can be transmuted into true poetry. Seldom in the broadsides is there a fuller picture of Elizabeth in the popular imagination; she is a pearl, "the onely star of light," a phœnix, God's own. Symbols are exhausted and coalesce.

When the balladist in 1586 eulogizes the death of the Earl of Bedford in *The poore people's complaynt: Bewayling the death of their famous benefactor, the worthy Earle of Bedford,* he introduces the queen in gracious dialogue with the earl in behalf of the poor. He concludes praying:

And, Lord, with thy mercy hould vp with thy hand
Thy faythfull handmayd, the Queene of *England.*
Lord blesse her, Lord keepe her, Lord lengthen her dayes.[65]

A lost ballad entitled *In praise of the quenes shippes* (entered on August 1, 1586)[66] suggests national pride in ships

---

[64] Lilly, pp. 183–185.
[65] *Shirburn Ballads,* p. 259.
[66] No. 1231.

that will be victorious over the Spanish galleons about two
years later; but 1586, in seeing the triumphant discovery
of the conspiracies of Savage, Ballard, Babington, and
others, gave immediate occasion for songs to the queen
protected by God. *A proper new Ballad breefely declaring
the Death and Execution of fourteen most wicked Traitors,
who suffered death in Lincolnes Inne feelde neere London:
the 20 and 21 of September, 1586,* has a journalistic quality
which makes one suspect that Deloney was commissioned
by Richard Jones and Edward Alde as special reporter for
the executions.[67] The preservation of the queen is the ultimate theme of the piece, and Deloney himself leads in the
familiar prayer that makes Elizabeth the bringer of "glorious daies" to England through the grace of God.[68] Even
more jubilant is this same patriot's *A most ioyfull Songe,
made in the behalfe of all her Maiesties faithfull and louing
Subiects: of the great ioy, which was made in London at the
taking of the late trayterous Conspirators, which sought opportunity to kyll her Maiesty, to spoyle the Cittie, and by forraigne inuasion to ouerrun the Realme: for the which haynous
Treasons, fourteen of them haue suffered death on the 20 &
21 of Sept. Also a detestation against those Conspirators and
all their confederates, giuing God the prayse for the safe
preseruation of her maiesty, and their subuersion. Anno
Domini. 1586.* The energy is fresh if the attitudes are worn:

They came together gladly all, and there did mery make,
And gaue God thankes with cheerefull hartes, for Queene
    Elizabeths sake.
In solempne Psalmes they sung full sweete the prayse of God
    on hie,
Who now and euer keepes our Queene from Traytors tyranny.
But when our noble gratious Queene did vnderstand this thing,

---

[67] The suggestion is made in Rollins, *History*, p. 275.
[68] *The Works of Thomas Deloney*, ed. F. O. Mann, Oxford, 1912, p. 467.

She writ a letter presently, and seald it with her Ring.
A Letter such of royall loue, vnto her Subiectes cares,
That mooued them from watry eyes, to shed forth ioyfull teares.
O noble Queene without compare, our harts doth bleed for woe,
To thinke that Englishmen should seeke, thy life to ouerthroe.[69]

A prayer for "our noble Queene" ends the ballad. *A godlie Dittie to be song for the Preservation of the Queene's most Excelent Majestie's Raigne* (printed in 1586) is also inspired chiefly by the collapse of Catholic plots. The line of demarcation between its spirit and some Protestant hymnology is faint.

> All English hearts rejoyce and sing,
>   That feares the Lord and loves our Queene;
> Yeld thanks to God, our heavenly King,
>   Who hytherto hir guide hath been.
> With faithfull hartes, O God! we crave
> Long life on earth her grace may have!
>   We laude and prayse
>   His name allwayes,
>   Who doth our Queene defend;
>   And still we pray
>   God, night and day,
>   To keep her to the end.
>
> .   .   .   .
>
> A Judith just shee still hath beene,
>   A loving prince to subjects all:
> She is our good and gracious Queene;
>   Lord blesse her, that shee never fall
> In any danger of hir foes,

---

[69] Pages 463-464. Rejoycing in very similar style and for the same favors from God is *A short Discourse: Expressing the substance of all the late pretended Treasons against the Queenes Maiestie, and Estates of this Realme, by sondry Traytors* (*Fugitive Tracts*, first series, no. 25). *A Godly Prayer for the safetie of her Highnesse Person* that precedes this ballad in the text is in the established style of broadside idealization; so, too, *Verses written vpon the Alphabet of the Queenes Maiesties name, and giuen to her Highnesse*, reprinted with the ballad in *Fugitive Tracts*.

But safely keepe her Lord from those!
  We laude and praise, &c.

.   .   .   .

If on our side God had not beene,
  When traitours sought much blood to spill;
This day of joy we had not seene,
  But had been subject to their will:
But God doth aye all those defend,
That on him doe only depend.
  We laude and praise, &c.

Let belles ring out, let joy abounde,
  Let earth and ayre bee fild with noyse;
Let drommes strike up, let trumpets sound,
  Let musicke sweete shew foorth our joys:
And let us all with one accord,
To see this day, joy in the Lord.
  We laude and praise, &c.[70]

The new year began with *The thankfull hartes of the poore Commons to our gracious quene &c* (entered on February 6, 1587); [71] and it saw the usual celebrations of Elizabeth's anniversary in November.[72] There was good reason for

---

[70] *Harleian Miscellany,* X, 278. One may feel sure that the following lost ballads of 1586 were very much like those just surveyed: *The quenes passage into the parlament. 23 novembris Anno 27 &c* (no. 2229); *A newe ballad of Reioycinge for the Revealinge of the quenes enemyes* (no. 2252); *The Commons crye of England against the queenes maiesties Enemyes* (no. 342); and *A prayer or thankesgyvynge made by the prysoners of Ludgate in ye 29 yere of the quenes Reign* (no. 2173).

[71] No. 2606.

[72] Titles of lost ballads suggest the celebrations: *A prayer and thancksgyvinge vnto God for the prosperous estate and longe Contynuance of the Queenes maiestie to be songe on the xvijth of November 1587* (no. 2168); *A newe yeres remembrance wherein we may [ween] howe muche we be beholden to ye quene* (no. 1921); and *A ballat of the peoples Reioycinge for the late orders appointed by her maiestie for their Relief* (no. 2065), perhaps, as suggested in the *Index,* "on the Act of General Pardon for all offences, not expressly excepted, committed before Sept. 30, 1586." I am noting only titles that indicate celebrations clearly of the queen; but in the *Index* there are not a few titles of lost ballads on the conspiracies of 1586 which probably contained treatments similar to those illustrated in this chapter.

them, for on February 8, 1587, Elizabeth executed Mary
Stuart. At least one balladist saw the episode as the practical politician desired. W. Kempe wrote in the same year
A Dutiful Invective, Against the moste haynous Treasons of
Ballard and Babington: with other their Adherents, latelie
executed. Together, with the horrible attempts and actions of
the Q. of Scottes: and the Sentence pronounced against her at
Fodderingay. Newlie compiled and set foorth, in English
verse: For a Newyeares gifte to all loyall English subiects.
In this "Ioyfull New-yeares Guift" Kempe runs on in
violent denunciation of traitors to the "soueraigne
Queene," God's true servant. They are damned for listen-
ing to the "*Siren* songs" of Mary and for being false to
their "peereles Prince." When Mary is judged guilty,
Elizabeth can hardly bring herself to execute the sentence:

Whereto our Queene with wonted grace and mercie beinge moued
Was lothe to yealde consent thereto, for that shee well her loued.

But God is with her! Kempe wonders how any one could
have opposed such a good queen

That like the Orient Sun doth shine thorowout the world most
    bright.
Hath not her Graces gouernment this eight and twentie yeares:
Bene had in admiration of al that thereof heares.
The fruite whereof doth plainely proue, she is the Lords an-
    nointed.[73]

The expected prayer follows.

But 1588 brought Elizabeth a glory that overshadowed
any embarrassment that followed upon the execution of a
sister queen. After the victory over the Armada her star
rose to its actual zenith, and with its ascendancy came a
prestige in the public mind that excelled that from any
other triumph of her reign.[74] With superb tact and politi-

---

[73] *Fugitive Tracts*, first series, no. 28.
[74] Again some titles of lost ballads suggest treatment of the queen for the

cal sense Elizabeth visited the troops at Tilbury and
stirred the hearts of her men. Two broadsides give a vivid
picture of her reception there and of her effect on the
soldiers. Thomas Deloney writes in *The Queenes visiting
of the Campe at Tilsburie with her entertainment there [the 8
and 9 of August 1588]* as follows:

> Her faithfull souldiers great and small,
>   as each one stood within his place:
> Vpon their knees began to fall,
>   desiring God to saue her Grace.
> For ioy whereof her eyes was filled,
>   that the water downe distilled.
> Lord blesse you all my friendes (she said)
>   but doe not kneele so much to me:
> Then sent she warning to the rest,
>   they should not let such reuerence be.
>
> Then casting vp her Princely eyes,
>   vnto the hill with perfect sight:
> The ground all couered, she espyes,
>   with feet of armed souldiers bright.
> Whereat her royall hart so leaped,
>   on her feet vpright she stepped.
> Tossing vp her plume of feathers,
>   to them all as they did stand:
> Chearfully her body bending,
>   wauing of her royall hand.
>
> .   .   .   .
>
> Then came the Queene on pranceing steede
>   atired like an Angell bright:

---

popular taste, and the intense loyalty to her as the personification of native
land: *A godlie prayer, for the preservation of the quenes maiestie, and for her Armyes
bothe by Sea and lande against the Enymies of the churche and this Realme of
England* (no. 1004); *A Joyfull sonnet of the Redines of the shires and nobilitie of
England to her maiesties service* (no. 1331); *A propper newe balled briefely shewinge
the honorable Cumpanyes of horsmen and footemen whiche dyverse nobles of Englande brought before her maiestie &c* (no. 245); and *The martiall shewes of horsemen
before her maiestie at Sainct James* (no. 1680a).

And eight braue footemen at her feete,
  whose Ierkins were most rich in sight.
Her Ladies, likewise of great honor,
  most sumpteuously did waite vpon her.
With pearles and diamonds braue adorned,
  and in costly cales of gold:
Her Guarde in scarlet then ride after,
  with bowes and arrowes stoute and bold.

.   .   .   .

Her Ladies she did leaue behind her,
  and her Guarde which still did minde her.
The Lord generall and Lord marshall,
  did conduct her to each place:
The pikes, the colours, and the lances,
  at her approch fell downe apace.

And then bespake our noble Queene,
  my louing friends and countriemen:
I hope this day the worst is seen,
  that in our wars ye shall sustain.
But if our enimies do assaile you,
  neuer let your stomackes faile you.
For in the midst of all your troupe,
  we our selues will be in place:
To be your ioy, your guide and comfort,
  euen before your enimies face.

This done the souldiers all at once,
  a mightie shout or crye did giue:
Which forced from the Assure skyes,
  an Eccoo loud from thence to driue.
Which filled her grace with ioy and pleasure,
  and riding then from them by leasure,
With trumpets sound most loyally,
  along the Court of guard she went:
Who did conduct her Maiestie,
  vnto the Lord chiefe generals tent.[75]

---

[75] *Works*, pp. 475–478. The date set into the title is after the *Index*, no. 2230.

This "Angell bright" inspired *A Ioyful Song of the Royall receiuing of the Queenes most excellent Maiestie into her highnesse Campe at Tilsburie in Essex: on Thursday and Fryday the eight and ninth of August. 1588*; it was entered on August 10,[76] the same day that Deloney entered his version of the visit. It supplements Deloney's picture in some respects; it parallels it in its simple idealization of the queen.

> Attend a while and you shall heare,
> What loue and kindnesse doth appeare,
> From the princely mind of our loue deare,
>   Elizabeth Queene of England.
> To cheare her souldiers one and all,
>
>   .   .   .   .
>
> To tell the ioy of all and some,
> When that her Maiestie was come,
> Such playing of phiphes and many a drum,
>   to welcome the Queene of England.
> Displaying of Ensignes verie braue,
> Such throwing of hats what would ye haue,
> Such cryes of ioy, God keepe and saue,
>   our noble Queene of England.
>
>   .   .   .   .
>
> What princely wordes her grace declarde,
> What gracious thankes in euery warde,
> To euery souldier none she sparde,
>   that serued anywhere for England.
>
>   .   .   .   .
>
> Then might she see the hats to flye
> And euerie souldier shouted hye,
> For our good Queene wee'l fight or dye,
>   on any foe to England.

---

[76] No. 1328.

And many a Captaine kist her hand
As she past forth through euerie band,

.   .   .   .

Where many a one did say and sweare,
    to liue and dye for England.
And would not aske one penny pay,
To charge her highnesse any way,
But of their owne would finde a stay,
    to serue her grace for England.[77]

This ballad ends with a sincere prayer for "our loue deare."

Dominus flavit, et dissipati sunt! All Protestant eyes in England saw the hand of the Lord in the storms that helped make an end of the proud Armada. Rejoicing for the victory echoed in broadsides for many years.[78] The title of another ballad entered on August 10, 1588, shows Thomas Deloney summarizing the prevailing view of the queen after the victory of Howard, Drake, and Hawkins: *A ioyful new Ballad, Declaring the happie obtaining of the great Galleazzo, wherein Don Pedro de Valdez was the chiefe, through the mightie power and prouidence of God, being a speciall token of his gracious and fatherly goodness towards vs, to the great encouragement of all those that willingly fight in the defence of his gospel and our good Queene of England.*

Gods holy truth,
    they meane for to cast downe:

---

[77] Collmann, pp. 162–165.

[78] In a broadside *Vpon the Death of Queen Elizabeth* (*Ballads from Manuscripts*, II, 98–99) is this amusing stanza:

In Eighty Eight how shee did fight
    Is knowne to all and some,
When the Spaniard came, her courage to tame,
    But had better haue stayd at home:
They came with Ships, filld full of Whipps,
    To haue lasht her Princely Hide;
But she had a Drake made them all cry Quake,
    & bang'd them back and side.

And to depriue our noble Queene,
  both of her life and crowne.

.   .   .   .

But God almightie
  be blessed euermore:
Who doth encourage Englishmen,
  to beate them from our shoare.

.   .   .   .

Our gracious Queene
  doth greete you euery one:
And saith, she will among you be,
  in euery bitter storme.

.   .   .   .

Lord God almightie,

.   .   .   .

Bless thou our Soueraigne
  with long and happie life.[79]

On August 31 Deloney entered *A new Ballet of the straunge
and most cruell Whippes which the Spanyards had prepared
to whippe and torment English men and women: whiche were
found and taken at the ouerthrow of certaine of the Spanish
Shippes, in Iuly last past, 1588*. It shows the familiar attitudes toward "our noble Queene and Countrie," and ends
with a prayer for her protection against Spaniards and
Catholics.[80] Deloney's *The ouerthrow of proud Holofornes,
and the triumph of vertuous Queene Iudith* (entered on
March 23, 1588) [81] must have had double meaning indeed
after his "*Iudith* (prudent princely Dame)" had disposed
of the Spanish Holofernes. It ends:

[79] *Works*, pp. 472–473. The date is after the *Index*, no. 1998.
[80] *Works*, pp. 479–482.
[81] No. 1805. It is identified in the *Index* with no. 1120, *The historye of Judith
and Holyfernes*, entered to Wm. Pekering in 1566–67.

Lo here behold how God prouides
for them that in him trust:

.   .   .   .

How often hath our Iudith sau'd,
and kept vs from decay:
Gainst Holofernes, Deuill and Pope,
as may be seen this day.[82]

Deloney's enthusiasm is more than matched in *A proper new ballade, wherein is plaine to be seene how god blesseth england for loue of o^r Queene*. The blessings of England are vigorously rehearsed:

The spanish spite, which made ye papiste boast,
hath done them little good;
god dealt with them as wth king Pharoes host,
who were drowned in ye flood,
Elizabeth to saue.
The lord him selfe wth streached arme
did quell ther rage y^t sought o^r harme;
ther threatning brathes ye lord did charme —
Elizabeth so braue.[83]

In *A hartie thankes giuing to god for our queenes most excellent maiestie*, one feels post-Armada enthusiasm running high in some ardent Protestant:

What Realme on earth
may be compared to this,
that hath ye gospell plainly taught?
it is a heauenly blisse!

.   .   .   .

In each towne and cittie her grace doth delight it,
to haue gods word preached at large.[84]

---

[82] *Works*, p. 361.

[83] *Ballads from Manuscripts*, II, 93–94. The only evidence for the date of this ballad that I find is the internal evidence noted by the editors.

[84] II, 110-111. I have found no certain date for this broadside, but think it not out of place here.

The patriotic balladist did not forget to warn traitors during the exciting days of 1588. He speaks in *A warning to all false Traitors by example of 14. Whereof vi. were executed in diuers places neere about London, and 2 neere Braintford, the 28. day of August, 1588*; so there is good occasion for recalling the fates of Felton, Campion, Parry, Throckmorton, and Babington to emphasize the lesson these new traitors give to those who still seek "to suck the blood, of our gratious Queene of England." "Our Queene" would be merciful; she

> pardoned them their greatest paine;
> Yet all her pitie was in vaine,
> For to aske mercy they did disdaine
> of the gratious Queene of England.
>
> But God, we see, dooth still defend
> Our gratious Queene unto the end,
> Gainst traitors that doe ill pretend
> to her and her realme of England.
> God graunt that we may thankfull be
> Vnto his glorious Maiestie,
> That so defendes the soueraignty
> of the vertuous Queene of England.[85]

"To hurt our Queene in trecherous wise" is made synonymous throughout with hurting England; it is the familiar attitude.

Celebrations of the victory over the Armada dominate the broadsides of 1588. From June 29 to November 27 twenty-four ballads on the Spanish Armada were licensed.[86]

---

[85] *Broadside Black-letter Ballads*, p. 61.

[86] Rollins, *History*, p. 192 n. Probably representative is *A Joyfull ballad of the Roiall entrance of Quene Elizabeth into her cyty of London the — Day of nouember 1588 and of the solemnity vsed by her maiestie to the glory of God for the wonderful ouerthrowe of the Spaniardes &c* (no. 2337; the first stanza is printed in *Notes and Queries*, tenth series, XI [1909], 147). The titles of six of these broadsides, which seem not to be extant, make clearer still the celebration of the queen that ran on into the new year: *A newe ballad of the famous and honorable*

Most of them no doubt glorified the English Judith with unrestrained enthusiasm.

In the nineties the broadsides about the queen, or those in which she incidentally appears, echo attitudes that have been illustrated with ballads evoked by the coronation, the Northern Rebellion, Catholic plots, and the Armada of 1588. *Varium et Mutabile* may now have seemed her motto to diplomats who sat opposite her; but the nation had long liked to take her official motto at face value and find her *semper eadem*. Elizabeth in bright satins and jewels would continue to defy age, to ride and dance, and even try to die standing. But during these fretful years everyone dumbly knew that *semper eadem* best described her inevitable end. The last decade of her life is a complex time in England; the mind of the period is upset by old and new domestic and foreign problems. But the simple broadsides still hail the breaking queen with deep devotion. Prayers, frequently incidental, for her long life are touched with pathos when one remembers her age.[87] Titles of apparently lost ballads suggest the portrait of Elizabeth dur-

commyng of *Master Candishes shippe Called the Desyer before the Quenes maiestie at her Court at Grenwich the 12 of november 1588 &c* (no. 854); *A Joyefull Songe or Sonnett of the royall receavinge of the queenes maiestye into the cyttye of London on Sondaye the 24th of November 1588. all alonge Flete Streete to the Cathedrall churche of Sainct Paule. &c.* (no. 1330); *An excellent dyttie of the Queenes comminge to Paules Crosse the 24th Daie of November 1588* (no. 790); *The ioyfull Tryumphes performed by dyuerse christian princes beyond the Seas for the happines of England and the ouerthrowe of the Spanishe Navye, shewinge also the Justinge at Westminster on the Coronacon Daie in the xxxjth yere of her maiesties reigne* (no. 1332); *A ballad wherein is Declared the great goodnes of God in preservinge our gratious soueraigne ladie from soe manye conspiracies &c* (no. 2929); and *A ballad of her maiesties Ridinge to her highe Court of parlamente* (no. 1099).

[87] See those in *A mournefull Dyttie on the death of certaine Judges and Justices of the Peace, and diuers other Gentlemen, who died immediatly after the Assises holden at Lincolne last past* (entered on May 21, 1590, as noted in no. 1826; reprinted in Lilly, pp. 197–200); *The crie of the poore for the death of the right Honourable Earle of Huntington* (printed in 1596; reprinted in Lilly, pp. 228–231); and *The Lamentation of Mr. Pages Wife Of Plimouth* (printed in 1591; reprinted in Deloney, *Works*, pp. 482–485).

ing these years. One may guess something of the contents of the following ballads: *A ioyfull newe ballad of our quenes goinge to the parliament shewing her most happie and prosperous reigne and the great care she hath for the government of her people made this yere 1593* (entered on March 18, 1593);[88] *The honnour of the tilthe. xvij° Novembris. 1593* (entered on November 21, 1593);[89] *A ballad of the trivmphes at the tilte and thanksgyvinge the xvijth of November 1594 for her maiesties xxxvij yeres Reigne* (entered on November 15, 1594);[90] *A most ioyfull newe ballad shewinge the happines of England for her maiesties blessed reigne and the subiectes ioy for the same* (entered on November 15, 1594);[91] *A newe Ballad of the honorable order of the Runnynge at Tilt at Whitehall the 17. of november in the 38 yere of her maiesties Reign* (entered on November 18, 1595);[92] *Englandes Tryvmphe Conteyninge Diuerse of those aboundant blessinges wherewith this our Realme hathe ben blessed by our moste gratious Queene Elizabethes Reigne* (entered on November 20, 1595);[93] *A triumphant newe ballad in honour of the Quenes maiestie and her most happie gouernement who hath reigned in great prosperitie 37. yeres* (entered on November 19, 1595);[94] and *A newe balled yoifullie shewinge our queenes goinge to the parliament howse the 24 of October 1597* (entered on October 31, 1597).[95] Elizabeth's accession days were occasions for displays by the nobility, of which the crowd found well-colored descriptions in the broadsides.

Besides celebrations in the queen's honor, the balladist still had foreign wars to inspire him to glorify her. When Calais was taken by the Spaniards on April 7, 1596, there was much distress in England. *Callis, his wofull Lamentation for her haplesse spoyle* is a violently anti-Spanish *cri de cœur* of the city which ends:

[88] No. 2024. [90] No. 2696. [92] No. 1144. [94] No. 2703.
[89] No. 1142. [91] No. 2429. [93] No. 720.   [95] No. 1334.

England, kinde and fayre,
God preserue and blesse thee!
For thy royall Queene,
    Lorde prolonge her dayes!
Flanders she hath holpe,
and poore *France* distressèd,
to her endlesse fame
    and eternall prayse.
She stands, like *Sion's* hill,
vnremo[v]èd still,
    in despite of *pope* and *Spaine.*
Their most accursèd hate
styrreth not her state,
    for the Lord doth hir maintaine.
Happye be shee ever;
ende hir glories never: —
    wofull *Callis* humblye prayes —
JESU styll defende her
and in *Englande* sende her
    manye yeeres and happye dayes.[96]

Some historians find fault with Elizabeth's care of her
fighting men, but, if the broadsides are to be trusted, she
seems to have held always their love and loyalty. Such
publicity as *The Quenes Ma. prayer at the goinge owt of the
navye. 1597* [97] helped of course; yet at least one ballad
reveals a wholly spontaneous devotion from her soldiers at
the end of the century. Says the soldier to "the girl he
leaves behind him" of the queen he serves:

[96] *Shirburn Ballads*, p. 244. The editor (p. 240) says that the ballad "seems
written, under suggestions from Court, to enflame the national courage at this
crisis by old animosity against, and ever present fear of, Spain." This aspect of
Callis, his wofull Lamentation introduces the subject of the political status of the
broadsides in Elizabeth's reign; Sir Stephen Slany in a letter to Lord Burghley
ascribes to Deloney *A certain Ballad, containing a Complaint of Great Want and
Scarcity of Corn within the Realm . . . bringing in the Queen, speaking with her
People Dialogue wise, in very fond and vndecent sort*, which, rightly or wrongly,
brought Deloney into trouble in 1596. See Mann's *Deloney*, pp. ix-x, 495.
Elizabeth and her counselors kept a careful eye on broadsides for their political
implications.   [97] *Ballads from Manuscripts*, II, 197.

Sweet loue, content thee; leave to perswade me:
  I shall come home to thee againe.
My Soueraigne's seruice may not be hindred.
  Sweet loue, plead not in vaine.
What gould could cause me thus to go from thee,
  but my sweet prince's cause?
Her graces binds me, with loyall duety,
  to fight for her christian lawes.
In these her proceedings yf I should be slacke,
the lord would through vengance and wrath on my back.
Her foes, most iniuriously, grudg at her grace;
come hell, and consume me, yf I turne my face.[98]

A sweetheart pleads in vain to Elizabeth's soldier. Even when William Wrench deserted and was executed, the balladist made his farewell represent at least the author's sentiments about the queen, although the reader finds at the end of the piece assurance that the good night was made with Wrench's "owne hand, after his condemnation, in *Newgate*." The following are representative verses from *A warning for all Souldiers that will not venture their lyves in her Maiestye's cause and their Countrie's right: wherein is declared the lamentation of William Wrench, who, for running away from his captaine, with other two more, were executed for the same fact, in severall places about London, vpon the viii. day of September last, 1600*:

> Let youngmen all that liue at ease
> take heed by me how they displease
> their vertuous Prince, as I haue done;
> but, for her sake, no dangers shunne.[99]

The popular imagination was captivated by the figure of Essex. Loyalty to Elizabeth does not come without a pang after his execution as a traitor. Before the unhappy

[98] *Shirburn Ballads*, pp. 237–238. The piece survives without a title, and is incomplete; its first line is "My deare, adewe! my sweet loue, farwell." The editor assigns it to one of the many over-sea enterprises of Elizabeth's reign, and (p. 236) suggests the Azores voyage of 1597.   [99] Page 202.

rebellion a balladist drew a largely imaginary picture of
this popular hero keeping St. George's Day in Ireland,
April 23, 1599. It is notable that Elizabeth is the maiden
queen in two out of three of her appearances in this *A new
ballade of the tryumpes kept in Ireland vppon Saint Georg's
day last, by the noble Earle of Essex and his followers, with
their resollution againe there*:

> Of ioyfull triumphes I must speake,
> Which our *english* friends did make,
> For that renownèd mayden's sake,
>   that weares the crowne of *England*.
>
> .   .   .   .
>
> The Seargeants there that day were seen
> In purple veluet, red, and greene,
> In honour of that mayden Queene
>   which weares the crowne of *England*.
>
> .   .   .   .
>
> S[ain]ct *George's* day thus had an end;
> And those which did it nobly spend —
> The lord preserue them, and defend
>   our gratious Queene of *England*.[100]

As the years passed it became increasingly tactful to compliment the queen as a virgin. When Essex was executed
for his rebellion against this "renownèd mayden" his
death was poignantly mourned in the ballads; but it was
reason for remembering earlier traitors and condemning
all of them. In *A lamentable new Ballad vpon the Earle of
Essex death*, which catches the predicament of the balladist,
the rebel is made to declare:

> I have deserved to dye, I knowe;
>   but never against my cuntrye's right,
>
> Nor to my Queene was never foe;
>   vpon my death, at my *good-night*.

___
[100] Pages 322–326.

Farwell, *Elizabeth*, my gracious Queene!
God blesse thee and thy counsell all.[101]

Loyalty to Elizabeth overshadows fondness for Essex in
*A lamentable Dittie composed vpon the death of Robert Lord
Deuereux late Earle of Essex* (printed in 1603):

Yet her Princely Maiestie
gratiously, gratiously,
Hath pardon giuen free
to many of them:
She hath released them quite,
And giuen them their right,
they may pray both day & night
God to defend her.[102]

In the year following the execution of Essex the balladists were rejoicing in the putting down of a notorious
Irish rebel who had no such claim on their affection as the
queen's tragic favorite had had. The familiar anti-papal
and anti-Spanish spirit is rampant throughout *A ioyful
new Ballad of the late victorye obtained by my Lord Mount
Joy and our Maiestie's forces in Ireland, against that arch-
traytor Tirone and his confederates, vpon the 24 of December
last. Also of the yeeldinge of the Towne of Kingsalt, with 3
or 4 other houldes, by Don John at Aquila, Generall of the
Spanish army, which was yeelded vp the 9 of January last
1602.* It concludes:

To god [give praise who us do]th still defende.
Lord, on this [land always] thy blessing sende;
Preserve our Queene, her Counsayle grave and wise;
confound her foes that doth the truth despise.[103]

---

[101] Page 330.
[102] Collmann, p. 107. There are other extant pieces hardly out of the broadside class that lament the death of Essex, but affection for the rebel usually gives
way, if reluctantly, to fidelity to the queen. See *Ballads from Manuscripts*, II,
23–37, 217–239 — where the versifiers equivocate amusingly.
[103] *Shirburn Ballads*, p. 128.

Interesting in its tendency to recall all the achievements of Elizabeth's reign with ardent idealization of her is *A pleasant newe Ballad, of the most blessed and prosperous Raigne of her Maiestye for the space of two and fortye yeeres, and now entring into the three and fortith to the great ioy and comfort of all her Ma[iestye's] faythfull subiects.*

> Ring out your bels!
> What should yow doe els?
> Stricke vp your Drums for ioy!
> The Noblest Queene
> that ever was seene
> In *England* doth Raigne this day.
> *The noblest Queene*
> *that evar was seene*
> In England *doth Raigne this day.*

.   .   .   .

> Three and forty yeares
> her grace writeth heare
> In glory and great renowne;
> *Elizabeth,*
> whose lyke on earth
> Wore never the *English* Crowne.

> To the glory of god
> she hath made a Rod
> Hir enemies to subdue;
> And banisht away
> all Papisticall play,
> And maintaynes the Ghospell true.

Her ships, her armor, her "Castles and Towres," and her forts are all admired as better than England has ever known.

> Those Rebels Route,
> that were so stoute,
> She hath quickly made them quaile.

By Sea and by lande,
  she hath strength at hand,
To make them stricke their sayle.

  The *Muscovite*
    with many a knight,
The *Swesians* and *Denmarke* kinge,
    To her good grace
    send hither, a-pace,
For many a needfull thing.

  The *Scots* can tell,
    The *Spaniards* knowe well,
The *Frenchmen* cannot denye,
    But her good grace
    toward every place
Doth carry a gratious eye.

  Now let vs take heede,
    seinge well we speede,
That our synnes do not annoy
    Our blessèd ioy,
    and chyefest staye,
Because we haue deserud it so.

  Yet god, that doth see
    her maiestye,
His servaunt in all assayes,
    His grace will giue
    that she maye lyve
Many prosperous yeares and dayes.

  All yow that giue eare
    this song to heare,
With dilligent dutye all praye
    that long vpon earth
    Elizabeth
Our Queene continue maye.
    That longe, &c.[104]

---

[104] Pages 179–181. This ballad, although dated 1600 by Clark, was "apparently . . . sung on each anniversary of the Queen's accession" (Rollins, *Notes*

But all knew that God would hardly grant them their "chyefest staye" much longer. The fear and unrest in the public mind on the eve of the queen's final decline is perhaps felt in *A most strange and trew ballad of a monst[r]ous child borne in Southampton vpon tuesdaye being the 16. day of March last, 1602, as it is verified by the maiestr[a]ts and officers of the same towne, witnesses of this most fearfull sight*:

> For God is angrye with vs all,
>
> .   .   .   .
>
> And pray vnto the Lord our god
>   to blot out of his minde
> Those synnes which yow committed haue,
>   that yow maye favour finde.
> Thy servaunt Queene *Elizabeth*,
>   Oh lord, guide with thy hand,
> That peace and plentye, all her reigne,
>   may flourish in her lande.[105]

Perhaps the blow that Essex gave England's "blessèd ioy" hastened her end. Her death on March 24, 1603, evoked grief that united poets high and low. But the last broadside that I shall now present for its reflection of Judith is *The plot of the play, called Englands ioy. To be Playd at the Swan this 6. of Nouember. 1602.* The play itself is lost, but the broadside gives a prose summary in nine divisions of this popular treatment of Elizabeth's

on the *Shirburn Ballads* [reprinted from *The Journal of American Folk-Lore*, vol. XXX, no. cxvi (July–September, 1917)], p. 374). Professor Rollins suggests that *A Comfortable songe or thanks gyving to be songe the xvijth Day of Nouember for the most gratious and happie Reigne of our souereigne lady quene Elizabethe &c* (entered on November 3, 1602) was perhaps a reissue of this ballad; he calls attention to two very similar pieces at the anniversary time in 1594 — nos. 2429 and 2696 in the *Index*. Certainly the piece has a content and tone appropriate for any of the later anniversary seasons, once the "three and forty yeres" is changed. The title just quoted is no. 335 in the *Index*.

[105] *Shirburn Ballads*, pp. 295–296.

reign.[106] Since this broadside epitomizes the entire picture
of Elizabeth that I have illustrated from the ballads of her
reign, I end the survey with *Englands ioy*:

First, there is induct by shew and in Action, the ciuill warres
of England from *Edward* the third, to the end of Queene *Maries*
raigne, with the ouerthrow of Vsurpation.

2   Secondly then the entrance of Englands Ioy by the Coronation of our Soueraigne Lady *Elizabeth*; her Throne attended
with peace, Plenty, and ciuill Pollicy: A sacred Prelate standing
at her right hand, betokening the Serenity of the Gospell: At her
left hand Iustice: And at her feete Warre, with a Scarlet Roabe
of peace vpon his Armour: A wreath of Bayes about his temples,
and a braunch of Palme in his hand.

3   Thirdly is dragd in three Furies, presenting Dissention,
Famine, and Bloudshed, which are throwne downe into hell.

4   Fourthly is exprest vnder the person of a Tyrant, the enuy of
Spayne, who to shew his cruelty causeth his Souldiers dragge in
a beautifull Lady, whome they mangle and wound, tearing her
garments and Iewels from off her: And so leaue her bloudy, with
her hayre about her shoulders, lying vpon the ground. To her
come certaine Gentlemen, who seeing her pitious dispoylment,
turne to the Throne of England, from whence one descendeth,
taketh vp the Lady, wipeth her eyes, bindeth vp her woundes,
giueth her treasure, and bringeth forth a band of Souldiers, who
attend her forth: This Lady presenteth *Belgia*.

---

[106] "The play or spectacle was frequently acted at the Swan Theatre in 1602
and 1603, and its fame lived long afterwards" (Sir Sidney Lee, "The Topical
Side of the Elizabethan Drama," in *Transactions of the New Shakspere Society*,
series I, pt. I [1887], 13). From a gossipy letter that John Chamberlain wrote to
Dudley Carleton on November 19, 1602, one gathers that a certain Richard
Vennar "baited" the London public with this sheet by promising a production
of *Englands ioy* in which gentlemen and ladies would take part, and that a large
and angry crowd mobbed the stage when Vennar slipped away with the money-
bags. See W. J. Lawrence, *The Elizabethan Playhouse and Other Studies*, second
series, Philadelphia, 1913, pp. 68 ff. The broadside does testify to what was the
popular view of Elizabeth in her last years. It proves that Vennar shrewdly
knew what would be good bait for a populace that admired its queen just this
side of idolatry.

5   Fiftly, the Tyrant more enraged, taketh counsell, sends forth letters, priuie Spies, and secret vnderminers, taking their othes, and giuing them bagges of treasure. These signifie *Lopus*, and certaine Iesuites, who afterward, when the Tyrant lookes for an answere from them, are shewed to him in a glasse with halters about their neckes, which makes him mad with fury.

6   Sixtly, the Tyrant seeing all secret meanes to fayle him, intendeth open violence and inuasion by the hand of Warre, whereupon is set forth the battle at Sea in 88. with Englands victory.

7   Seuenthly, hee complotteth with the Irish rebelles, wherein is layd open the base ingratitude of *Tyrone*, the landing there of *Don Iohn de Aguila*, and their dissipation by the wisedome and valour of the Lord *Mountioy*.

8   Eightly, a great triumph is made with fighting of twelue Gentlemen at Barriers, and sundrie rewards sent from the Throne of England, to all sortes of well deseruers.

9   Lastly, the Nine Worthyes, with seuerall Coronets, present themselues before the Throne, which are put backe by certaine in the habite of Angels, who set vpon the Ladies head, which represents her Maiestie, an Emperiall Crowne, garnished with the *Sunne*, *Moone* and *Starres*; And so with Musicke both with voyce and Instruments shee is taken vp into Heauen, when presently appeares, a Throne of blessed Soules, and beneath vnder the Stage set forth with strange fireworkes, diuers blacke and damned Soules, wonderfully discribed in their seuerall torments.[107]

I have shown the reiterated themes in broadside praise of Elizabeth because they reveal directly an idealization that is the secure, if homely, base for refinements in the formal poetry which I am yet to present. Preposterous to a modern skeptic, they make Elizabeth God's favorite queen; yet they reveal an attitude of mind deeply akin to

[107] From the reduced facsimile of the broadsheet in the collection of the Society of Antiquaries (Lemon, no. 98), in Lawrence, opposite p. 68.

Est mihi supplicij causa fuisse piam.

Many daughters haue don well but thou surpassest them all

The Lord had ne'edone on my [...]

Woodstock

I S. Inuent.

THE FRONTISPIECE OF THOMAS HEYWOOD'S
Englands Elizabeth, 1631

that which is behind the true poet's eye "in a fine frenzy
rolling." They show, however bad their style, the popular
mind discovering in the actual ruler and woman such
achievements and attributes as lead it to hail her as the
ideal queen, as God's elect princess because of "twoo principall exploytes of her Maiestie since shee came to the
crowne — to weete, establishment of religion and peace."[108]
It is very significant that she is widely regarded as having
had God's special guidance in the "establishment of religion and peace." By becoming identified more and more
with Protestantism during years of relative freedom from
religious discord such as had darkened Mary's reign Elizabeth came to seem God's elect princess. How were the
masses of Englishmen otherwise to account for her miraculous preservation through two turbulent reigns and her
escape from countless foes year after year for two normal
lifetimes? In those days, God's loving care was the only
answer. A modern historian who dismisses her preservation as mere "luck" tends to find too much, or too little,
in names — to forget that "God" symbolized the mystery
perhaps more richly for Elizabethans than "luck" does for
him. A mute consciousness that the hallowed forms of the
past were dissolving and uncertainty as to what would re-
place them, especially after the chaos under Edward and
Mary, led Englishmen to adore a queen who brought bal-
anced evolution and sobriety to her people. They saw a
single weak woman effect the seeming miracle. It was
wholly natural that they should think of her as particularly guided by their God, and so celebrate her. Treason
against her seemed treason against the true God, against
the state that a brilliant virgin queen personified during
years when English patriotism was pulsing with fresh
fervor. From the outset the new energies in life and art
that characterized the Renaissance had taken a moral ac-

[108] *Partheniades*, in *Ballads from Manuscripts*, II, 83.

cent in England. In the broadside portrait of the queen in
terms of Biblical character and story — as God's chosen
Judith to bring peace and plenty to England — one can
see how deeply moral the new vigor in thought and feeling
remained among the masses during the great age. And all
the while blending admirably with the crown that the Lord
was felt to be giving her in particular was the halo of divine
right that hung over her head as a heritage.

The ascription of divine favor that dominates in the
broadside view of Elizabeth has a vital part in the growth
of the legend in poetry infinitely above the ballads. This
ascription to her of God's full favor, this belief in her as an
English Judith, was deeply and widely rooted even by the
seventies, and supports the poetic deification in after years.
It gave some inner reason for "that willing suspension of
disbelief" in the pretty fictions at court — Gloriana, Cynthia, Astræa, and so on. It made them persist in the poetic
faith of vigorous men of action who were aware of the
rough nature of things as they actually are. George Gascoigne in his *Certayne Notes of Instruction* declared: "The
first and most necessarie poynt that euer I founde meete
to be considered in making of a delectable poeme is this,
to grounde it upon some fine inuention." [109] Today the
"invented" Elizabeth that the poets seemed to find
equally adorable under a dozen different names appears as
perhaps their most absurd conceit. In a world in which
most men have changed their minds about God and his
particular favor for any people, especially for kings and
queens, it is hard to feel the full value then of such an
attitude toward a woman who certainly had none of the
saint about her. But the view is dominant in the Elizabethan mind. If one keeps a sympathetic eye for a view
which the broadsides prove to have prevailed throughout
her age, the refined legend about the queen and lady will

[109] *Elizabethan Critical Essays,* ed. G. Gregory Smith, Oxford, 1904, I, 47.

be something more than just an extravagant literary convention. Luckily, one does not have to prove whether Elizabeth was or was not God's pet princess, whether she was or was not a virgin, whether she was or was not a great governor even. The fact is that she was believed by most of her subjects to be blessed by God as a great virgin queen, and that this belief was potent enough to build a legend of her in the minds and hearts of her people.

The substratum of popular admiration and loyalty in the broadside ballads is not to be divorced from the power and influence that the legend has at large over most of the best poetic imaginations of the age. Gloriana and Belphœbe, for all the gorgeous pagan finery with which their maker liked to adorn them — just such as Elizabeth herself loved — are goddesses in their inception and essence deeply English. The elevation of Elizabeth by the balladists to God's elect queen for his chosen isle is a strong native warp for all the fine weavings of Spenser and the court poets. This popular idealization prepares the public mind for the sophisticated song that first appears admirably in *The Shepheardes Calender* and in Lyly's dramas. The establishment of Elizabeth as a favored "handmaid of the Lord" in a national mind, gave to courtly epithets like Spenser's "hevenly borne" and "th' idole of her Makers great magnificence" something more than the coolly poetic sound they have for a modern skeptic. This popular acclaim of Elizabeth as God's unique instrument for England's good partly explains the quantity and quality of the praise bestowed on her, and the persistence of much of it into the next age.

In the study of Elizabeth idealized as Elisa, Diana, and Gloriana, it is always to be remembered that the Judith of the broadsides is an elder cockney cousin of these court ladies; in her homely style she testifies to their honest English stock. The plain petticoat of ballad homespun that

Eliza first wears is always a stout support for the brocades
and jewels with which her poets adorn her. Court poets
did not transform Elizabeth into Gloriana without having
heard the burden of many a ballad-monger's song ringing
in the London streets —

> God blesse and keep our noble queen,
> Whose like on earth was neuer seen!

Makers of the broadsides were notoriously inspired by
English ale; and court poets drank many imported wines,
chiefly Italian and French vintages put up in old bottles
molded in the great Christian and pagan past. But neither
balladist nor court poet disdained the other's preferred
drink. The latter consumed not a little ale between times,
just as he read not a few "abhominable ballets" for all his
outward contempt of them. Both alike loved England,
and the intoxicating effect of both wine and ale, better
brews than some later times have known, inspired in both
balladist and Platonist, alike patriots, a vision of Elizabeth
favored of God to lead her land to a new self-fulfilment.
As one follows with Nichols in the paths of the progresses
of the queen, it is amusing to discover that, although her
majesty liked to boast of her Italianate tastes, care was
always taken to have the buttery well stocked with English
ale wherever she tarried. After she left Cambridge on
Thursday, August 10, 1564, "a saying was, 'if provision
of beer and ale could have been made, her Grace would
have remained till Friday;' her Highness was so well
pleased with all things."[110]

[110] John Nichols, *The Progresses and Public Processions of Queen Elizabeth*,
2d ed., 1823, I, 171.

CHAPTER II

Deborah in Progress

WILLIAM CAMDEN, perhaps the most distinguished chronicler of the reign of Elizabeth, says that it began "with happy acclamations and most ioyfull applause of the people." He declares that "neither did the people ever embrace any other Prince with more willing and constant mind and affection, with greater observance, more joyfull applause, and prayers reiterated, whensoever she went abroad during the whole course of her life, then they did her." [1] In the preceding chapter I have shown how the London populace expressed itself about Elizabeth in the broadside ballads. I shall now review some memorials of her progresses to towns, castles, and universities to show her image as it was reflected in the popular mind "whensoever she went abroad." Celebrations from two sources appear in these memorials. I shall direct chief attention to the speeches composed by amateurs or hack writers to greet the queen when she visited in the country towns. The other materials, written by skilled poets to entertain her and her court when she passed on to the castles of the nobility, are a part of the sophisticated idealization to which I shall turn in later chapters. This work of literary artists for noble hosts of the queen appears to dominate in the memorials of her progresses after 1590. I recognize such material in this review of progress verse because it suggests how popular and cultivated idealization of Elizabeth intertwined in a land in which rural and urban people,

[1] *Annals*, p. 2.

humble and noble, were bound together in their love of her.

But before I follow the paths of the queen in progress to town and university, the "happy acclamations and most ioyfull applause of the people" upon her accession merit notice in verse other than the coronation broadsides which I have already illustrated. Her first unofficial progress was from Hatfield to Charterhouse on November 23, 1558, when she was welcomed with enthusiasm by the people. Interesting is the voice of London, her chief city, and the one in traditional alliance with the English monarch, as it was heard the day before the coronation on January 15, 1559. The following is a contemporary expression:

So that if a man shoulde say well, he could not better tearme the Citie of London that time, than a stage wherein was shewed the wonderfull spectacle, of a noble hearted Princesse toward her most loving People, and the People's exceding comfort in beholding so worthy a Soveraigne, and hearing so Prince like a voice, which could not but have set the enemie on fyre, since the vertue is in the enemie alway commended, much more could not but enflame her naturall, obedient, and most loving People, whose weale leaneth onely uppon her Grace and her Governement.

"Nere unto Fanchurch" a "chylde in costly apparell" spoke these verses:

O pereles Soveraygne Quene, behold what this thy Town
  Hath thee presented with at thy fyrst entraunce here;
Behold with how riche hope she ledeth thee to thy Crown,
  Beholde with what two gyftes she comforteth thy chere.

The first is blessing tonges, which many a welcome say,
  Which pray thou maist do wel, which praise thee to the sky;
Which wish to thee long lyfe, which blesse this happy day,
  Which to thy kingdome heapes, all that in tonges can lye.

The second is true hertes, which love thee from their roote,
  Whose sute is tryumphe now, and ruleth all the game.

Which faithfulnes have wone, and all untruthe driven out;
  Which skip for joy, when as they heare thy happy name.

Welcome therefore, O Quene, as much as herte can thinke;
  Welcome agayn, O Quene, as much as tong can tell;
Welcome to joyous tonges, and hartes that will not shrink:
  God thee preserve we praye, and wishe thee ever well.

The verses were received with a great shout.

Next came an elaborate pageant, "The uniting of the two Howses of Lancastre and Yorke." Henry VII was impersonated by a performer enclosed in a red rose, and his queen, Elizabeth, by another enclosed in a white rose. The identity of the new queen's name with that of her grandmother was featured, and "unitie was the ende whereat the whole devise shotte." Homely verses pointed the moral. The final flower of York and Lancaster "thanked the Citie, praysed the fairenes of the worke, and promised that she would doe her whole endevour for the continuall preservation of concorde, as the Pageant did emport." Fifteen Latin sentences showed the longing of the people for peace under the new rule, as these two examples prove:

  Princeps ad pacem natus non ad arma datur.
  Filia concordiæ copia, neptis quies.

The "Seate of worthie Governaunce" was complimented for her "Pure Religion, Love of Subjects, Wisdom, and Justice." An oration heralded the coming in of "everlasting continuance of quyetnes and peace." In a third pageant eight children spoke in verse the "eight Beatitudes expressed in the v chapter of the Gospel of St Matthew, applyed to our Soveraigne Lady Quene Elizabeth." The city gave her a crimson satin purse with a thousand marks of gold in it.

The Quenes Majestie, with both her handes, tooke the purse, and aunswered to hym againe merveylous pithilie; and so pithilie, that the standers by, as they embraced entirely her gracious aunseer, so they merveiled at the cowching thereof; which was in wordes truely reported these:

"I thanke my Lord Maior, his Brethren, and you all. And wheras your request is that I should continue your good Ladie and Quene, be ye ensured, that I will be as good unto you as ever Quene was to her People. No wille in me can lacke, neither doe I trust shall ther lacke any power. And perswade your selves, that for the safetie and quietnes of you all, I will not spare, if need be, to spend my blood. God thanke you all."

Whichte aunswere of so noble an hearted Pryncesse, if it moved a mervaylous showte and rejoysing, it is nothyng to be mervayled at, since both the heartines thereof was so wonderfull, and the woordes so joyntly knytte.

At the "Little Conduit in Cheape" Truth was represented as the liberated daughter of old Father Time, and the queen received "the boke of Truth." The "Causes of a ruinous Commonweale" were contrasted with the causes of a flourishing one to compliment the queen who was to bring a golden age. A Latin oration hailed the virtues of the new queen as those the divine Plato gave to the prince of a happy state. After hearing Latin verses of praise, Elizabeth advanced to find a richly dressed personage representing a queen, with above her head, "Debora the judge and restorer of the house of Israel, Judic. iv." A child in simple verses developed the comparison between the ancient Hebrew prophetess and the new English queen. The full appositeness of such verses the future hid even from patriotic eyes.

In war she, through God's aide, did put her foes to fright,
    And with the dint of sworde the hande of bondage brast.
In peace she, through God's aide, did alway mainteine right;
    And judged Israell till fourty yeres were past.

As Elizabeth passed by "St. Dunstones church, where the children of thospitall wer appointed to stand with their governours," she promised to remember the love and loyalty of the poor. At Temple Bar she found images of "Gotmagot the Albione, and Corineus the Briton." The "onely stay" of the people heard their sentiment expressed in verses of farewell:

As at thyne entraunce first, O Prince of high renown,
Thou wast presented with tonges and heartes for thy fayre;
So now, sith thou must nedes depart out of this towne,
This citie sendeth thee firme hope and earnest prayer.

For all men hope in thee, that all vertues shall reygne,
For all men hope that thou none errour wilt support,
For all men hope that thou wilt trueth restore agayne,
And mend that is amisse, to all good mennes comfort.

Clearly the populace embraced Elizabeth as a Protestant savior sent to bring harmony and peace to a nation exhausted by discord. The tactful and circumspect queen, when the speaker had finished, answered merely, "Be ye well assured I will stande your good Quene." The chronicler is impressed by her mindfulness of God's favor by which "Princes be set in their seate," first by her prayer on leaving the Tower when she compared her delivery to Daniel's from the "crueltie of the gredy and rageing lyons"; and again, when she received at the "Little Conduit in Cheape" the Bible in English, kissed it, laid it upon her breast, and promised to read it "most diligentlye." The interplay of affection between queen and people is summarized:

Thus the Quenes Hyghnesse passed through the Citie, whiche, without any forreyne persone, of itselfe beawtifyed itself, and receyved her Grace at all places, as hath been before mentioned, with most tender obedience and love, due to so gracious a Quene and Soveraigne Ladie. And her Grace lykewise of her side, in all her Graces passage, shewed herselfe generally an ymage of a

woorthye Ladie and Governour; but privately these especiall
poyntes wer noted in her Grace as sygnes of a most princelyke
courage, whereby her loving subjectes maye ground a sure hope
for the rest of her gracious doinges hereafter.

.   .   .   .

... How many nosegayes did her Grace receive at poore
womens handes: how ofttimes stayed she her chariot, when she
sawe any simple body offer to speake to her Grace: a branche of
rosemary geven to her Grace with a supplication by a poore
woman about Flete Bridge, was seen in her chariot til her Grace
came to Westminster, not without the marveylous wondring of
such as knew the presenter, and noted the Quenes most gracious
receiving and keeping the same.

.   .   .   .

As at her first enterance she as it were declared herselfe prepared to passe through a Citie that most entierly loved her, so
she at her last departing, as it were, bownde herselfe by promis
to continue good Ladie and Governor unto that Citie whiche by
outward declaracion did open their love to their so loving and
noble Prince in such wyse, as she herselfe wondered therat.[2]

In this coronation year, as in the many years that followed, loving hearts outside of London welcomed the
queen. I shall now follow the queen in progress to some
of her towns, universities, and castles.[3]

Early in the coronation year Elizabeth was winning the
love of her people beyond the court group and the City.
On April 25, 1559,

[2] I quote from the reprint of *The Passage of our most drad Soveraigne Lady
Quene Elyzabeth through the Citie of London to Westminster, the daye before her
Coronation, Anno 1558-9*, in Nichols, *Progresses*, I, 38–60. The chroniclers bear
similar testimony to the welcome that the people gave Elizabeth.

[3] I have made no attempt to tell of every visit which the queen made during
the reign. Guided by "A Court Calendar" in E. K. Chambers, *The Elizabethan
Stage*, Oxford, 1923, IV, 75–130, for dates, and by his "Pageantry" (I, 106–148),
I have drawn representative materials from Nichols, some of which are now in-
accessible.

the Queen in the afternoon went to Baynard's Castle, the Earl
of Pembroke's Place, and supped with him, and after supper she
took a boat, and was rowed up and down in the River Thames;
hundreds of boats and barges rowing about her; and thousands
of people thronging at the water-side, to look upon her Majesty;
rejoycing to see her, and partaking of the musick and sights on
the Thames; for the trumpets blew, drums beat, flutes played,
guns were discharged, squibs hurled up into the air, as the Queen
moved from place to place. And this continued till ten of the
clock at night, when the Queen departed home. By these means
shewing herself so freely and condescendingly unto her people,
she made herself dear and acceptable unto them.[4]

On July 2, "the City of London entertained the Queen
at Greenwich with a muster, each company sending out a
certain number of men at arms . . . to her great delight
and satisfaction; whose satisfaction satisfied the Citizens
as much; and this created mutual love and affection."
There was skirmishing and running at tilt, and on July 10
at Greenwich, came elaborate military celebrations. At
Nonsuch in early August "a great supper made for her"
was followed by a play by the children of Paul's; and
that by "a costly banquet, accompanied with drums and
flutes."[5]

In 1560 Elizabeth was in progress to Greenwich, Lambeth, Oatlands, Sutton, Winchester, Basing, and Windsor;
but poetic memorials are missing. In the next year she
was in Essex, Suffolk, and Hertfordshire. Four Italian
verses over the house door of New Hall in the parish of
Boreham, a royal mansion inherited from Henry VIII,
may commemorate Elizabeth's visit there in 1561; but
they may have been added to Henry's "arms in a garter,
supported by a lion and a griffin," during later years of
the ascendancy of "la piu lucente stella":

4 Nichols, I, 67.
5 I, 69–74.

Viva, Elizabetha.

In terra la piu savia regina,
En cielo la piu lucente stella,
Virgine magnanima, dotta, divina,
Lagiadra, honesta, e bella.[6]

When at Harwich in 1561,

the Queen accepted of an Entertainment from the Borough;
lodging, as it is said, for several days at a house about the middle
of the High-Street. And being attended by the Magistrates at
her departure as far as the Windmill out of Town, she graciously
demanded of them, what they had to request of her; from whom
. . . she received this answer, "Nothing, but to wish her Majesty
a good journey." Upon which she turning her head about, and
looking upon the Town, said, "A pretty Town, and wants
nothing;" and so bad them farewell.[7]

And when she came from Enfield to St. James's beyond
Charing Cross, from "Islington thither the hedges and
ditches were cut down to make the next way for her.
There might be ten thousand People met to see her; such
was their gladness and affection to her."[8]

In 1563 the queen was at Windsor Castle and Eton to
escape the plague. There on September 19 she was presented with complimentary Latin verses by twenty-three
Eton boys. She was lavishly lauded; "Epigramma 32"
hails her: "O rosa, lux mundiq, sine qua tua terra peribit."[9]

At King's College Chapel in 1564 the queen heard a
sermon preached by Dr. Perne on a text from chapter 13
of Paul's Epistle to the Romans. He divided his dis-

---

[6] I, 94 n.
[7] I, 97 n.
[8] I, 104.
[9] *De aduentu gratissimo ac maximé exoptato Elisabethæ . . . suas Ætonensium
scholarum maximé triumphans ouatio,* British Museum MS. Royal 12 A. XXX,
fol. 20. See below, p. 430.

course into three parts, "speaking, *de authoritate principis, virtutibus principis, obedientiâ subditorum*"; he denounced the pope, and showed how Elizabeth exemplified the three virtues, "requisite in a Prince, *prudentiam, magnificentiam, & clementiam.*" She was much pleased, and sent word that it was the "first Sermon she had ever heard *ad clerum*, and the best." [10] This lauding of Elizabeth in many Protestant sermons through the reign, preached before her or not, is a factor in the popular exaltation of her that must not be forgotten as one sees Judith and Deborah portrayed in broadside and progress verse. In them she was fervidly idealized in Biblical terms, if one may judge from some surviving examples.[11] Such discourses constantly touched the deepest hearts of most of her subjects. It is a Deborah or Judith that the sermons paint; and if the painting was sometimes not to the sitter's taste she would speak out in blunt rebuke, as readers of Nichols and Harington know.

At this time in August, 1564, Elizabeth was making a visit to Cambridge, partly in compliment to Cecil, who

---

[10] Nichols, I, 184–185.

[11] See such praise in Thomas White, *A sermon Preached at Pawles Crosse on Sunday the ninth of December. 1576*, 1578, sig. F3ᵛ; Matthew Hutton, *A sermon Preached at Yorke, before the right Honorable, Henrie Earle of Huntington*, 1579, sigs. *3–*3ᵛ; Peter White, *A Godlye and fruitefull Sermon against Idolatrie*, 1581, sig. A3ᵛ; John Rainolds, *A Sermon vpon part of the Prophesie of Obadiah*, 1584, sig. C1ᵛ; John Rainolds, *A sermon vpon part of the eighteenth psalm*, Oxford, 1586, sigs. A4, B2ᵛ; William James, *A sermon preached at Paules Crosse the IX. of Nouember, 1589*, 1590, sig. H1ᵛ; Robert Temple, *A Sermon teaching discretion in matters of religion*, 1592, sig. B8; John Dove, *A Sermon preached at Pauls Crosse the 3. of Nouember 1594*, [1594], sig. C5ᵛ; Thomas Playfere, *A most excellent and heavenly sermon: Vpon the 23. Chapter of the Gospell by Saint Luke*, 1595, sig. E3ᵛ; Adam Hill, *The crie of England. A Sermon preached at Paules Crosse in September 1593*, 1595, sig. C1ᵛ; J. Tanner, *A Sermon preached at Paules Crosse the first day of Iune. 1596*, 1596, sigs. B7, E7ᵛ–E.8; William Westerman, *Two sermons of assise*, 1600, sig. ²C2; Francis Marbury, *A sermon preached at Paules Crosse the 13. of Iune, 1602*, 1602, sigs. B5ᵛ, E6ᵛ–E8ᵛ; and Marbury's *A fruitful sermon necessary for the time, preached at the Spittle vpon the Tuesday in Easter weeke last*, 1602, sigs. C8ᵛ, D3ᵛ–D4.

had been made chancellor of the university. The *Tri-umphs of the Muses. Or, The Grand Reception and Enter-tainment of Queen Elizabeth at Cambridge* [12] preserves an account of the reception which an academic community gave to this Deborah who was herself a Latinist. Mr. William Master of King's welcomed her before the "West door (which was, on the walls outward, covered with verses)" with an elaborate address in Latin in which he celebrated her virginity. "'Praising virginity,' she said to the Orator, 'God's blessing of thyne heart; there continue.'" She complimented him when he had ended, and modestly excused herself from an answer in Latin "for fear she should speak false Latin; and then they would laugh at her." Plays by students from the colleges entertained her; and disputations on the subjects "Monarchia est optimus status reipublicæ?" and "Frequens legum mutatio est periculosa?" were designed to compliment her. At King's College she was greeted in an oration, and was presented with "a fair book, covered with red velvet, containing all such verses as [the] company had made of her Graces coming. . . . Which book she received with a mild coun-tenance, and delivered to one of her footmen." Souvenir volumes of such verses in "Greek and Latin, Hebrew, Caldee, and English, which were made of her coming, and otherwise set up in divers places of the town," were given her. Orations in Latin and Greek welcomed her to other colleges, and she replied graciously, answering the Greek verses at Christ's in Greek. One conclusion of the dispu-tations of the afternoon was, "Civilis magistratus habet authoritatem in rebus ecclesiasticis." It no doubt en-couraged her graciousness when she delivered a Latin speech to the university in which she declared:

[12] I quote from Nichols, I, 151–182, where the piece is printed from manu-script, together with "Further Particulars of the Queen's Entertainment" (I, 183–189).

"And I am perswaded to this thing by two motives:

"The first is, the increase of good letters; which I much desire, and, with the most earnest wishes, pray for. The other is, as I hear, all your expectations."

She counseled the students to study if they would win fortune and her favor, and pledged her support to the university in a speech nicely designed to inspire her academic audience, especially after her initial apology for the "womanly shamefacedness" that might deter her from delivering her poor efforts. A cheer, "Vivat Regina," she answered with "Taceat Regina." She departed on Thursday, August 10, 1564, so pleased with Thomas Preston's farewell oration that she "openly called him — *her scholar* . . . offered him her hand to kiss," and even gave him £20 *per annum* for his admirable acting in the tragedy of *Dido* and for "genteelly and gracefully" disputing before her. A virgin queen at ease in Latin and Greek must have stimulated a new enthusiasm for learning and achievement in the ambitious students who heard her speeches at Cambridge and saw her reward Preston.[13]

In the next year the common people of Coventry compliment their queen without the aid of Latin and Greek. When the recorder gives her a purse with £100 of gold in it, the mayor declares that there is a great deal more therein — "the hearts of all your loving subjects." "'We thank you, Mr. Mayor,' said she; 'it is a great deal more indeed.'" Mr. John Throckmorton testifies to their happiness in having a prince "that loveth learning and justice" and is also "plentifully endued with all wisdom and virtue." Her profound learning and policy are seldom to be found "in any man comparable, much less in any woman."

[13] Learned memorials of the visit to Cambridge appear in the idealizing verses in *Regina literata Siue De Serenissimæ Dominæ Elizabethæ . . . in Academiam Cantabrigiensem aduentu. . . . Anno. 1564. Aug. 5. narratio Abrahami Hartuelli Cantabrigiensis,* 1565. See sigs. F4–F6ᵛ, especially.

She is sent by God "as an excellent and divine jewel" to a "happy, fortunate people." He hopes that she may be a mother to the kingdom, and encourages her as follows:

The popular course of the inhabitants, their greedy taste for your Majesty, the ways and streets filled with company of all ages, desirous of having the fruition of your blessed countenance, the divers shews and stages provided to the utmost of their powers, as not satisfied with one sight of your Royal person; the houses and habitations themselves, lately arisen from their naked barns to a more lively and fresh furniture, doth sufficiently declare the same I speak; the joyful hearts, the singular affections, the ready and humble good-will of us your true, poor, hearty subjects.[14]

Such plain English compliment contrasted with that given her when she visited Oxford, August 31–September 6, 1566, which she would not have neglected since the Cambridge visit of 1564 had not the plague at Oxford prevented. Again she heard Latin and Greek orations and disputations designed to compliment her. Again plays filled the evenings. She was delighted with the acting of Richard Edwards's *Palamon and Arcite*. Walls were decorated with Greek, Latin, and Hebrew verses in her honor. She received souvenir copies of them. Again she delivered a Latin oration that pledged her devotion to her people and to their learning "to the very great delight and rejoicing of many hundred then present." When she departed the walls of St. Mary's Church, All Souls, and University College were hung with innumerable sheets of verses bemoaning her going. Mr. Roger Marbeck spoke "an eloquent oration" to her in which he stressed the new hope of learning under her rule. Elizabeth, after "many thanks to the whole University," bade farewell, and "left such impressions in the minds of scholars, that nothing but emulation was in their studies; and nothing left un-

[14] Nichols, I, 192–196.

touched by them whereby they thought they might be advanced by her, and become acceptable in her eye." [15]

November 17, 1570, is a notable date in the popular idealization of Elizabeth because then the nation united, probably under force of the putting down of rebellion and the pope's excommunication, to make Accession Day a national holiday for thanksgiving and festival. Hitherto celebrated with bell-ringing, it was hereafter kept as a great holiday throughout the reign. It came to be called "the Birth-day of the Gospel," and held a place in several subsequent reigns. In 1570 "sermons in churches, ringing of bells, tilting, with all the extraordinary signs of joy and triumph" marked the day. The year had been ushered in with such verses as these by Dr. Thomas Wilson:

> "Ecce! duodecimus Regni nunc incipit annus;
> Quem Tibi, quem Regno det Deus esse sacrum.
> Hactenus est series felix, talisque videtur
> Qualis in Elysiis dicitur esse locis.
> Quæ superest series sit par, vel lætior esto,
> Si modo fata dari prosperiora queant.
> Talis es, ut merito valeas, regnesque beata,
> Regno nempe tuo stella salutis ades.
> Nescio si Dea sis, mihi numen habere videris,
> Tam bene nos Anglos Diva benigna regis.
> Quod si sola potes sine sensu vivere mortis,
> Sola sis, æternum vivere digna solo.
> Sed licet ex cœlo es, mortali in corpore vivis,
> Ortaque temporibus, tempore cuncta cadunt.
> Pignore sed vives ter felix Mater adulto,
> Sic potes æternum vivere Diva, Vale." [16]

On January 23, 1571, the "ter felix Mater" went "to dine with Sir Thomas Gresham, in Bishopsgate-street, and gave name to the Royal Exchange." [17] The prosperity that her

[15] I, 206-217.
[16] I, 274-275.
[17] I, 275.

subjects had hoped for [18] now had an official home. That
prosperity the recorder of Warwick remembered in his
rehearsal of the blessings of her reign when, to the great
delight of the citizens, she visited his town in 1572. He
praised "the restauracion of God's true religion, the
speedie chaunge of warres into peace, of dearth and famine
into plentie, of an huge masse of drosse and counterfait
monye into fyne golde and silver, to your Hieghnes' gret
honour." The bag of sovereigns which he finally gave the
queen was evidence of the new wealth. She accepted the
gift with reluctance more polite, perhaps, than genuine.
Certainly "Mr. Griffyn, the Preacher" pleased her less
when he presented Latin verses, the initial and final letters
of which, taken in sequence, spelled out "Tu Elisabeta viro
nubis, o mater eris"; for Elizabeth notoriously disliked to
have subjects meddle with the matter of her marriage and
an heir. Other Latin verses ended more tactfully with
"Deo regente, reges." And here at Warwick "it pleased
her to have the countrey people, resorting to see her,
daunce in the Court of the Castell, her Majesty beholding
them out of her chamber wyndowe; which thing, as it
pleasid well the country people, so it seemed her Majesty
was much delyghted, and made very myrry." [19]

The people gave her a hearty welcome at Sandwich in
the next year. Upon "every post and corner, from her
first entrye to her lodginge, wer fixed certen verses, and
against the court gate all these verses put into a table and
there hanged up." Military exercises and reviews honored
her.

"Mrs. Mayres, and her sisters the Jurats' wives, made the
Quenes Majestie a banket of clx dishes on a table of xxviii
foot longe in the Scole-howse; . . . and in the Schole-howse

[18] See the coronation verses which declared, "We trust wealth thou wilt
plant, and barrennes displace" (Nichols, I, 50).
[19] I, 312-319.

garden Mr. Isebrand made unto her an Oration, and presented
to her Highnes a cupp of silver and guylt, . . . to whom her
Majestie answered this, *Gaudeo me in hoc natum esse, ut vobis et
Ecclesie Dei prosim*; and so entered into the Scole-howse,
wheare she was very merrye." [20]

When the queen came to Bristol in 1574 she was lauded
for the peace which she had brought to England under
God's guidance. Fame met her at High Cross and declared of the news of her coming:

No sooner was pronounst the name, but baebs in street gan leap;
The youth, the age, the ritch, the poor, cam runnyng all on heap,
And, clapping hands, cried maynly out, "O blessed be the owre!
Our Queen is commyng to the Town, with princely trayn and
    poure."
Then collors cast they o'er the walls, and deckt old housis gaye;
Out flue the bags about afayrs that long a hording laye.

At the next gate, Salutation, Gratulation, and Obedient
Good Will, impersonated by boys, drew their swords and
stood ready to defend "(against all dissencions) a pesable
Prynce." Salutation spoke:

All hayll, O Plant of Grace, and speshall Sprout of Faem,
Most welcom to this Western coest, O perll and princely daem.
As loe a custom is whear humble subjects dwels,
When Prynce aprocheth neer their vew for joy to ring their bels.
So all that beareth lief in Bristow now this day
Salutes the Queen from deepth of breast with welcom every way.

Military shows and salutes honored the queen "that gives
the Whit and fayr Red Roes" by condemning dissension
and lauding peace. She sent two hundred crowns "to
make the souldiors a banket." The sentiment of all
Bristol hearts was caught in the following verses:

[20] I, 338–339.

O England, joy with us,
And kis the steps whear she doth traed, that keeps her country
thus
In Peace and rest, and perfait stay; whearfore the God of Peace,
In Peace, by Peace, our Peace presarve, and her long lief
encrease.

In a mournful ditty the city bade farewell to the "Lords
Anointed," to "the deer Lady of this Land." [21]

On July 9, 1575, Elizabeth began her third and most
celebrated visit to Kenilworth Castle, but the common
people had little voice in the "princely pleasures" there.
The Kenilworth masques, the work of trained imaginations to tickle courtly tastes, are elaborate minglings of
old romances, folk survivals, and classical water myths.

The people spoke out in enthusiastic welcome when the
queen removed from Kenilworth to Worcester by way of
Lichfield, Stafford Castle, Chillington, and Hartlebury
Castle. Worcester furbished itself up to receive its royal
guest with due ceremony on August 13, 1575. At Hallow
Park Elizabeth hunted, and divided her spoils, two bucks,
between the two bailiffs. The "dilectable" speeches appear to be lost. But they probably were "dilectable," for
the queen replied as follows to a loyal parting speech:

"'M'rs, I Thank you all very hartely for y' paynes; and I thank
you for the greet cheer you made to my men, for they talk
greatlie of it. And, I pray you, com'end me to the whole Citie,
and thank them for their verry good will and paynes. And, I
assure you, you all pray so hartily for me, as I fear you will by

---

[21] Nichols (I, 393-407) reprints this Bristol material chiefly from *The Firste
Parte of Churchyarde's Chippes, contayning Twelve seueral Labours*, 1575. Thomas
Churchyard, that honest old hack writer who more than spanned Elizabeth's
reign, seems to have been a sort of "literary camp-follower" for some few of the
pageants and progresses. It is worth noting that this semi-official progress poet
was also a veteran broadside writer. He speaks of Elizabeth for city and town
alike, even as London broadsides agree with occasional verses at Bristol in
idealizing her as a virgin princess of peace, guided by Jehovah.

y^r prayers make me lyve too long. But I thank you all; and so God be with you!'"

The chronicler adds: "And so departed with teres in her eyes; and the people with a lowd cry sayd, 'God save y^r Majestie!'" [22]

In a long Latin prose oration at Woodstock, 1575,[23] Laurence Humphrey praises Elizabeth's peace, prudence, and piety. He mixes parallels from Biblical history with ancient history and myth. Elizabeth is a "Debora Christianissima"! Latin verses from Humphrey's pen mark the accession day, November 17, 1575, and pay the familiar homage to the queen who with God's guidance has given England true religion and checked the accursed pope. A few of the verses will suggest the tone of the poem:

> Post tenebras lucem dedit, & post nubilia solem.
> Illi omnis sit honos, laus & benedictio soli.
> O metamorphosis grata, o mutatio fœlix:
> Te Deus elegit solus, Regina, ministram:
> Hic te sublimem provexit honoris ad arcem,
> Unxit, constituit, Caput & Diademate cinxit.
> Ille tuum solium fulcit firmatque Coronam,
> Ille tuæ solus produxit stamina vitæ,
> Bisque Novem tibi jam Regnam stabilivit in annos,
> Jamque novus rediit (Domino volvente) November.
> Non opus hoc hominis, non Papæ chrisma manusve:
> At manus, at digitus Domini, cui gloria detur:
> Illi omnis sit honos, laus & benedictio soli.
> Perge age, Virginei Lumen Splendorque decoris,
> Cur sceptrum teneas, quis te præfecerit Anglis,

---

[22] Nichols, I, 543. The oration that welcomed Elizabeth to Worcester is still another instance of familiar praise of her as God's chosen queen (see I, 545–548). At Woodstock she heard *The Tale of Hemetes the Heremyte*, which George Gascoigne later rendered into Latin, French, and Italian and dedicated to her as a new year's gift. The frontispiece shows him presenting the book to his queen. See below, pp. 188–189.

[23] I, 588–599.

Cur sic Imperii cursum tot proroget annos,
Specta, quoque vocat, generosa mente sequaris.
Ut te glorificat, sic glorificabis & illum,
Quo magis ille tuum Nomenque diesque peremet.[24]

Deborah's progresses in 1578 were extensive. When she was at Audley End Cambridge University complimented her. Burghley ordered an oration full of

thanks and praise to Almighty God, for his long blessings, delivered to the whole Realm by her Majesty's government; and particularly to the two Universities, which were kept by her, as by a Nurse, in quietness to be nourished in piety, and all other learning; free from all outward troubles, as rebellions, and such other innumerable calamities, as other countries were then subject unto.[25]

At Audley End Gabriel Harvey presented her *Gratulationes Waldenses*, containing Latin and Greek poems by several hands, native and foreign, in her honor. It held speeches and verses sent from Cambridge. The vice-chancellor gave her a pair of gloves embroidered in gold with these verses:

In αποφθεγμα Sereniss.
Principis Elizabethæ
SEMPER VNA.
VNA quod es SEMPER, quod semper es Optima Princeps,
   Quam bene conveniunt hae duo verba tibi:
Quod pia, quod prudens, quod casta, quod innuba Virgo
   Semper es, hoc etiam SEMPER es VNA modo.
Et Populum quod ames, Populo quod amata vicissim
   Semper es, hic constans SEMPER et VNA manes.
O utinam quoniam sic SEMPER es, VNA liceret,
     VNA te nobis SEMPER, Eliza, frui.[26]

---

[24] I, 586.
[25] II, 110.
[26] II, 112.

Her motto, *Semper Eadem*, was admirably calculated to fix her rule in the affection of a people desirous of a secure and constant government. It is frequently echoed in the poetry of the age.

After she left Audley End, Elizabeth was welcomed in Suffolk and Norfolk, and again faithful Churchyard chronicled the entertainment of her. At Hartford Bridge the lord of the manor of Erlham gave her golden spurs and verses of devotion. The reception at Norwich, where Elizabeth was from August 16 to August 22, is especially notable. The mayor welcomes her in a Latin oration as "hujius Regni lumen (ut David olim fuit Israelitici)," and gives her a cup of silver containing £100 in gold. The queen answers him:

"We hartily thanke you, Maister Maior, and all the reste, for these tokens of good-will, neverthelesse Princes have no neede of money: God hath endowed us abundantly, we come not therefore but for that whiche in right is our owne, the heartes and true allegeaunce of our subjects, whiche are the greatest riches of a kingdome: whereof as we assure ourselves in you, so doe you assure yourselves in us of a lovyng and gratious Soveraigne."

However, "the cover of the cup lifted up, hyr Majestie saide to the footeman, 'Looke to it, there is a hundreth pound.'" Rain prevents the public reading of a speech in which King Gurgunt reviews English history to the glory of the Tudor rose and assures her that Norwich hearts "full fast with perfect love to thee do cleave." The gates are decorated with the scutcheon of Saint George and with the city's and the queen's arms. Beneath red and white roses united are these verses:

> Division kindled stryfe,
> Blist Union quenchte the flame:
> Thence sprang our noble Phænix deare,
> The pearlesse Prince of Fame.[27]

[27] II, 141–143.

Pageants at Norwich give an unusually full understanding of the idealization of Elizabeth by her people in the provinces, its causes and its quality. The first pageant is presented by the weavers on a large stage with the following inscription:

The causes of this Commonwealth
are,
God truely preached.
Justice duely executed.   The people obedient.
Idlenesse expelled.   Labour cherished.
Universall Concorde preserved.

A boy representing the commonwealth speaks:

> Most gracious Prince, undoubted Soveraigne Queene,
>   Our only joy next God, and chiefe defence:
> In this small shewe our whole estate is seene;
>   The welth we have, we finde proceede from thence.
> The idle hande hath here no place to feede,
> The painefull wight hath stil to serve his neede.
>
>   .   .   .   .
>
> We bought before the things that now we sell,
>   These slender ympes their workes do passe the waves,
> Gods peace and thine, we holde and prosper well,
>   Of every mouth the handes the charges saves.
> Thus through thy helpe and ayde of power divine,
>   Doth Norwich live, whose harts and goods are thine.

"Poore Norwich" (one of "five personages apparelled like women") has "hungred to gaine the sight" of her, and begs her favor:

> What should I say? Thou art my joy next God, I have none
>   other,
> My Princesse and my peerlesse Queene, my loving Nurse and
>   Mother.

My goods and lands, my hands and hart, my limbes and life are
    thine,
What is mine own in right or thought, to thee I do resigne.

Deborah appears to tell how God helped her to slay Sisera.
She commends and blesses her superior. Next comes
Judith to exclaim:

> Oh floure of grace, oh prime of Gods elect,
>   O mighty Queene and finger of the Lord,
> Did God sometime by me poore wight correct,
>   The Champion stoute, that him and his abhord:
> Then be thou sure thou art his mighty hand,
> To conquere those which him and thee withstand.

Then Hester, after recalling Hamon, concludes for these
Biblical Amazons:

> Dost thou not see the joy of all this flocke?
>   Vouchsafe to viewe their passing gladsome cheare,
> Be still (good Queene) their refuge and their rocke,
>   As they are thine to serve in love and feare:
> So fraude, nor force, nor foraine Foe may stand
> Againste the strength of thy moste puyssaunt hand.

The fifth person, Martia, recalls that she was once queen
of the land for thirty-three years. She is now roused to
life by Norwich's welcome to

> "the Pearl of Grace;
> . . . the Jewell of the Worlde, hir peoples whole delight,
> The Paragon of present time, and Prince of earthly might."

Martia's father-in-law built Norwich, town and castle;
and she now rises to greet this queen whose virtues surpass
those of all pagan goddesses. A ditty is sung to soft music
as the queen enters the gates. It varies but little the conventional compliment of having Jove decide the famous
quarrel among his goddesses in favor of Elizabeth.[28]

[28] II, 143-150.

On Tuesday, August 19, the queen hunts, and later hears
a Latin oration by the minister of the Dutch church. He
praises her and presents a cup worth £50. She has been,
as Joseph was, led by the Lord "from prison and deceite";
and she is "wise as the serpent, and meeke as the dove."
On Wednesday she hears an oration by the minister of the
grammar school in Norwich. Her goodness waters the
land as the Nile, Egypt, and as Pactolus, Lydia — save
that it is of infinitely more worth. He declares:

We certainely now inhabite, and leade our lives in those most
happie ilands of the which Hesiodus maketh mention, which not
only abounde with all manner of graine, wool, cattel, and other
aydes of mans life, but muche more with the most precious
treasure of true religion and the word of God, in the whiche
onlye the mindes of men have reste and peace. There bee that
call Englande another worlde, whiche I thinke maye bee moste
true in this our age: for whereas all landes on everye side of us
are afflicted with most grievous warres, and tossed with floudes
of dissention, we only, your Highnesse governing our sterne, do
sayle in a most peaceable haven, and severed from the worlde of
mischiefes, do seeme after a sorte to be taken up into a heaven
of happinesse.

When the oration ends, she says to the speaker:

"It is the best that ever I heard; you shal have my hande;"
and pulled off hir glove, and gave him hir hand to kiss; which,
before kneeling on his knee, he arose and kissed: and then she
departed to the Court, without any other shew that night; but
that she sente backe to know his name.[29]

"The nexte night, beyng Thursdaye, there [is] an ex-
cellent princely maske brought before hir after supper, by
Mayster Goldingham, in the Privie Chamber; it [is] of
gods and goddesses, both strangely and richly apparelled."
In this masque the deities of antiquity bring gifts to the
English Deborah. Ceres, Bacchus, and Pomona cannot

[29] II, 150–159.

appear because they are "tyed by the tyme of the yeare."
"Onely Himineus denyeth his good-will, eyther in presence, or in person" to the queen who persists in a single
life that gives her people, they repeat, no assurance of an
heir. Jupiter and Juno testify especially to the love of her
subjects. Mars offers a "fayre payre of knyves" and
declares:

> And though, oh Queene, thou beest a Prince of Peace.
> Yet shalt thou have me fastly sure at neede.

The verses which Venus speaks praise the queen's beauty,
of course. The white dove which she gives "being cast
off, [runs] directly to the Queene, and being taken up and
set upon the table before hir Majestie, [sits] so quietly as
if it had bin tied." Pallas presents a "booke of Wisdome,"
but admits that it can teach this princess nothing. Neptune's gift of a "great artificiall fishe, and in the belly
thereof a noble pike, which he [throws] out before hir
Majestie." His pledge of loyalty in 1578 is a curious
prophecy if one remembers his rôle in the defeat of the
Armada in 1588.

> Can sea or earth devise to hurte thy hap,
> Since thou by Gods doest sit in Fortunes lap?

> As Heaven and Earth have vowed to be thine,
>   So Neptunes seas have sworne to drench thy foes,
> As I am God, and all the waters mine,
>   Still shalte thou get, but never shalt thou lose:
> And since on earth my wealth is nought at all,
> Accept good-will, the gifte is very small.

Diana's bow and silver arrows are given to the "chastest
Dame in these our happy dayes." Cupid comes last to
present an arrow of pure gold "meete for the noblest
Queene" and able to pierce any "King or Caesar" she
may fancy. When the sun is overclouded once during

the visit, a bad conceit carries a sincere compliment to the "Virgine pure" who makes Apollo thus retire. She it is who

> the darkenesse drave of Poprye quite away:
> And, by Religion, hath restord the bright and lightsome day.

And the same clumsy hand gives good reasons why three great goddesses should pay tribute to Elizabeth. A Latin dialogue, "Gloria Civilis an bellica maior," is spoken to compliment her, and Greek verses of welcome show a provincial city anxious to please a learned princess. Mr. Goldingham congratulates the city upon its good fortune in having in it this paragon of queens, but his Latin verses show no new attitudes.[30]

Churchyard did service at this entertainment of Elizabeth in Suffolk and Norfolk in 1578, and he was anxious that his efforts should achieve immortality along with the work of Goldingham and Garter, from whom I have just been quoting. Hence his printing *A Discourse of the Queenes Majestie's Entertainment in Suffolk and Norfolk: With a Description of many Things then presently seene.* In a letter to the reader he testifies to the sincerity of the country folk in Suffolk and Norfolk, to their deep devotion to their guest. He speaks for these subjects in not a few verses in his usual flat style. Mercury comes from "Jove, or just Jehova, Lord of might" to announce the various shows that his master has appointed for the entertainment of one most dear to him. Cupid's bow is given to Elizabeth by Chastity because "the Queene [has] chosen the best life . . . to learn to shoote at whome she pleased, since none coulde wounde hir Highnesse hart." Chastity defeats poor Cupid and then speaks a eulogy of herself which ends, of course, with obeisance to the queen of chastity. A philosopher abuses Cupid until Riot and Wantonness carry

[30] II, 159–178.

him off. Venus is condemned as a strumpet. Modesty,
Temperance, Good Exercise, and Shamefastness, as the
waiting maids of Chastity, come in and sing. Modesty
exalts the chaste life that is a "pretious pearle" and sits
and rules "in regall throne." Another elaborate show by
Churchyard presents Manhood, Beauty, Good Favor,
Desert, and Good Fortune — all with verses turned to
compliment the queen.[31]

When Elizabeth departs from Norwich she is asked to

> receive thy subjects heartes,
> In fixed faith continually thine owne:
> Who ready rest to lose their vitall partes
> In thy defence, when any blast is blowne.
> Thou arte our Queene, our rocke, and only stay
> We are thine own to serve by night and day.[32]

Two parting orations to the "Nurce of Religion, Mother
of the Commonwealth, Beautie of Princes, Solace of . . .
Subjectes" agree in pledging her the "wonderfull love,"
the "sincere affection, and unfayned good-will" that she,
endowed by the majesty of God, stirs in the hearts of her
subjects. She answers in good part according to one witness: "'I have laid up in my breast such good will, as I
shall never forget Norwich;' and proceeding onward, did
shake hir riding-rod, and said, 'Farewel, Norwich,' wyth
the water standing in her eies." [33] This visit to Norwich
led Churchyard to exclaim in concluding his account:
"Suche . . . a Soveraigne Layde we have, that can make
the crooked pathes streighte where she commeth, and
drawe the hearts of the people after hyr wheresoever she
travels." [34]

[31] II, 179–211.
[32] II, 165.
[33] II, 166.
[34] II, 215.

In 1582 the queen, while at Hampton Court, passed through Kingston. The town hall, built about this period, has this inscription, from which the date is obliterated:

"Vivat Regina Elizabetha, in qua fides,
prudentia, fortitudo, temperantia,
et justicia elugent luculente
anno R. Elizabethæ...." [35]

George Peele's *The Device of the Pageant borne before Wolstane Dixie, Lord Mayor of the Citie of London* (on October 29, 1585) contains smooth verses that unite the country and London in idealization of Elizabeth. They present London, Magnanimity, Loyalty, the Country, the Thames, the Soldier, the Sailor, Science, and four Nymphs singing in turn their love and devotion. At least London and the Country must be heard.

London.

New Troye I hight, whom Lud my Lord surnamed,
  London, the glory of the Western side;
Throughout the world is lovely London famed,
  So far as any sea comes in with tide;
    Whose peace and calme under her Royal Queene,
    Hath long been such as like was never seene.
Then let me live to caroll of her name,
  That she may ever live, and never dye;
Her sacred shrine set in the house of Fame,
  Consecrate to eternal memorie.
    My peerless Mistresse, Soveraigne of my peace,
    Long may she joy with honour's great increase.

.   .   .   .

The Country.

For London's aid the Country gives supplie
  Of needful things, and store of every graine:

---

[35] II, 392.

London, give thanks to Him that sits on high,
Had never towne lesse cause for to complaine.
And love and serve the Soveraigne of thy peace,
Under whose raigne thou hadst this rich encrease.[36]

Elizabeth was received in state by the town of Windsor
on August 10, 1586. On her birthday, September 7, the
mayor, Edward Hake, delivered *An Oration conteyning an
expostulation aswell with the Quenes Highnesse faithful subjects for their want of due consideration of God's blessings
enjoyed by means of her Majestie: as also with the unnatural
English, for their disloyaltie and unkindnesse towards the
same their Soveraygne.*[37] The speech is perhaps the best
example of such praise of the queen as I have glanced at in
earlier orations. The speaker, remembering the "seas of
miseries [that] possessed and wel neere overflowed this
little but moste noble Ilande" before Elizabeth rescued it,
declares that she has been upheld "by the extraordinary
and very express hand of God." He summarizes the
blessings she has brought:

First, therefore, and above all, we have and enjoy by her Majesty, the most glorious of all glorious jewels, the true and sincere
Worde of GOD, with the free, open, and universal preaching and
professing thereof: . . .

The nexte blessing (as the effecte of faith and of God's
Woorde) that falleth out in order to bee spoken to, is worldly
and external peace. From which, well used, springeth plentie.
And where the abuse of these hath wrought among us, namely,
in disordered persons, pride and dissolution, these things have
notwithstanding, by a great blessing of godly government, bin
so moderated with such mixture of those foure chiefe and car-
dinall vertues, Prudence, Fortitude, Justice, and Clemencie,
besides all other heroicall vertues shining in her Majesty, . . .
the moste peacefull, milde, and gentle Soveraigne, that ever
raigned in this lande.

[36] II, 448-449.
[37] I quote from the oration as it is reprinted in Nichols, II, 461-480.

She should be contrasted with the pope and Rome.

See if there be not in this her gratious Majesty, a mirror of excelling virtues, and (as it were) a lodge of heavenly graces, constant firmnes, innocent hands from [*sic*] corruption, high equitie,
clement and mercifull behaviour, faithfulnes of minde, zeal, and
tender harte, princelie magnanimitie; and in briefe, a nature en-
riched with all admirable ornaments of devine and heavenly
blessinges?

Hake is happy that in

this our England (as it were in a little Goshen), neither feeling
dint of sword, nor hearing sounde of droomme, nor fearing either
slaughter or depilation of the Oppressour, sit us still every man
in his owne home, having freedome at the full to praise God in
his sanctuary, and safety at the full to follow our affaires in the
Commonwealth.

The oration is typical of many delivered before Elizabeth
in progress or in London; Deborah brings sweet peace to a
troubled land and nurtures true religion.

The ballads have already shown the glorification of the
queen when in 1588 the nation made war to save the peace
which Hake prized. They have shown how

shee went in person to Tylbury; where her presence and princely
encouragement, Bellona-like, infused a second spirit of love,
loyaltie, and resolution into every souldier in her armie, who being as it were ravished with their Soveraygnes sight, that as well
commaunders as common souldiers quite forgate the ficklenesse
of Fortune and the chance of Warre, and prayed heartily the
Spanyardes might land quickly; and when they knew they were
fled, they beganne to lament.[38]

The stirring words she spoke to her soldiers at Tilbury
have a downright directness of style unknown to her in
most exigencies of state.

[38] II, 535. Impressive echoes of the queen's rousing words are heard in
Richard Leigh, *The copie of a letter sent out of England to Don Bernardin Mendoza*,
1588, sig. C4[v]; and in Thomas Nun, *A comfort against the Spaniard*, 1596, sig. C2.

My loving People, we have been perswaded by some that are careful of our Safety, to take heed how we commit our Self to armed Multitudes, for fear of Treachery; but I assure you, I do not desire to live to distrust my faithful and loving People. Let Tyrants fear, I have always so behaved my self, that under God, I have placed my chiefest Strength and Safeguard in the loyal Hearts and good Will of my Subjects, and therefore I am come amongst you, as you see, at this time, not for my Recreation and Disport, but being resolved, in the midst and heat of the Battle, to live or die amongst you all, to lay down for my God, and for my Kingdom, and for my People, my Honor, and my Blood, even in the Dust, I know I have the Body but of a week and feeble Woman, but I have the Heart and Stomach of a King, and of a King of *England* too, and think foul Scorn that *Parma* or *Spain*, or any Prince of *Europe* should dare to invade the Borders of my Realm; to which, rather than any Dishonor shall grow by me, I my self will take up Arms, I my self will be your General, Judge, and Rewarder of every one of your Vertues in the Field. I know, already for your Forwardness, you have deserved Rewards and Crowns; and we do assure you, in the Word of a Prince, they shall be duly paid you. In the mean time, my Lieutenant General shall be in my stead, than whom never Prince commanded a more Noble or worthy Subject, not doubting but by your Obedience to my General, by your Concord in the Camp, and your Valor in the Field, we shall shortly have a famous Victory over those Enemies of my God, of my Kingdoms, and of my People.[39]

James Aske described the visit of the queen to Tilbury and the famous victory in his *Elizabetha triumphans; Conteyning the damned practizes, that the divelish Popes of Rome have used ever sithence her highnesse first comming to the Crowne, by moving her wicked and traiterous subjects to Rebellion and Conspiracies, thereby to bereave her majestie both of her lawfull seate, and happy Life. — With a Declaration of the manner how her Excellency was entertained by her*

---

[39] *Cabala, Sive scrinia sacra: Mysteries of State and Government*, 3d ed., 1691, pp. 343–344.

souldyers into her Campe Royall at Tilbery, in Essex: And of the overthrow had against the Spanish Fleete.[40]   It but duplicates the broadside portrait of Judith and Deborah on the field of battle — and the thing is too barbarous in style to merit quotation.

Back in London, the victorious Deborah,

going as it were in triumph, went with a very gallant traine of Noblemen thorow the streets of *London*, which were hung with blew cloth, and the companies of the Citie standing on both sides with their banners in goodly order, being carried in a Chariot drawn with two horses . . . to *Pauls* Church (where the banners taken from the enemy were hung forth to be seene) gave most humble thanks to *God*, and was present at a Sermon wherein the glory was given to *God* onely. To the Lord Admirall she assigned certaine rents for his service, and many times commended him and the Captaines of her ships, as borne for the preservation of their Countrey. The rest She graciously saluted by name as oft as she saw them, as men of passing good desert (wherewith they held themselues well rewarded) and those that were hurt and poore, she rewarded with reasonable pensions. The learned both at home and abroad, congratulating the victory with hearts leaping for joy, wrote triumphall poems in all Languages.[41]

It is time to leave this English Deborah on the London stage where thirty years before "was [first] shewed the wonderfull spectacle, of a noble hearted Princesse toward her most loving People, and the People's exceding comfort in beholding so worthy a Soveraigne."

Elizabeth's star was at its actual zenith just after the Armada victory in 1588. The resplendent figure of the queen and woman did not cease thereafter to draw the love of her people, as the broadsides printed after 1588 have testified. Her progresses among them continued almost

---

[40] It is reprinted in Nichols, II, 545–582.
[41] Camden, pp. 372–373. See below, p. 289.

until she made her progress to the grave. But verse echoing the affectionate voice of the people during these later years seems to be mostly lost;[42] what survives is chiefly the work of cultivated poets engaged by noble hosts to entertain the queen and a courtly audience at their castles.[43]

The portrait of Elizabeth in progress is like that of Judith in the broadsides; an English Deborah, triumphant over all enemies through Jehovah's special guidance, gives His chosen people unexampled quiet and prosperity. This Deborah who is at ease in Greek and Latin is a beautiful virgin whom her subjects praise at times in these languages; but her learning and her virginity do not impress the popular imagination so constantly as her peace and her preservation of "Pure Religion." Those blessings give "exceeding comfort" to provincial and London hearts alike. Although the towns make clumsy use of pagan

[42] In August, 1591, the queen was at Chichester; but the corporation book which contained a full account of her reception there is lost (Nichols, III, 96). In September, 1592, the queen made a farewell visit to Oxford. From the memorials which I have had opportunity to examine, I conclude that her entertainment there was like that she was given back in 1566 — orations, disputations, Latin verses, and the like. See Nichols, III, 144-167. In 1593 the speech of the recorder of London after the election of Sir Cuthbert Buckle to be lord mayor, contained familiar praise of Elizabeth's justice, plenty, and peace (III, 228-231). See a similar speech in 1594 (III, 254-260). Churchyard's *A pleasant conceite*, presented to the queen on new year's day at Hampton Court, 1593-94, shows this old semi-official progress poet still speaking for the people (III, 237):

> These Townes and all, the People dwelling there,
>   And all the rest, that love theyr Country well:
> And all true harts, and subjects ev'ry where,
>   That feare their God, and doe in England dwell,
> Salute with joy, and gladnes this new yeere,
> Our gracious Queene, and Soveraigne Lady deere.
> All wished haps, and welcome fortunes to,
> Still waites on her, as handmaides ought to doe.
> With long good life, with peace and perfect rest,
> And all good gifts, that ever Prince possest.

[43] I refer to such compliment as the queen heard at Theobalds, Cowdray, and Elvetham in 1591; at Bisham, Sudeley, Rycote, Ditchley, and Woodstock in 1592; at Theobalds in 1593; and at Harefield Place in 1602.

myth to compliment her, some Biblical parallel comes to
the provincial mind when it is most sincere.[44]

One should remember that the progresses and processions not only gave Elizabeth welcome recreation in the
country; they had a constant part in her policy of winning
and holding the affections of her people. The coronation
dialogue between queen and people set the key for her
public demeanor throughout the remainder of her reign.
However much she bared the coarser side of her complex
character to maids and counselors, Elizabeth was always
gracious and radiant before her people. She was careful to
show herself often to them in all her splendor. She celebrated merry holidays with them. In progress she was
always easy of approach, ready to hear of any injury, at-
tentive to the humblest suppliant.[45] She received gifts
graciously, and left appealing mementos behind her, even
when she could not afford to follow Castiglione's counsel
of princely liberality. She was careful to keep public expectation at a high pitch by the uncertainty of her royal
pleasure as to just what host she would honor next. By
progresses and processions among the masses, and by
favoring masques, jousts, and tournaments among the
nobility, Elizabeth grappled to her the hearts of all her
people with hoops of steel.[46]

[44] Professor Robert Withington (*English Pageantry*, Cambridge, Mass.,
I [1918], 202) notes the absence of classical characters in the coronation show.
Historical and Biblical figures naturally displace foreign deities on this deeply
patriotic occasion.

[45] See below, pp. 216–217. Effective as a gesture of Christian humility was
the queen's observance of Maundy Thursday. Under 1560, Nichols (I, 83–85)
notes: "Maunday Thursday, the Queen kept her Maundy in her Hall at the
Court in the afternoon; and then gave unto twenty women so many gowns, and
one woman had her best gown; and her Grace washed their feet: and in a new
white cup she drank unto every woman, and then they had the cup. The same
afternoon she gave unto poor men, women, and children, whole and lame, in
St. James's Park, being two thousand people, and upwards, *2 d.* apiece."

[46] See the admirable chapter, "'The Affability of Their Prince,'" in Professor
J. E. Neale's *Queen Elizabeth*, New York, 1934, pp. 202–216.

One should remember, too, that the progresses, processions, and spectacles with which Elizabeth won and held her people had medieval precedents and contemporary parallels. Perhaps she, a close student of history, did not forget that Roman emperors, usually far less worthy of the affection of their subjects, had made use of sports, games, and barbaric spectacles to dazzle and hold the populace. The English tradition which she expanded went back to William of Normandy's mobile courts, impressively organized in progression from one lord's castle to another. Wolsey had surrounded his master — and himself — with magnificent display as a shrewd political measure. Across the channel, Catherine was using amusements and spectacles to entertain the crowd and to distract Protestants and Catholics from civil war; the young French king was about a long progress in 1564–1566. And the entertainment of Alençon at Antwerp in 1581–82 featured allegorical devices that parallel some of the progress shows for Elizabeth.[47] In an age when comparatively few people could read, the power and dignity of the prince needed to be made real for the masses by the sight of him in rich array, heralded by song and dance. Pageants and festivals diverted the attention of the people from past troubles and present changes, and they gave the queen needed relaxation. These were sound political reasons for Elizabeth's progresses and processions. The wisdom of her policy in visiting town and university and castle alike throughout her long and popular reign is best seen when it is contrasted with her successor's course of centering his display upon a court group, in spite of his extensive progresses. The music of the Jacobean masque was not finally so sweet, at least for a ruler's ears, as the simple songs of devotion which Elizabeth heard when she visited towns like Norwich, or when the London balladist caught her attention.

[47] See Nichols, II, 354–385.

Nor were her people reluctant idolaters. Of course not
many a subject "whined away himself for the love of
Queen *Elizabeth*," as Francis Osborne declares a certain
tailor did,[48] and the troubles, financial and otherwise, of
the queen's hosts were very real, but local loyalty repeatedly assented to drains on its treasury to help entertain
her. Burghley's great expense as host at Theobalds he dismissed with the declaration that to please her majesty he
"never would omit to strain [himself] to more charges than
building it." [49]   His attitude is like that of most noble
servants in whom Elizabeth knew how to inspire complete
devotion to herself as England personified. Englishmen
felt that they were celebrating the waxing glory of their
native land when they honored their Deborah as she moved
among them. They found no hospitality too rich for her.
She represented the new greatness of their nation in its
increasing consciousness of strength. Mere flattery and
convention do not obscure the deepest notes heard in the
progress and ballad verse. And no merely vain woman
could have commanded her gracious replies to the compliments paid her. Elizabeth knew that she was the happy
personification of a happier nationality which her people
were making articulate through their poets. Their song in
her praise for nearly half a century is proof that she was a
wise politician who knew the source of her power — a
pleased people. It is proof, too, that she did not give them
politics alone.

Now that the ballads and the progress memorials have
borne united testimony to the popular admiration and
awe which supports every great idealization of a national
figure, I pass naturally, by way of a national drama, into
a study of Elizabeth idealized by the more cultivated
imagination of the age. Eliza and the beautiful court

[48] *The Miscellaneous Works*, 11th ed., 1722, I, 58.
[49] Nichols, I, 205 n.; see I, xxvii.

ladies whom I shall soon introduce must not make one
forget the homely charm of their cockney and country
cousins, Judith and Deborah. They prove that Gloriana
was, as Gloriana herself boasted, "mere English."

CHAPTER III

Eliza in the Drama

T
HE portrait of Eliza in the drama, which is finished in plays by Lyly, Peele, Jonson, Dekker,
and Shakespeare, is begun in crude sketches
attached to late moralities and interludes, most
of which were performed before the playhouses were built.
Such rough strokes appear in prologues, or in epilogues
that are formal concluding prayers. At first they have
little or no organic relation to the plays themselves, as the
following quotation from Thomas Ingelend's *The Diso-*
bedient Child (*ca.* 1560) will suggest:

> *Here the rest of the Players come in and kneele downe*
> *all togyther, eche of them sayinge one of these verses.*

And last of all to make an ende,
O God to the we most humblye praye,
That to Queene Elizabeth thou do sende
Thy lyvely pathe and perfecte waye!
Graunte her in health to raygne
With us many yeares most prosperouslye,
And after this lyfe for to attayne
The eternall blysse, joye, and felycytie!

.   .   .   .

And that we thy people, duely consyderynge
The power of our Queene and great auctorytie,
Maye please thee and serve her without fayntynge,
Lyvynge in peace, rest, and tranquilytie.
GOD SAVE THE QUEENE.[1]

---

[1] Pages 58–59, *Early English Poetry, Ballads, and Popular Literature of the*
Middle Ages, vol. XXII (1848), ed. J. O. Halliwell, Percy Society. The prayer

VISIT OF QUEEN ELIZABETH TO BLACKFRIARS, JUNE 16, 1600

From the painting by Marcus Gheeraerts in the collection of Col. F. J. B. Wingfield Digby, Sherborne Castle, Dorset

Similar prayers appear at the end of *Tom Tyler and his Wife* (not later than 1563),[2] *Apius and Virginia* (not later than 1567–68),[3] *Cambyses King of Persia* (not later than 1570),[4] *The Play of Patient Grissell* (1558–1561),[5] and *Common Conditions* (not later than 1576).[6]

When the playwrights let their actors speak prologues or concluding prayers more or less in character, they took a step forward not only in the creation of Eliza but in dramatic technique as well. After Damnation has made away with the wicked souls in Thomas Lupton's (?) *All for Money* (not earlier than 1558 or later than 1577), Godly Admonition, Virtue, Humility, and Charity moralize the play. Virtue leads in a prayer:

Let vs praye for the Queenes Maiestie our soueraigne gouernour,
That she may raigne quietly according to Gods will:
Whereby she may suppresse vyce and set foorth Gods glorie and honour.
And as she hath begon godly, so to continue still.[7]

Peace prays in *Impatient Poverty* (entered in the Stationers' Register, 1560);[8] Exercitation also prays in W. Wager's

---

as for Queen Elizabeth may be an interpolation for an audience that is elsewhere in the play reminded to "serve the King." Unless otherwise noted, I date plays throughout this study according to dates of production as given in E. K. Chambers, *The Elizabethan Stage*, 1923.

² Ed. G. C. Moore Smith and W. W. Greg, Malone Society Reprints, 1910, lines 924–928.

³ Ed. J. S. Farmer, Tudor Facsimile Texts, 1908, sig. E3ᵛ.

⁴ Ed. J. S. Farmer, Tudor Facsimile Texts, 1910, sig. F4ᵛ.

⁵ Ed. W. W. Greg and R. B. McKerrow, Malone Society Reprints, 1909, lines 2104–2113.

⁶ Ed. C. F. Tucker Brooke, Elizabethan Club Reprints, New Haven, 1915, lines 1899–1902.

⁷ Ed. J. S. Farmer, Tudor Facsimile Texts, 1910, sig. E3ᵛ.

⁸ Ed. J. S. Farmer, Tudor Facsimile Texts, 1907, sigs. E2–E2ᵛ. Although the first edition of this play may be no later than the reign of Edward VI, as Sir Edmund Chambers (IV, 20) thinks, it is fitting that Peace should follow Prosperity and speak this prayer at the end of the 1560 edition of the interlude.

The Longer Thou Livest, the More Fool Thou Art (ca. 1559).[9]
Assurance, after a prayer for God's church and congrega-
tion by Edification, ends *New Custom* (not earlier than
1558 or later than 1573) by praying for "our noble Quêene
Elizabeth." [10] At the end of Wager's *Enough is as Good
as a Feast (ca.* 1560) Satan carries off Covetousness on
his back, and Enough and Contentation pray for Elizabeth.[11] Nobility, Clergy, and Civil Order close John
Bale's *King Johan* (Elizabethan revision between 1560
and 1563) with praise and prayers for the queen who is a
"lyghte, to other princes all for the godly wayes," and
who subdues papists and Anabaptists.[12] At the end of the
same author's *A nevve Comedy or Enterlude concernyng thre
lawes, of Nature, Moises, and Christe* (1562) Fides Christiana prays for Elizabeth.[13] Prayers for her conclude
Richard Edwards's *Damon and Pythias* (1565) and promise
her true friends.[14] Equity and Charity join Constancy to
end *King Darius* (not later than 1565) with a prayer for
her.[15] Toward the end of *Jacob and Esau* (not later than
1558) Rebecca prays for Elizabeth.[16] In the concluding
dialogue between Truth and Duty in John Pickering's
The History of Horestes (1567–68) Duty calls upon all to

[9] Ed. J. S. Farmer, Tudor Facsimile Texts, 1910, sig. G4.

[10] Ed. J. S. Farmer, Tudor Facsimile Texts, 1908, sig. D4^v.

[11] Ed. Seymour De Ricci, Henry E. Huntington Facsimile Reprints, New
York, 1920, sig. G2^v.

[12] Ed. J. H. P. Pafford and W. W. Greg, Malone Society Reprints, 1931,
pp. 133–134. The date is after the editors, p. xvii.

[13] Sig. L1^v. This rare 1562 edition (British Museum C.34.f.4) of Bale's play,
the first known edition of which is dated 1538, has, after the concluding prayer
for Elizabeth, "A songe vpon Benedictus" in which the queen appears as the
restorer of God's law (sig. L2^v).

[14] Ed. J. S. Farmer, Tudor Facsimile Texts, 1908, sigs. H3^v–H4.

[15] Ed. J. S. Farmer, Tudor Facsimile Texts, 1909, sig. H4.

[16] Ed. J. S. Farmer, Tudor Facsimile Texts, 1908, sig. G4^v. *"'Jacob and
Esau' was licensed in 1557–8, and was probably printed soon afterwards, so that the
1568 edition is not likely to be the first one, but no other impression is extant"*
(editor's preliminary note).

pray for the queen.[17] Virtuous Life, Honor, and Good
Fame unite at the end of Ulpian Fulwell's *Like will to Like*
(*ca.* 1568) to pray for "our noble and gracious Queen." [18]
Fortune, making the last speech in *The Rare Triumphs of
Love and Fortune* (1582 ?) after the dissension with Venus
has been resolved, prays for her.[19] So, too, the Judge
toward the end of *The Pedlar's Prophecy* (not later than
1594).[20] In Robert Wilson's *The Three Lords and Three
Ladies of London* (*ca.* 1589) a "Lady very richly attyred,
representing London, hauing two Angels before her, and
two after her," speaks a preface, a part of which follows:

> This blessing is not my sole benefit,
> All England is, and so preseru'd hath bene,
> Not by mans strength, his pollicie and wit,
> But by a power and prouidence vnseene.
> Euen for the loue wherwith God loues our Queen:
> In whom, for whom, by whom we do possesse
> More grace, more good, than London can expresse.
>
> And that hath bred our plenty and our peace,
> And they doo breed the sportes you come to see.

At the marriage of the three lords and the three ladies a
song is sung that contains the following verses:

> Strowe the faire flowers and herbes that be greene,
> To grace the gaiest wedding that euer was seene.

If London list to looke, the streetes were nere so cleene,
Except it was when best it might, in welcome of our Queene.

And Pomp, one of the three lords of London, leads in a
prayer for this queen who brings all blessings.[21] In *A*

---

[17] Ed. J. S. Farmer, Tudor Facsimile Texts, 1910, sig. E4. Sir Edmund
Chambers (III, 466) thinks that this play was the court *Orestes* of 1567–68.

[18] *The Dramatic Writings of Ulpian Fulwell*, ed. J. S. Farmer, 1906, p. 52.

[19] Ed. W. W. Greg, Malone Society Reprints, 1930, lines 1850–1851.

[20] Ed. W. W. Greg, Malone Society Reprints, 1914, lines 1555–1558. Chambers (IV, 41) thinks that the play reads "like a belated piece of *c.* 1560–70."

[21] Ed. J. S. Farmer, Tudor Facsimile Texts, 1912, sigs. A2ᵛ, I2ᵛ, I4.

Looking Glass for London and England (*ca.* 1590) London is rebuked for her many sins, and the glass is so held that Jonas can conclude the play with the following verses:

> O turne, O turne, with weeping to the Lord,
> And thinke the praiers and vertues of thy Queene
> Defers the plague which otherwise would fall.
> Repent, O London, least for thine offence
> Thy shepheard faile, whom mightie God preserue,
> That she may bide the pillar of his Church
> Against the stormes of Romish Antichrist.
> The hand of mercy ouershead her head,
> And let all faithfull subiects say, Amen.[22]

Honesty in the last speech of *A Knack to Know a Knave* (1592) prays that "God cut then [*sic*] off that wrong the Prince or Comnmnaltie [*sic*]," and begs that

> her dayes of blesse neuer haue end,
> Upon whose lyfe so many lyues depend.[23]

Mucedorus (not later than 1598) ends with a dialogue in which Envy refuses to "praise a womans deeds" until Comedy calls for a prayer for Elizabeth; then Envy heart-ily offers praise and prayer.[24]   Clearly the late moralities and interludes, most of which were produced before the Armada year, portray the queen very much as she is drawn in broadside and progress verse.   She is favored of the Protestant God; and she brings her land peace and plenty.

But the mature Eliza of the drama is also the flower of the Tudors whom patriotic Englishmen linked with the glory of Arthur and Brut.   After a passing glance at *The Contention between Liberality and Prodigality* (1601), it

---

[22] *The Plays and Poems of Robert Greene*, ed. J. C. Collins, Oxford, 1905, I, 214.

[23] Ed. J. S. Farmer, Tudor Facsimile Texts, 1911, sig. G4.

[24] Ed. J. S. Farmer, Tudor Facsimile Texts, 1910, sig. F4ᵛ. Quarto 2 of this play shows a prologue and conclusion made to compliment King James. See *The Shakespeare Apocrypha*, ed. C. F. Tucker Brooke, Oxford, 1908, pp. 105, 126.

will be well to trace that side of Eliza's ancestry. This moralizing play shows that the virtues of the queen could be linked closely with the content of a drama. The play is still near in style and content to such immature work as has just been reviewed.[25] Prodigality is arraigned before Elizabeth. The trial is on "the fourth day of February, in the three & fortie yeere of the prosperous raigne of Elizabeth our dread Soueraigne." Prodigality concludes his plea:

> The Prince is mercifull, of whose great mercy,
> Full many haue largely tasted already:
> Which makes me appeale thereto more boldly.

At the end "*Vertue, Equitie, Liberalitie, Iudge, and all come downe before the Queene, and after reuerence made, Vertue speaketh*" an epilogue offering the show to the queen as her "*humble vassall, . . . With feare and loue.*" [26]

It is, of course, in the history play that the dramatist found his best chance to develop Eliza as a symbol for the new nationalism which her rule was fostering. *Gorboduc*, which "was shewed before the Quenes most excellent Maiestie, in her highnes Court of Whitehall, the .xviij. day of Ianuary, Anno Domini. 1561," [27] was a sermon on the evils of civil war in Britain and the dangers to the land

[25] Chambers (IV, 26) thinks it unnecessary to assume with Fleay that this play of 1601 was a revival of an Edwardian play just because "prince" is made to refer to Elizabeth. Chambers does recognize that "the characters are mainly abstract and the style archaic for the seventeenth century," and that "it is conceivable that the *Prodigality* of 1567-8 had been revived." See Greg's prefatory remarks (pp. v–vi) in his edition of the play from which I quote.

[26] Ed. W. W. Greg, Malone Society Reprints, 1913, lines 1247 ff.

[27] Chambers, III, 457. There is a good discussion of this aspect of *Gorboduc* in Professor Mary Martha Purdy's *Elizabethan Literary Treatment of the Proposed Marriages of Queen Elizabeth*, an unpublished University of Pittsburgh thesis, 1928, pp. 205–215. Miss Purdy (pp. 196–198) finds verses in the 1561 edition of *Godly Queen Hester* which may indicate that this early interlude was reworked to apply to the marriage question for Elizabeth, figured as Hester, "a virgin puer" who excels in "learninge and litterature." To Miss Purdy's

when a prince remained without issue. Elizabeth went her own way to leave an empire as her descendant; but a dramatist who preached the need of union in her name to avoid war and dissension was certain to please if he let the direct succession problem alone. An excellent illustration of Eliza as the happy heir of the nation's fancied or actual past in whom all discords are resolved appears in *The Misfortunes of Arthur*, which was presented to her majesty by the "Gentlemen of *Grayes-Inne* at her Highnesse Court in Greenewich" on February 28, 1588. The introduction, "penned by Nicholas Trotte" to excuse the efforts of the unpoetic lawyers who staged the play, shows the center of their devotion to be

> a Queene, for whom her purest gold
> Nature refind, that she might therein sette
> Both priuate and imperiall vertues all.
>
> .   .   .   .
>
> How sutes a Tragedie for such a time?
> Thus. For that since your sacred Maiestie
> In gratious hands the regall Scepter held
> All Tragedies are fled from State, to stadge.

At the outset of the first act the spirit of Gorlois foretells the great troubles ahead that must avenge the deep wrongs that he has suffered. But he sees promise in the heavens of

> A happier age a thousand yeares to come:
> An age for peace, religion, wealth, and ease,
> When all the world shall wonder at your blisse:
> That, that is yours.[28]

---

excellent study I am indebted for several references; but my ideas about the idealization of Elizabeth, sometimes parallel with Miss Purdy's about the virgin queen, were developed independently of it.

[28] Ed. H. C. Grumbine, Berlin, 1900, pp. 112–113, 120.

And at the end of the play the ghost of Gorlois comes
forward again to speak:

> Let future age be freé from *Gorlois* Ghost.
> Let *Brytaine* henceforth bath in endlesse weale.
> Let *Virgo* come from Heauen, the glorious Starre:
> The Zodiac's ioy: the Planets chiefe delight:
> The hope of all the yeare: the ease of Skies:
> The Aires reliefe, the comfort of the Earth.
>   That vertuous *Virgo* borne for *Brytaines* blisse:
> That pierelesse braunch of *Brute*: that sweête remaine
> Of *Priam's* state: that hope of springing *Troy*:
> Which time to come, and many ages hence
> Shall of all warres compound eternall peace.
>   Let her reduce the golden age againe,
> Religion, ease and health of former world.
> Yea, let that *Virgo* come and *Saturnes* raigne,
> And yeares oft ten times tolde expirde in peace.
> A Rule, that else no Realme shall euer finde,
> A Rule most rare, vnheard, vnseéne, vnread,
> The sole example that the world affordes.
>   That (*Brytaine*) that Renowme, yea that is thine.
> B'it so: my wrath is wrought.[29]

Robert Greene lets Friar Bacon in *Frier Bacon and Frier
Bungay* (*ca.* 1589) prophesy about the "pierelesse braunch
of *Brute*" that should ultimately come to bless a united
England:

> *Bacon.* I find by deepe praescience of mine Art,
>   Which once I tempred in my secret Cell,
>   That here where *Brute* did build his *Troynouant*,

---

[29] Page 190. A speech "penned by William *Fulbecke gentlemen*" to be spoken
in the second scene of the last act instead of this one by Thomas Hughes looks
over the centuries of turmoil in Britain to the "thrice happie daies" of the
"goddesse of the Angels land" (pp. 195–196). Perhaps such lost history plays
as *I The Conquest of Brute* (Chambers, III, 288), *King Arthur* (III, 333), and
Owen Tudor (III, 448) contained similar celebration of the Tudor princess
descended from Brut and Arthur.

From forth the Royall Garden of a King,
Shall flourish out so rich and faire a bud,
Whose brightnesse shall deface proud *Phoebus* flowre,
And ouer-shadow *Albion* with her leaues.
Till then, *Mars* shall be master of the field:
But then the stormy threats of wars shall cease;
The horse shall stampe as carelesse of the pike,
Drums shall be turn'd to timbrels of delight;
With wealthy fauours plenty shall enrich
The strond that gladded wandring *Brute* to see,
And peace from heauen shall harbour in these leaues,
That gorgeous beautifies this matchlesse flower.
Apollos Hellitropian then shall stoope,
And *Venus* hyacinth shall vaile her top,
Iuno shall shut her gilliflowers vp,
And *Pallas* Bay shall bash her brightest greene;
Ceres carnation, in consort with those,
Shall stoope and wonder at *Diana's* Rose.[30]

England "girt in with the ocean" was the chief mari-
time power after 1588. Dramatists found Eliza a fit sym-
bol for the national pride in the victory of that year. The
Armada is proudly alluded to in Robert Greene's *Orlando
Furioso* (*ca.* 1591, and "plaid before the Queenes Maiestie"
according to the edition of 1594);[31] and in George Peele's
The Battle of Alcazar (*ca.* 1589) King Sebastian warns
Stukeley:

I tell thee, Stukeley, they are far too weak
To violate the Queen of Ireland's right;
For Ireland's Queen commandeth England's force.
Were every ship ten thousand on the seas,
Mann'd with the strength of all the eastern kings,
Conveying all the monarchs of the world,
T' invade the island where her highness reigns,
'Twere all in vain, for heavens and destinies
Attend and wait upon her majesty.

[30] *Plays and Poems*, II, 77.   [31] I. i. 87.

Sacred, imperial, and holy is her seat,
Shining with wisdom, love, and mightiness:
Nature that everything imperfect made,
Fortune that never yet was constant found,
Time that defaceth every golden show,
Dare not decay, remove, or her impair;
Both nature, time, and fortune, all agree,
To bless and serve her royal majesty.
The wallowing ocean hems her round about;
Whose raging floods do swallow up her foes,
And on the rocks their ships in pieces split,
And even in Spain, where all the traitors dance
And play themselves upon a sunny day,
Securely guard the west part of her isle;
The south the narrow Britain-sea begirts,
Where Neptune sits in triumph to direct
Their course to hell that aim at her disgrace;
The German seas alongst the east do run,
Where Venus banquets all her water-nymphs,
That with her beauty glancing on the waves
Distains the cheek of fair Proserpina.
Advise thee, then, proud Stukeley, ere thou pass
To wrong the wonder of the highest God;
Sith danger, death, and hell do follow thee,
Thee, and them all, that seek to danger her.[32]

It is Eliza's peace that the dramatists most frequently
praise. In a history like *The Tragedy of Locrine* (*ca.* 1591)
the author does not miss his chance to allude to a peace
which contrasted with the "Lamentable Tragedie of
Locrine, the eldest sonne of King *Brutus*, discoursing the
warres of the *Britaines*, and *Hunnes*, with their discom-
fiture." Atey speaks at the end of the play:

> Lo here the end of lawlesse trecherie,
> Of vsurpation and ambitious pride,
> And they that for their priuate amours dare

---

[32] *The Works of George Peele*, ed. A. H. Bullen, 1888, I, 259–260.

Turmoile our land, and see their broiles abroach,
Let them be warned by these premisses,
And as a woman was the onely cause
That ciuill discord was then stirred vp,
So let vs pray for that renowned mayd,
That eight and thirtie yeares the scepter swayd,
In quiet peace and sweet felicitie,
And euery wight that seekes her graces smart,
wold that this sword wer pierced in his hart.[33]

Allusion to Elizabeth in Latin history plays shows the far
reach of the love of her peace. Nemesis speaks in Matthew
Gwinne's *Nero Tragædia Nova* (not later than 1603):

> *At hic alumna pacis, imperij salus,*
> *Dea mititatis, hominum amor, regum decus,*
> *ELISA regnat; vix scias magis an suos*
> *Amet, an ametur à suis; maior loco,*
> *An melior animo; faciat, an foueat magis*
> *Probos, fideles aulicos: Patres suos*
> *Magis an sequatur: an præeat: illi parem*
> *Laudem an poeta fingat, an Princeps ferat.*
> *Tam fama, facta, fata, disparia, vt magis*
> *Nihil esse possit, quàm Anglica Neroni Dea,*
> *Temporibus illis ista, bona summè malis.*
> *Nos ergo eamus: Vos vel exutis malo*
> *Nerone, vestris vel bonis plausum date.*[34]

George Salterne's *Tomumbeius siue Sultanici in Ægypto
Imperij Euersio* (not later than 1603) is dedicated to the
virgin Eliza in Latin verses;[35] and the drama *Sapientia
Salomonis* (1565–66), acted before the queen by the
Westminster boys, has its prologue and epilogue turned to

---

[33] Ed. R. B. McKerrow, Malone Society Reprints, Oxford, 1908, lines
2269–2280.

[34] *Nero Tragædia*, 1603, sig. T3. Chambers (III, 332) takes the "*ELISA
regnat*" of this epilogue as evidence that the date of this play is not later than
1603.

[35] Bodleian MS. Rawlinson Poet. 75, fol. 3.

compliment her.[36]   The epilogue of Thomas Legge's
Richardus Tertius (March, 1580) follows the happy union
of York and Lancaster down to Elizabeth —

> Elizabethā, patre dignā filiā,
> Canosq vencentem seniles virginem.
> Quæ regna tot Phœbi phractis cursibus
> Cōmissa rexit pace fœlix Anglia.
> quam dextra supremi tonantis protegat
> illus et vitam tegendo protrahet.[37]

The True Tragedy of Richard the Third (not later than
1594) also has at the conclusion a survey of England's
rulers from the "ioyning of these Houses both in one, by
. . . braue Prince Henry the seauenth" on to

> Worthie Elizabeth, a mirrour in her
> age, by whose wise life and ciuill gouernment, her
> country was defended from the crueltie of
> famine, fire and swoord, warres, fearefull messengers.
> This is that Queene as writers truly say,
> That God had marked downe to liue for aye.
> Then happie England mongst thy neighbor Iles,
> For peace and plentie still attends on thee:
> And all the fauourable Planets smiles
> To see thee liue, in such prosperitie.
> She is that lampe that keeps faire Englands light,
> And through her faith her country liues in peace:
> And she hath put proud Antichrist to flight,
> And bene the meanes that ciuill wars did cease.
> Then England kneele vpon thy hairy knee,
> And thanke that God that still prouides for thee.
> The Turke admires to heare her gouernment,
> And babies in *Iury*, sound her princely name,
> All Christian Princes to that Prince hath sent,

---

[36] British Museum MS. Additional 20061, fols. 3–3ᵛ, 33–33ᵛ. This manuscript is the presentation copy to the queen, stamped with the royal arms and her initials.

[37] Ed. W. C. Hazlitt, *Shakespeare's Library*, 2d ed., V (1875), 220.

After her rule was rumord foorth by fame.
The Turke hath sworne neuer to lift his hand,
To wrong the Princesse of this blessed land.
Twere vaine to tell the care this Queene hath had,
In helping those that were opprest by warre:
And how her Maiestie hath stil bene glad,
When she hath heard of peace proclaim'd from far.
Ieneua, France, and *Flanders,* hath set downe,
The good she hath done, since she came to the Crowne.
For which, if ere her life be tane away,
God grant her soule may liue in heauen for aye.
For if her Graces dayes be brought to end,
Your hope is gone, on whom did peace depend.[38]

Eliza appears of full stature in the plays to which I now turn. The conception of peaceful Elizabeth as the "piere-lesse braunch of *Brute*" that dominates in the histories merges with the homely view of her as the "wonder of the highest God" that prevails in the moral interludes. A gracious virgin queen who incarnates all virtues is the result of this union when a cultivated playwright turns to popular drama. The conclusion of *Histriomastix* (1589?, 1599) presents this Eliza by the name of Astræa to suggest her golden age of peace.

Enter PEACE, BACCHUS, CERES *and* PLENTY, *bearing the* Cornu copiæ, *at the one doore. At the other* POVERTY *with her at-tendants; who, beholding* PEACE *approach, vanish.*

.   .   .   .

They begin to sing, and presently cease.

A Song.

With Lawrell shall our Altars flame,
In honour of thy sacred name.

---

[38] Ed. W. W. Greg, Malone Society Reprints, 1929, lines 2192–2223.

Enter ASTRÆA *ushered by* FAME, *supported by* FORTITUDE *and*
RELIGION, *followed by* VIRGINITY *and* ARTES.

> *Peace.* No more:
> Be dumbe in husht observance at this sight:
> Heere comes *Amazements* object, wonders height,
> *Peaces* patronesse, *Heavens* miracle,
> *Vertues* honour, *Earths* admiration,
> *Chastities* Crowne, *Justice* perfection,
> Whose traine is unpolute *Virginity*,
> Whose *Diadem* of bright immortall *Fame*
> Is burnisht with unvalued respect,
> Ineffable wonder of remotest lands;
> Still sway thy gratious Scepter! I resigne;
> What I am is by Thee, my selfe am thine!

At this point Astræa "*mounts unto the throne.*" A marginal
gloss, "*Q. Eliza,*" in the original gives a pointer hardly
needed, for the verses that follow could of course describe
only her.

> Mount, Emperesse, whose praise for Peace shall mount,
> Whose glory, which thy solid vertues wonne,
> Shall honour *Europe* whilst there shines a Sunne!
> Crown'd with Heavens inward beauties, worlds applause;
> Thron'd and reposd within the loving feare
> Of thy adoring Subjects: live as long
> As Time hath life, and *Fame* a worthy tongue!
> Still breath our glory, the worlds *Empresse*,
> *Religions* Gardian, *Peaces* patronesse!
> Now flourish Arts, the Queene of *Peace* doth raigne;
> *Vertue* triumph, now shee doth sway the stemme,
> Who gives to *Vertue* honours Diadem.
> All sing *Pæans* to her sacred worth,
> Which none but Angels tongues can warble forth:
> Yet sing, for though we cannot light the Sunne,
> Yet utmost might hath kinde acceptance wonne.

Song.
Religion, Arts and Merchandise
triumph, triumph:
Astræa rules, whose gracious eyes
triumph, triumph.
O're *Vices* conquest whose desires
triumph, triumph:
Whose all to chiefest good aspires
then all triumph.[39]

More graceful than this compliment to Eliza as Astræa
is that which Thomas Nashe paid "*Peaces* patronesse" in
Summer's Last Will and Testament (1592) when she was on
summer progress. Toward the beginning of the play
Summer declares:

This month haue I layne languishing a bed,
Looking eche houre to yeeld my life and throne;
And dyde I had in deed vnto the earth,
But that *Eliza*, Englands beauteous Queene,
On whom all seasons prosperously attend,
Forbad the execution of my fate,
Vntill her ioyfull progresse was expir'd.
For her doth Summer liue, and linger here,
And wisheth long to liue to her content.

At the end departing summer makes the following re-
quests:

And finally; O words, now clense your course,
Vnto *Eliza*, that most sacred Dame,
Whom none but Saints and Angels ought to name,
All my faire dayes remaining I bequeath,
To waite vnto her till she be returnd.

---

[39] Ed. Richard Simpson, *The School of Shakspere*, New York, 1878, II, 84–87.
Chambers (IV, 17) thinks that this masque-like conclusion is "no doubt . . . an
addition, constituting an alternative ending for a court performance before
Elizabeth." The old ending shows Plenty, Pride, Envy, War, and Poverty
entering and resigning their several scepters to Peace "sitting in Maiestie."

Autumne, I charge thee, when that I am dead,
Be prest and seruiceable at her beck,
Present her with thy goodliest ripened fruites,
Vnclothe no Arbors where she euer sate,
Touch not a tree thou thinkst she may passe by.
And, Winter, with thy wrythen frostie face,
Smoothe vp thy visage, when thou lookst on her;
Thou neuer lookst on such bright maiestie:
A charmed circle draw about her court,
Wherein warme dayes may daunce, & no cold come;
On seas let winds make warre, not vexe her rest,
Quiet inclose her bed, thought flye her brest.
Ah, gracious Queene, though Summer pine away,
Yet let thy flourishing stand at a stay;
First droupe this vniuersals aged frame,
E're any malady thy strength should tame:
Heauen raise vp pillers to vphold thy hand,
Peace may haue still his temple in thy land.
Loe, I haue said; this is the totall summe.
Autumne and Winter, on your faithfulnesse
For the performance I do firmely builde.[40]

The "Epilogue, at the Presentation before Queen Elizabeth. By Malcilente," which Ben Jonson wrote for *Every
Man out of his Humour* (1599) is a beautifully phrased
tribute to the English Astræa. It gains particular force in
being spoken by a severe critic of the follies of the court.

Never till now did object greet mine eyes
With any light content: but in her graces
All my malicious powers have lost their stings.
Envy is fled my soul at sight of her,
And she hath chased all black thoughts from my bosom,
Like as the sun doth darkness from the world.
My stream of humour is run out of me,
And as our city's torrent, bent t'infect
The hallow'd bowels of the silver Thames,

---

[40] *The Works of Thomas Nashe*, ed. R. B. McKerrow, III (1910), 237, 291–292.

Is check'd by strength and clearness of the river,
Till it hath spent itself even at the shore;
So in the ample and unmeasured flood
Of her perfections, are my passions drown'd;
And I have now a spirit as sweet and clear
As the more rarified and subtle air: —
With which, and with a heart as pure as fire,
Yet humble as the earth, do I implore,
O heaven, that She, whose presence hath effected
This change in me, may suffer most late change
In her admired and happy government:
May still this Island be call'd Fortunate,
And rugged Treason tremble at the sound,
When Fame shall speak it with an emphasis.
Let foreign polity be dull as lead,
And pale Invasion come with half a heart,
When he but looks upon her blessed soil.
The throat of War be stopt within h'er land,
And turtle-footed Peace dance fairy rings
About her court; where never may there come
Suspect or danger, but all trust and safety.
Let Flattery be dumb, and Envy blind
In her dread presence; Death himself admire her:
And may her virtues make him to forget
The use of his inevitable hand.
Fly from her, Age; sleep, Time, before her throne;
Our strongest wall falls down, when she is gone.[41]

In *Cynthia's Revels* (1600–01) Jonson clothed a vigorous
satire of the court in an elaborate compliment to the virgin
Eliza. She is a "goddess excellently bright" above and
beyond the foibles and affectations that infect her court.
With daring self-assurance Jonson has his Cynthia approve
the censures of Crites, who only aims to make her court
more virtuous. Her proud speeches reflect some of Eliza-

---

[41] *The Works of Ben Jonson*, ed. W. Gifford and F. Cunningham, 1875, II,
198–200.

beth's own imperious command over the loves of her lords
and ladies, her impatience with cant and license. The
queen and the satirist were no Puritans, but they were at
one in condemning scandal, hypocrisy, and undisciplined
love. Nor did Jonson need to doubt her approval of the
satire when he deified her in the second of the concluding
masques and vowed his aim to be, "*with refined voice*," to

> *report*
> *The grace of Cynthia, and her court.*[42]

Cynthia was the "bright mirror of true Chastitie" for
patriotic dramatists.

The prologue that was "*pronounced* before the Queenes
Maiestie" when Dekker's *The Shoemaker's Holiday* (1599)
was performed at court was as follows:

> As wretches in a storme (expecting day)
> With trembling hands and eyes cast vp to heauen,
> Make Prayers the anchor of their conquerd hopes,
> So we (deere Goddesse) wonder of all eyes,
> Your meanest vassalls (through mistrust and feare,
> To sincke into the bottome of disgrace,
> By our imperfit pastimes) prostrate thus
> On bended knees, our sailes of hope do strike,
> Dreading the bitter stormes of your dislike.
> Since then (vnhappy men) our hap is such,
> That to our selues our selues no help can bring,
> But needes must perish, if your saint-like eares
> (Locking the temple where all mercy sits)
> Refuse the tribute of our begging tongues.

---

[42] II, 359. Gifford (II, 361–362) writes that the "fulsome compliments paid
to the 'obdurate virgin' of threescore and ten, the hoary-headed Cynthia of
Whitehall, must have appeared infinitely ridiculous, if the frequency of the
practice had not utterly taken away the sense of derision." When one comprehends the profoundly adequate symbol that Cynthia was for her age, Gifford's
judgment about language "grossly adulatory" seems "infinitely ridiculous."

Oh graunt (bright mirror of true Chastitie)
From those life-breathing starres your sun-like Eyes,
One gratious smile: for your celestiall breath
Must send vs life, or sentence vs to death.[43]

No doubt the "deere Goddesse" liked Hammon's words to the Lord Mayor when Rose declares she means "to liue a maide":

Nay chide her not my Lord for doing well,
If she can liue an happie virgins life,
Tis far more blessed than to be a wife.[44]

The inevitable match between Rose and Lacy is effected by royal will — by the queen's royal ancestor "yet a bachelor."

In *Old Fortunatus* (1599) Eliza and Virtue become identical.

The Prologue at Court: Enter two old men.
1. Are you then trauelling to the temple of Eliza?
2. Euen to her temple are my feeble limmes trauelling. Some cal her Pandora: some Gloriana, some Cynthia: some Delphœbe, some Astræa: all by seuerall names to expresse seuerall loues: Yet all those names make but one celestiall body, as all those loues meete to create but one soule.
1. I am one of her owne countrie, and we adore her by the name of Eliza.

The old men laud their goddess and conclude:

2. My pure loue shines, as thine doth in thy feares:
I weepe for ioy to see so many heads
Of prudent Ladies, clothed in the liuerie
Of siluer-handed age, for seruing you,
Whilst in your eyes youthes glory doth renue:
I weepe for ioy to see the Sunne looke old,

---

[43] *The Dramatic Works of Thomas Dekker*, pub. John Pearson, 1873, I, 7.
[44] I, 35.

To see the Moone mad at her often change,
To see the Starres onely by night to shine,
Whilst you are still bright, still one, still diuine:
I weepe for ioy to see the world decay,
Yet see Eliza flourishing like May:
O pardon me your Pilgrim, I haue measurd
Many a mile to find you: and haue brought,
Old Fortunatus and his family,
With other Cipnots (my poore countrie men)
To pay a whole yeeres tribute: O vouchsafe,
Dread Queene of Fayries, with your gracious eyes,
T'accept theirs and our humble sacrifice.

    1. Now ile beg thee too: and yet I need not:
Her sacred hand hath euermore beene knowne,
As soone held out to straungers as her owne.

    2. Thou doest incourage me: Ile fetch them in,
They haue no princely gifts, we are all poore,
Our offrings are true hearts, who can wish more? [45]

After Fortune has deferred to Virtue at the end of the play, Virtue speaks:

    Fortune th'art vanquisht: sacred deitie,
O now pronounce who winnes the victorie,
And yet that sentence needes not, since alone,
Your vertuous presence Vice hath ouer-throwne,
Yet to confirme the conquest on your side,
Looke but on Fortunatus and his sonnes
Of all the welth those gallants did possesse,
Onely poore Shaddow is left comfortlesse,
Their glorye's faded and their golden pride.
    Sha. Onely poore Shaddow tels how poore they died.
    Vert. All that they had, or mortall men can haue,
Sends onely but a Shaddow from the graue.
Vertue alone liues still, and liues in you,
I am a counterfeit, you are the true,

---

[45] I, 83–84.

I am a Shaddow, at your feete I fall,
Begging for these, and these, my selfe and all.
All these that thus doe kneele before your eyes,
Are shaddowes like my selfe, dred Nymph it lyes
In you to make vs substances. O doe it,
Vertue I am sure you loue, shee woes you to it.
I read a verdict in your Sun-like eyes,
And this it is: Vertue the victorie.
    All. All loudly cry, Vertue the victorie.
    Vert. Vertue the victorie: for ioy of this,
Those selfe same himmes which you to Fortune sung
Let them be now in Vertues honour rung.

The Song.

Vertue smiles: crie hollyday,
Dimples on her cheekes doe dwell,
Vertue frownes, crie wellada,
Her loue is Heauen, her hate is Hell.
Since heau'n and hell obey her power,
Tremble when her eyes doe lowre.
Since heau'n and hell her power obey,
Where shee smiles, crie hollyday.
    Hollyday with ioy we crie,
    And bend, and bend, and merily,
    Sing hymnes to vertues deitie:
    Sing hymnes to Vertues deitie.

As they all offer to goe in, Enter the two old men.

THE EPILOGUE AT COURT

    1. Nay stay, poore pilgrims, when I entred first
The circle of this bright celestiall Sphære,
I wept for ioy, now I could weepe for feare.
    2. I feare we all like mortall men shall proue
Weake (not in loue) but in expressing loue.
    1. Let euery one beg once more on his knee,
One pardon for himselfe, and one for mee,
For I intic'd you hither: O deere Goddesse,

Breathe life in our nombd spirits with one smile,
And from this cold earth, we with liuely soules
Shall rise like men (new-borne) and make heau'n sound
With Hymnes sung to thy name, and praiers that we
May once a yeere so oft enioy this sight,
Til these yong boyes change their curld locks to white,
And when gray-winged Age sits on their heads,
That so their children may supply their Steads,
And that heau'ns great Arithmetician,
(Who in the Scales of Nomber weyes the world)
May still to fortie two, and one yeere more,
And stil adde one to one, that went before,
And multiply fowre tennes by many a ten:
To this I crie Amen.
    All. Amen, Amen.
    1. Good night (deere mistris) those that wish thee harme,
Thus let them stoope vnder destructions arme.   .
    All. Amen, Amen, Amen.[46]

A view of the portrait of Eliza in the popular drama [47] has led from the prayer at the end of *The Disobedient Child* to this at the end of *Old Fortunatus.* Several passing allusions to her, certain or possible, suggest that the portrait was omnipresent in a dramatist's consciousness.

[46] I, 173-175.
[47] Plays designed especially for presentation at court I consider when I formally examine the idealization of Elizabeth in the poetry of the cultivated imagination. I glance at two now — Lyly's *Campaspe* and *Sapho and Phao.* *Campaspe* (1584) is an elaborate allegory in which Elizabeth seems to be figured in Alexander, "a great prince, whose passions and thoughts do . . . far exceede others in extremitie" (*The Complete Works of John Lyly*, ed. R. W. Bond, Oxford, 1902, II, 331), and yet rise free of fettering love. The play is full of witty euphuistic compliment that might tickle Eliza's ears. *Sapho and Phao* (March 3, 1584) is a "medley of classical suggestion . . . made to serve the author's main purpose of flattering the Queen by an allegorical representation of the relations between herself and her suitor, the Duc d'Alençon" (II, 366). Sapho renounces Phao with magnanimity. She triumphs over Venus, and even Cupid himself disowns his mother to sit in her lap. Elizabeth's dictatorship in matches at court is suggested by Sapho's words to Cupid: "I will direct thine arrowes better. Euery rude asse shall not say he is in loue. It is a toye made for Ladies, and I will keepe it onely for Ladies" (II, 414).

Whereby great *Sydney* and our *Spencer* might,
With those *Po*-singers being equalled,
Enchaunt the world with such a sweet delight,
That their eternall Songs (for euer read)
May shew what great *Elizaes* raigne hath bred.
What musicke in the kingdome of her peace,
Hath now beene made to her, and by her might,
Whereby her glorious fame shall neuer cease.[48]

Death. I, now will *Death* in his most haughtie pride,
Fetch his imperiall Carre from deepest hell,
And ride in triumph through the wicked world,
Sparing none but sacred *Cynthias* friend,
VVhom *Death* did feare before her life began:
For holy fates haue grauen it in their tables,
That *Death* shall die, if he attempt her end,
Whose life is heauens delight and *Cynthias* friend.[49]

Hear, hear, O, hear Iarbas' plaining prayers,
Whose hideous echoes make the welkin howl,
And all the woods Eliza to resound![50]

Nay, hearers hong vpon his melting tong,
While sweetly of his Faiery Queene he song,

---

[48] From the epistle to "the right honourable, the *Lady* Mary, *Countesse of* Pembrooke" which precedes Samuel Daniel's *Cleopatra* (not later than 1593) (pp. 26–27, *The Complete Works in Verse and Prose of Samuel Daniel*, ed. A. B. Grosart, III [1885]).

[49] *Solimon and Perseda* (ca. 1589–1592), ed. J. S. Farmer, Tudor Facsimile Texts, 1912, sig. I2ᵛ. Professor F. S. Boas in a note on this play (*The Works of Thomas Kyd*, Oxford, 1901, p. 445) takes "*Cynthias* friend" as an allusion to Elizabeth.

[50] IV. ii. 8–10 of *The Tragedy of Dido Queen of Carthage* (not later than 1593) (p. 194, *The Life of Marlowe and the Tragedy of Dido Queen of Carthage*, ed. C. F. Tucker Brooke, 1930). Professor Tucker Brooke's footnote on "Eliza" in this passage is in part as follows: "This would seem to be an intentional echo of the many praises of Queen Elizabeth under the title of Eliza. 'The two names [i.e. *Eliza* and *Elissa* (Dido)] were regarded as equivalent, and Gabriel Harvey and many others refer to the Queen as Elissa. . . .' (McKerrow)."

While to the waters fall he tun'd [her] fame,
And in each barke engrau'd Elizaes name.[51]

Our radiant queen hates sluts and sluttery.[52]

That very time I saw (but thou couldst not)
Flying between the cool moon and the earth
Cupid, all arm'd. A certain aim he took
At a fair Vestal, throned by the West,
And loos'd his love-shaft smartly from his bow,
As it should pierce a hundred thousand hearts.
But I might see young Cupid's fiery shaft
Quench'd in the chaste beam of the wat'ry moon,
And the imperial vot'ress passed on,
In maiden meditation, fancy-free.[53]

No hart shall intertaine a murthrous thought,
Within the sea imbracing continent,
Where faire *Eliza* Prince of pietie,
Doth weare the peace adorned Diadem.[54]

Yet let not vs maydens condemne our kinde,
Because our vertues are not all so rare:

---

[51] *The Returne from Pernassus* (1598–1602?), lines 222–225 (p. 84, *The Pilgrimage to Parnassus with the Two Parts of the Return from Parnassus*, ed. W. D. Macray, Oxford, 1886).

[52] *The Merry Wives of Windsor* (1599–1600?), V. v. 50 (*The Complete Works of Shakespeare*, ed. G. L. Kittredge, Boston, 1936). In 1702 John Dennis set down a tradition that the play was written at the order of the queen who wanted to see Falstaff in love. The tradition may give ground for taking the verse as an allusion to her exacting preference for virginity.

[53] *A Midsummer Night's Dream* (1595), II. i. 155–167. This passage is generally accepted as an allusion to the English Diana. It fits happily into the atmosphere of a play in which the moon has an important rôle.

[54] Robert Yarrington, *Two Lamentable Tragedies* (not earlier than 1594 or later than 1601), ed. J. S. Farmer, Tudor Facsimile Texts, 1913, sig. K3. The copy of *Fedele and Fortunio or Two Italian Gentlemen* (*ca.* 1584) which came to the Folger Shakespeare Library from the Mostyn sale of 1919 contains a verse "Prologue before the Queene," and an "Epilogue at the Court" signed "M.A." Modern editions are from the copy in the Chatsworth collection which is without the prologue and the epilogue. See Chambers, IV, 13.

For we may freshly yet record in minde,
There liues a virgin, one without compare:
Who of all graces hath her heauenly share.
In whose renowme, and for whose happie daies,
Let vs record this Pæan of her praise.[55]

"*Religions* Gardian, *Peaces* patronesse" — epitomizes
the character of Eliza in the popular drama. The moral
interludes show how close akin she is as "*Religions* Gardian" to Judith and Deborah of broadside and progress
verse. As "*Peaces* patronesse" she is the ultimate heroine
of patriotic history plays.

One should remember that good dramatic technique did
not encourage inserted praise of the queen. Prologues,
epilogues, and prayers were appendages. Allusions were
likely to be out of character or tone. *Histriomastix* and
Old Fortunatus show, however, that it was possible to
resolve the organic movement of a play into a happy
compliment to Eliza. Lyly and Peele wrote charming

---

[55] Robert Wilmot, *The Tragedie of Tancred and Gismund* (1566?), ed. W. W. Greg, Malone Society Reprints, 1914, lines 578–584. In *Sir Giles Goosecap* (not earlier than 1601 or later than 1603; ed. J. S. Farmer, Tudor Facsimile Texts, 1912) Will declares (sig. A4) that the Lady Eugenia "is the best scholler of any woman but one in England." Dramatists took care to except Elizabeth and her court if rulers and courts were being unfavorably represented. See the epilogue of *Cambyses* (sig. F4ᵛ) which asks that the history of a wicked king be not taken amiss. Note *Damon and Pythias* (sig. A2):

> Wherein talkyng of Courtly toyes, wee doo protest this flat,
> Wee talke of Dionisius Courte, wee meane no Court but that.

I have avoided presenting many moot allusions. Clear, but quite conven-
tional, references to Elizabeth appear in Shakespeare's *Henry V*, Prologue.
V. 29–30; in Robert Yarrington's *Two Lamentable Tragedies*, sig. I2; in *Captain
Thomas Stukeley*, ed. J. S. Farmer, Tudor Facsimile Texts, 1911, sigs. D1ᵛ, E4ᵛ;
in *A Larum for London*, ed. W. W. Greg, Malone Society Reprints, 1913, lines
888–892; and in *A Warning for Fair Women*, ed. J. S. Farmer, Tudor Facsimile
Texts, 1912, sigs. I1–I1ᵛ. Professor G. C. Moore Smith (*Modern Language
Review*, III [1907–1908], 146–149) finds a compliment to Elizabeth in *Lingua*
(III. v), which he would date 1602, in the references to "our dread Queen
Psyche" whose words charmed all her hearers.

court plays that were conceived and executed as idealizations of her.

Perhaps the deepest celebration of Elizabeth as "*Peaces patronesse*" is that which is implicit in Shakespeare's plays on English history. Shakespeare was too orthodox a workman to reject the conventional prayer, prophecy, and incidental allusion.[56] But if one takes a patriotic Elizabethan's point of view the histories, especially the Henry plays, sound a far more pervasive pæan to Eliza than that at the end of *The True Tragedy of Richard the Third*. Shakespeare's portrait of his ideal sovereign, Henry V, was for a contemporary patriot a reflection of the virtues of the reigning sovereign, Henry's descendant. Elizabeth, now by avoiding the evils of internal dissension and ill-advised foreign conquest, now by stimulating the arts of peace, was bringing the harmonious England that the histories glorified. The popular audience that cheered Hal's prayer and leadership on the eve of Agincourt did not forget Elizabeth's words on the eve of the Armada of 1588. It liked to hear Hal declare himself a Welshman because Elizabeth was hailed as a Welsh princess sprung of Arthur's line. Cambridge and Grey complimented her government in praising that of Henry V.[57] All patriots knew that Elizabeth's justice and wisdom matched his. She, like Hal, could meet a trying impasse in government with a witty or humorous trump. Both loved fun mixed with the serious duties of kingship. Hal's wooing of the French Catherine interested keenly an audience that had been keyed to a pitch over the French matches proposed for their queen. She, who had her own mind in such matters, must have relished Hal's words about kissing before marriage:

[56] See, respectively, the epilogue for *2 Henry IV*, Cranmer's prophecy in *Henry VIII*, and the "fair Vestal, throned by the West" of *A Midsummer Night's Dream*.   [57] *Henry V*, II. ii. 25 ff.

O Kate, nice customs cursy to great kings. Dear Kate, you and I cannot be confin'd within the weak list of a country's fashion. We are the makers of manners, Kate; and the liberty that follows our places stops the mouth of all find-faults.[58]

Elizabeth's shrewd sense and her mastery of statecraft contrasted, too, with the weak piety of Henry VI. Richard III could be made a Marlovian villain with impunity because he had usurped the throne that was destined for "*Peaces* patronesse." Elizabeth and all her subjects heard Richmond's speech at the end of *Richard III* with an understanding one must share to know the full import of Shakespeare's history plays:

> We will unite the White Rose and the Red.
>
> .   .   .   .
>
> O, now let Richmond and Elizabeth,
> The true succeeders of each royal house,
> By God's fair ordinance conjoin together!
> And let their heirs (God, if they will be so)
> Enrich the time to come with smooth-fac'd peace,
> With smiling plenty, and fair prosperous days!
> Abate the edge of traitors, gracious Lord,
> That would reduce these bloody days again
> And make poor England weep in streams of blood!
> Let them not live to taste this land's increase
> That would with treason wound this fair land's peace!
> Now civil wounds are stopp'd, peace lives again:
> That she may long live here, God say amen! [59]

It is forever memorable that the drama flowered under the shadow of Eliza's peace, that "dear nurse of arts, plenty, and joyful births." [60]

Furthermore, Elizabeth was a vitally important patroness of the drama, and her personal tastes mirror its temper

[58] V. ii. 293–298.
[59] V. v. 19–41.
[60] *Henry V*, V. ii. 35.

and range.[61] For almost twenty years before the public theaters arose Elizabeth encouraged and patronized plays and entertainments at court and on progress to her towns and universities. Early actors invoked her protection against a persecuting Lord Mayor. Because the queen loved drama the Privy Council fought for concessions in favor of the struggling theater. The Chapel Royal boy players enjoyed the direct patronage of the court. Elizabeth's tastes were broad enough to nurture the rich and varied growth that matured before she made her exit. Academic plays of Senecan model were performed before a queen who herself translated a chorus from the second act of the pseudo-Senecan *Hercules Oetaeus*.[62] When she visited Oxford and Cambridge, Sophocles, Plautus, and Seneca entertained her. Her scholars and actors did not go unencouraged and unrewarded, as her favor to Thomas Preston at Cambridge in 1564 reminds one.[63] Elizabeth

[61] See the admirable paragraph which Chambers (I, 3–6) writes in this connection.

[62] This royal work, which survives in manuscript (Bodleian Library MS. e Museo 55, fol. 48), was printed (I, 102–109) in Horace Walpole's *A Catalogue of the Royal and Noble Authors of England, Scotland, and Ireland*, ed. Thomas Park, 1806. See Chambers, III, 311. A 1559 Oxford edition of *The sixt tragedie of . . . Seneca, entituled Troas, . . . Newly set forth in Englishe by Iasper Heywood* is dedicated to Elizabeth as a new year's gift. Heywood (sig. A3) writes: "*I thought it should not be vnpleasant for your grace to se some part of so excellent an author in your owne tong (the reading of whom in laten I vnderstande delightes greatly your Maiesty) as also for that none may be a better iudge of my doinges herein, then who best vnderstandeth my author.*" The *Phœnissæ* of Euripides which was printed at Strassburg in 1577 in parallel Greek and Latin texts is dedicated (sig. A2) by the translator to Elizabeth. William Gager's *Meleager* (February, 1582) has an epistle (Oxford ed., 1592, sig. F6), "Apollo προλογίζει ad serenissimam Reginam Elizabetham 1592," with the following verses:

> *Regina salue virgo, terrarum Dea,*
> *Cæliq, cura, sæculi, ac mundi stupor.*
> *O singulare pectoris studium tui!*

On sig. F6ᵛ there is a "Prologus in Bellum Grammaticale ad eandem sacram Maiestatem."

[63] See above, p. 71.

liked, too, the sophisticated blend of classical myth and Renaissance wit that John Lyly perfected for the delectation of the court. Her tastes were happily catholic. Plays acted at court of which there is record prove that she favored both classical and native drama of almost every kind that her people enjoyed.[64]

Just as she gave her applause to "tragedy, comedy, history, pastoral, pastoral-comical, historical-pastoral, tragical-historical, tragical-comical-historical-pastoral, scene individable, or poem unlimited," so in her public life she played almost every kind of drama that the age loved. She was its true child in her superb sense of the dramatic and the theatrical and in her energy for playing a variety of rôles in official and social life.[65] Her many marriage projects and attentions to handsome courtiers illustrated almost every style of romance on a regal scale. The Alençon episode showed her wits for acting a romantic rôle so convincingly that she distressed the nation — even herself — with her seeming sincerity in her most extraordinary *affaire d'amour*. There was high tragedy in the last act with Essex. Only her loyalty to her greatest part made her equal to her duty as a rebel's ruler. Her greatest part was that to which she was inalienably pledged when she took the wedding ring of England in Parliament at the outset of her reign. Whatever absurd or sordid rôles policy forced her to act, to that wedding vow she was faithful unto death. She symbolized England wedded to its own self-realization. Her acting of this rôle in the greatest of English history plays held the national audience more than any mere stage piece could, and won her international renown. All true Englishmen saw their most thrilling drama in the story of the lovely princess who all alone made a

---

[64] See the instructive "Court Calendar" in Chambers, IV, 75-130.

[65] See F. E. Schelling, *The Queen's Progress and Other Elizabethan Sketches,* Boston, 1904, pp. 5-11.

perilous passage to the crown, put down all rebels and escaped all plots, executed the false Duessa for the nation's sake, defeated the deadly Spanish dragon single-handed, and contrived always to be "*Religions* Gardian, *Peaces* patronesse" to her loving husband, England.[66] For many years age seemed not to wither nor custom to stale the infinite variety and skill with which she played the many parts for which fate cast her in this drama. The stage was all the while a "secular temple, [that] provided from time to time a communion of patriotism instead of the old communion of faith."[67] Her subjects traveled often to that "temple of Eliza." Their devotions have been heard. The conventional prayers carry genuine sincerity; the custom of praying for the sovereign is established if not engendered in such plays as I have reviewed. In the playhouse commons and nobles united to express their love of England's new glory when they adored Eliza. Eliza leads one naturally from Judith and Deborah to their aristocratic court cousins. It will be seen that "some [poets] cal her Pandora: some Gloriana, some Cynthia: some Delphœbe, some Astræa: all by seuerall names to expresse seuerall loues: Yet all those names make but one celestiall body, as all those loues meete to create but one soule."

[66] See, in this connection, *Englands ioy*, above, pp. 54-56.
[67] Émile Legouis and Louis Cazamian, *A History of English Literature*, New York, 1930, p. 392.

CHAPTER IV

Fayre Elisa, Queene of Shepheardes All

I PASS now into a study of the idealization of Queen Elizabeth by the cultivated poets of her age. As everyone knows, much of the poetry of that age was early nurtured at court. Poets there addressed sophisticated readers of whom the queen was the center. Almost all non-dramatic poetry before 1603 was conditioned by the pioneering of Lyly, Sidney, and Spenser. Their portrait of "fayre Elisa, queene of shepheardes all" is of first interest; hence I turn at once to their pastorals.

In viewing the pastoral portrait of Elizabeth and other refined images of her, I take as a sustained approach that of Spenser in his "particular intention" for his elaborate compliment to Elizabeth in *The Faerie Queene*. He tells Ralegh that he will celebrate her first as a "most royall queene or empresse," and then as a "most vertuous and beautifull lady." [1] But of course the line between her two "persons," between her public character and her private character, can nowhere be heavily drawn through the complicated idealization which the queen and lady under-

---

[1] *The Complete Poetical Works of Edmund Spenser*, ed. R. E. N. Dodge, Boston, 1908, p. 136. In his prefatory letter to Ralegh Spenser writes: "In that Faery Queene I meane glory in my generall intention, but in my particular I conceive the most excellent and glorious person of our soveraine the Queene, and her kingdome in Faery Land. And yet, in some places els, I doe otherwise shadow her. For considering she beareth two persons, the one of a most royall queene or empresse, the other of a most vertuous and beautifull lady, this latter part in some places I doe express in Belphœbe, fashioning her name according to your owne excellent conceipt of Cynthia, (Phœbe and Cynthia being both names of Diana.)."

goes in the poetry of the age. More than in the broadside
ballads will the "most vertuous and beautifull lady" be
seen to stimulate the imaginations of courtly poets; but
the qualities of the virgin "lady" and the achievements of
the "most royall queene or empresse" are not ultimately
to be separated. They fuse inextricably in the best poetry.
Yet Spenser's point of view is helpful now in studying the
idealization of Elizabeth in pastoral poetry from 1558 to
1603, and it will be equally so when the sisters of Elisa
appear. I shall consider the pseudo-pastoral masques and
dramas of the reign only in so far as the imaging of the
queen and lady in them seems to prelude or to echo the
idealization of her in formal eclogues and in free lyrics.
After showing this characterization of the queen and lady,
I shall relate it to the *raison d'être* of pastoral poetry.

It is not necessary to tarry over the elaborate history of
the pastoral from Stesichorus, Theocritus, Virgil, Cal-
purnius, and Ausonius, through Dante, Petrarch, Boc-
caccio, Mantuanus, Sannazaro, Montemayor, Ronsard,
and Marot to its introduction as a Renaissance genre into
England by Buchanan, Barclay, Googe, and Turbervile.
It is, however, important to remember the native stock
upon which the foreign importations were budded — indigenous ballads with pastoral qualities, half a dozen
homely shepherd plays, Henryson's *Robene and Makyne*
with its fresh and native accents, and the three mediocre
semi-pastorals in *Tottel's Miscellany* of 1557. For this
native song, after the Virgilian or Renaissance eclogue
that celebrates a royal patron is grafted on it, bears fruit
in the patriotic music of Colin's hymn to "fayre Elisa,"
Rowland's to "Beta," and Watson's to the "*beauteous
Queene of second Troy.*"

"Traces of pastoral influence appear in English drama
in the seventies, in a masque of wild men at court in 1573,
and in Gascoigne's use of such a personage as Sylvanus or

the '*hombre salvagio*' in the queen's entertainments at
Kenilworth two years later." [2] But few of the devices in
the elaborate Kenilworth compliment to the queen, which
are built chiefly of classical myth, can be regarded as
formally pastoral in nature. This elaborate tissue of compliment spoken out of doors by Sibella, nymphs, various
classical deities including Diana, Eccho, and so on, is to be
regarded as "an unconscious preparation for an eager acceptance of the real pastoral when it comes" — as verse
in which "the Virgin Queen, with the symbolic flattery of
pagan myth, adds to the significance of the pastoral idea
to the Elizabethan court and people." [3] Such material
with its mythological disguise and semi-rural background
is a forerunner of formal eclogues, masques, and lyrics
which idealize the queen.

The "first mask or entertainment of undoubted pastoral
nature" [4] was Sidney's *The Lady of May*. This "lively
little pastoral idyl" [5] was performed before "Her Most
Excellent Majestie walking in Wansteed Garden, as she
passed downe into the grove," in May, 1578 or 1579, during another visit to Leicester; but it was not printed until
it appeared at the end of *Arcadia* in 1598. The "Suiter"
seeks justice before the queen:

> *Most gracious Soveraigne,*
> *To one whose state is raised over all,*
> *Whose face doth oft the bravest sort enchaunt,*
> *Whose mind is such, as wisest minds appall,*
> *Who in one selfe these diverse gifts can plant;*
> *   How dare I wretch seeke there my woes to rest,*
> *   Where eares be burnt, eyes dazled, harts opprest?*

---

[2] F. E. Schelling, *Elizabethan Drama 1558–1642*, Boston, 1908, II, 144–145.
[3] H. A. Eaton, *The Pastoral Idea in English Poetry in the Sixteenth Century*,
an unpublished Harvard University thesis, 1900, chap. v, pp. 11–12.
[4] Chapter v, p. 18.
[5] Schelling, II, 98.

Your state is great, your greatnesse is our shield,
Your face hurts oft, but still it doth delight,
Your mind is wise, your wisedome makes you mild,
Such planted gifts enrich even beggers sight:
So dare I wretch, my bashfull feare subdue,
And feede mine eares, mine eyes, my hart in you.

After this courtly speech the queen is called upon to decide
whether the Lady of May should prefer Therion or Espilus
as suitor. "*Lalus the old shepheard*" declares "by my
white Lambe [she is] not three quarters so beautious" as
is the queen. The May Lady pays homage to "the beauti-
fullest Lady these woods have ever received." Therion
and Espilus enter into a singing contest for the love of the
May Lady before this "most excellent Ladie," and Therion
concludes the first round:

Great sure is she, on whom our hopes do live,
Greater is she who must the judgement give.

The singing match concludes:

Espilus kneeling to the Queene.
Judge you to whom all beauties force is lent.

Therion.
Judge you of Love, to whom all Love is bent.[6]

Then comes praise from "*Dorcas* an olde shepheard" in
courtly prose. Finally the May Lady, after giving judgment for Espilus, takes leave of her majesty with a complimentary farewell. *The Lady of May* contains courtly
compliment, artificial in style and design, turned off, however, with a typical pastoral device, the singing-match.
When the May Lady does obeisance to Elisa, a formal
device fuses with native tradition. Classical shepherds
contrive a compliment to the loveliest English May Lady

---

[6] *The Complete Works of Sir Philip Sidney*, ed. Albert Feuillerat, Cambridge,
II (1922), 330–334. The date is discussed in Chambers, III, 492.

— the beautiful and beneficent sovereign "to whom all
Love is bent."

About the time that Elizabeth heard *The Lady of May*,
Spenser effected in his April eclogue a very happy fusion
of home and foreign material for hymning "fayre Elisa,
queene of shepheardes all." His eclogue ultimately gave
pattern for similar celebrations, as will be seen. Colin's
patriotic song shows at the beginning of the poetic maturity
of the age the chief qualities in the queen's public and private characters which inspire the pastoral portrait. The
"Virgins that on Parnasse dwell" are invoked to help

> "to blaze
> Her worthy praise
> Which in her sexe doth all excell.
>
> "Of fayre Elisa be your silver song,
> That blessed wight:
> The flowre of virgins, may shee florish long
> In princely plight.
> For shee is Syrinx daughter without spotte,
> Which Pan, the shepheards god, of her begot:
> So sprong her grace
> Of heavenly race,
> Nor mortall blemishe may her blotte.
>
> "See, where she sits upon the grassie greene,
> (O seemely sight!)
> Yclad in scarlot, like a mayden queene,
> And ermines white.
> Upon her head a cremosin coronet,
> With damaske roses and daffadillies set:
> Bayleaves betweene,
> And primroses greene,
> Embellish the sweete violet.
>
> "Tell me, have ye seene her angelick face,
> Like Phœbe fayre?
> Her heavenly haveour, her princely grace,
> Can you well compare?

The redde rose medled with the white yfere,
In either cheeke depeincten lively chere.
    Her modest eye,
    Her majestie,
Where have you seene the like, but there?"

Before this "flowre of virgins" sprung "of heavenly race" classical deities bow. Phœbus is "amazed"; Cynthia, "dasht"; Calliope, the other Muses, and the Graces celebrate her. Henry VIII and Anne Boleyn as Pan and Syrinx attest the domestication of such foreign deities. And it is Elisa's peace that all honor, virgins most appropriately:

"Chloris, that is the chiefest nymph of al,
Of olive braunches beares a coronall:
    Olives bene for peace,
    When wars doe surcease:
Such for a princesse bene principall.

"Ye shepheards daughters, that dwell on the greene,
    Hye you there apace:
Let none come there, but that virgins bene,
    To adorne her grace.
And when you come whereas shee is in place,
See that your rudenesse doe not you disgrace:
    Binde your fillets faste,
    And gird in your waste,
For more finesse, with a tawdrie lace."

After a heightening of the idyllic atmosphere by a charming flower stanza, the song ends with a skilful bid for Colin's reward from Elisa.

"Bring hether the pincke and purple cullambine,
    With gelliflowres;
Bring coronations, and sops in wine,
    Worne of paramoures;
Strowe me the ground with daffadowndillies,

And cowslips, and kingcups, and loved lillies:
   The pretie pawnce,
   And the chevisaunce,
Shall match with the fayre flowre delice.

"Now ryse up, Elisa, decked as thou art,
   In royall aray;
And now ye daintie damsells may depart
   Echeone her way.
I feare I have troubled your troupes to longe:
Let Dame Eliza thanke you for her song:
   And if you come hether
   When damsines I gether,
I will part them all you among." [7]

Thenot and Hobbinol in dialogue complete the frame for the encomium.

But clearly the frame surrounds a genuine pastoral painting of Elisa, virgin queen of peace. The oils and the technique show the dual nature of Spenser's poetry very significantly — a duality which justifies one in calling him "the first of a series of English writers who combined the traditions of regular pastoral with the wayward graces of native inspiration." [8] The encomium on the queen has its prototype perhaps in Virgilian eclogue in which shepherds sing extravagant praise of Caesar. [9] This convention had been revived by Continental poets to compliment princes of the Italian and French Renaissance. But Spenser's compliment in its air of fresh simplicity and in its genuine feeling suggests the authentic tone of Theocritus because of the second element in his eclectic pastoral genius. He sets Latin, French, and Italian im-

---

   [7] Lines 43–153.
   [8] W. W. Greg, *Pastoral Poetry and Pastoral Drama*, 1906, p. 84.
   [9] It is interesting to note that E. K. points out that "Thenots Embleme," *O quam te memorem, virgo?*, and "Hobbinols Embleme," *O dea certe!*, are from Virgil. E. K.'s gloss on the emblems is in itself a quaintly turned compliment to Elisa.

portations to native music, even as Henryson in *Robene and Makyne* seems to have acclimatized the foreign pastourelle. The outworn convention of celebrating a sovereign in a stiff eclogue is rejuvenated by Spenser's patriotism as it centers upon Elizabeth, virgin queen of peace and brilliant Renaissance lady. The maiden queen of the broadsides who was particularly chosen of God to lead his favored people into peace and plenty, triumphant over all enemies, is closely akin to this Elisa "of heavenly race." However full of pagan myth and of complex harmony these musical stanzas may be, English ears heard within them some notes very like those of the ballads that sing the queen as Jehovah's special care. The popular songs of the time "influenced the whole pastoral lyric output, and gave grace and charm to the most frigid forms of eulogy and personal compliment." [10] The rustic simplicity of the ballad survives obviously in the verse of "August." Lodowick Lloyd's *A Dittie to the tune of Welshe Sydanen, made to the Queenes maj.*[11] is transmuted into a perfect portrait of Elisa.

Spenser's art in acclimatizing the pastoral will be evident after a closer glance at one or two of his strokes in this portrayal of Elisa. It is classified by E. K. as a "recreative" eclogue. The queen is gracefully complimented by being hymned in a spring month; as her years were to go, she was still comparatively young. E. K. tells us that the "Ladyes of the Lake be Nymphes"; classical myth and Arthurian romance mingle curiously to do Elisa homage. Decked out in spring flowers, she seems a genuine English May queen, akin to Sidney's May Lady. E. K. declares that by "the mingling of the redde rose and the white is meant the uniting of the two principall houses of Lancaster and of Yorke: by whose longe discord and deadly debate

[10] Eaton, chap. x, p. 27.
[11] See above, pp. 26–28.

this realm many yeares was sore traveiled, and almost cleane decayed."[12] This is a recurring conceit in verse that celebrates the queen. It was a happy accident for the poetic imagination of the time that the Tudor princess and virgin queen could be thus symbolized, and most appropriately in pastoral poetry, by the rose, a flower rich in poetic associations. The *rosa* had done high service in Italian Renaissance verse, now as the symbol of virginity, now as suggestive of all the fugitive loveliness of life. For centuries of medieval devotion the rose had symbolized a far holier virgin than the one that patriotic Englishmen were adoring.[13] The "damaske roses," the "primroses

[12] *Works*, p. 21.

[13] Ancient, medieval, and Renaissance poets made extensive use of the rose to suggest virginity and the fragility of beauty. The last were heirs to the very influential *Le Roman de la Rose* in which the medieval lady is elaborately idealized with the rose as a symbol —

> C'est cele qui tant a de pris,
> Et tant est digne d'estre amée
> Qu'el doit estre Rose clamée.

One notes "que la comparaison de la femme aimée avec une rose, développée dans le *Dit de la Rose*, petit poème peut-être antérieur à l'ouvrage de Guillaume, est en tout cas familière aux poètes lyriques et aux romanciers courtois les plus anciens, par exemple à Gautier d'Arras (*Eracle*, vers 2394 et suivants)" (Joseph Bédier and Paul Hazard, *Histoire de la Littérature Française Illustrée*, Paris, I [1923], 72). For Elizabethan use of the rose to symbolize virginity, see *The Phœnix Nest 1593*, ed. H. E. Rollins, Cambridge, Mass., 1931, pp. 101–102, 198–199. Such a graceful poem as Drayton's "Singe wee the Rose" (*Works*, ed. J. W. Hebel, Oxford, I [1931], 491–492) shows how easily the rose could figure the mistress of an Elizabethan's fancy. It is a short step from Nicholas Breton's "The Rose the Queene," concluding "Of highest trees the hollye is the Kinge, And of all flowres faire fall the Queene the Rose" (*Works in Verse and Prose*, ed. A. B. Grosart, Edinburgh, 1879, I, *t*, 16) to Spenser's figuring the Tudor queen as a rose. One should recall the coronation pageant, "The uniting of the two Howses of Lancastre and Yorke" (see above, p. 63). Henry Goldingham's *The Garden Plot, An Allegorical Poem, Inscribed to Queen Elizabeth*, survives in an unfinished manuscript; but it would appear that all the flowers of the court garden are to retire before the crossing of the "Whyte Rose," the "vyrgin flower," and the red rose. A compliment to the virgin Tudor rose is probably figured, although the poem may be "intended to represent Elizabeth's court, to some fair flower of which he [the author] might have been attached" (*The*

greene" (the "chiefe and worthiest" says E. K. in his gloss on the February eclogue), or the "redde rose medled with the white yfere" were full of foreign and native associations when used to describe a virgin descended from York and Lancaster. This domestication of the rose of classical, Renaissance, and medieval poetry in Colin's hymn to Elisa is a fair token of the subtle blending of native and imported materials in Spenser's idealization of Elizabeth, and of her power to attract symbols of the beautiful and the good in sovereignty and womankind.

Colin's "flowre of virgins" who shames Olympian deities by her magnificence, this "mayden queene" famed for her peace, is the prototype of numerous similar encomiums. Whatever the truth may be about the influence of *The Shepheardes Calender* before the publication of the first three books of *The Faerie Queene* in 1590 brought the earlier poem anew before the public,[14] one does not find much formal pastoral poetry lauding Elizabeth until about that year and thereafter. However, Elisa has rôles in several pseudo-pastoral court dramas before she is glorified

---

Garden Plot, ed. Francis Wrangham, 1825, p. xv). The author would hardly inscribe a poem to Elizabeth without intending to compliment her first as the "fair flower." She must have been pleased with the following lines (p. 58):

    Of all the flowers Batchelers bouttons ys beste
    And beste becomes to matche wythe maydenher.

[14] The question of the influence of *The Shepheardes Calender* before 1590 was debated at length by the late Professors Edwin Greenlaw, C. R. Baskervill, and Dr. J. J. Higginson. Greenlaw argued against its influence in *Publications of the Modern Language Association of America*, XXVI (1911), 419–451; and in *Studies in Philology* (U. of N. C.), XI (1913), 3–25. Greenlaw, in arguing (p. 449) that the several religious satires of the *Calender* give the poem its central unity and chief burden — a plea for a united front against Rome — might have observed that his interpretation makes the April praise of Elisa something of a call to arms around the "mayden queene" who personified the new church for Protestant Englishmen. The praise is, too, a tactful internal support for the gloss which he interprets as so "artfully constructed as to minimize . . . the danger such plain speaking threatened an unknown poet anxious to succeed at court."

in the lyrics of the next decade. And there are one or two interesting appearances in formal pastoral verse.

In England, as in Italy, the way was prepared for the pastoral drama proper by the appearance

of mythological plays, introducing incidentally pastoral scenes and characters, and anticipating to some extent at any rate the peculiar atmosphere of the Arcadian drama.

The earliest of these English mythological plays, alike in date of production and of publication, was George Peele's *Arraignment of Paris*, 'A Pastorall. Presented before the Queenes Majestie, by the children of her Chappell,' no doubt in 1581, and printed three years later.[15]

It has the nature of a masque in that the whole composition is an elaborate compliment to Queen Elizabeth or "Zebeta," a name which "Peele probably borrowed along with one or two other hints from Gascoigne's Kenilworth entertainment of 1575." [16] Whatever Peele's sources, his compliment in having the celebrated quarrel over the apple for the fairest settled by Diana's giving it to the "*Nymph* ELIZA" is essentially of a piece with a type of compliment which I have already noted. The Kenilworth material and the April eclogue show Olympian deities displaced by Elisa's majesty. It is chiefly her virginity, too, that Peele compliments, first by having Pallas, Juno, and

---

[15] Greg, p. 216. Chambers dates the play *ca.* 1584.

[16] Greg, pp. 216–217 (following Ward). Professor F. E. Schelling (*Modern Language Notes*, VIII [1893], 103–104) argues that the compliment was suggested by lines in George Gascoigne's *The Grief of Joye* (*Complete Works*, ed. J. W. Cunliffe, Cambridge, II [1910], 526), a work dedicated to the queen as a new year's gift, and printed in 1576:

> This *Queene* it is, who (had she satt in feeld,
> When *Paris* judged, that *Venus* bare the bell,)
> The prize were hers, for she deserves it well.

Perhaps the encomium on Elizabeth in *The Shepheardes Calender* encouraged the compliment here. Eaton (chap. vii, p. 26) sees a possible parallelism between the flower list in Peele's play (I. i. 57 ff.) and that in the April eclogue.

Venus bow to Diana as the just judge of the quarrel.
Diana calls Elisa a nymph that "honour[s] Dian for her
chastity" and praises especially her justice and peace.
Peele takes some care to develop the claim of each goddess
to the apple so that the compliment to Elisa, when she is
awarded it, shall have the fullest force. Pallas assents to
Diana's judgment, praising Zabeta and the day of her
birth. Venus declares:

> To this fair nymph, not earthly, but divine,
> Contents it me my honour to resign.

Juno retires:

> To her whom Juno's looks so well become,
> The Queen of Heaven yields at Phœbe's doom;
> And glad I am Diana found the art,
> Without offence so well to please desart.

The three Fates *"lay down their properties at the* Queen's
feet" with Latin speeches of deference. Atropos exclaims:

> Live long the noble phœnix of our age,
> Our fair Eliza, our Zabeta fair!

Diana offers more

> Praise of the wisdom, beauty, and the state,
> That best becomes thy peerless excellency.[17]

The epilogue summarizes the tone of the praise:

> OMNES SIMUL. *Vive diu felix votis hominumque deumque,*
> *Corpore, mente, libro, doctissima, candida, casta.*

In this earliest semi-pastoral drama Elisa inspires praise
of the same type as that introduced by the formal April
eclogue; an extravagant use of classical myth appears
beside material of apparently indigenous growth.[18]

---

[17] V. i. 105–160.
[18] See Greg, p. 234.

The portrait of Elisa in court drama by Peele and Lyly is difficult to isolate with complete clarity; first, because any true pastoral devices are thoroughly mixed with mythological elements; and second, because the complicated allegories, especially in Lyly's plays, give refractions of Elisa that make the exact intentions of that dramatist a matter for debate. But whenever Lyly's plays seem to portray Elisa they must have some attention because their portrayal underlies true pastoral praise by other court poets, and because it is an important antecedent to praise of the queen's virginity later in the reign.[19]

Gallathea (not earlier than 1584 or later than 1588) is a charming and sophisticated tissue of compliment and restrained satire written chiefly to be heard by the maiden queen, surely more or less figured in Diana with her train of virgin nymphs. The prologue is turned to Elizabeth in Lyly's most flattering style, but the present interest is the character of Diana, chaste goddess of the hunt, in whom the queen was expected to see herself pleasingly mirrored.

> *Cupid.* What is that *Diana*? a goddesse?
> what her Nimphes? virgins? what her pastimes? hunting?
> *Nymph.* A goddesse? who knowes it not?
> Virgins? who thinkes it not? Hunting? who loues it not?[20]

It is the strife between Diana and Venus and her son that makes one know that the play was designed to tickle, not without a light scratch, perhaps, the prejudices of the virgin autocrat of the court. Telusa, Eurota, and Ramia, Diana's nymphs, are all caught by Venus and Cupid; and Diana's invective against her nymphs in love must have seemed to court ladies an expurgated version of what they had actually heard from the queen, contriving to love, as they often did, in spite of the royal Diana.[21]   Finally

---

[19] I follow Greg (pp. 225 ff.) in considering *Gallathea, Loves Metamorphosis,* and *The Woman in the Moone* as Lyly's pseudo-pastoral plays.

[20] I. ii. 8–11.   [21] See III. iv. 1 ff.

Cupid is caught. There is tart and clever dialogue between him and Diana. Elizabeth's control of love at court seems epitomized in Diana's declaration: "Thou shalt be vsed as *Dianaes* slaue, not *Venus* sonne. All the worlde shall see that I will vse thee like a captiue, and shew my selfe a Conquerer." [22] And poor Cupid, put to work untying love knots, gives the goddess only such a thrust as would please rather than irritate a queen who always welcomed the adulation of a handsome courtier or a marriage proposal from a prince for whom she had a political use:

Cupid. . . . The time may come *Diana*, and the time shall come, that thou that settest *Cupid* to vndoe knots, shalt in-treate *Cupid* to tye knots, and you ladies that with solace haue behelde my paines, shall with sighes intreate my pittie.

.   .   .   .

Telusa. *Diana* cannot yeelde, she conquers affection.
Cupid. *Diana* shall yeeld, she cannot conquer desteny.[23]

In Venus's prayer for revenge on Diana there is criticism of her as one who

hateth sweet delights, enuieth louing desires, masketh wanton eyes, stoppeth amorous eares, bridleth youthfull mouthes, and vnder a name, or a worde constancie, entertaineth all kinde of crueltie.[24]

More of the like anon. Diana, content to stand by Neptune's judgment and surrender Cupid to his mother, sounds like Elizabeth — and certainly pleased her.

Diana. I account not the choyse harde, for had I twentie *Cupids*, I woulde deliuer them all to saue one Virgine; knowing loue to be a thing of all the vainest, virginitie to be a vertue of all the noblest.

[22] III. iv. 91–93.   [23] IV. ii. 72–89.   [24] V. iii. 29–32.

.   .   .   .

Venus. . . . *Diana* cannot forbid him to wounde.
Diana. Yes, chastitie is not within the leuell of his bowe.
Venus. But beautie is a fayre marke to hit.[25]

Thus Venus turns Diana a compliment with the same
breath that threatens her. And, if the epilogue is rather
surprisingly pro-Venus, one may remember that Elizabeth
and her court delighted in an atmosphere of love full of all
the ambiguities that wit could sport with.[26] Furthermore,
the play's dominant deference to virginity is caught even
in such details as Neptune's demanding "the fairest and
chastest virgine" for the sacrifice, and in Hæbe's farewell
praise of virgins and of the "pompe of Princes Courts, . . .
where chastitie honoreth affections and commaundeth,
yeeldeth to desire and conquereth." [27]

Loves Metamorphosis (1589–1590?) [28] shows a similar
blending of mythological and pastoral materials in its reflection of Elizabeth, but, as compared with *Gallathea*, it
is distinctly more critical of the queen's insistence upon
her single way of life as the right way for the whole court.

The attitude towards love of Ceres and her nymphs, respectively, is almost a reversal of that of Diana and hers: and Cupid
is no longer a petulant boy, playing truant, making mischief,
caught and punished for it; but a great god with a temple at
which Ceres offers homage, and wielding a dread power of
physical punishment.[29]

The defense of Ceres's position as champion of virginity is
but slight in comparison with the attack. Her nymphs,

[25] V. iii. 72–81.

[26] See the dialogue between Phillida and Gallathea, III. ii.

[27] V. ii. 33–38.

[28] Bond (III, 295–298) thinks that the play was first produced by the Paul's
boys in 1586–1588, revived by them in its present form in 1599 or early in 1600,
and transferred to the Chapel children before the year was far advanced.

[29] III, 294. See *Gallathea*, III. iv. 16 ff. "That the Queen is represented in
the person of Ceres has been generally allowed," says Bond (III, 297).

Nisa and Celia, do sing in her honor before her sacred tree
on the "haruest holyday" and offer two white doves to her
whose heart is virgin. Ceres boasts of her power over
Erisichthon, and he, repentant for his offenses, praises her.
Nisa, Celia, and Niobe do wittily protest in the name of
virginity when their lovers are restored by Cupid. And
Celia speaks an amusingly sophistical speech designed to
please the queen; for she blandly forgets that no "roses"
would ever appear did not less philosophical maids than
herself take the poet's advice to go breed; she forgets that
"frail beauty must decay" just as surely in the maid who
scorns a man as in the most complaisant wife. But the
attack on Ceres's position is vigorous and sustained.
Erisichthon cuts the sacred tree, declaring that he has no
regard for "your goddesse, which none but pieuish girles
reuerence." [30] Ceres's distressed nymphs lament his crime
with a wavering confidence in the power of their mistress.
It is the omnipotent god Cupid, however, who, angry because of the disrespectful opinion of him which Ceres's
nymphs hold, attacks Ceres in penetrating speeches —
Ceres who "doest but gouerne the guts of men, I the
hearts." [31] Finally, Ceres effects a compromise with Cupid
that is far more to his honor than to hers. She is driven
to plead:

My sweete Nymphs, for the honor of your sex, for the loue of
Ceres, for regard of your own countrie, yeeld to loue; yeeld, my
sweete Nymphes, to sweete loue.[32]

Cupid tells her that he has tormented all her nymphs
with love because "they thought it impossible to loue."
Humbled, yet declaring that though to love "be no vice,
yet spotlesse virginitie is the onely vertue," Ceres suggests

[30] I. ii. 78–79.
[31] V. i. 8–9.
[32] V. iv. 110–112. See II. i. 38 ff.

the queen who insisted, in spite of all marriages at court, upon exalting the virgin ideal. The politic Cupid demands:

> Why, *Ceres*, doe you thinke that lust followeth loue? *Ceres*, louers are chast: for what is loue, diuine loue, but the quintescens of chastitie, and affections binding by heauenly motions, that cannot bee vndone by earthly meanes, and must not be comptrolled by any man? [33]

He finally declares:

> You see, Ladies, what it is to make a mocke of loue, or a scorne of *Cupid*: see where your louers stand; you must now take them for your husbands; this is my iudgement, this is *Ceres* promise.[34]

The promise from Ceres shows how far she is fallen; yet it may be remembered that love adjusted to such a sane political end as the provision for new citizens for the state could not finally displease the queen who was not just a prejudiced spinster, but a wise governor bent on disciplining the energies of her court for the strength of England. However, the half-despairing cry of an aging queen still seeking to rule in her fashion the surging new blood at court may be echoed in Ceres's last speech but one — "these louers mind nothing what we say." [35] Perhaps the veiled drift of the whole sophisticated court allegory is summed up in Petulius's chorus-like speech:

> A straunge discourse, *Protea*, by which I find the gods amorous, and Virgins immortall, goddesses full of crueltie, and men of vnhappinesse.[36]

About Lyly's intent in his third and last pseudo-pastoral drama, *The Woman in the Moone* (not earlier than 1590 or later than 1595?) there is considerable disagreement.[37] I

---

[33] II. i. 122–126. Cupid suggests problems in Spenser's *Hymnes*.
[34] V. iv. 45–48.   [35] V. iv. 181.   [36] V. ii. 1–3.
[37] See Alfred Mézières, *Prédécesseurs et Contemporains de Shakspeare*, 2ᵉ édit., Paris, 1863, pp. 75–76, for an interpretation that makes Pandora a hostile portrait of the queen; for less certainty about Pandora as a satirical portrait,

confess my inability to fathom the exact intent of this un-
reserved satire of women which would make "fayre
Elisas" and all "foolish, fickle, franticke, madde." It may
be the culmination of satirical intentions in *Gallathea* and
Loves Metamorphosis; it may be applicable to woman in
general and associate itself merely with the conventional
satire in the early *Anatomy of Wit*. Certainly *The Woman
in the Moone* was an amazingly stupid move for favor if
Lyly was still seeking advancement. It was a most reck-
less move if he was determined to speak out in anger at
lack of desired reward.

In 1587 verses celebrating Elizabeth in the established
pastoral patterns appeared in the middle of Angel Day's
*Daphnis and Chloe Excellently describing the weight of af-
fection, the simplicitie of loue, the purport of honest meaning,
the resolution of men, and disposition of Fate, finished in a
Pastorall, and interlaced with the praises of a most peerlesse
Princesse, wonderfull in Maiestie, and rare in perfection,
and celebrated within the same Pastorall, and therefore termed
by the name of The Shepheards Holidaie*. Lesbian swains of
the fifth century sing the praises of Elisa! She is the flower
of a peerless line; she is God's particular care; she is Dian's
favorite; the gods have endowed her with all gifts; her
"virgin sway" brings every blessing.[38] This anachronistic
celebration of Elisa in an Elizabethan rendering of a late
Greek pastoral romance is inserted with some technical
skill, and an Elizabethan pastoral tone is felt in spite of the
rather wooden verses. Day's modern editor well observes

---

see Bond, *Works*, II, 256–257; III, 236; and Albert Feuillerat, *John Lyly*, Cambridge, 1910, pp. 232–233. Professor Feuillerat notes that Pandora is a complimentary name for Elizabeth in Warner's *Albion's England* (chap. xxxiii) and in
the prologue of *Old Fortunatus*. It is also a wholly complimentary name for her
in Peele's *Descensus Astrææ* (*Works*, I, 362), in George Whetstone, *An Heptam-
eron Of Civil Discourses*, 1582, sig. ¶2; and in the National Library of Wales
MS. 3040 B (= Mostyn MS. 132), pp. 111–112.

[38] Ed. Joseph Jacobs, London, 1890, pp. 101 ff.

that the "book appeared just on the eve of the Armada,
and reflects accurately enough the idealization of the
Queen, regarded not in her personal characteristics, but as
the nation personified." [39]

In the varied flowering of English literature in post-
Armada years pastoral verse enjoyed a new popularity
which culminated, it would seem, in the pastoral anthology, *England's Helicon* (1600). Sidney's pastoral romance,
Arcadia, was newly influential after its printing in 1590.
By that same year Spenser had transformed Elisa into
Gloriana and Belphœbe. Portraits such as I have been ex-
hibiting in imitations of classical and Renaissance eclogues
and in the drama are painted with renewed enthusiasm
after the glorious Armada in 1588. Native English rhythms
and backgrounds that suggest the English countryside are
felt in the free pastoral lyric of these later years. In them
"fayre Elisa, queene of shepheardes all" has a radiance
that makes any satirical portraiture in Lyly seem pale;
she is a finished symbol of ideal sovereignty and womanhood for her shepherds.

An early, if incidental, post-Armada appearance of
Elisa is in George Peele's *An Eglogue. Gratulatorie. Entituled: To the right honorable, and renowmed Shepheard of
Albions Arcadia: Robert Earle of Essex and Ewe, for his
welcome into England from Portugall* (1589). Piers pipes
gayly to welcome home the "*renowmed Shepheard of
Albions Arcadia*," who, even as lamented Sidney, "Pallas'
peerless knight," served Elisa, has

> served, and watch'd, and waited late,
> To keep the grim wolf from Eliza's gate;
> And for their mistress, thoughten these two swains,
> They moughten never take too mickle pains. [40]

---

[39] Page xxx.
[40] *Works*, II, 273.

Peele's *Eglogue* illustrates well how felicitously the conceit
of Elizabeth as a great royal shepherdess figured her sway
over devoted servants and poets. In the next year Thomas
Watson published *Melibœus* in Latin, and in the same year
he assured himself of satisfaction with the Englishing by
translating it himself. Heralded as a consolation for Walsingham's daughter, the eclogue turns awkwardly into a
song of comfort for Elisa, bereft of her counselor. The
daughter is told to help

> with vs, and eurie countrie wight,
> to chace all grieuance from *Dianaes* minde:
> From drad *Diana*, earths and heauns delight,
> *Diana*, glorie of hir sexe and kinde;
> *Diana*, wondrous mirrour of our daies;
> *Diana* matchlesse Queene of *Arcadie*;
> *Diana*, whose surpassing beauties praise
> Improous hir worth past terrene deitie;
> *Diana*, *Sibill* for hir secret skill;
> *Diana*, pieties chief earthlie friend;
> *Diana*, holie both in deede and will;
> *Diana* whose iust praises haue no end.[41]

Spenser is summoned with glowing tribute to comfort
Diana — "for well shee likes thy vaine." Elisa in Watson's imagination is a virgin goddess, the paragon of all
virtues.

This Diana or Elisa is hymned as Beta in the third
eclogue of Drayton's *Idea The Shepheards Garland* (1593).
Her virginity and her peace especially inspire this admirable imitation of Colin's song. Patriotic Drayton
skilfully introduces *"fayre silver Thames"* into the pastoral
setting. Again a *"Queene of Virgins"* with the favor of
"Blessed Angels" shames Olympian deities. Three stanzas
will suggest the song:

[41] *Poems*, ed. Edward Arber, English Reprints, 1870, pp. 171–173.

O see what troups of Nimphs been sporting on the strands,
And they been blessed Nimphs of peace, with Olives in their hands.
How meryly the Muses sing,
That all the flowry Medowes ring,
And Beta *sits upon the banck, in purple and in pall,*
And she the Queene of Muses is, and weares the Corinall.

.   .   .   .

Make her a goodly Chapilet of azur'd Colombine,
And wreath about her Coronet with sweetest Eglentine:
Bedeck our Beta *all with Lillies,*
And the dayntie Daffadillies,
With Roses damask, white, and red, and fairest flower delice,
With Cowslips of Jerusalem, and cloves of Paradice.

.   .   .   .

Beta *long may thine Altars smoke, with yeerely sacrifice,*
And long thy sacred Temples may their Saboths solemnize,
Thy shepheards watch by day and night,
Thy Mayds attend the holy light,
And thy large empyre stretch her armes from east unto the west,
And thou under thy feet mayst tread, that foule seven-headed beast.[42]

Richard Barnfield's *The Affectionate Shepheard* was published in November, 1594. In the next year Barnfield writes in the letter "To the curteous Gentlemen Readers" prefacing his *Cynthia. with certaine Sonnets, and the Legend of Cassandra*:

In one or two places (in this Booke) I vse the name of *Eliza* pastorally: wherein, lest any one should misconster my meaning (as I hope none will) I haue here briefly discouered my harmles conceipt as concerning that name: whereof once (in a simple Shepheards deuice) I wrot this Epigramme.

> *One name there is, which name aboue all other*
> *I most esteeme, as time and place shall proue:*
> *The one is* Vesta, *th'other Cupids Mother,*

---

[42] *Works*, I, 57–58.

The first my Goddesse is, the last my loue;
Subiect to Both I am: to that by berth;
To this for beautie; fairest on the earth.[43]

The title piece, *Cynthia*, is an adaptation of the medieval
dream poem with an elaborate infusion of classic myth and
allegory, all designed to compliment Cynthia, the "sacred
Virgin" — Elisa. In his *The Encomion of Lady Pecunia:
or The praise of Money* (1598) this young courtier-poet
cleverly points his verses to open the money-bags of
"ELIZA," unmistakably his actual sovereign, who is declared "*Queene of Diamonds*" even if Pecunia be "*Queene
of harts.*" The pastoral "Ode," which appears in the 1595
volume with the "Epigramme" in which he assures one
that he "discovers" his "conceipt" intended in the name
"*Eliza,*" seems to be designed to please the royal Elisa.
In this "Ode" the poet comes upon a love-sick shepherd
— whose heart shortly breaks:

> ELIZA written I might see:
> In Caracters of crimson blood,
> (VVhose meaning well I vnderstood.).[44]

If the heart of this "Youngest Swaine of Summers Queene"
(Barnfield was born in 1574) is riven by some fair cruel
maid of his fancy whom he would have the reader think
the true "*Eliza,*" perhaps it is also to be understood as
riven to compliment the Elisa who was the prototype of
any shepherd's ordinary Eliza.

In 1595 appeared "the first attempt in English at writing original eclogues in Vergilian metre"[45] — Francis
Sabie's *Pans pipe, three pastorall eglogues, in English
hexameter. With other poetical verses delightfull.* "Thestilis Ode" in Sapphics concludes the volume. It is poor
poetry, but the idealization is notable. The old quarrel of

---

[43] *Poems. 1594–1598*, ed. Edward Arber, The English Scholar's Library,
1882, p. 44.   [44] Page 66.   [45] Greg, p. 114.

Juno, Venus, and Minerva is given a new development, at least for the pastoral. The goddesses contend, not for the apple, but for the possession of Elisa. Clever Jove, blind to theological anachronism, gives judgment:

> This is my iudgment, sweet *Eliza*, Ladies,
> shall be mine onlie.
>
> O what great and huge miracles Iehouah
> Aiding, she hath wrought here, many yeares which prest vs,
> From Romish *Pharaohs* tyrannous bondage, she
> safely releas'd vs.
>
> Since that bright day-star shady night expelling,
> Which hath brought day-light ouer all this Iland:
> That *Moses* which her people through the sea led,
> As by the drie land.
>
> From craggie mountaines water hath she made
> With *manna*, *nectar*, manie yeares she fed vs:
> Thus hath she long time, noble *Ioue* assisting,
> mightily led vs.
>
> O from what *Scillas* she preserued hath
> From spanish armies Ioue hath her protected,
> Thy force O Romish Prelate, and wiles hath she
> wiselie detected.
>
> Her realme in quiet many yeares she ruled
> Her subiectes saftie verie much regarding,
> Punishing rebels, she reformeth vices,
> Vertue rewarding.
>
> The plow-man may now reap his haruest in ioy,
> Each man may boldly lead a quiet life here
> We shepheards may sit with our heard in field, and
> merilie pipe here.
>
> A Phœnix rare she is on earth amongst vs,
> A mother vs her people she doth nourish
> Let vs all therefore, with one heart, pray *Ioue* that
> long she may flourish.[46]

---

[46] Ed. J. W. Bright and W. P. Mustard (reprinted from *Modern Philology*,

One wonders how Dr. Johnson would have spoken out
before this "irreverent combination" of "trifling fictions"
and "awful and sacred truths." The verses are not to be
honored by further association with *Lycidas*; but their
failure as poetry does not keep them from showing baldly
that the pastoral idealization of Elizabeth is based on significant facts of her reign. Elisa turns suddenly into the
Judith or Deborah of homely broadside encomium —
"seuerall loues" meeting "to create but one soule."

Drayton singing of Beta was clearly echoing Spenser's
song to Elisa; and Barnfield perhaps complimenting Elisa
was a professed disciple of "that excellent Poet, Maister
Spencer, in his *Fayrie Queene*." [47] Colin's song is in the
background of Sabie's Sapphics. In the year they appeared, 1595, Spenser published *Colin Clouts Come Home
Againe*, written several years earlier. In pastoralism that
is "more a point of view than a set disguise, or, at least,
[a] mask . . . worn lightly and removed at will," [48] Spenser
glorifies Elisa with such soaring idealism as to make all
competitors seem feeble in their outbursts. Colin, deeply
disillusioned with the ugly vanities of court life, is, in the
final analysis, celebrating a rarefied image of the actual
Elizabeth in his own mind's eye more than any mortal
woman. Colin rouses his "sleepie Muse" to tell Hobbinol
of the glories of Elisa's court revealed to him when Ralegh,
the "Shepheard of the Ocean," took him there. Elizabeth's kingdom by land and sea is figured in an elaborate
conceit of Cynthia as shepherdess of all. Colin and his
friend journey until they come into her presence. Colin
despairs of describing her by rich similes:

---

vol. VII, no. 4), Chicago, 1910, pp. 31–32. The editors (p. 9) note that part of
the eclogue is a paraphrase of a Latin poem, "Iouis Elizabeth" appearing in
Lyly's *Euphues and his England* (*Works*, II, 216–217; see below, pp. 238–239).

[47] *Poems*, p. 44.

[48] Dodge, in *Works*, p. 686.

"But vaine it is to thinke, by paragone
Of earthly things, to judge of things divine:
Her power, her mercy, and her wisedome, none
Can deeme, but who the Godhead can define.
Why then do I, base shepheard bold and blind,
Presume the things so sacred to prophane?
More fit it is t' adore, with humble mind,
The image of the heavens in shape humane." [49]

He lauds the lovely nymphs of Cynthia's train: "Theana"
is "the well of bountie and brave mynd," "the ornament
of womankind"; "Marian" is "the Muses only darling";
"Mansilia" is the "paterne of true womanhead, And onely
mirrhor of feminitie"; "Neæra" is "the blosome of grace
and curtesie"; "Phyllis" is a "floure of rare perfection";
"Charillis" is a "paragone Of peerlesse price, and ornament of praise" —

"the pride and primrose of the rest,
Made by the Maker selfe to be admired,
And like a goodly beacon high addrest,
That is with sparks of heavenlie beautie fired." [50]

And Rosalind had first been praised in the following vein:

"The beame of beautie sparkled from above,
The floure of vertue and pure chastitie,
The blossome of sweet joy and perfect love,
The pearle of peerlesse grace and modestie:
To her my thoughts I daily dedicate,
To her my heart I nightly martyrize:
To her my love I lowly do prostrate,
To her my life I wholly sacrifice:
My thought, my heart, my love, my life is shee,
And I hers ever onely, ever one:
One ever I all vowed hers to bee,
One ever I, and others never none." [51]

---

[49] Lines 344–351.   [50] Lines 560–563.   [51] Lines 468–479.

But when Aglaura asks Colin for a description "of great Cynthiaes goodnesse and high grace," he seems to belie his pledges to Rosalind by soaring as follows:

"More eath," quoth he, "it is in such a case
How to begin, then know how to have donne.
For everie gift and everie goodly meed,
Which she on me bestowd, demaunds a day;
And everie day in which she did a deed
Demaunds a yeare it duly to display.
Her words were like a streame of honny fleeting.
The which doth softly trickle from the hive,
Hable to melt the hearers heart unweeting,
And eke to make the dead againe alive.
Her deeds were like great clusters of ripe grapes,
Which load the braunches of the fruitfull vine,
Offring to fall into each mouth that gapes,
And fill the same with store of timely wine.
Her lookes were like beames of the morning sun,
Forth looking through the windowes of the east,
When first the fleecie cattell have begun
Upon the perled grasse to make their feast.
Her thoughts are like the fume of franckincence,
Which from a golden censer forth doth rise,
And throwing forth sweet odours mounts fro thence
In rolling globes up to the vauted skies.
There she beholds, with high aspiring thought,
The cradle of her owne creation,
Emongst the seats of angels heavenly wrought,
Much like an angell in all forme and fashion."

Perhaps Cuddy's sense of humor is aware of the amusing side of such a flight as this in the name of a mere mortal, even if the lady be a queen among a dozen "gorgeous dames" who inspire similar songs:

"Colin," said Cuddy then, "thou hast forgot
Thy selfe, me seemes, too much, to mount so hie:
Such loftie flight base shepheard seemeth not,

From flocks and fields to angels and to skie."
   "True," answered he, "but her great excellence
Lifts me above the measure of my might:
That, being fild with furious insolence,
I feele my selfe like one yrapt in spright.
For when I thinke of her, as oft I ought,
Then want I words to speake it fitly forth:
And when I speake of her what I have thought,
I cannot thinke according to her worth.
Yet will I thinke of her, yet will I speake,
So long as life my limbs doth hold together,
And when as death these vitall bands shall breake,
Her name recorded I will leave for ever.
Her name in every tree I will endosse,
That, as the trees do grow, her name may grow:
And in the ground each where will it engrosse,
And fill with stones, that all men may it know.
The speaking woods and murmuring waters fall,
Her name Ile teach in knowen termes to frame:
And eke my lambs, when for their dams they call,
Ile teach to call for Cynthia by name.
And long while after I am dead and rotten,
Amongst the shepheards daughters dancing rownd,
My layes made of her shall not be forgotten,
But sung by them with flowry gyrlonds crownd.
And ye, who so ye be, that shall survive,
When as ye heare her memory renewed,
Be witnesse of her bountie here alive,
Which she to Colin her poore shepheard shewed." [52]

Thestylis asks Colin why he left the presence of such a
goddess and her nymphs. His satirical answer throws the
cool truth about Elizabeth and her court as much out of
focus as the hymn just quoted. And yet one feels that
Melissa rightly declares that Colin " 'now full deeply
[has] divynd Of love and beautie ' " —

[52] Lines 590–647.

"Beautie, the burning lamp of heavens light,
    Darting her beames into each feeble mynd." [53]

It might be argued, perhaps with secret sophistry, that, if any relative proportion is to be kept, the hyperbole in Spenser's praise of Cynthia is logically necessary when his idealizing imagination beholds its queen after bestowing superlatives on a dozen of her maids — not to mention its first love, Rosalind. But the final rationale of this glorification of Elisa or Cynthia is to be found in the profoundly Platonic cast of Spenser's imagination. The essence of Renaissance Platonizing was the abstraction of lovely ideas from their earthly manifestations, now here, now there, for a sustained adoration that yet expressed itself in sensuous imagery draped upon some "shape humane." It was but a copy, mirror, or reflection of what was revealed to the imagination "fild with furious insolence." Elizabethan poets spoke out often in an elaborate language of metaphor and hyperbole that was not necessarily stale, insincere, and hollow because a composite of ancient, medieval, and Renaissance conceits. The vocabulary of love can never be a new thing under the sun. And Spenser's language through all these verses that celebrate Rosalind, a dozen court ladies, and Cynthia is surely the speech of a poet in love with the essence of feminine beauty more than with any particular copy of it. Whether or not Spenser ever got a clear-sighted political view of Elizabeth such as Bacon surely had, or Machiavelli would have had, need not be of interest now.[54] The final interest is that in the actual queen and lady Spenser found a manifestation of what he felt to be the beautiful and the good in a queen and woman which was potent enough to stimulate lofty hymns addressed ultimately to the ideal. The figure of a brilliant virgin queen of great actual achievements neces-

[53] Lines 873–874.
[54] See below, pp. 360–361, 405.

sarily worked like magic upon an imagination that worshipped virtue and beauty. In lauding many ladies from
Rosalind on to Cynthia Spenser, if understood, is but
adoring the incarnation of feminine loveliness, almost as
fragrant under one name as another, but particularly
sweet as the Tudor rose.

It may seem a drop from Elisa as the subject of Spenser's
lofty Platonizing to pastoral materials which were occasioned by the progresses of the latter years of her reign.
But the pastoral idealization in them ranges all the way
from the artless compliments of actual shepherds to the
dainty songs of sophisticated court poets, Spenser's fellows. The first kind of compliment reveals pastoral illusion
fading before homely actuality; the second, pastoral illusion giving a very charming tone to the Elizabethan song,
a genre that "best accomplished the blending of the genius
of the people and the artistic sense awakened by humanism." [55] Both kinds of compliment lead beyond the range
of this chapter, but they may properly be introduced here.

The speeches when the queen visited Theobalds in May,
1591; Cowdray in August, 1591; Elvetham in the same
year; and Bisham and Sudeley in the next, are full of interesting compliment decked out in motley rural and
mythological dress. In at least one graceful pastoral lyric
the idealization of Elisa transcends conventional pastoral
poetry. At Elvetham the queen heard this "Dittie of the
six Virgins Song" as they "walked on before her towards
the house, strewing the way with flowers, and singing a
sweete song of six parts":

> With fragrant flowers we strew the way
> And make this our chiefe holliday:
> For though this clime were blest of yore,
> Yet was it neuer proud before,

---

[55] Legouis and Cazamian, p. 312.

O beauteous Queene of second Troy,
Accept of our vnfained ioy.

Now th'ayre is sweeter then sweet balme,
And Satyrs *daunce about the palme:*
Now earth, with verdure newly dight,
Giues perfect signe of her delight.
   O beauteous Queene of second Troy,
   Accept of our vnfained ioy.

Now birds record new harmonie,
And trees doe whistle melodie:
Now euerie thing that nature breeds,
Doth clad it selfe in pleasant weeds.
   O beauteous Queene of second Troy,
   Accept of our vnfained ioy.[56]

The refrain, less happily turned than the verses that pre-
cede it, at least has an echo of the patriotic refrains of much
broadside eulogy of the queen.[57] When the queen came to
Bisham in 1592, after a rather conventional speech by a
"wilde man," she was amused by a prose dialogue in
praise of her virginity. "At the middle of the Hill sate
PAN, and two Virgins keeping sheepe, and sowing in their
Samplers, where her Maiestye stayed and heard this."
The witty and humorous dialogue is spoken in a fresh
English country scene that is closer to Theocritus than to
Renaissance artificiality. There is little native music to
give life to the mixture of myth and pastoral suggestions
in Ceres's song which follows on the dialogue; but the song
does have an actual English hillside for its background.
Actuality breaks the pastoral illusion in compliments to

[56] Lyly, *Works*, I, 439. Bond (I, 524) is inclined to think this song by Thomas
Watson, who signs it in *England's Helicon 1600, 1614*, ed. H. E. Rollins, Cambridge, Mass., 1935, I, 47.
[57] The "thirde daies entertainement" brought the familiar "In the merrie
moneth of May" (Lyly, *Works*, I, 447–448), which so pleased royal ears that it
was encored. It may be taken as representative of the best pastoral verse
written not to compliment directly, but to entertain the queen.

the queen at Sudeley. "At her Majesties entrance into the Castle, an olde Shepheard" spoke:

Vouchsafe to heare a simple shephard: shephards and simplicity cannot part. Your Highnes is come into Cotshold, an uneven country, but a people that carry their thoughtes, levell with their fortunes; lowe spirites, but true harts; using plaine dealinge, once counted a jewell, nowe beggery. These hills afoorde nothing but cottages, and nothing can we present to your Highnes but shephards.

Thus this actual English shepherd suggests in a few words his native background, turns a courtly compliment or two, and concludes becomingly as follows:

This lock of wooll, Cotsholdes best fruite, and my poore gifte, I offer to your Highnes; in which nothing is to be esteemed, but the whitenes, virginities colour; nor to be expected but duetye, shephards religion.

Courtly shepherds or "makers" and actual Cotswold shearers praise Elisa's virginity with their respective tokens. The conventional pastoral devices appear side by side with such ingenious actuality, however; for the next to come before the queen is "APOLLO running after DAPHNE," chiefly to enable her to take refuge with "the Queene of chastety." [58]

The Elisa who appears in two important courtly anthologies in 1600 and 1602 is far removed from the actual queen one visualizes before the Cotswold shepherd with his gift of virgin wool. In *A Poetical Rhapsody* of 1602 Elisa figures in at least two of the eclogues which are written more or less under the influence of Spenser. The fourth piece in the opening group in the volume, "Pastorals and Eglogues," is headed: "*A* DIALOGVE *betweene two shepheards*, Thenot, *and* Piers, *in praise of* ASTREA, *made*

---

[58] I quote from the Bisham and Sudeley speeches as they are reprinted in Bond's *Lyly*, I, 471–488.

by the excellent Lady, the Lady Mary *Countesse of* Pembrook, *at the Queenes Maiesties being at her house.*" The two shepherds praise Astræa in stanzas like the following:

> *Then.*   ASTREA is our chiefest ioy,
>   Our chiefest guarde against annoy,
>   Our chiefest wealth, our treasure.
> *Piers.*   Where chiefest are, three others bee,
>   To vs none else but only shee;
>   When wilt thou speake in measure? [59]

In an "Eglogue" signed by Francis Davison an appeal is made to Astræa to show pity on a poor shepherd, Eubulus, who has fallen on evil days and lost her favor. Here a portrayal of Elisa would seem to be but a vehicle for an earnest personal plea. The eclogue is composed with admirable care for the natural background, and there is some poignant feeling in the complicated stanzas of the shepherd's lament, as the following will suggest:

> Thou flowret of the field that erst didst fade,
> And nipt with Northerne cold didst hang the head.
> Yee Trees whose bared bowes had lost their shade,
> Whose with'red leaues by western blasts were shed
>   Yee gin to bud and spring againe,
>   Winter is gone that did you straine.
>   But I, that late
>   With vpright gate
> Bare vp my head, while happy fauour lasted;
>   Now olde am growne,
>   Now ouerthrowne,
> With wo, with griefe, with wailing now am wasted.
>
> .   .   .   .
>
> Nor I, alas, do wish that her faire Eyes,
> Her blessed-making Eies should shed a teare,

---

[59] *A Poetical Rhapsody 1602-1621*, ed. H. E. Rollins, Cambridge, Mass., I (1931), 16.

Nor that one sigh from her deere Breast should rise,
For all the paines, the woes, the wrongs I beare.
   First let this weight oppresse me still,
   Ere shee, through mee taste any ill.
            Ah if I might
            But gaine her sight,
And shew hir, e're I die, my wretched case!
            O then should I
            Contented dy;
But ah I dy, and hope not so much grace.[60]

In such verses reality again breaks through pastoral illusion to show an imperious Elizabetha Regina, and in no
such happy way as in the Cotswold shepherd's compliment. Astræa is a great goddess whose disfavor is deadly
— but one whose good is to be sought whatever the price
a poor servant has to pay.[61]

   In *England's Helicon* of 1600, an anthology that crowned
pastoral lyricism in Elizabethan England, there is an in-
gathering of lyrics portraying "fayre Elisa, queene of
shepheardes all" from the several sources that I have been

---

[60] I, 32-34. For Eubulus as Secretary William Davison in disgrace, see the
Rhapsody, II (1932), 102-104.

[61] Perhaps an actual love affair between some shepherd and a nymph of
Elisa's court upon which the "queene of shepheardes all" as usual frowned is
shadowed in another one of the "Pastorals and Eglogues" signed by Francis
Davison. It is "Strephons Palinode," introduced with the following summary:
"Strephon, *vpon some vnkindenes conceiued, hauing made shew to leaue* VRANIA,
*and make loue to another Nymph, was at the next solemne assembly of shepheards,
not onely frowned vpon by* VRANIA, *but commanded with great bitternesse out of her
presence: Whereuppon, sory for his offence, and desirous to regaine her grace whom
he neuer had forsaken, but in shew, vpon his knees he in this Song humbly craues
pardon: and* VRANIA *finding his true penitence, and vnwilling to loose so worthy a
seruant, receiues him againe into greater grace and fauour than before*" (*A Poetical
Rhapsody*, I, 21). The poem that precedes this one, signed by Walter Davison,
and presented as "A Roun-de-lay in inuerted Rimes, betweene the twoo friendly
Riuals, Strephon and Klaius, in the presence of Vrania, Mistris to them both,"
may be designed to shadow Walter and his brother Francis as friendly rivals for
the royal favor. These poems are among four grouped in sequence in *A Poetical
Rhapsody*, the Countess of Pembroke's "A Dialogue . . . in praise of Astrea,"
clearly to the queen, coming first.

reviewing. In this anthology all the lyrics are made to fit
pastoral patterns. In it appear Colin's portrait of Elisa,
Rowland's of Beta, and Watson's song for the "*beauteous
Queene of second Troy*" — the three best songs to Elisa.
In it also are Sidney's "Song . . . sung before the Queenes
most excellent Maiestie" by Espilus and Therion, Barnfield's "Sheepheards Ode," and "Ceres Song in emulation
of Cinthia." [62] "A Canzon Pastorall in honour of her
Maiestie," signed by Edmund Bolton, shows a new conceit for Elisa's glory that may well conclude this exhibition
of Elisa in the pastoral poetry of her reign. I quote the
second half of the poem:

> Loe Matron-like the Earth her selfe attires
> In habite graue,
> Naked the fields are, bloomelesse are the brires,
> Yet we a Sommer haue,

---

[62] Elizabeth may be complimented in "The Sheepheards praise of his sacred
Diana," a pseudo-pastoral song in *England's Helicon* (I, 100-101) reprinted from
The Phœnix Nest of 1593 along with these others from various sources praising
Elisa. Certainly it raises the problem of allegorical compliments that might be
intended for Elizabeth, but about which it is now impossible to be certain, as a
sophisticated Elizabethan reader accustomed to ambiguous allegory perhaps
was. Yet I believe that "The Sheepheards praise," when read in sequence with
the pastoral idealizations which I have assembled and particularly with those
with which it appears in *England's Helicon*, will be seen to paint the familiar
portrait of Colin's "Cynthia, the Ladie of the Sea." Elizabeth as mistress of the
seas after 1588 and Elizabeth as defying time were frequent figures in the verse
praising her, as chapter vii will show. Such lines as "She beauty is, by her the
faire endure," and "In her is vertues perfect Image cast," have parallels in such
Platonic idealization as I noted in *Colin Clouts Come Home Againe*. Professor
Rollins in his edition of *The Phœnix Nest* (p. 167) writes: "The Malone copy
of the *Helicon*, in the Bodleian Library, is signed 'S. W. R.' (Sir Walter Raleigh)
but has a cancel with the name 'Ignoto' pasted over it. In the British Museum
copy the original signature has been erased, and the cancel is missing. The
Davison manuscript (MS. Harleian 280, fol. 99) attributed the poem to W. R.,
and Hannah included it, somewhat doubtfully, in his *Poems of Sir Walter
Raleigh*, 1875, 1892, pp. 77-78. Bond, on insufficient evidence, attributed it to
Lyly, in whose *Complete Works*, III, 478, he reprinted it." Miss Agnes M. C.
Latham, Ralegh's most recent editor, although reprinting this piece among the
"Doubtful Poems" (*The Poems of Sir Walter Ralegh*, 1929, p. 111), yet writes

Who in our clime kindleth these liuing fires,
        Which bloomes can on the briers saue.
No Ice dooth christallize the running Brooke,
No blast deflowres the flowre-adorned field,
Christall is cleere, but cleerer is the looke,
Which to our climes these liuing fires dooth yield:
        Winter though euery where
        Hath no abiding heere:
On Brooks and Briers she doth rule alone,
The Sunne which lights our world is alwayes one.[63]

So much for a view of the pastoral idealization of Elisa, "most royall queene or empresse" and "most vertuous and beautifull lady," by her shepherds in various masques, eclogues, court dramas, and free lyrics.[64] Clearly Elizabeth's peace and her virginity, perhaps the most distinctive

---

(p. 194) that it seems to her to be "so much in Ralegh's manner that I regret the necessity of placing it among the doubtful poems." Although no one seems to have read the poem as Ralegh's praise of the queen, it is of a piece with much of his poetry that does clearly reflect his "fantastic courtship" of her, of which Miss Latham writes with comprehension. See below, chapter vii.

[63] *England's Helicon*, I, 22.

[64] I have subordinated pastoral drama in this chapter, but I might well call attention to one or two late appearances of Elisa in the drama after Peele and Lyly. Chambers (*Elizabethan Stage*, III, 464–465) thinks that William Percy's *The Faery Pastorall* (dated 1603) may have been originally produced by Paul's boys before 1590 and revised by the author after 1599 in hope of a revival. See the conventionally complimentary "Prologue before the Court" (*The Cuck-Queanes . . . The Faery Pastorall or Forrest of Elues by W—— P—— Esq.*, From a MS. in the Library of Joseph Haslewood, 1824, pp. 95–96) and Florida's speech (p. 124) in thankfulness for the preservation of her virginity:

        Then Prayse to Joue, and to that virgin Queene
        Dread Mistris of our woodes.

Perhaps a song to Diana's victory over Cupid in II. ii. (pp. 120–121) may be meant to please the queen. A deal of Elizabethan pastoral poetry has been lost, as a glance at Greg's list (*Pastoral Poetry*, p. 119) will indicate. Elisa probably figured in much of it if one is to judge by the rôle she plays in what is extant. Perhaps the last reference to Elisa *in vita* is in William Basse's second of three pastoral elegies published in 1602 which Greg (p. 114) calls "the last work of the kind to appear in Elizabeth's reign." It is an earnest prayer for "fayre Elisa," now almost seventy (*The Poetical Works*, ed. R. W. Bond, 1893, p. 65).

qualities of her public and private characters, are most repeatedly celebrated. I have not tried to lay down a fixed
definition of pastoral poetry because formal definition is
not essential. I have been examining some three out-
growths of foreign graftings upon native English stock:
the Renaissance eclogue with its ultimate ancestry in
Virgil and Theocritus, now made to subserve the end of
courtly compliment to Elisa; the loose interweaving of
pastoral machinery and mythological disguises into
masque-like memorials of the queen's progresses, or into
court drama of eulogistic or satirical intent; and the free
song which creates an Arcadian atmosphere invigorated
by the fragrance of the English countryside.

Three spiritual notes characterize the pastoral. One is . . .
exaltation of content, connecting itself on the one side with the
longing for renewed simplicity of manners, on the other with a
vivid sense of the uncertainty of all human advantages. . . .
    Then there is the note of love; the one serious preoccupation
of pastoral life, . . .
    And finally, there is the note of delight in, and refreshment
from, natural beauty.[65]

Each of these three qualities of the pastoral has significant
affinities for Elizabeth and for the poets who idealized her
as "fayre Elisa, queene of shepheardes all."
    The queen herself once neatly revealed the attitude of
mind that "does appear to be a constant element in the
pastoral as known to literature . . . the recognition of a
contrast, implicit or expressed, between pastoral life and
some more complex type of civilization." [66] Captive at
Woodstock, she, "hearing vpon a time out of hir garden
at Woodstocke, a certeine milkmaid singing pleasantlie,

    [65] I quote from Sir Edmund Chambers's admirable introduction to his *Eng-
lish Pastorals*, 1906, pp. xxxix–xli.
    [66] Greg, p. 4.

wished hir selfe to be a milkemaid as she was, saieng that hir case was better, and life more merier than was hirs in that state as she was." [67] Pastoral poetry is not to be separated from disillusion with urbane existence and a longing for escape to a simple and happy rural life, once known, or imagined. In luxurious Alexandria Theocritus remembered the Sicilian hills of his youth; and Elizabethan court poets desired escape from many sordid actualities. The Arcadia to which Sidney and his fellows journeyed was far from the fresh and downright world of Theocritus, but the instincts that urged their journeying were close to the genesis of pastoral poetry in any age. The pastoral is most appealing when a deep desire for a life closer to the fresh soil leads, as most notably in Theocritus, to passionate identification with its first fruits. Men like Ralegh knew that "ruin, weariness, death, perpetually death, [stood] grimly to confront the other presence of Elizabethan drama which [was] life." [68] But they were vigorous enough to behold the actual scene, struggle with it in London, Flanders, or the New World, rest from it with the pretty fictions of Arcadia, and return to the struggle. The pastoral fiction was for Elizabeth and her poets a brave beauty added to the richness of life and veiling the ugliness of their particular death in life, about which they had no final illusions. It was inevitable that a queen who was an adept in sustaining various pretty fictions at her brilliant court and in her progresses should be idealized in the pastoral dreams of her poets. For the queen epitomized her age in her delight in the various arts, the pastoral masquerade among them, that embellished mortality for it.

The actual queen and lady whom poets crowned "fayre Elisa, queene of shepheardes all" stimulated the other

[67] *Holinshed's Chronicles of England, Scotland, and Ireland*, IV (1808), 133.
[68] Virginia Woolf, *The Common Reader*, 1925, p. 82.

distinct sentiments of pastoral poetry — love of love and of nature. The queen's political maneuvering in the name now of matrimony, now of virginity, is a curious gloss or caricature on such toying with love as is the stock in trade of the conventional Phillis. This brilliant royal virgin playing with love and wedlock before two generations of poets was uniquely suited to be a true shepherd's queen in every sense of the term. It was a happy accident that English poets had an actual queen who embodied the conventional shepherd's queen in her personal tastes and in much of her public style. Inevitably she attracted many pastoral conceits. Virgil and his Renaissance imitators had shown how pastoral machinery could be turned to the compliment of royalty. About 1579 Elizabeth was reaching a climax in her exciting game of diplomacy and love. She must have roused both the patriotic fervor and the cultivated fancy of her poets. It is small wonder that she inspired in Spenser a beautiful English lyric woven inextricably of high patriotism and traditional pastoral conceits. Sidney, too, knew how to weave courtly compliment to Elisa into such an indigenous pastoral design as a May lady. It became increasingly tactful to adore Elisa's virginity; but the virgin ideal was anyway one of profound attraction for a Renaissance mind questioning the authority of the Queen of Heaven only to meet the appeal of her elder sister, the pagan Diana. The English Diana, increasingly fussy about the virginity of her nymphs, must have multiplied the number of virgin nymphs in English verse. The continuous hymning of chastity in English pastoral drama began under an autocratic virgin queen even if the form saw its maturity after her. If "love *in vacuo* is the beginning and end of the pastoral romance proper," [69] then pastoral love was particularly at home at Elisa's court, so officially sacred to Diana. The love casu-

[69] Greg, p. 154 (quoting Sir Walter Raleigh).

istry of which Elizabethan poetry is full had an old and
complex ancestry, the traditional eclogue being in its tree.
In the pastoral and in the sonnet the pagan spirit of the
age sported with the paradoxes and ambiguities of love,
however rebuked by its Christian conscience, and with a
surprising zest for both the "hony" and the "gaule" of
love. Just such ambiguous allegorizing as now confounds
the curious scholar and critic — compliments mixing love
of mistress, of friend, of queen, and of mere conceits —
delighted less than it puzzled the readers for whom Barnfield threw a loose pastoral disguise over this love and
that. The romantic love that Elisa stimulated and sublimated matched the conventional conceits to which her
poets were attached throughout her reign.

But romantic love is not the only theme of love sounded
on the English shepherd's pipes as he plays before "fayre
Elisa." From Colin's song to "Thestilis Ode" in almost
all the pastoral poetry that sings Elisa there is a recurring
amor patriæ — a country happily personified by Elisa
during years of intense political fervor. One group of
court poets had as an avowed aim the lifting of English
poetry to the level of Continental achievement. Necessarily the praise of royalty in Italian and French eclogues
stimulated patriotic imitation by Elisa's shepherds, especially since she was uniquely fitted to suggest pastoral
conceits, themes, and moods. Patriotic celebration of
Elizabeth is most blatant in the broadsides. But when
Francis Sabie concludes *Pans pipe* with a vigorous encomium on Elisa as Jehovah's chosen queen, Protestant
patriotism breaks through pastoral illusion and shows that
Elisa is but another name for the English Judith of the
ballads. One suspects that love of the England that Elizabeth personifies is deeper than devotion either to Jove or
Jehovah in poets who in the pastorals and broadsides
praise Elisa in the name of both of those deities. Yet men

were really serving the two gods in Elizabethan England.[70]
Naturally they invoked both pagan and Christian favor
for Elisa who personified England.

The note of *amor patriæ* which Elisa evokes, now in a
fresh song by Colin, now in a stiff classical eclogue awkwardly resolved into a homely broadside eulogy, is profoundly related to the third spiritual quality of the pastoral
— "delight in, and refreshment from, natural beauty."
Elizabethans enjoyed nature with little scientific interest
in her ways. One will not find among the flowers with
which Colin and Rowland adorn Elisa and Beta much
evidence of that exact observation of the English flora
which poets of the Romantic Revival show. And yet both
Colin and Rowland contrive to make one feel that they
mean English flowers to bedeck Elisa, and their nymphs
to dance around her on an English green. Chaucer's
"Prologue" lines are inimitably fragrant with an English
spring in spite of their conventional pattern. Such love
of English landscape was stimulated by the vigorous patriotism of the times; and a brilliant virgin queen who all her
life took keen pleasure in the out-of-doors was a magnet
for the pastoral fancy of her poets as it transformed Sicilian or Continental landscape into English countryside.
To her talent for dance and music, itself a requisite for
any true shepherd's queen, Elizabeth added a great delight in a favorite English sport, the chase; thus, as well

---

[70] The mingling of things pagan and Christian in Elizabethan literature is
amusingly evident in "Coridons Song" toward the end of Lodge's *Rosalynde*
(p. 137, *Complete Works*, ed. Hunterian Club, 1883, I) in which a "*country
Lasse*" is promised relief of her sorrow — her virginity — by a shepherd boy:

> *And fore God Pan did plight their troath,*
> *and to the Church they hied them fast.*

> *And God send euerie pretie peate*

> .   .   .   .

> *so kinde a friend to helpe at last.*

as by her virginity, she suggested Diana to her shepherds, the poets.[71]

English pastoral poetry flowers most freely, and perhaps most beautifully, in short songs of which Marlowe's "Come Live with Me" is the classic example. In such a piece one hears the three essential notes of the pastoral spirit which I have been associating with the Elizabethan mind as it idealized the public and private characters of Elizabeth. And the song to Elisa beginning "*With fragrant flowers we strew the way*" echoes these notes. Six virgins sing a love song to the "*beauteous Queene*" whose peace has blessed "*second Troy*" as it has never been blessed before. They strew her way with "*fragrant flowers*" as "Satyrs *daunce about the palme*" and "*birds record new harmonie*" in an English Arcadia far from care.

[71] The 1575 edition of George Turbervile's *The noble arte of venerie or hunting* contains interesting pictures and verses in this connection. On sig. F5ᵛ the queen is seen in a forest with courtiers around her and dinner being spread on the ground. Verses following describe the serving of a repast "on pleasant gladsome greene" for a queen or king; and on sigs. F7–F7ᵛ are verses addressed directly to Elizabeth. See scenes with the game before her on sigs. F8, I3; also representations of her hawking in Turbervile's *The Booke of Faulconrie or Hauking*, 1575, sigs. F1, G8ᵛ.

CHAPTER V

Diana

FAYRE Elisa, queene of shepheardes all," reigns
not only over pastoral lyricism. Variously named,
she is queen of other types of lyric poetry which
flower under her rule. As a beautiful virgin lady
who commands the lives and loves of her "sort of goodly
knights," she has surprising kinships with the sovereign
lady of chivalric romance — even with the Holy Virgin,
that blessed lady who held the final adoration of every
"parfit gentil knight." This "queene of shepheardes all"
is in peculiar ways an archetype of the fashionable sonnet
mistress of the nineties. She becomes a unique center for
Platonic idealism imported from Italian courts. To suggest the unity of these several concepts of Elizabeth, I
wish to introduce at once three sisters of Elisa — the
royal Diana, the royal Laura, and the royal Idea. It is
necessary to isolate the ladies somewhat in order to ana-
lyze the body of verse and prose in which they have their
immortality, but I hope to emphasize the intimate rela-
tionship of concepts that together gave expression to many
of the cultural ideals of Elizabethan England.

It is chivalric sentiment at the court of Queen Elizabeth
that finally accounts for the idealization of her as Diana.

Before meeting Diana directly it is well to recall the
nature of Elizabethan chivalry.

The late Professor W. H. Schofield introduced his excellent study of chivalry in English literature — in Chaucer,
Malory, Spenser, and Shakespeare — by remembering
that chivalry is "less an institution than an ideal," [1] as

[1] *Chivalry in English Literature*, Cambridge, Mass., 1912, p. 3.

Léon Gautier had made clear in his *La Chevalerie*. Professor Schofield then quoted John Addington Symonds's memorable description of that ideal. Because chivalry at the court of Queen Elizabeth had distinctly an ideal being, and because Symonds's penetrating description of the mature chivalric ideal is a happy touchstone with which to study Elizabethan chivalry, I shall further imitate Schofield by recalling it at the outset of this chapter. Symonds wrote as follows:

Chivalry is not to be confounded with feudalism. Feudalism was a form of social organisation based upon military principles. Chivalry was an ideal binding men together by participation in potent spiritual enthusiasms. Feudalism was the bare reality of mediæval life. Chivalry was the golden dream of possibilities which hovered above the eyes of mediæval men and women, ennobling their aspirations, but finding its truest expression less in actual existence than·in legend and literature. The pages of feudal history tell a dismal tale of warfare, cruelty, oppression, and ill-regulated passions. The chivalrous romances present sunny pictures of courtesy and generosity and self-subordination to exalted aims. . . . Chivalry, though rarely realised in its pure beauty, though scarcely to be seized outside the songs of poets, and the fictions of romancers, was the spiritual force which gave its value to the institutions and the deeds of feudalism. Whatever was most noble in the self-devotion of Crusaders, most beneficial to the world in the foundation of the knightly orders, most brilliant in the lives of Richard, the Edwards, Tancred, Godfrey of Bouillon, most enthusiastic in the lives of Rudel, Dante, Petrarch; most humane in the courtesy of the Black Prince; most splendid in the courage of Bayard; in the gallantry of Gaston de Foix; in the constancy of Sir Walter Manny; in the loyalty of Blondel; in the piety of St. Louis — may be claimed by the evanescent and impalpable yet potent spirit which we call Chivalry.

Regarding Chivalry, not as an actual fact of history, but as a spiritual force, tending to take form and substance in the world

at a particular period, we find that its very essence was enthusiasm of an unselfish kind. The true knight gave up all thought
of himself. At the moment of investiture he swore to renounce
the pursuit of material gain; to do nobly for the mere love of
nobleness; to be generous of his goods; to be courteous to the
vanquished; to redress wrongs; to draw his sword in no quarrel
but a just one; to keep his word; to respect oaths; and, above all
things, to protect the helpless and to serve women. The investiture of a knight was no less truly a consecration to high unselfish
aims for life than was the ordination of a priest.[2]

The England of Elizabeth inherited a generous portion
of this "impalpable yet potent spirit," of this "enthusiasm
of an unselfish kind" that rejoiced in the service of *Dieu
et les dames*. Of course I cannot evoke that evanescent
spirit from all Elizabethan literature.[3] But there is much
evidence that it had not died in Elizabeth's England,
however changed it was to new times and needs. If metrical romances did decline in favor about 1575, there was
thereafter a notable vogue for French prose "books of
chivalry" and for translations of late Spanish romances,[4]
and it coincided in time with the years when the popularity and brilliance of Elizabeth's reign were at their
height — the eighties and the early nineties. The ordinary
reader was familiar with the stories and customs of chivalry through old-fashioned and new-fashioned romances,
through chronicles, plays, ballads, and local traditions.
Sophisticated readers were enjoying Malory anew. His
romantic and nationalistic attitude toward chivalry must
have made a deep appeal to aristocratic tastes. Through-

---

[2] *An Introduction to the Study of Dante*, 1899, pp. 255–257.
[3] I appeal to Professor Schofield's lectures on chivalry in Spenser and Shakespeare for witness to its presence; the impalpable spirit did come when that distinguished scholar summoned it from those vasty deeps.
[4] See Professor R. S. Crane's *The Vogue of Medieval Chivalric Romance During the English Renaissance*, an abstract of a University of Pennsylvania thesis,
Menasha, Wisconsin, 1919, for a good study of the subject. My generalizations
at this point are based upon it.

out the *Morte Darthur* "true love is exalted as a noble in-spiration to valour." [5] The book is full of calls to patriotic service that were not lost on English knights who won the Armada victory some hundred years after Malory tried to summon the discordant nobility of the fifteenth century to service for a united England. The author of *The Knight's Tale* and *Troilus* was still a well of chivalric sentiment un-defiled for Spenser and the readers of *The Faerie Queene*. In the birthright of every gentle English reader was a wealth of chivalric sentiment variously modified from Gower to Hawes.

The Faerie Queene and *Arcadia* are the most eloquent monuments of the survival and revival of chivalric senti-ment under Elizabeth, however transformed by new times for a new political order. The popularity of *Arcadia* shows how Renaissance taste liked its heritage of medieval show and sentiment blended with Greek romance. In it the old stories from the Amadis series and late Greek romances were made over to inculcate typical Elizabethan ideals of conduct and character. Pyrocles and Musidorus are Elizabethan knights about ideal Elizabethan adventures in a land in which the pastoral and the chivalric are mingled after Montemayor's formula. In *Arcadia* and *The Faerie Queene* is still to be found the essence of Eliza-bethan chivalry, which sought to fashion for action in public life "a gentleman or noble person in vertuous and gentle discipline." The deep impress of Sidney, the "presi-dent of noblesse and of chivalry" to whom Spenser dedi-cated *The Shepheardes Calender*, of his character and his writings on the chivalric temper of his age, is comparable only, perhaps, to that which the greater poet, if not the greater man, made with his epic.[6] Chivalry in *The Faerie*

---

[5] Schofield, p. 108.

[6] Elizabethan chivalric ideals we prefer to find in Sidney's life, rather than to thread the mazes of his chivalric pastoral; and his career is truly a finer expres-

Queene is a colossal and elusive subject indeed; and I can
do no more than suggest wherein Spenser modified inherited chivalric ideals for Renaissance tastes. He absorbed the chivalry of Malory and of Chaucer, but he
infused, as Schofield observed, the conception of the perfect knight as a gentleman molded to virtuous and gentle
discipline. Even Spenser's word "virtue" had been im-
pregnated with new intellectual significance in England
since Chaucer's day. It resembles more the Italian *virtù*.
And "discipline," a word that Chaucer uses only once,
and Malory not at all, "signifies more than the outward
precept or expert usage of earlier days: it insists on mental
comprehension of underlying motive." [7] The source of
this new conception of mental force as essential to the
complete knight's armor was, of course, the Italian Renaissance. "If one idea could be picked out as the dominant
thought in Italian courtesy books, it was that the outward
graces of man should all be cultivated by education." [8]

---

sion of Elizabethan chivalry than any poet or critic can effect. He had the
"courtier's, scholar's, soldier's, eye, tongue, sword." He was "th' observ'd of
all observers — quite, quite down." He is John Addington Symonds's brave
medieval knight in service to *Dieu et les dames* after he has gone to school at the
Italian Renaissance and learned of Castiglione to be a loyal courtier and scholar-
poet as well as a gallant lover and soldier. Any final estimate of the place of
chivalry in Elizabethan life would have somehow to gauge the profound impress
which Sidney's character and deeds made on the actions and ideals of the most
important men and women of the age. Tributes to him, in number and in fulness of admiration, are second only to those to Elizabeth. The idealization of
him as a masculine type of perfection is a significant parallel to the legend about
the queen. The queen who personified English well-being for all her shepherds is
linked with her famous courtier in an allusion in the eloquent "Epitaph upon the
Right Honourable Sir Phillip Sidney, Knight: Lord Governor of Flushing,"
written by Sir Walter Ralegh and printed in *Astrophel* (Spenser, *Works*, p. 713):

> Whence to sharpe wars sweet honor did thee call,
> Thy countries love, religion, and thy friends:
> Of worthy men the marks, the lives, and ends,
> And her defence, for whom we labor all.

[7] Schofield, p. 151.
[8] Lewis Einstein, *The Italian Renaissance in England*, New York, 1902, p. 110.

George Pettie, in the preface to his translation of Guazzo's
Conversations, commends learning in soldiers, and declares
that "it is only it which maketh you gentlemen, and seeing
that the only way to win immortality is either to do things
worth the writing, or write things worth the reading." [9]
A virtuous and cultivated knight in action for glory —
that is the chivalric ideal now. Such a knight, as every
reader of Castiglione's *Cortegiano* knows, finds his prince's
court the natural place at which to run for the "immortal
garland." The Elizabethan "parfit gentil knight" is a
scholar and a courtier, thanks to schooling in Italy. He
delights to spend his days in the service of England, in the
service of his princess — "to win worthy place through
due deserts and comely carriage," as Spenser says. [10]

Sidney and Spenser are the supreme exemplars of Elizabethan chivalry in their lives and in their writings. Sidney
was even there to embody visibly the remodeled chivalric
ideal for his friend when he began *The Faerie Queene*.
Shakespeare universalized chivalric ideals, [11] and brought
them home to men's bosoms in dramas familiar to all of
us. However, it is Spenser's or Sidney's chivalry — intellectual and courtly — that is of chief concern as I pass to
a study of a revival of chivalric idealism which is inseparable from the figure of Elizabeth.

But first I shall introduce William Segar as an additional
witness to the distinguishing quality of Elizabethan chivalry — the conception of a true knight as an educated
gentleman who serves his prince and state and rises by his
individual worth and noble deeds to an immortality of
fame. Segar will also prove that discriminating Elizabethans did not condemn romances, as did Ascham and
his over-zealous brethren. Segar may remind one, too,

---

[9] Quoted in Einstein, pp. 109–110.
[10] Quoted in Schofield, p. 156.
[11] Schofield, p. 263.

how love of adventure which, along with religious enthusiasm, was of the essence of medieval chivalry, found a
fortunate stimulus in Elizabethan voyaging. William
Segar's *Honor Military, and Ciuill, contained in foure
Bookes* was printed in 1602. Its four books treat respectively of "Justice, and Iurisdiction Military"; of "Knighthood in generall, and particular"; of "Combats for life,
and Triumph"; and of "Precedencie of great Estates, and
others." Coming at the very end of Elizabeth's reign, and
treating subjects "not handled heretofore in our English"
by armorists, so Segar tells the reader in his dedication, it
is good authority for any final information about mature
chivalric form and practice in Elizabethan England. "The
Authors Intention" is a notable defense of learning as the
crowning virtue of a good knight. Segar says that

the endeuour of Gentlemen, ought be either in Armes or learning, or in them both. And in my poore conceit, hardly deserueth
he any title of honour, that doth not take pleasure in the one or
the other.[12]

He adds a little essay on the importance of learning for an
Elizabethan knight who would rise by personal merit. It
is clear evidence of contact with Italian courtly ideals that
have already appeared as typical of the chivalry of Sidney
and Spenser. When Segar writes his chapter "How enterprises aduenturous ought to be admired, but not discredited," he shows how Elizabethan voyaging nourished
chivalric love of adventure — and he gives a good answer
to Ascham and all squinting moralists.

True it is, as hath bene formerly said, that many enterprises
in times past attempted and atchieued aboue the expectation of
men, are now thought rather fabulous then faithfully reported:
either because we that now liue did not know, or see them, or

[12] Sig. R5ᵛ.

that ignorant men cannot conceiue howe they might be done, or that want of courage doth disable them to take the like actions in hand. Yet most certaine it is, that diuers histories commonly reputed vaine fables, were at the first begun vpon occasion of matter in effect true, although some writers afterwards, to shew the excellencie of their inuention, or make their workes more vendible, haue added many fancies and fictions which are not indeede worthy to bee beleeued. And who so shall well consider how difficult a thing it is to write an history of so great trueth and perfection, as cannot be controlled, will easily excuse these writers that haue taken in hand matter so farre from our knowledge and vnderstanding. For like vnto all other men, mooued with loue, hate, profit, or other priuate passion, they are either willing or ignorantly induced to encrease or extenuate the actions and merits of those men, of whom their histories haue discoursed. Howsoeuer that bee, I verely thinke the Acts and enterprises of *Vlysses*, *Æneas*, *Hector*, and other famous captaines (of whome Poets and profane Writers haue written so many woonders) were indeed of notable men, and some part of their doings such, as writers haue made mention. Much lesse doe I doubt, that some egregious acts atchieued and written in the bookes of *Amadis de Gaule*, *Ariosto*, *Tasso*, King *Arthur* of England, and such others doe containe many things, which deserue not to be discredited. But omitting to meddle with time so long since past, and with countreys so farre from our Climate, wee will remember some few Actions which worthy men of our owne Nation or our neighbours (as that of *Hernando Cortez*, *Pisarro*, and others) haue (within our knowledge) to the eternizing of their fame and honour, perfourmed. The greater part of which enterprises haue bene atchieued in this present age, and shall no doubt hereafter (when men are lesse industrious) be thought rather fabulous, then matters credible.

Let vs therefore say no more of matter so long before our dayes, and begin with actions notable performed by men of our owne Countrey, and they (for the most part) persons of such qualitie, as were not forced with distresse, but with desire to aduance the honour of their Countrey.

He recounts the "actions notable" of Anthony Jenkinson, Sir John Hawkins, Sir Humphrey Gilbert, Sir Richard Grenville, Sir Francis Drake, and other great Elizabethan voyagers. He remembers the glorious voyage of 1588, and declares:

These and other notable aduentures and victories were aboue the common opinion of men, attempted, and atchieued by worthie and excellent Captaines of our countrey: and the chiefe of them within the raigne of our sacred Soueraigne, by whose counsell and princely prudence they were begun and ended.[13]

Exactly what stimulus was given to the chivalric spirit by the presence of "our sacred Soueraigne," from "whose counsell and princely prudence" Segar would not separate the "notable aduentures and victories" of her "worthie and excellent" knights? What was Diana's character?

In studying the nature of Diana one should remember the two characters which Elizabeth had for the imagination of her most chivalric poet. Spenser compliments her in *The Faerie Queene* first as a "most royall queene or empresse," and then as a "most vertuous and beautifull lady." Perhaps one may think of Gloriana or Elizabetha Regina as attracting such chivalric loyalty as a sovereign would command, and of Belphœbe or Elizabeth Tudor as inspiring the personal devotion of her knights to the "most vertuous and beautifull lady." I shall call this lady Elizabetha Virgo — or Diana — for reasons that will appear. But it must be remembered that the lady was every inch a queen for her knights.

Segar may properly introduce Elizabetha Regina as a magnetic center for chivalric idealism. His book on chivalric practice during her reign is dedicated to her:

Considering (most sacred, and most *mighty Princesse*) *that the duety of euery Subiect is, not onely to obey, but also to the vttermost*

[13] Sigs. E5ᵛ–E6ᵛ.

of his power, in his degree and qualitie, to aduance the Honour of his Prince and Countrey; I haue according to my poore talent en-deuoured, in discharge of my duetie, for the place of Seruice which I holde vnder your Maiestie, by your most Gracious fauour, to frame these Discourses concerning Armes, Honor, and the Princely Magnificence of your Maiesties Court, *a subiect proper to* Armor-ists, *and men of my profession, not handled heretofore in our English by them, or any other to my knowledge: Yet fit to be knowen of all Noble and worthy personages, being perswaded that as your Maiestie hath bene a Mirrour to all the world for excellent gifts of Minde, Person, and Fortune: So your Raigne most happie both for victorious Armes, and flourishing Arts, which shall remaine glorious to all posteritie, may haply receiue some Honourable note from hence, which I most heartily desire, as the chiefest scope of my dessein.*

And so most humbly beseeching your Maiestie to vouchsafe that your poorest Seruant may in all duetie, and humble deuotion pros-trate himselfe, and his Labours, at your most Sacred feete, I be-seech the Almightie God to graunt your Maiestie to exceede all other Princes in length of life, in perfect health, in prosperous Raigne, and all felicitie.

Your Maiesties

Most humble and obedient seruant,

W. Segar *Norroy.*[14]

After a description of foreign chivalric shows, the third book, "Combats for life, and Triumph," culminates in a proud description of combats, jousts, tournaments, and triumphs under Elizabeth.

Yea certaine it is, that neither *France, Spaine, Germany* or other Nation Christian was euer honoured with so many Militarie triumphes, as *England* hath bene, chiefly in the raigne of her Maiestie who now liueth; as hereafter shal appeare. For besides other excellent triumphal Actions, and Militarie pastimes since her Maiesties raigne, a yeerely (and as it were ordinary) triumph hath bene celebrated to her Highnesse honour, by the noble and

[14] Sig. *2.

vertuous Gentlemen of her Court; a custome neuer before vsed
nor knowen in any Court or Countrey. And albeit (as hath bene
formerly remembred) the Triumphes of *Germany* were of great
pompe and notable, yet because they were furnished with the
whole number of Princes and Nobilitie of that Nation, (and the
celebration rare) they seeme to me lesse admirable then our
owne, which haue continued more then 30. yeeres yeerely, without intermission; and performed chiefly (and in effect onely) by
the Princes, Lords and Gentlemen dayly attendant vpon her
Maiesties Royal person. Whereby the honour of those Actions
is indeed due to her Highnesse Court onely.[15]

I shall look first at a few memorials of the chivalric
exaltation of Elizabetha Regina at the anniversaries of her
accession.[16] Herr Lupold von Wedel of Kremzow, who
visited England in 1584–85, left some vivid pictures of the
queen and her knights on such an occasion;[17] but Peele's
easy verses give more brilliant glimpses of such scenes. In
*Polyhymnia Describing, The honourable Triumph at Tylt,
before her Maiestie, on the 17. of Nouember last past* (1590)
thirteen couples of brave Elizabethan knights joust on this
holiday

> In honour of their peerless sovereign,
> High mistress of their service, thoughts, and lives.

The following verses suggest the scene:

> All with a Burning Heart greets he [Carey] her grace,
> Whose gracious countenance he his heaven esteems,
> And to her sacred person it presents,
> As who would say, "My heart and life is hers,
> To whom my loyalty this heart prefers."

---

[15] Sig. Q5[v].
[16] See Nichols, I, 63; III, 443, 522–526 for records of striking accession and
anniversary celebrations.
[17] See *Queen Elizabeth and Some Foreigners*, ed. Victor von Klarwill, 1928,
pp. 328–332.

.   .   .   .

And all was done in honour of their queen.

.   .   .   .

   And now had England's queen, faire England's life,
Beheld her lords, and lovely lordly knights,
Do honour's service to their sovereign.[18]

Cumberland is dressed "in virgin's colours"; "lovely
Compton" also wears white; and "to't they [all] go" to
"do their royal mistress honour's right." Peele glorifies
this queen of chivalry on a later anniversary in *Anglorum
Feriæ, Englandes Hollydayes, celebrating the 17th of Novemb.
last, 1595, beginninge happyly the 38 yeare of the raigne of
our soveraigne ladie Queene Elizabeth.* After many verses
that sing her preservation and blessings he begs Clio's aid
to describe adequately the scene

That all may see how well she is beloved,
What troop of loyal English knights in arms,
Right richly mounted and appointed all,
In shining arms accoutred for the war,
Small number of a number numberless,
Held justs in honour of her holiday,
Ready to do their duties and devoir
Against the mightiest enemy she hath,
Under what clime soe'er his colours wave,
And with keen sword and battle-axe in hand
To wound his crest, whatever foe he be
That any way in her dishonour braves.
   Among this stirring company of knights,
That at the tilt in fair habiliments
Gan show themselves, renowmèd Cumberland,
Knight of the Crown, in gilded armour dight,
Mounted at Queen Elizabeth's approach,
Inflamed with honour's fire, and left his hold
Kept by a dragon, laden with fair spoils:
And there his duty done, and large device

---

[18] *Works,* II, 287–300.

Made by his page known to her majesty,
Whose gracious eye reflecting on this earl
Was like Prometheus' life-infusing fire,
Behold, he stands impatient of delay,
Awaiting there his friendly foe's approach!
Daring he stands, true knight and challenger,
And hardly brooks the time of their address
That shortly came in duty all devote,
To solace with their martial exercise
Their princely mistress, to whose worthiness
That day's device and days of all their lives
Right humbly were and purely dedicate.

Essex and Sussex appear in rich array; then Bedford and
Southampton.

Southampton ran
As Bevis of Southampton, that good knight,
Had justed in the honour of the day;
And certes Bevis was a mighty man,
Valiant in arms, gentle and debonair;
And such was young Wriothesley, that came
As if in duty to his sovereign
And honour's race for all that he had done,
He would be of the noblest over-run.
Like to himself and to his ancestors,
Ran Bedford, to express his readiness,
His love to arms, his loyalty to her
Whose burning eyeballs did retain the heat
That kindled honour's fire at their hearts;
Bravely ran Bedford, and his staves he brake
Right happily for his high mistress' sake.

Compton and Carey are followed by

three redoubted knights and men-at-arms,
Old Knowles his offspring, gallant cavaliers;
And such they show'd as were King Arthur's knights
He whilom used to feast at Camelot,
Or three of great King Priam's valiant sons

Had left Elysium and the fields of Mars
To celebrate Eliza's holiday:
They ran as if three Hectors had made way
To meet Achilles, Ajax, Diomede.

Toward honor's goal they all go, fired by the "radiant beams" from their "princely mistress."

Young Howard, ramping lion-like, came on,
Anchor of Howard's honourable house,
His noble father's hope, his mother's joy.
Loyal and lovely was this fair young knight,
Gracious in his beginnings at the tilt,
Pleasing to her to whom he did present
His person and the service of that day,
And all the days and minutes of his life:
Bravely he bare him in his mistress' eye,
And brake his staves and let the shivers fly.

   .   .   .   .

Long may they run in honour of the day!
Long may she live to do them honour's right,
To grace their sports and them as she hath done,
England's Astræa, Albion's shining sun!
And may she shine in beauty fresh and sheen
Hundreds of years, our thrice-renownèd queen!
Write, Clio, write; write, and record her story,
Dear in heaven's eye, her court, and country's glory.[19]

"Albion's shining sun" inspired her Bevises to displays of devotion on many occasions other than her anniversaries; but I shall invite attention to only a few of them.

There were, of course, notable chivalric devices in the celebrated spectacles at Kenilworth in 1575, although classic myth and native Arthurian water legend did chief service there to compliment the English Diana. Leicester even made an ineffectual effort to revive the Knights of the Round Table to honor his guest. Nationalistic en-

[19] II, 348–355.

thusiasm associated all the Tudors, and especially the "*beauteous Queene of second Troy*," with Arthur's line.[20] Because Elizabeth was a Welsh princess of Arthurian descent she could lay impressive claim to his original empire by land and sea, as Dr. Dee clearly proved. The third chapter in the second book of *Honor Military, and Ciuill* is an account of Knights of the Round Table — "The maner of making Knights about the yeere of Christ 500. neere which time King Arthur reigned in England." He ends his third book with descriptions of knightly life under the Tudor princess whom all patriotic Englishmen hailed as the ultimate flower of Arthur's stock. The compliment is notable, if implicit. It is made more appropriate in that Arthur's knights are described as sea knights in this chapter, which immediately precedes the passage that I quoted to show how chivalric energy vented itself in Elizabethan voyaging. At Kenilworth the Lady of the Lake rose from the water to honor the "*beauteous Queene*" whose own sea knights were extending her empire over seas Arthur's men had never dreamed of. The jumble of pagan myth and chivalric show in which the Lady appeared was wholly to the fancy of the age. It knew not the correct taste of Mr. Addison as Bishop Hurd lets him express it to Dr. Arbuthnot.[21]

Segar describes various tournaments, among them, a "notable Tourneament on horsebacke, solemnized within her Maiesties pallace at Westminster: which became the more rare and memorable, because it was performed in the night"; also "An honourable Challenge . . . brought before her Maiestie, by the Earle of *Arundell*, calling himselfe *Callophisus*, who with his assistant Sir *William Drurie*,

[20] This fashion has been studied by the late Professor Greenlaw in *Studies in Spenser's Historical Allegory*, Baltimore, 1932, and by Professor C. B. Millican in *Spenser and the Table Round*, Cambridge, Mass., 1932.
[21] *Hurd's Letters on Chivalry and Romance*, ed. Edith J. Morley, 1911, p. 65.

challenged all commers. *Anno 1580.*"[22] But "farre exceeding" these affairs "in princely pompe and qualitie of Actors" were the chivalric entertainments in 1581 when Elizabeth "most roiallie feasted and banketted" the noblemen from the French king who came to win this "difficile lady" for Alençon. "Maister Philip Sidneie, and maister Fulke Greuill," with two other knights, "calling themselues the foure foster children of desire," attacked only to be defeated, the fortress of "perfect Beautie," which was defended by twenty-two knights, including "sir Thomas Perot" and "maister Anthonie Cooke" as Adam and Eve, and Sir Henry Lee as the unknown knight. Each one of the challengers ran six courses against his defendant, and they all "performed their parts so valiantlie on both sides, that their prowesse hath demerited perpetuall memorie." When the triumph was continued the next day, the challengers and defendants "did verie noblie, as the shiuering of the swords might verie well testifie: and after that to the barriers, where they lashed it out lustilie and fought couragiouslie, as if the Gréeks and Troians had dealt their deadlie dole." Then came a last speech to the queen "signifieng the humble hearted submission of the foure foster children of desire." "For witnesse thereof they present this oliue branch to your presence, in token of your triumphant peace, and of their peaceable seruitude, whereby they present themselues as bondmen by those bonds, which the losse of life can onelie loose." So invincible was the castle of this "perfect Beauty" that it did not yield even to Virtuous Desire, although cannons bombarded it with sweet powder and perfume. Her majesty gave them all such "praise and great thanks" that they "thought themselues rewarded according to their owne wishing."[23]

[22] *Honor Military, and Ciuill,* sig. R2.
[23] *Holinshed's Chronicles,* IV, 434–445.

Further, if accidental, association of this "most un-matched Princesse" with her ancestor Arthur is seen in the record of a prolusion of "Prince Arthur, with his Knights of the Round Table." This show was exhibited in 1587 at the expense of Hugh Offley, a rich London merchant. "Perfect Beauty" just chanced to see it as she passed by; but she declared that "'in her life she never saw a more stately company of archers.'"

They, approaching near to her Majesty, did their duty upon their knee, praying God long to prosper and preserve her Majesty; whereupon she most graciously bowed her body, and gave them most hearty thanks, saying, "she would love, maintain, and advance, her Citizens of the City of London;" and so prayed to God to bless all her good subjects therein.[24]

In 1594 the queen was an honored guest of the gentle-men of Gray's Inn. The elaborate compliments she heard then survive in the burlesque entertainment, *Gesta Grayorum; or, the history of the high and mighty Prince Henry, Prince of Purpoole, Arch Duke of Stapulia and Bernardia, Duke of High and Nether Holborn, Marquis of St. Giles and Tottenham, Count Palatine of Bloomsbury and Clerkenwell, Great Lord of the Cantons of Islington, Kentish Town, Paddington, and Knights-Bridge, Knight of the Most Heroical Order of the Helmet, and Sovereign of the same: who reigned and died A. D. 1594. — Together with a Masque, as it was presented (by his Highness's command) for the Entertainment of Q. Elizabeth, who, with the Nobles of both Courts, was present thereat.* Messages to Prince Henry and his replies disguise but thinly Elizabeth and her European affairs. All is turned to compliment her directly or indirectly. The Prince's "Sixth Councellor" would persuade to "Pass-times and Sports," and cries out against his sober predecessors: "'What! nothing but tasks?

[24] Nichols, II, 529-530.

nothing but working-days? No feasting, no music, no dancing, no triumphs, no comedies, no love, no ladies?'" [25] The Prince immediately heeds such good suggestions. In what follows, Elizabeth's own love of fun is reflected — and the high spirits of her followers. The Prince makes a speech that indirectly compliments the queen and directly felicitates himself and his fellows on the charm of their devices. After telling that men say that he as a sovereign is unappreciated and has a hard lot, he asks: "'What Prince ever found in his subjects, in matters of weight, more love, more loyalty, more readiness, more service? When we have been inclined to solace, what liveliness, what alacrity, what ingenious devices, sports, jollities, what variety of pleasure!'" [26] The articles of the noble order conclude: "'Lastly, all the Knights of this honourable Order, and the renowned Sovereign of the same, shall yield all homage, loyalty, unaffected admiration, and all humble service, of what name or condition soever, to the incomparable Empress of the Fortunate Island.'" [27] To her is addressed the sea masque performed on this occasion. In it she is elaborately idealized as "Cynthia, the Ladie of the Sea." It and the sports of Prince Henry show how chivalric materials were blended with pagan myth and English history, past and present, to idealize the "incomparable Empress."

If the knights of the "Most Heroical Order of the Helmet" frolicked to compliment and amuse their lady Elizabeth, those of the noble Order of the Garter served her in all high seriousness in many a rich chivalric show. Segar proudly describes this order first in his accounts of the many orders of knights. Elizabeth was equally proud of her position as the official head of this most distinguished

[25] III, 295.
[26] III, 304.
[27] III, 287.

survival of the institutions of English chivalry. Throughout the reign it played a prominent part in the social and
diplomatic life of the court. Especially on April 23, the
birthday of its patron saint, the English St. George, did
English knights offer high service to their first lady. Their
very collars of enameled roses, white and red, set with
jewels, suggested the Tudor flower whom they loved.
Leicester saw that the feast of St. George was observed at
Utrecht in 1586. There "was a most sumptuous cloth and
chayre of estate for the Queenes Majestie, with her armes
and stiles thereon, and before it a table covered with all
thinges so requisite, as if in person shee had beene there." [28]
Shakespeare's "English John Talbot" in his speech on the
"sacred name" of a knight of St. George shows what a
good bridge the order was to unite Elizabethan patriotism
with high chivalric idealism. An inferior, but patriotic,
poet has left verses which illustrate how such idealism,
Protestant zeal, and fervid patriotism were fused in the
name of St. George and his princess. Richard Vennar's
*A Prayer for the prosperous Successe of hir Majestie's
Forces in Ireland* has ardent petitions for God's preservation of Elizabeth:

Circumuent that rebellious *Sissira*, that thy judgement (like a
naile), may pierce into the braine of his malitious practises: that
our *Soueraigne* may sing with *Debora* after the victorie, having
with *Hester* preserued hir people, and with chast *Judith* cut off
the head of harme pretending *Holofernes*. And as to thy seruant
Moyses, under-prop the arme of hir Generall with thine own
powre, the head corner stone of the Temple. Stand still, O
Sonne of God, and give thy people victory. Let the traiterous
vaissaile be confounded, thy seruant *Elizabeth* preserved, and
thy selfe above all glorified. Graunt this, O Father! for thy
Sonne Jesus Christ his sake. Amen   R. V.

---

[28] II, 456.

SAINT GEORGE FOR ENGLAND.
[*And below a Cut of the Saint this Motto,*]
Conculcabis Leonem et Draconem.   Psal. 90.

A Virgin Princesse and a gentle Lambe,
  Doomb'd both to death to gorge this vgly beast:
This valiant victor like a Souldier came,
  And of his owne accord, without request:
With never daunted spirit the Fiend assail'd,
Preserv'd the Princesse and the Monster quail'd.

.   .   .   .

Saint George the Dragon, Jesus Sathan kill'd;
  Saint George the Princesse and the Lambe preserv'd:
Jesus his bitter combat hath fulfill'd,
  And by the Divel's death his Church reserv'd:
That spotlesse Dame whose ravishment was sought
By tirant's rage that bloudy ruine brought.

Saint George's Knight, goe noble Mountjoy on,
  Bearing thy Saviour's badge within thy breast:
Quell that Hell's shape of divellish proud Tirone,
  And cover with the dust his stubborne crest:
That our deere Princesse and hir land be safe,
Such power to him, oh Jesus Christ vouchsafe.[29]

Peele's *The Honour of the Garter* was addressed to the
Earl of Northumberland when the queen made him a
knight of St. George in 1593. The poet, after the conventional medieval formula, has a marvelous dream. "Fast
by the stream where Thame and Isis meet," he hears
strange noises, and straightway sees in the heavens a
garter glistening brightly on great King Edward's leg.
Renown, Honour, and Time appear, Time with a book in
his hand wherein are written the names of famous knights
of the order. They are lavishly described; but the review
of celebrities, past and present, culminates, of course, in a
vision of the virgin queen.

[29] III, 541-542.

Under the glorious spreading wings of Fame,
I saw a virgin queen, attired in white,
Leading with her a sort of goodly knights,
With garters and with collars of Saint George:
"*Elizabeth*" on a compartiment
Of gold in bysse was writ, and hung askew
Upon her head, under an imperial crown.
She was the sovereign of the knights she led:
Her face, methought, I knew, as if the same,
The same great empress that we here enjoy,
Had climb'd the clouds, and been in person there;
To whom the earth, the sea, and elements
Auspicious are.

Then King Edward congratulates the new knights
That at this day their honour have received
Under Elizabeth, England's great sovereign, —

.   .   .   .

created by a Queen
Peerless for wisdom and for majesty.[30]

Herr Johann Jacob Breuning von Buchenbach, a veteran
traveler and diplomat, sought in vain to get his ducal

[30] *Works*, II, 333–335. See the portrait of Elizabeth in William Teshe's
Verses on the Order of the Garter (*Ballads from Manuscripts*, II, 115–129). The
manuscript of this work (British Museum MS. Harleian 3437), dated 1582, contains drawings of the arms of various knights as they appear in review before
their sovereign lady. See, too, the association of Elizabeth with St. George in
Gerard de Malynes, *Saint George for England, allegorically described*, 1601,
sigs. A2–A3. Further association of Elizabeth with chivalric survivals appears
in John Bossewell, *Workes of Armorie*, 1597, sig. C3ᵛ; John Ferne, *The blazon of
gentrie*, 1586, sig. Kk1; John Leland, *A Learned and True Assertion of the original,
Life, Actes, and death of . . . Prince Arthure, King of great Brittaine. . . . Newly
translated into English by Richard Robinson*, 1582, sig. B1; throughout Lodowick
Lloyd, *The Triplicitie of Triumphes*, 1591, which is dedicated to Elizabeth; and
in *Vincentio Saviolo his Practise. In two Bookes. The first intreating of the Vse
of the Rapier and Dagger. The second, of Honor and honorable Quarrels*, 1595,
which concludes an extended defense of the prowess of women in art and arms
with praise of the "Sunne of Christendome, and the onely Starre wherby all
people are directed to the place which aboundeth in peace, religion and vertue"
(sig. Mm3ᵛ).

master into the Order of St. George. But he left some vivid
pictures of its sovereign. The following is a part of his
portrait of St. George's "Virgin Princesse" at the age of
sixty-three:

Her Majesty was this time dressed in a red robe interwoven
with gold thread, and on her head was the usual royal crown of
pearls. She wore a collar that looked almost exactly like that
worn by the Knights of the Order on St. George's Day. Everything was studded with very large diamonds and other precious
stones. Over her breast, which was bare, she wore a long filigree
lace shawl, on which sat a hideous large black spider that looked
as if it were natural and alive. Many might have been deceived
by it.[31]

When that ill-fated knight, Essex, set sail for Ireland in
1599, old Thomas Churchyard wrote *The fortunate farewell to the most forward and Noble Earle of Essex, one of the
Honorable Privie Counsel, Earle High Marshal of England,
Master of the Horse, Master of the Ordinance, Knight of the
Garter, and Lord Lieutenant General of all the Queenes
Majestie's Forces in Ireland.* Patriotic Churchyard looked
to this popular knight of the Garter for victories of "*Eliza's
ships*" on "Irish seas." [32]

Moving now into a review of Elizabetha Virgo as the
object of chivalric idealism, I shall examine on the way
some materials which show various elements from old
romance used to praise Elizabetha Regina (really inseparable from Elizabetha Virgo), especially in occasional
verse. The soldier poet, George Gascoigne, dedicated in
verse and in prose his translations of *The Tale of Hemetes
the Heremyte* to the queen. Hemetes, once a great knight,
but now made blind and cast out of Venus's temple, tells
a tale of fair Gandina, whose lover Contarenus had been
reft away by enchantment directed by a cruel father.

[31] *Queen Elizabeth and Some Foreigners*, p. 394.
[32] Nichols, III, 434.

Apollo's priest had declared that all complications would be resolved when "two of the most valyaunt knightes [had fought], two of the most constant lovers [had met], & the most vertuous lady in the world [had been] theare to looke on." Elizabeth has now seen Contarenus fight with one Loricus, faithful in adversity to a noble mistress who could never be his. That constant Loricus has now met the loyal Gandina while the "most vertuous lady in the world" has looked on; and the old hermit's sight has been restored because he has beheld what his "harte delighteth in, a ladie in whome enhabiteth the most vertue learnyng, and beawtie, that ever was in creature." [33] Thus is romantic narrative made to compliment Elizabeth as the supreme lady of all loyal knights. In 1601 Thomas Morley edited *Madrigales. The Triumphs of Oriana, to Five and Sixe Voyces, composed by divers several Authors.*[34] Twenty-odd pastoral lyrics sing gracefully the glory of Elizabeth, this time named for Oriana, who was the daughter of Lisuarte, an imaginary king of England. Oriana was beloved of the celebrated Amadis of Gaul as the fairest and most faithful woman in the world. In the *Madrigales* "Fair Oriana" is Diana's favorite nymph, a "Fair Queen of Peace and Plenty," and every singer's first mistress.

On September 20, 1592, at Ditchley, Elizabeth heard songs which show a similar blending of romance with Renaissance lyricism. The chief conceit was to have an old knight (Sir Henry Lee, it would appear) freed from a deep enchantment by his queen's revealing the secrets of certain pictured emblems that hung on walls around him. After dinner, two liberated ladies sang a pretty lyric laud-

[33] I quote from the reprint of the *Tale* in the *Works*, II, 473–510. For interpretation, see E. K. Chambers, *Sir Henry Lee*, Oxford, 1936, pp. 85–91. See below, p. 432.

[34] Reprinted in *An English Garner*, VI (1883), 29–40. Perhaps the last song in Nicholas Yonge's *Musica Transalpina* (1597) celebrating "faire ORIANA" (sig. D4ᵛ) suggested Morley's compliment.

ing the "Heauenlie Goddesse" who had delivered them and their knights from imprisonment in trees. Then they began a prose *débat*, in which one maintained the cause of constancy, and the other that of inconstancy. Finally Inconstancy was converted by a greater power than reason — the radiant presence of a queen with the motto *Semper Eadem*. The final song rejoiced in the

> Happie houre, happie daie,
> That Eliza came this waie

to free her knights and ladies, now pledged to constancy to her. The next day the chaplain made an oration that lauded Eliza and told of the long and devoted service of the old and retired knight Loricus. Ill, he has sent to the queen his last will and testament. But shortly a page announces that she has wrought a miracle; Loricus has his health again. The chaplain has besought him to bless God for his new health, but Loricus has declared: "Truthe . . . yet whosoeuer blesseth her, blesseth God in her: and euer blessed be God for her." Grateful Loricus makes her a legacy of the whole Manor of Love, with all its appurtenances, detailed in the technical language of a legal conveyance.[35]

Clearly Elizabetha Regina stimulated enough chivalric idealism for one to find fresh meaning in Spenser's tribute to Cleopolis, the capital of Gloriana's Faery Land:

> And well beseemes all knights of noble name,
> That covett in th' immortall booke of fame
> To be eternized, that same to haunt,
> And doen their service to that soveraigne dame,
> That glory does to them for guerdon graunt:
> For she is hevenly borne, and heaven may justly vaunt.[36]

---

[35] I base my summary of the Ditchley entertainment upon Chambers, *Sir Henry Lee*, pp. 145–149, 276–297.
[36] *The Faerie Queene*, I. x. 59.

The chivalric idealism which was revived by Elizabetha Regina upon whom I have been concentrating attention, was aroused in large part by the most impressive attribute of the "most vertuous and beautifull lady" — her virginity. The materials to which I now turn illustrate more exactly the idealization of the virgin Elizabeth Tudor — Elizabetha Virgo. I have earlier noted how at Bisham and Sudeley in 1592 compliment was paid to the virgin, even with a gift of virgin wool from a Cotswold shepherd.[37] Court poets were too enamored of pagan myth not to name this virgin Diana or Cynthia. But the pagan names should not mislead one. A medieval ideology underlay the fashions of Italianate Elizabethans; the exaltation of their virgin queen links itself with medieval love of virginity and gets expressed in semi-medieval forms. A rather charming poem that leads in the right direction is Richard Barnfield's *Cynthia* (1595). It is an adaptation of the medieval dream type. Classical myth and medieval allegory are amusingly dovetailed into each other. In a lovely Spenserian dale with a "trickling streame" the poet enjoys a grand dream in which Jove solves the celebrated quarrel as to who merits the golden apple by giving it, with the approval of all goddesses, to the English "sacred Virgin." Praise of her concludes:

> Thus, sacred Virgin, Muse of chastitie,
> This difference is betwixt the Moone and thee:
> Shee shines by Night; but thou by Day do'st shine:
> Shee Monthly changeth; thou dost nere decline:
> And as the Sunne, to her, doth lend his light,
> So hee, by thee, is onely made so bright:
> Yet neither Sun, nor Moone, thou canst be named,
> Because thy light hath both their beauties shamed:
>   Then, since an heauenly Name doth thee befall,
>   Thou VIRGO art: (if any Signe at all).[38]

---

[37] See above, pp. 155–156.   [38] *Poems*, p. 52.

Elizabetha Virgo was complimented in an amusing debate poem, usually attributed to Sir John Davies. It was spoken before the queen in 1602 when she was royally entertained at Cecil's "newe house in the Strand." In "A Contention betwixt a Wife, a Widdow, and a Maide" the three ladies debate cleverly the virtues of their respective states. Ultimately the maid carries off all honors, but not until keenly amusing points have been made by the wife and widow, who are eventually set against each other that battle may be deflected from the maid. The following speech from the maid wins full capitulation from both wife and widow; and the three journey to "*Astreas* shrine" to make obeisance and offerings to the "Goddess" who "hath both wiues and widdowes lou'd, Though she would neither wife nor widdow be":

> To spotlesse maids this gift is giuen,
> To liue in incorruption from their birth;
> And what is that but to inherit heauen
> Euen while they dwell vpon the spotted earth?
>
> The perfectest of all created things,
> The purest gold, that suffers no allay;
> The sweetest flower that on th' earths bosome springs,
> The pearle vnbord, whose price no price can pay:
>
> The Christall Glasse that will no venome hold,
> The mirror wherein Angels loue to looke,
> *Dianaes* bathing Fountaine cleere and cold,
> Beauties fresh Rose, and vertues liuing booke.
>
> Of loue and fortune both, the Mistresse borne,
> The soueraigne spirit that will be thrall to none;
> The spotlesse garment that was neuer worne,
> The Princely Eagle that still flyes alone.
>
> She sees the world, yet her cleere thought doth take
> No such deepe print as to be chang'd thereby;
> As when we see the burning fire doth make,
> No such impression as doth burne the eye.[39]

---

[39] *The Complete Poems of Sir John Davies*, ed. A. B. Grosart, 1876, II, 84–85.

In 1590 Sir Henry Lee, grown old in service as "Master of her Highnesse Armorie," resigned his office as the queen's champion in all her anniversary tilts and tourneys. Loyal knights then actually raised an altar to the sacred English virgin who was to be deified in "A Contention." The material is of climactic interest.

On the 17. day of Nouember, *Anno 1590.* this honourable Gentleman, together with the Earle of *Cumberland,* hauing first performed their seruice in Armes, presented themselues vnto her Highnesse, at the foot of the staires vnder her Gallery window in the Tilt yard at *Westminster,* where at that time her Maiestie did sit, accompanied with the *Vicount Turyn* Ambassador of *France* [*sic*], many Ladies, and the chiefest Nobilitie.

Her Maiesty beholding these armed Knights comming toward her, did suddenly heare a musicke so sweete and secret, as euery one thereat greatly marueiled. And hearkening to that excellent melodie, the earth as it were opening, there appeared a Pauilion, made of white Taffata, containing eight score elles, being in proportion like vnto the sacred Temple of the Virgins Vestall. This Temple seemed to consist vpon pillars of Pourferry, arched like vnto a Church, within it were many Lampes burning. Also, on the one side there stood an Altar couered with cloth of gold, and thereupon two waxe candles burning in rich candlesticks, vpon the Altar also were layd certaine Princely presents, which after by three Virgins were presented vnto her Maiestie. Before the doore of this Temple stood a crowned Pillar, embraced by an Eglantine tree, whereon there hanged a Table; and therein written (with letters of gold) this prayer following.

Elizæ. &c.

Piæ, Potenti, Fœlicissimæ virgini,
Fidei, Pacis, Nobilitatis vindici,
Cui Deus, Astra, Virtus,
Summa deuouerunt
omnia.
Post tot Annos, tot Triumphos,

Animam ad pedes positurus
Tuos,
Sacra Senex
affixit Arma.
Vitam quetam, Imperium, famam
Æternam, æternam,
precatur tibi,
Sanguine redempturus suo.
Vltra columnas Herculis
Columna moueatur Tua.
Corona superet Coronas omnes,
vt quam cœlum fœlicissimè
nascenti Coronam dedit,
Beatissima moriens reportes cœlo.
Summe, Sancte, Æterne,
Audi, exaudi,
Deus.[40]

It is time to seek a comprehension of devotion that raised altars to the virgin Elizabeth.

Segar is an appropriate witness to the Elizabethan's desire for favor of *les dames* as a first reason for deeds of

---

[40] Segar, sigs. R3–R3ᵛ. After the charming lyric, "My golden locks time hath to siluer turnd," with its ending —

> Goddesse, vouchsafe this aged man his right,
> To be your Beadsman now, that was your Knight —

the "Vestall maydens" presented the "Goddesse" with gifts which included a "vaile of white exceedingly rich and curiously wrought." See Chambers, *Sir Henry Lee*, pp. 135–144. The central episode of Peele's *Polyhymnia* (*Works*, II, 300) is the poet's sketch of this adoration of the English Diana:

> Old Henry Lee, Knight of the Crown, dismounts;
> And in a fair pavilion hard at hand,
> Where holy lights burn'd on the hallow'd shrine
> To Virtue or to Vesta consecrate,
> Having unarm'd his body, head and all,
> To his great mistress his petition makes;
> That, in regard and favour of his age,
> It would so please her princely majesty
> To suffer him give up his staff and arms,
> And honourable place wherein he served.

chivalric valor. He tells of numerous jousts and tournaments under Elizabeth's ancestors in such a way as to
prove that English knights had always been animated by
a desire "to serue their Ladies by the honorable aduentures of their persons." [41]

A glance at several kinds of love which underlay love of
Elizabeth as a "sacred Virgin" will throw light on the
chivalric idealization which I have been reviewing, especially such adoration as her knights gave her in "A Contention" and when Sir Henry Lee resigned his post. In
studying this lady as evocative of chivalric idealism,
which persisted in the English imagination beneath Renaissance fashions, one should remember first that the medieval economy made ample room for profane love, however
much it exalted sacred. Renaissance lovers found it easier
to serve Venus and Diana because their immediate ancestors had done homage both to Venus and the Holy
Virgin.

It is, of course, in the institution of courtly love, inseparable from the development of medieval chivalry, that the
place of woman in chivalric idealism is most significantly
revealed. I must needs be brief about large matters; I
shall merely point out some cardinal tenets of the courtly
love system, as illustrated especially by Chaucer, which
Elizabeth as lady and queen was peculiarly fitted to revive
in her knights. In courtly love, as Andreas Capellanus
formulated it, the lady was perfect in all spiritual and
physical attributes and of exalted position. She commanded absolute devotion from her lover, who was bound
to submit to her will, however "cold, disdainful, capricious,
and domineering" she chose to be. [42] Chrétien but refined
Capellanus's doctrine with conceits too familiar to men-

---

[41] See sigs. L5, N2ᵛ, N3ᵛ, O5, P1ᵛ.

[42] W. G. Dodd, *Courtly Love in Chaucer and Gower*, Boston, 1913, p. 12. I
have relied chiefly on this study in summarizing the nature of courtly love.

tion, but some of which are surprisingly appropriate if applied to Elizabeth. As he left the system, so it remained in essentials. The perfect lady was beautiful, gracious, and worthy of all devotion. Her knight was truthful, courteous, gentle, humble, loyal, and constant. He left off all "vileinye," avoided pride, dressed well, was as merry and joyful as possible, and generous in giving and spending, especially for his lady's pleasure. It was well if he was of noble rank, yet troubadour lovers were not always so. Eleanor of Aquitaine was loved by Bernart de Ventadorn, the son of a serving man. Now it is immediately obvious that the attributes of Elizabeth and her devoted knights parallel strikingly these essential ones of medieval courtly lovers. Everyone knows what unending service, loyalty, and devotion she inspired, then exacted from her courtiers and servants. Their expressions have been heard in some of their poetry. But the indigenous ancestry of their service and devotion will be more apparent if I associate with it a few lines from Chaucer which focus well these attributes of a true courtly lover. The knight in black in *The Book of the Duchess* attributes every good quality of mind and heart to his lady. If she is superior and indifferent, he remains no less her true and devoted servant:

> purely tho myn owne thoght
> Seyde hit were bet serve hir for noght
> Than with another to be wel.

Finally his lady came to understand that he

> ne wilned thing but good,
> And worship, and to kepe hir name
> Over al thing, and drede hir shame,
> And was so besy hir to serve.[43]

Pandarus answered any questioning of such service to a "difficile lady":

[43] Quoted in Dodd, p. 112.

Nay, nay, but ever in oon be fresh and grene
To serve and love his dere hertes quene,
And thenke it is a guerdon hir to serve
A thousand-fold more than he can deserve.[44]

Surely one reason why Elizabeth's courtiers served their
"dere hertes quene" long and well was because much of
the literature that they inherited gave examples of unselfish and devoted service to a lady. The courtly ideal of
true love, if modified, was yet alive in noble Elizabethan
hearts. Thurio is "degenerate and base" when he aban-
dons Silvia with the words,

> *I hold him but a fool that will endanger*
> *His body for a girl that loves him not.*

Shakespeare's own view is closer to that in Sonnet 116.[45]
The faithful shepherd Silvius tells Rosalind "what 't is
to love." It is "*to be all made of sighs and tears,*" "*of faith
and service.*"

> *It is to be all made of fantasy;*
> *All made of passion, and all made of wishes;*
> *All adoration, duty, and observance,*
> *All humbleness, all patience, and impatience,*
> *All purity, all trial, all observance.*[46]

If "perfect and unfaltering obedience to his lady was in-
cumbent upon every [courtly] lover," [47] what ideal of love
other than the courtly could so well have been nurtured
by a virgin princess whose political wisdom advised that
she entrench herself in the hearts of her nobility? Loyalty
to the lady as inculcated by countless songs and romances
of chivalry could be of incalculable value to the politician,

[44] *Troilus and Criseyde*, i, st. 117; quoted in Dodd, p. 125 n.
[45] Noted in Schofield, p. 248.
[46] Quoted in Schofield, p. 249. Cf. (p. 241), "Chivalric love manifestly pre-
figured that which Shakespeare exalted."
[47] Dodd, p. 63.

as will appear. The belief that true honor and courtesy
might arise from low station, and be best proved by noble
deeds, is in Chaucer and Shakespeare alike.[48] It certainly
got emphasis at a court whose princess kept its aristocratic doors open to individual merit if ever sovereign did.
The old courtly love doctrine that a true lover should go
on expeditions to foreign lands to win glory and gain the
favor of his "lady sovereign" was, of course, one to revive
with knights like Ralegh in your service. With less secrecy
than their ancestors in courtly love practice had needed to
show, knights who stayed at home were welcome to solace
themselves by confessing their devotion and despair in
"songs, compleintes, roundels, virelayes" [49] to this

> Auctor of norture, lady of plesaunce,
> Soveraine of beaute, flour of wommanhede.[50]

This Tudor Emilia did not object to hearing such music —
far from it. Fortunately, too, the darker aspects of courtly
love doctrine faded out of its ideals as they were revived
around her. Its Ovidian base and illicit end were suppressed in devotion to a virgin lady whom few mere subjects — save a Leicester in his conceited moments —
dreamed of actually possessing. Had she not with a ring
ceremony been inalienably wedded to their "dear, dear
land" at the outset of her reign? Increasingly she appeared to all knights as an unattainable virgin lady to be
adored as the embodiment of the best ideals of courtly
love. It suited Elizabetha Regina's tastes and purposes
perfectly to be so loved outside of wedlock. A happy twist
to orthodox courtly love doctrine. The royal tercel in
The Parlement of Foules chose the formel eagle "not as his
mate, but as his lady sovereign" [51] — to serve her ever.

[48] Schofield, pp. 260–261.
[49] *The Franklin's Tale*, l. 948; quoted in Dodd, p. 114.
[50] *Womanly Noblesse*; quoted in Dodd, p. 99.
[51] Dodd, p. 123.

Curiously pat description of how every knight chose this
virgin Tudor rose for his adoration. "Sovereign" in
every sense. At the same time, Elizabeth's autocratic
restriction of all court marriages and her premium on
single life endorsed the ideal of unwedded love — now
refined into one of pure loyalty to a virgin princess, who
embodied a native land to which she was bringing unique
peace and prosperity.

So much for Elizabeth as a happy stimulus to a courtly
lover who began idealizing his lady in the name of Venus.
Before inquiring further into devotion to the English
Diana, one should remember that chivalric idealization of
Elizabeth by the knights of her court was encouraged because she was the most distinguished knight of them all.[52]
Records show that the queen consorts, wives and daughters
of knights, and some other women of exalted position had
in the fourteenth and fifteenth centuries been received into
the Order of the Garter — were designated "Dames de la
Fraternité de St. George." [53] From 1558 to 1603 the head
of the Order was a virgin lady who finally fought and
mortally wounded the dread Spanish dragon, St. George's
greatest enemy. On the eve of her victory she rode as a
lady knight among her troops at Tilbury and spoke to
them simple words that fired them with courage and ardor
to fight with her.[54] For Armada knights, she surely sur-
passed the wife of Robert the Norman, or those women
who, armed like men, once rode on a crusade. Spenser

[52] In a Fugger news-letter from Venice, January 15, 1590 (*The Fugger News-Letters*, second series, ed. Victor von Klarwill, 1926, pp. 199–200), the corre-spondent declares the King of Navarre thinks her "a Knight, . . . because of her gay and indomitable spirit, of which she has more than is to be found in other women. She has valiantly defended herself against the power of such great and mighty foes, against two of the greatest Kings in the world, whom she previously insulted, and she has preserved her realm despite attempts to split it into factions, to propagate discord, and to invade it with a powerful Armada."

[53] *The Encyclopædia Britannica*, 14th ed., 1929, XIII, 433.

[54] See above, p. 89.

and his circle of course preferred Britomart to Bradamante;
a good deal might perhaps be said about their kinship.[55]
Shakespeare's oblique vision when he portrayed the warrior maid Joan was only English.   Segar wrote later of
her as "a certaine mayden called *Iohan*, a woman of so
rare wit and valour in Armes, as was reputed more then a
mortall creature, or rather some enchantresse of singular knowledge." [56] Elizabeth's fearlessness and personal
courage — she slept, report says, with a dagger by her
side — and her remarkable escapes from all plots to kill
her encouraged the song of her as a "Maiden Queene, and
yet of courage stout," as James Aske described her.[57]
Surely the English God maintained such a lady knight.

    I come now to the crux of this inquiry into the causes of
the revival of chivalry that made the English Diana.
Every true knight of medieval romance served two ladies
— a profane and a sacred — his "lady sovereign" and the
Queen of Heaven. His descendants in the sixteenth century discovered in Elizabetha Regina their noblest "lady
sovereign," as I have shown. But can one explain the
ceremonies when Sir Henry Lee resigned his post without
believing that to this "Maiden Queene" these descendants
unconsciously transferred some of the adoration which by
right of strict inheritance was due a far holier virgin? It
is a delicate matter. I trespass on sacred ground that cannot be explored with scientific precision. Yet I think the
evidence justifies the belief that so it was.

    In the first place, one must always remember that the
medieval lover did not give one heart to Venus and his
mistress, and another to the Blessed Virgin. Ecclesiastical
forms notoriously did service along with profane, feudal,
and classical ones in amorous verse addressed to a mis-

[55] See below, p. 359.
[56] Sig. G6.
[57] Nichols, II, 548.

tress. And the church in turn found it wise to clothe
scriptural truth in chivalric dress — most memorably,
perhaps, in the *Ancren Riwle*.[58] A troubadour's song to
his lady is often astonishingly like his next to the Virgin.
Chaucer most cleverly of all poets applied religious ideas
to courtly love, as *Troilus and Criseyde* stands to witness.[59]
The fifty-first balade of Gower's *Cinkante Balades* is addressed to the Virgin, and is an "excellent example of the
mystical expressions of love and devotion to Christ and
Our Lady in which the language of chivalrous love was
employed." [60] In fact, "adaptations of all the important
features of the mediaeval Christian worship may be found
in the erotic literature of the time." [61] Nor is it strange
that "no strict line was drawn between the figures of romance and religion, . . . because both embodied men's
ideals and were together ever present in mediæval minds."[62]
An ideal knight was daring to madness, he was burning
with zeal for delivery of the oppressed and rescue of the
Holy City, and he exalted chastity. Some orders professed
celibacy.[63] Even a sensuous courtly lover, if in practice he
departed far from the church's view of the chastity of
virginity as higher even than that of marriage or widow-
hood, exalted constancy and steadfastness of affection in
his illicit love; and so he knew virtues that acquainted him
with the ideals of pure virginity.

Although idealization of a profane lady and idealization
of the Blessed Virgin Mary merge inextricably in the
medieval consciousness, it does behoove one to remember
how extensively the Holy Virgin was herself glorified and

[58] W. H. Schofield, *English Literature from the Norman Conquest to Chaucer,*
1925, pp. 403–408.
[59] See Dodd, pp. 199 ff.
[60] Page 40.
[61] Page 18.
[62] Schofield, *English Literature,* p. 406.
[63] *Hurd's Letters,* p. 93.

what attributes won to her all hearts. It was popular devotion that nurtured the cultus of the virgin. With the
crusades she began to overshadow the Trinity itself.
"The Virgin even had the additional charm of the public
that she was popularly supposed to have no very marked
fancy for priests as such; she was a queen, a woman, and a
mother, functions, all, which priests could not perform." [64]
No wonder the greatest medieval poem ends with a canticle
in her honor.

Perhaps because the Anglo-French did not vent their
emotions on worldly love so much as did the French of the
Continent, they turned their passion particularly toward
the Holy Virgin. Her "they endowed with all bodily
grace and beauty of form, and offered themselves as her
faithful servitors with the rapture of religious joy. Thus
most permanently did the spirit of Provençal poetry manifest itself in England. Nowhere was the cult of the Virgin
more developed: in her honour numerous poems were composed." [65] Glorification of the Virgin in England during
the thirteenth and fourteenth centuries must have grown
apace in a soil that produced such various praise of virginity as Aldhelm's discourses to nuns, the violent diatribe
against marriage in *Holy Maidenhood*, and the exquisite
eulogy of maidenhood in *The Pearl*. Isolated poems of a
homiletical character magnified God and the Virgin with
mystical fervor.[66] While pious and devout women were
adoring Christ, devotees from St. Bernard to Richard
Rolle were "pouring forth their emotions in 'love-longing'
to the Holy Virgin." [67] "Many are the orisons and saluta-
tions to Our Lady, the Ave Marias short and long, separate and in sequences, original and translated, that were

[64] Henry Adams, *Mont-Saint-Michel and Chartres*, Boston, 1913, p. 101.
[65] Schofield, *English Literature*, p. 133.
[66] Page 384.
[67] Page 408.

written in the thirteenth and fourteenth centuries." [68]
The rôle that the Virgin had in such a miracle play as the
York fragment (no. 49), *The Coronation of Our Lady*,
brought her virtues home visually to her people. I need
not underscore the significance of her continuous appearances in romances of chivalry, none the less notable because they are often in formal prayers such as that of the
distressed maid in *La Bone Florence de Rome* — or Chaucer's
own at the end of *Troilus and Criseyde*. One meets
her everywhere as "Marie bryght"; "seynt Marie";
"Marie mylde"; "hevene quene"; "that swete flour";
"Sweet flower of Paradise"; "Maiden, mother mild";
"Lady, flower of allë thing, *rosa sine spina*"; "Lady,
queen, of paradise, *electa*"; "Maiden mild, mother." [69]
The following verses from a Middle English hymn to
the Virgin admirably characterize her:

> Heil be þou goodli grou*n*d of grace!
> Heil blessid sterre upon þe see!
> Heil of coumfortis in euery caas!
> Heil þe cheeuest of charitee!
> Heil welle of witt and of merci!
>
> .   .   .   .   .   .
>
> Heil be þou virgyne of virgins!
> Heil blessid modir! heil blessid may!
> Heil norische of sweete ihesus!
> Heil cheefest of chastite, forsþoe to say! [70]

In juxtaposition with these verses from a sacred hymn
to the blessed virgin Queen of Heaven one should place
some profane "hymns" to the blessed virgin queen of

[68] Page 438.

[69] These characteristic epithets are drawn from *Ancient English Metrical
Romances*, ed. Joseph Ritson, Edinburgh, II (1885), 94, 96, 54, 60; and from
Schofield, *English Literature*, pp. 438-439.

[70] *Hymns to the Virgin & Christ*, ed. F. J. Furnivall, Early English Text
Society, 1867 (reprinted 1895), p. 5.

England. An humble broadside of 1563, already once
heard, has added meaning now:

> Loe here the pearle,
>   Whom God and man doth loue:
> Loe here on earth
>   The onely starre of light:
> Loe here the queene,
>   Whom no mishap can moue
> To chaunge her mynde
>   From vertues chief delight!
> Loe here the heart
>   That so hath honord God,
> That, for her loue,
>   We feele not of his rod:
> Pray for her health,
>   Such as good subiectes bee:
> Oh Princely Dame,
>   There is none like to thee! [71]

From the ingenuous appeal of these verses to Elizabeth as
a "pearle," as an "onely starre of light" to Sir John
Davies's Platonic *Hymnes of Astræa* is a leap; yet all of his
graceful acrostics which laud Elizabeth's various attributes sound a note of reverential adoration not wholly dissimilar. The seventh hymn sings Elizabeth as the "Rose
of the Queene of Loue belou'd"; I quote verses from the
first two hymns in which her virginity is sung.

HYMNE I.
Of Astræa.

E arly before the day doth spring,
L et us awake my Muse, and sing;
I t is no time to slumber,
S o many ioyes this time doth bring,
A s time will faile to number.

---

[71] See above, pp. 9–10.

B ut whereto shall we bend our layes?
E uen vp to Heauen, againe to raise
T he Mayd, which thence descended;
H ath brought againe the golden dayes,
A nd all the world amended.

. . . .

HYMNE II.
To Astræa.

E ternal Virgin, *Goddesse* true,
L et me presume to sing to you.
I oue, euen great *Ioue* hath leasure
S ometimes to heare the vulgar crue,
A nd heares them oft with pleasure.

B lessèd *Astræa*, I in part
E nioy the blessings you impart;
T he peace, the milke and hony,
H umanitie, and civil *Art*,
A richer dower then money.

R ight glad am I that now I liue,
E uen in these dayes whereto you giue
G reat happinesse and glory;
I f after you I should be borne,
N o doubt I should my birth-day scorne
A dmiring your sweet storie.[72]

Some descendant of the Welsh bards, trying to keep his
balance before this virgin rose of Arthur's line, declared

[72] *Poems*, I, 129–130. When this "Eternal virgin" returned to the heaven
from whence she descended, all England wept the loss of its "*Perle* of choyse"
(Nichols, III, 641 n.; from a "scarce Poem, entitled, 'Newes, &c. of Sir Francis
Drake,' 1587"). It mourned the going of its "virgin scepter-swaying Mother"
(John Nichols, *The Progresses, Processions, and Magnificent Festivities of King
James the First*, 1828, I, 2); its "Virgin Mother and a Maiden Queene" as a
"starre from earth to heauen ascended" (I, 15); and repeatedly as the loveliest
Tudor rose. "Brittain's Lacrimæ" may remind one now of the mortality of this
"Eternal Virgin" and emphasize her rank (Nichols, *Elizabeth*, III, 652):

> Weepe, little Isle, and for thy Mistris death
> Swim in a double sea of brackish waters:

there never was a maid like her except one who bore God in her womb —

> Iechyd yn i bowyd byth
> i lana ei svtt o lin Seth
> a bvn ni bv /r/ioed i bath
> ond vn y chwrdd Duw/n/ i chroth.[73]

But in John Dowland's *The Second Book of Songs or Airs* (1600) there are verses that suggest an actual substitution of the English virgin for the Catholic in the hearts of ardent Protestant knights. They are of high interest:

> Time's eldest son, Old Age (the Heir of Ease,
> Strength's Foe, Love's Woe, and Foster to Devotion)
> Bids gallant Youth in martial prowess please!
> As for himself, he hath no earthly motion;
> But thinks Sighs, Tears, Vows, Prayers, and Sacrifices,
> As good as Shows, Masks, Jousts, or Tilt devices.
>
> Then sit thee down! and say thy *Nunc dimitis!*
> With *De profundis, Credo,* and *Te DEUM!*
> Chant *Miserere,* for what now so fit is
> As that, or this, *Paratum est cor meum!*
> O that thy Saint would take in worth thy heart!
> Thou canst not please her with a better part.
>
> When others sing *Venite exultemus!*
> Stand by, and turn to *Noli emulari!*
> For *Quare fremuerunt,* use *Oremus!*
> *Vivat ELIZA!* for an *Ave MARI!*
> And teach those Swains that live about thy cell;
> To sing *Amen,* when thou dost pray so well! [74]

> Weepe little world, weepe for great ELIZABETH;
> Daughter of warre, for Mars himself begate her,
> Mother of peace, for she bore the latter.
> She was and is, what can there more be said,
> In earth the first, in heaven the second Maid.

[73] National Library of Wales MS. 3039 B, p. 288, stanza 9.

[74] *An English Garner,* IV (1882), 524–525. On the authorship of this lyric, see Chambers, *Sir Henry Lee,* pp. 142–143.

In *Westward Ho!* Eustace declares that the Blessed Virgin Mary's prayers have saved Amyas; but Frank replies that the prayers of "that most pure and peerless virgin" Elizabeth have done so. Kingsley seems to have exaggerated not much more than Diana's poets who cried "*Vivat Eliza!* for an *Ave Mari!*"

It may appear absurd to the superficial observer, but interesting and ironic to the more thoughtful one, that the English iconoclasts while wrecking the image of the Queen of Heaven turn to adoring that which they model after the queen of England. The rationale of the change has tangled roots that reach back from the frequent appearance of Diana in Renaissance literature to her birth in elemental folklore. They nourish the exaltation of virginity in much Elizabethan verse.[75] They involve the religious and political exigencies of the state that Elizabeth had to rule. Elizabethan poetry is full of compliments to virgin goddesses and ladies. I cannot pause with them; those to the virgin Elizabeth alone are legion.[76] Enough have been heard in various verses to reveal the far-flung reach of idealization of her virginity as she half unconsciously reminded her chivalric knights of the Blessed Virgin, or

[75] One might draw illustrations from Thomas Lodge, Giles Fletcher, William Browne, Sir John Davies, Richard Barnfield, Michael Drayton, and many others. To Catholic temperaments like Henry Constable's and Nicholas Breton's virginity made a deep appeal. See Breton's description of a virgin in *The Good and the Badde* (*Works*, II, r, 11-12). See "The praise of Chastitie" in the aristocratic anthology, *The Phœnix Nest* of 1593 (pp. 20-23). See, too, "The ioy of Virginitie" in *A Handful of Pleasant Delights (1584)*, ed. H. E. Rollins, Cambridge, Mass., 1924, pp. 42-43, and the interesting note on p. 102. Nowhere, of course, is love of the virginal in woman more conspicuous than in Spenser of the *Amoretti*; his "maidenliness" Coleridge pointed out. No wonder this most chivalric of Elizabethan poets paid the "arch-maiden" his "lady sovereign" her most magnificent compliment. Such love of virginity descended directly to inspire *Comus*, the author of which no doubt found Spenser his best teacher of this "sage and serious" doctrine.

[76] The most amusing praise of Diana that I have discovered is in Phineas Fletcher's *The Purple Island* at the end of canto iii. When the poet comes to

consciously of Diana, Astræa, Minerva, the vestal virgins, and so on. But a fuller understanding of the idealization of Elizabeth as Diana comes if one views it for a moment as the result of the ardent patriotism of her half-Catholic subjects in alliance with her political and religious policies.

Elizabeth came to a throne which was far from secure. Somehow she had to unify the nobility to the support of her government and to still the religious turmoil of the preceding reign. She needed to seize upon every possible aid if she was to steady her throne and bring health and harmony to England. She was an eminently practical statesman. She always used what was at hand to secure what the immediate occasion demanded. Feudalism had broken down in the fourteenth century when heavily armed foot-soldiers proved that armed knights were hopelessly of the past. But the ages that knew the evils of a feudal society, which, disintegrating in the fifteenth century, cleft England in twain, had still envisaged the ex-

---

describe the reproductive parts of the island (*The Poetical Works of Giles and Phineas Fletcher*, ed. F. S. Boas, Cambridge, II (1909), 42–44) he cries:

> Forbear, my maiden song, to blazon wide
> What th' Isle and Natures self doth ever strive to hide.

He admits that from two "fair Isles"

> in Loves delight agreeing,
> Another little Isle is soon proceeding;

but he hurries on:

> Here oft not Lust, but sweetest Chastitie,
> Coupled sometimes, and sometimes single, dwells;
> Now linkt with Love, to quench Lusts tyrannie,
> Now Phœnix-like alone in narrow cells:
>   Such Phœnix one, but one at once may be:
>   In *Albions* hills thee, *Basilissa*, thee,
> Such onely have I seen, such shall I never see.

Fletcher concludes the canto with what appears to be an allusion to the Essex tragedy, and by singing of the "royall maid," "the shepherds Queen," who found no joy after

> she a deare Deers side unwilling rented;
> Whose death she all too late, too soon, too much, repented.

alted ideals of chivalry, as Malory proves. Chivalry had
shown the world the need "'of noble service willingly rendered. It [had] upheld courage and enterprise in obedience
to rule, it [had] consecrated military prowess to the service
of the Church, glorified the virtues of liberality, good
faith, unselfishness and courtesy, and above all, courtesy
to women.'" [77] Would not a lone princess in her need
evoke and utilize this rich fund of idealism that embraced
the very loyalties which a wise statesman in her predicament would want to inspire? Since her father's reign
feudal discord had rent England anew. Chivalric loyalty
to a sovereign was again at low ebb. Perhaps Elizabeth
remembered William's system in which contentious nobles
were harmonized into a subservient support for monarchy
by grants in return for their loyalty and service. Perhaps
she remembered that the revival of English self-conscious-
ness in the fourteenth century had been effected with the
aid of tactful appeals to chivalric devotion made in the
name of old British heroes of romance. Her grandfather
had begun to establish a new nobility based on individual
achievement and service to the crown. Her father had
continued the work, and he had known how to arouse
great devotion among his subjects by personal charm and
by rich entertainments that capitalized the pomp and
circumstance of glorious chivalry. It was certainly not her
father's structure at its best that Elizabeth inherited —
far from it. Yet at least the masses hailed her upon her
accession with a devotion the depth of which she was quick
to sense and respond to. She had, too, discovered during
her dark days a few trusty friends. Elizabeth had these
aids, and she had unique wits of her own. Something of
what happened, especially on her progresses, has been
seen. Tournaments and jousts like those Peele described
drew the nobility to the support of her throne. Energies

[77] *The Encyclopædia Britannica*, 11th ed., Cambridge, XV (1911), 859.

that had recently wrecked the state were shrewdly sublimated to its service by a virgin princess who soon mastered
all the arts of stimulating chivalric loyalty to a "lady
sovereign." Machiavelli had bitterly opposed feudal aris-
tocracy as disruptive of the unified state. This economical
Tudor princess soon found that she could turn such energies within her nobility to the formation of the harmonious
state which was her goal. Somehow, during the best years
of her reign, she brought the centrifugal energies of all her
people into rough but effective counterpoise with the
centripetal. The old feudal ardor of the nobility, the new
rising religious zeal of all classes, for a few fortunate years
got directed into devotion to "this blessed plot, this earth,
this realm, this England." Rare achievements both in the
arts of peace and of war were possible. Of course no one
will ever be able to say finally just how far the queen alone
effected the fugitive harmony. It was a full coöperative
achievement in which Elizabeth was more than a mere
catalytic agent.

The fact that England's ruler was now a brilliant virgin,
skilled in various arts and delighting in sports, conditioned
profoundly the revival of chivalric loyalty to the crown.
Even if chivalry as an institution had lost its pristine fas-
cination when the Crusades failed, its exaltation of honor,
loyalty, and courage still cast a spell by various mediums,
as Sidney, Spenser, and Segar remind one. Even if formal
courtly love had been long dead, the cult of Laura had
risen from its fertile ashes. Every *courtois* lover in Elizabethan England knew and venerated the tradition which
made absolute loyalty and devotion to the loved lady, rewarded or not, his cardinal virtue. His first lady was now
Elizabeth. Elizabeth was "mere English." She was England beautifully embodied. His first and final loyalty was
to England's Elizabeth. Hence such a lady had a perfect
ascendancy over the hearts of all her knights. What the

presence of this lady knight did to inspire and discipline a
great number of untrained men in the Armada crisis, has
been seen. Not for a moment did she forget her peculiar
power when she disciplined a Leicester, a Ralegh, an
Essex. She could inspire them to action in the name of
loyalty to herself — to England; she could and she did
with no mincing words rebuke and restrain the pride,
haughtiness, or quick wrath which such knights inherited
along with belief in a lover's complete devotion to a lofty
mistress. Medieval "mesure" she could teach in language
any man could understand, and to his complete confusion
because the teacher was his "lady sovereign" who could
actually give life or death to the lover. Her rigorous social
autocracy exacted all the chivalric virtues from the Hot-
spurs of the court; it rebuked all their feudal faults. She
could even make a final sacrifice of her affection as a
courtly lady to her duty as a just sovereign, and execute
Essex. Segar is emphatic in pointing out that the sovereign
makes knights in England; [78] and Coke in noting that the
English knight "'is by creation and not by descent.'" [79]
Elizabeth regarded knighthood as an exceedingly high
honor. She based its bestowal upon individual merit and
achievement with remarkable consistency. Nor was she
forgetful of her policies when in the enthusiasm of the
Armada eve she knighted a loyal lady — Mary, wife of
Sir Hugh Cholmondeley, of Vale Royal — "the bold lady
of Cheshire." [80] But she conferred knighthood sparingly.[81]
Camden speaks with disapproval when Essex in France

[78] Sig. G1v.

[79] *The Encyclopædia Britannica*, 14th ed., XIII, 432.

[80] Agnes Strickland, *Lives of the Queens of England*, IV (1851), 571. Miss
Strickland followed Nichols, *James*, III, 406, though she gives an inexact refer-
ence. See, too, *Notes and Queries*, eighth series, IX (1896), 124–125, where the
Newcastle Chronicle is the authority.

[81] Contrast the policy of the French king with his Order of St. Michael —
which Segar (sig. G6) does not commend.

presumptuously "knighted many"; [82] and that overween-
ing noble greatly angered his mistress by his liberties in
creating knights. What a fine diplomatic tool she could
make of the honor of admission to the noble Order of
St. George is very amusingly shown in the history of
Count Frederick of Württemberg and Möpelgard. From
Elizabeth he sought in vain for full Garter honors for
eleven years; unwise James quickly satisfied him.[83] Acceptance of any honors from foreign princes Elizabeth
regarded as an act of disloyalty to herself. When Sir
Nicholas Clifford and Sir Anthony Shirley accepted
knighthood in the Order of St. Michael without consulting
her, she "commanded them to make a resignation and
send backe their ornaments, and procure their names to
be blotted out of the Memorials of that Order." [84] Of
Thomas Arundell's having been made a count of the Holy
Roman Empire by Rudolph II she expressed herself as
follows:

"Betweene Princes and their Subiects there is a most straight
tye of affections. As chaste women ought not to cast their eye
upon any other than their husbands, so neither ought subiects to
cast their eyes upon any other Prince, than him whom *God* hath
given them. I would not have my sheepe branded with another
mans marke; I would not they should follow the whistle of a
strange Shepheard." [85]

Sir Robert Naunton declares that the queen prevented
Sidney's election to the sovereignty of Poland "not out of
emulation of his advancement, but out of feare to lose the
jewell of her time." [86] This "parfit gentil knight" said
that he preferred rather to be a subject to Queen Elizabeth

[82] *Annals*, p. 399.
[83] See *Queen Elizabeth and Some Foreigners*, pp. 347–423.
[84] Camden, p. 435.
[85] Page 469.
[86] *Fragmenta Regalia*, 1824, p. 66.

than a sovereign beyond the seas.[87] It is clear that this sovereign lady capitalized chivalric loyalty to herself for high political ends. The cohesion and the weakening of the Elizabethan state actually parallel closely the youth, maturity, and decline of its virgin queen as the adored mistress of all English knights.

One may now inquire further into the power of Elizabeth's virginity to arouse chivalric loyalty which was of priceless value in keeping her nobility in leash and in regulating the religious zeal of her people. Elizabeth wrought her spell over the loyalties of her Renaissance knights because she played at serving Venus all the while that she abode in fealty to Diana. The paradox of a life full of marriage schemes and handsome favorites on the one hand, and of constant exaltation of virginity on the other, suited perfectly the divided tastes of the age. In 1579 Elizabeth was a very brilliant virgin lady playing her most exciting marriage game. When Sir John Davies published his *Hymnes of Astraea* in 1599 she was no longer the match of Europe, but she still was about as brilliant as rare wits and decoration could make a queen — and her favorites were as handsome as ever. Almost to the very last she paradoxically wedded amorousness to virginity. Hence she held the fancy of poets who read *Hero and Leander* one day and celebrated the charm of chastity on the next. Because the medieval knight had shared his heart between Venus and the Blessed Virgin Mary, it was easier for his Elizabethan descendant to raise his song now to his own profane mistress, now to his Renaissance princess, and now to the "blessed virgin" who was his queen. The age loved passionate experience and seldom feared it. But it was an age when intelligence did seek to keep pace with range of feeling. So it came to admire in-

[87] Thomas Fuller, *The History of the Worthies of England*, ed. P. A. Nuttall, 1840, II, 142.

creasingly the conquest of affection which it thought it saw in its queen's perpetual virginity. Most immediate experience of the passion of love in a robust age leads to an exaltation now of Venus, now of Diana. In all the atmosphere of love which prevailed at her court Elizabeth contrived to play with Cupid, yet never to be captured by him. Poets less clever at the game naturally turned to her in their disillusion as their only constant mistress, as a uniquely chaste lady high on a pedestal above mundane desire and deceit. To courtiers and poets she appeared to triumph over the tangles of love in which they were often painfully caught. To those around her who often knew too well the sea of troubles that can surge in the wake of love's pleasure, she seemed to drive Plato's steeds perfectly. Remaining aloof from all entangling alliances, yet never ceasing to sport with love, she came to embody the conquest of desire for a poet who often, like luckless Ralegh, loved at court not wisely but too well. She came to stand for patriotic restraint of passion. What many Englishmen longed to achieve, she illustrated. Here is one secret of the growth of the cult of the virgin queen. In her control over all marriages at court she was playing the rôle of a wise governor more than that of a prejudiced spinster. She demanded that affection be given first to England as she personified it. She directed a maximum of amorous energy into action for the greater glory of that England. Marriage was but an institution for propagating such citizenship as would never endanger Tudor authority.[88] As this royal virgin escaped from all political nets woven in the name of love, and yet never ceased to make curtsies to Cupid, Englishmen gradually realized that love of England was the constant love of her life. She was faithful to the ring ceremony that had dramatically begun

[88] In this connection, see Diana's speech to her nymphs in Lyly's *Gallathea*, III. iv. 16–53; and Cupid's speeches, IV. ii.

her reign. More and more her single life seemed admirable as the country grew into unique achievements under her rule. She countered the orthodox view of woman that nagged her for many years — the conviction that even a queen was but another Eve needing a royal Adam. She tactfully triumphed over all precedent and prejudice that insisted that a queen should first be a wife and a mother. For many years Englishmen begged Elizabeth for an heir of her body. When the fullness of time brought none, but gave instead unprecedented national health, her minstrels gallantly exalted her vicarious virginity into a symbol of feminine constancy and purity inseparable from the new fruition in the life of England. The tense hostility to the Alençon match shows that in having taken no husband Elizabeth had divined the temper of rising English nationalism better than it had known itself.

In Elizabeth's England a very ancient conviction still had a standing hallowed from the darkest antiquity. That the virgin way of life is somehow the more blessed one, and the one that brings man nearer to divinity, was a belief that a dominant church had nurtured with particular favor for centuries. Now came a "mere English" princess who persisted in exalting her virginity when official allegiance to that church had been severed, and when hostility to it was increasingly synonymous with love of country and loyalty to its queen. Human devotion changes more slowly than its objects shift. From 1558 to 1603 the virgin queen of England was the object of a love not dissimilar in quality from that which for centuries had warmed English hearts that looked to the virgin Queen of Heaven for all grace. The Blessed Virgin Mary had for ages been the fountain head of mercy and favor for all who appealed to her. No matter how humble or sinful the subject, he could yet obtain her favor if he but called on her. Her gifts were rich to those who served her — her miracles, innumerable.

She especially protected the poor and the friendless, the humble and the oppressed. She was the best leech for the sick; they should all seek her for health and bliss. Especially did medieval minstrels claim her protection.[89] But now the church in which this Holy Virgin was so glorified appeared more and more as a mortal enemy to the life of England and its own virgin queen. The English virgin queen stood at the head of the new national church. If she was technically a profane virgin, she was yet contriving to give her people in relative peace and prosperity more tangible goods than the virgin Queen of Heaven had often provided when her namesake sat on the English throne. That this English virgin's justice was tempered with rare mercy, all her subjects agreed.

In her Progress she was the most easie to be approached; Private Persons, and Magistrates, Men and Women, Countrey people and Children, came joyfully and without any fear, to wait upon her, and to see her. Her ears were then open to the Complaints of the afflicted, and of those that had been any way injured. She would not suffer the meanest of her People to be shut out from the places where she resided, but the greatest and the least were then in a manner levelled. She took with her own hand, and read with the greatest goodness the Petitions of the meanest Rusticks. And she would frequently assure them, that she would take a particular care of their Affairs; and she would ever be as good as her word. She by her Royal Authority protected those that were injured and oppressed: She punished the Fraudulent, False, Perfidious and Wicked. In all this variety of Affairs she was able to keep her temper, and appear with an equal and uninterrupted serenity and humanity to all that came nigh her; *She was never seen angry with the most unseasonable, or uncourtly Approach: She was never offended with the most impudent or importunate Petitioner....* Nor was there any thing in the whole course of her Reign that more won the hearts of the People, than this her wonderful

[89] Schofield, *English Literature*, pp. 18, 327–328.

ACCOMODATIO

PRÆCEDENTIS TY-
PI AD SERENISSIMAM REGINAM
NOSTRAM, VERSICVLIS U-
bíque in speciem arboris digesta vtrinque li-
teris maiusculis terminatis ex quibus bre-
vis ista precatiuncula conficitur.

ELIZABETHAM REGINAM DIV NOBIS
SERVET IESVS INCOLVMEM: AMEN.

```
                Ecce beato S
             Lux nos dedisse maxim E,
           Illustris   illa    creditu R,
         Sæpiterno quæ celebrada cult V,
       Anglia,   insigni  generata stirp E
     Beata virgo, cum regnare cœpera T:
     Eam parem  patulæ  dixeris  arbor I;
       Tempestate gravi subito ruent E,
        Huius se folijs tegunt volucre S,
          Adeuntq; bruta pro cubit V;
           Magnu invame omnibu S:
            Regina princeps.profug I
             Eius celebrat nome N:
              Gentibus ipsa la C,
             Inclyta    virg O,
            Non negat ijs simu L
            Alma  nutrix man V,
           Miserit auxiliu M:
          Det deus itaqu E,
         Impleat  annu M,
          Vivat & integr A,
     Nullibi vnquam deficiens supremu M:
    Omnibus auxilium,quæ exhibuit pi E,
   BIS  locupletur ò patriæ colume N.
```

Emblem.

ANDREW WILLET, *Sacrorum emblematum centuria una* [1596?]

facility, and condescention, and the strange sweetness and pleasantness with which she entertained all that came to her.[90]

This virgin's royal hands even came directly to heal the "*Complaints of the afflicted.*" William Tooker dedicated to her his *Charisma siue donum sanationis* (1597). The title-page continues:

SEV *Explicatio totius quæstionis de mirabili*um Sanitatum Gratia, in qua præcipuè agi*tur de solenni & sacra curatione strumæ, cui Reges Angliæ ritè inaugurati, diuinitùs medicati sunt, & quam Serenissima* ELIZABETHA, *Angliæ, Franciæ, & Hiberniæ* REGINA, *ex cælesti gratia sibi concessa, Applicatione* manuum suarum, & contactu morbidarum partium, non sine Religiosis ceremonijs, & precibus, cum admirabili & fælici successu indies sanat.

The ten chapters of this treatise discuss in detail the divine gift of royal healing — its scriptural base, its presence in early royal nurses of God's church, and its flowering in chaste and godly Elizabeth (*Elizabetham Reginam cæteris omnibus antecellere hac gloria*).[91]

If Elizabeth was vowed to "perpetual virginity," she was yet mystically married to England. With consummate tact she repeatedly spoke to her subjects as beloved children of this union. They called her constantly their "Mother of peace," their "Virgin Mother and a Maiden Queene." The "mother" concept of Elizabeth was early encouraged by Isaiah 49: 23 — "For kynges shalbe thy nursyng fathers, and queenes shalbe thy nursyng mothers." Dozens of times this scriptural figure was turned to glorify Elizabeth; it fused prettily with her conceit that she was

---

[90] Edmund Bohun, *The Character of Queen Elizabeth*, 1693, pp. 349–350.

[91] Sig. A3ᵛ. For further testimony to the queen's power in healing, see William Clowes, *A right frutefull and approued Treatise, for the Artificiall Cure of that Malady called in Latin Struma, and in English, the Evill, cured by Kinges and Queenes of England*, 1602, sigs. A2ᵛ, A3ᵛ, A4, G4–H1ᵛ, I2ᵛ.

the virgin mother of her people, joined in holy wedlock to their state. At least a voice or two must be heard:

whose hart is not greatly moued to glorifie God, who hath giuen vs, so faithful & constant a nurse & louing mother, & so wōderfully defended and preserued her, and by & vnder her most happy gouernment hath made vs so many yeares together, without feare the free possessors of most vnspeakable ioy, in the participation of incomparable heauenly treasure and most flourishing earthly prosperitie.[92]

Another cries out that

her Highnesse is the most louing Mother and Nurse of all her good Subiectes, and is lykewise the husband of the common weale, maried to the Realme, and the same by ceremony of Ring as solemnly signified, as any other mariage.[93]

The rising Protestant spirit that insisted with St. Paul that it is better to marry than to burn was silenced; for before this uniquely chaste virgin queen who was yet England's faithful spouse, raised up by God "as a mother in Israell / to trauell with and bring forthe our churche againe," [94] it could pay sincere homage to an ideal its conscience was increasingly uneasy with. More than her

---

[92] Josias Nichols, *Abrahams faith*, 1602, sigs. B1–B1ᵛ.

[93] Anthony Munday, *A VVatch-vvoord to Englande*, 1584, sig. A3. See like sentiment in Thomas Norton, *To the Quenes Maiesties poore deceiued Subiectes of the North Countrey*, 1569, sig. A7ᵛ; William Averell, *A meruailous combat of contraries*, 1588, sigs. E3, F2ᵛ; Francis Bradley, *A godly sermon preached before the right Worshipfull Eduuard Cooke Esquier*, 1600, sig. A6ᵛ; Thomas Tymme, *A preparation against the prognosticated dangers of this yeare, 1588*, 1588, sig. A2ᵛ; Anthony Anderson, *The shield of our Safetie*, 1581, sig. A3; Thomas Cooper, *An admonition to the people of England*, 1589, sig. Ii4ᵛ; Richard Mulcaster, *The first part of the elementarie*, 1582, sigs. *2–*2ᵛ; John Phillip, *The Life and Death of Sir Philip Sidney*, 1587, sig. B1ᵛ; John Foxe, *An abridgement of the booke of acts and monumentes of the church: . . . abridged by Timothe Bright*, 1589, sig. ¶8ᵛ; John Calvin, *Sermons . . . vpon the Epistle of Saincte Paule to the Galathians* [translated by Arthur Golding], 1574, sig. ¶4ᵛ.

[94] Walter Travers, *A full and plaine declaration of Ecclesiasticall Discipline*, 1574, sig. A2ᵛ.

AN ENGRAVING OF QUEEN ELIZABETH BY WILLIAM ROGERS

people realized, she encroached upon the Blessed Virgin in their hearts. Hallowed epithets came to her. Her people called her their "pearl," their "star," their "rose." [95]

That patriotic Englishmen unconsciously half shifted their affection for a sacred Virgin to a profane is interestingly suggested in *The monument of matrones: conteining seuen seuerall Lamps of Virginitie, or distinct treatises; whereof the first fiue concerne praier and meditation: the other two last, precepts and examples, as the woorthie works partlie of men, partlie of women.* It appeared in 1582 "*compiled for the* necessarie vse of both sexes out of the sacred *Scriptures, and other approoued authors,*" by Thomas Bentley, a student of Gray's Inn. For Elizabeth, Bentley has made "readie these seuen Lamps of your perpetuall virginitie"; he offers his "diuine exercises of the church, vnto your Maiestie the most naturall mother and noble

---

[95] Liber XVII of *Batman vppon Bartholome, His Booke De Proprietatibus Rerum* (1582) is "De Arboribus et Herbis." Chapter 136, which gives a full description of the *rosa* has (sig. Hhh3ᵛ) the following significant passage: "*Dodoneus* writeth of ten kinde of Roses, among the which, the Eglantine rose, and Muske rose, yeolow and white. There is one rose growing in *England*, is worth all these, *Rosa sine spina*: which royall Rose growing in hir proper soyle, is borne vp of a well settled stalke, and armed with such thornes, as are apparant to so gentle a kinde, the leaues of Lilye hiew, called the Orient gréene, notwithstanding, subiect to flawes of dreadfull blastes, as all our common Roses be to tempesteous windes. Zeale constraineth me somwhat to speake of so wholsome a floure, chéerefull in sight, mild in kinde, and mercifull in iustice, by whose meanes, as the smell of the rose is comfortable to the sence, so much more is this Rose, for *Englandes* whole prosperitie." After a defense of godly life and the abused clergy, Batman prays: "God graunt ẙ view of this note to the royall Rose, that the Cleargie be no more oppressed." Professor B. J. Whiting kindly drew my attention to this passage in Batman.

Elizabeth even seems to have had her "rose window." In Robert Miller Christy's *The Progresses of Queen Elizabeth Through Essex, and the Houses in Which She Stayed* (Colchester, 1917; reprinted from *The Essex Review*, XXVI [1917], 115–129, 181–197) there is a reproduction of a roundel of painted glass in a window at "Tuke's" in Layer Marney, which seems to commemorate a visit of the queen, September 3–5, 1580. A Tudor rose with apparently faded petals is surmounted by a crown and the royal cypher. See the discussion in Christy, p. 21. See above, pp. 134–135.

nursse thereof; the cause of a virgine to a Virgine." Elizabeth's translation of Margaret of Navarre's *A Godly
Medytacyon of the christen sowle* is in the "second lamp"
that contains also prayers and meditations made by "sundrie vertuous Queenes." The "third lamp" contains
prayers and meditations "to be properlie vsed of the
QVEENES *most excellent Maiestie, as especiallie* vpon the
17. daie of Nouember, being the daie of *the gladnesse of hir
hart, and memorable feast of* hir coronation: so on all other
daies *and times at hir Graces* pleasure." Striking prayers,
some worked out on Elizabeth's name, appear in the
"lamps." Joined to the third are the "Heast" and "Vow"
that I reproduce. Some of the dedicatory Latin verses
deserve quotation:

Lampas Virginitatis.

Ecce tibi lucet, Princeps clarissima, lampas:
In tenebris gressus dirigat illa tuos.
Si quæris librum cur lampada virginis istum
Inscribam: causas dico fuisse duas.
Vna est, quòd talem præfert ecclesia lucem,
Expectans sponsum virgo pudica suum.
Altera, quòd manibus virgo reginea librum
Sumit, cui veræ lampadis instar erit,
Dum Domino litat, & sacris indicit honorem,
Nuncupat & Christo vota secunda suo.
Anna sibi lucem, sibi Debora prætulit istam:
Inq̃ suis Princeps ELIZABETHA *malis.*[96]

Elizabeth missed no chance to catch the veneration due
"sacred virginity," as students of her life know. She often
dressed in white, a virgin's color; and her speeches as frequently commended virginity. Fate favored her not only
in her birth; she died on the eve of the Virgin's annunciation. Dekker mourned for her in *The VVonderfull Yeare*
(1603): "Shee came in with the fall of the leafe, and went

[96] Sig. [A4ᵛ].

The KINGS Heart, or GODS
familiar speech to the
QVEENE:
Collected out of the holie Pfalmes of good
King DAVID, as they are learned-
lie expounded by THEODORE
BEZA:

Wherein almightie GOD (after a diuine fort fpea-
king vnto hir Maieftie, as he fometimes did vnto Dauid,
though not in fo myfticall maner) doth firft declare his
mercifull prouidence in preferuing hir, and his gratious
goodneffe in exalting hir to the Crowne, exhorting hir
therewithall, humblie to acknowledge his fouereigntie
ouer all earthlie powers, and to worfhip him. Secondlie, he defcribeth vnto hir Grace, the woorthie properties that are required to bee in euerie godlie Prince,
and wife Gouernour, for the maintenance of his glorie,
and their eftates. Thirdlie, he exhorteth hir Maieftie to
the faithfull difcharge of hir office and dutie in his feare
and feruice, to the increafe of vertue, and fuppreffing of
vice. And fo fhewing the commodities that will infue
thereby to hir and hir people, he fourthlie promifeth, not
onelie to be hir continuall defender againft all hir enimies; but alfo to bleffe hir, and hir Realme, with manie
large, fweet and comfortable benefits, both corporall &
celeftiall, and to make hir partaker of all his ancient mercies, promifed long fince to hir father Dauid ; namelie,
vpon this condition : if finallie fhe perfeuere in the
perfect loue and due obedience of hir
spirituall spoufe Chrift
Iefus.

¶ The

¶ The firft Chapter of
the HEAST.

ELIZABETH, thou
Virgin mine, the KINGS
Daughter, and faireft a-
mong women ; moft full
of beautie and maieftie :
attend a litle to my Heaſt,
and marke what I fhall
fay. Thou art my Daugh-
ter in deede, this daie haue
I begotten thee, and e-
fpoufed thee to thy king
CHRIST, my Sonne ;
crowned thee with my
gifts, and appointed thee QVEENE, to reigne vpon my
holie mount Zion.

Behold, I which am the onlie Lord (by full right
and authoritie) of all men ; and do my felfe gouerne
the Empires and kingdoms, as the greateft king of
all, and moft mightie Monarch of the whole world :
euen I the moft high God, and celeftiall father, haue
elected thee a chofen veffell of high honour and price in
my houfe, and to that end haue mightilie preferued
thee, and miraculouflie deliuered thee out of fo manie
& fo great dangers, and now at the laft haue brought
into thy fubiection the people, ouer whome thou haft
authoritie.

It is I, and none other, which haue confecrated
thee vnto my felfe ; and annointed thee with holie oile,
to be the Queene, the Mother, and the Nurffe of my
people in Ifrael : and who onlie haue giuen thee this
moft excellent and goodlie heritage, which thou poffef-
feft in peace.

Thee

The Queenes Vow, or
felfe-talke with
GOD:
Collected out of the Pfalmes of the princelie
Prophet King DAVID, as they are pa-
raphraſticallie expounded by that
godlie learned man, THEO-
DORE BEZA.

Wherein the Queenes Maieftie, after a moft Chriftian maner, euen with Dauds fpirit, his fweet words, and diuine
fentences, firft inciteth & prepareth hir hart and mind to
deuotion. Secondlie acknowledgeth the omnipotent
power of God ouer all kings, kingdoms, and creatures :
and, after a true rehearfall of his manifold benefits befto-
wed vpon hir from hir birth, with an acknowledgement
of hir fouereigntie to come onelie from the Lord, fhe
thirdlie confeffeth hir vnwoorthineffe, and reioiceth
greatlie in his protection and mercie towards hir, fince
hir comming to the Crowne. Fourthlie, hauing his won-
derous works and benefits, done for hir preferuation, in
great admiration, fhee not onelie yeeldeth condigne
thanks for the fame, but exhorteth all creatures, both in
heauen and earth, to praife God together with hir. And
fo laftlie fhe bindeth hir felfe as it were by a folemne oth,
vow and promife, to confecrate hir life wholie to the true
worfhip and fincere feruice of God, in all holie obedience to his lawes, to the glorie of God,
and full difcharge of hir dutie,
both in hir Court and
Realme.

⚹The

∗ The firft part of the
VOW.

ABBONI, my hart
fo boileth within mee,
that I muft nædes
burft foorth that, which
it hath conceiued; euen
a magnifical Vow of a
QVEENE confecrated
to the KING of heauen
himfelfe, and that with
fuch zeale and feruen-
cie, that no penne may
ſæme to be able to at-
taine vnto the voice of
the fpeaker.

Therefore, O my God, I being now prepared with
my whole hart ; with my whole hart and mind, I faie,
haue great defire to fpeake vnto thee : and in this my
prefent moft happie eftate, to call into my remembrance thy woonderfull works, wrought and brought
to paffe by thine almightie power for me, from my
conception, euen vntill this houre.

Neither will I do it, O Lord, with my mouth onlie,
as hypocrites vfe to do; but I will vnfeinedlie teftifie
thee my God to be mine onlie maker, redæmer, præfer-
uer, and Sauiour, with praife that fhall proceed euen
from the dæpe bottome of my hart.

Go to then my tongue, go to my mouth, I faie ; bæ
thou no longer dumbe ; but open thy felfe wide,
to fpeake out the moft excellent praifes
of my God, and make thy har-
tie Vowes, and faie :
as followeth.

The

away in the Spring: her life (which was dedicated to Virginitie,) both beginning & closing vp a miraculous Mayden
circle: for she was borne vpon a Lady Eue, and died vpon
a Lady Eue." [97]

In the calendar of the Catholic Church November 19
had been allotted to St. Elizabeth of Hungary. In 1568
her feast, along with thirty-seven others, was formally
omitted from the reformed breviary.[98] Patriotic English
courtiers seized on this saint's day as another way to compliment their Elizabeth, and celebrated it in her name as a
court festival. Richard Brakenbury writes to Lord Talbot
on November 20, 1590: "Thene the 19 day, beynge *Saynt
Elyzabeth's daye*, th' Erle of Comberland, th' Erle of Essex,
and my L. Burge, dyd chaleng all comers, sex courses
apeace, whiche was very honorably performed." [99]

Nicholas Sanders charged that Protestants were con-
temptuous of the Virgin's Nativity and *"insteede thereof
most solemnly doe celebrate the birth-day of Q. Elizabeth"*:

To the great contempte of the B. Virgin you make the 7. day of
September an holiday, which is the Even of the B, [*sic*] *Virgines*
Nativity. This 7. you solemnize most devoutly: this day you
significantly note in your Calender with red letters, but the day
of the Nativity of the B. *Virgine* you express onely in blacke
Characters &c.

Thomas Holland replied:

Because on the Even English subiectes giue thanks to God, and
shew some ioy of thankfulnesse for the comfortable Nativity of

---

[97] *The VVonderfull Yeare 1603*, ed. G. B. Harrison, 1924, p. 25.

[98] Miss Strickland (IV, 614) suggested that Pius V, "as some have insinu-
ated," struck the name of St. Elizabeth out of the calendar deliberately to indicate his ill-will to Queen Elizabeth. Cf. Nichols, *Elizabeth*, III, 69 n. The facts,
which I have ascertained through the generous help of Mr. John V. Curry, S.J.,
and the Reverend Edward A. Ryan, S.J., do not bear out this idea.

[99] III, 69-70. In a clash in 1563 with her Lords over the question of a successor Elizabeth declared that "the marks which they saw on her face were not
wrinkles but the pits of smallpox; she might be old, but God could send her
children as He had done to Saint Elizabeth" (Neale, p. 120).

Queene *Elizabeth*, happy in regiment; *Ergo* on the day next en-
suing immediatly they contemne to celebrate the Nativity of
the *B. Virgine.* Even as much as one shoulde saye: Some yeares
the 25. of March falleth on Easter Even: *Ergo* the celebration of
the feast of the *Annunciation* of the *B. Virgine* worketh a contempt of the solemnization of Christ our Saviours Resurrection.

Sanders charged further:

In the chiefest temple in all London for the accomplishment of the
sacred office of the church that day (a thing incredible wel most to be
herd) That Antiphone or Himne that was accustomably in the end
of the service songe by the Quier in the honor of the blessed Virgin,
is now converted (as it is reported by common fame) to the laude
and honor of Queene Elizabeth, thereby to sounde her praises.

Holland retorted:

To this I answere by negation, denying vtterly that any such
forme of Antiphone is vsed in Pawles Church at London, or in
any other Cathedral church or chappell of this Realme: Yet will
I not deny but that there is an Antiphone songe in Paules a little
before the conclusion of service both at morne and even the 17.
of November, but this Antiphone is meere Eucharistical, in-
dited only to this purpose to giue God thankes for the happy
regimente of Queene *Elizabeth*, noe waies tending to her com-
mendations, further then to glorifie God for her happy and
peaceable regiment, vvhich [God] hath lent vs this 41.
yeares, which God graunt she may long continew & prosper in.

He declares that if "noting with greate red letters" be an
appropriate

condition to signifie an Holy day in these times aswell this
Accuser may conclude that the dayes of the entring of the Sonne
into *Aries, Taurus, Gemini*, &c. to each, I say, of the 12. Signes
are Holy-daies. For all the titles of these days are limmed with
red inke by our Astronomers direction in all our printed Calen-
ders. . . . The distinguishing of *Aries* and *Taurus*, and the rest
of the 12. Signes by their red letters therein will easily dischardge

me without the force of a Mallet out of the brakes of this obiection.[100]

Elizabeth even seems to have been associated with the medieval legend of the fierce unicorn that could be taken only by a chaste maiden acting as decoy. The legend has hoary origins and amazing mutations.[101] In the Middle Ages it served both profane and sacred ends. "Nos chan-

[100] Thomas Holland, Πανήγυρις D. Elizabethæ, ... A sermon preached at Pauls in London the 17. of November Ann. Dom. 1599. ... VVherevnto is adioyned an Apologeticall discourse, whereby all such sclanderous Accusations are fully and faithfully confuted, wherewith the Honour of this Realme hath beene vncharitably traduced by some of our adversaries in forraigne nations, and at home, for observing the 17. of November yeerely in the forme of an Holy-day, and for the ioifull exercises, and Courtly triumphes on that day in the honour of her Maiestie exhibited, Oxford, 1601, sigs. L2–L3, R2–R2ᵛ. Holland, "Doctor of Divinity, & her Highnes Professor thereof in her Vniversity of Oxford," defends at length and with scriptural citations, the keeping of the "Queenes Nativity" and Accession Day. His sermon comparing the "Regia virgo" to the Queen of Sheba and Solomon follows Latin verses exalting her arms. The following titles will suggest further the enthusiastic observance of November 17: Edmund Bunny, Certaine prayers and other godly exercises, for the seuenteenth of Nouember: Wherein we solemnize the blessed reigne of our gracious Soueraigne Lady Elizabeth, 1585; Thomas White, A Sermon Preached at Paules Crosse the 17. of Nouember An. 1589. In ioyfull remembrance and thanksgiuing vnto God, for the peaceable yeres of her Maiesties most gratious Raigne ouer vs, now 32, 1589; John Howson, A sermon preached at S.ᵗ Maries in Oxford, the 17. day of November, 1602. in defence of the Festivities of the Church of England, and namely that of her Maiesties Coronation, Oxford, 1602 (Bishop Howson [sigs. C3–C3ᵛ] declares that the "Church of England hath ... auctority sufficient to institute, if it so please, the celebration of the Nativity, and inauguration of her excellent Maiestie, with publike sermons, common praiers, & thanksgiving for her godly & peaceable raigne, & the vnspeakeable blessing received by her, the chosen instrument of God for our good"); John Whitgift, A Most godly and Learned Sermon, Preached at Pauls Crosse the 17 of Nouember, in the yeare of our Lorde. 1583, 1589; Isaac Colfe, A sermon preached on the Queenes day. Beeing the 17. of Nouember. 1587. at the towne of Lidd in Kent, 1587; John King, A sermon preached in Yorke the seuenteenth day of Nouember in the yeare of our Lorde 1595. being the Queenes day, Oxford, 1597 (in Lectures vpon Ionas, Oxford, 1597, sigs. Xx7ᵛ–Yy3ᵛ); John Prime, The consolations of Dauid, breefly applied to Queene Elizabeth: in a Sermon preached in Oxford the 17. of Nouember, Oxford, 1588; and the same preacher's A sermon briefly comparing the estate of King Salomon and his Subiectes togither with the condition of Queene Elizabeth and her people. Preached in Sainct Maries in Oxford the 17. of Nouember, Oxford, 1585.

[101] See Odell Shepard, The Lore of the Unicorn, Boston, 1930.

sonniers et nos romanciers courtois comparent souvent à la licorne le chevalier dompté par Amour et par la Dame." [102] "An Elegie, or friends passion, for his Astrophill. Written vpon the death of the right Honorable sir Philip Sidney knight, Lord gouernor of Flushing" by Matthew Roydon appeared in *The Phœnix Nest* of 1593. In this poem it seems likely that "the 'burly Beare' and his fellows are allegorical: the bear may represent Leicester, the lion Lord Burghley, the unicorn Queen Elizabeth." [103] Paul Hentzner tells of a unicorn's horn eight spans and a half long and valued at above £10,000 which was in the queen's bedchamber at Windsor Castle when he visited England in 1598. [104] In Hakluyt's account of Frobisher's second voyage one learns that on "another small Iland here was also found a great dead fish, . . . having a horne of two yardes long growing out of the snoute or nostrels. This horne is wreathed and straite, like in fashion to a Taper made of waxe, and may truely be thought to be the sea Unicorne. This horne is to be seene and reserved as a Jewell by the Queenes Majesties commandement, in her Wardrope [*sic*] of Robes." [105] Perhaps Frobisher's was the "horne" that was in the maiden queen's chamber when Hentzner told of the wonders of her England.

Surmounting all the symbols of virginity that Elizabeth attracted was the halo of divine right, which was not completely dissipated from around the head of the English sovereign until Charles I was executed. "Great is the

[102] Bédier and Hazard, I (1923), 44.

[103] The suggestion is Professor Rollins's (*The Phœnix Nest*, p. 118).

[104] *A Journey into England in the Year MDXCVIII* (p. 45, ed. Horace Walpole, Aungervyle Society Reprints, first series, Edinburgh, vol. I [1881]).

[105] *The Principal Navigations*, Everyman's Library ed., 1910, V, 209–210. Churchyard reported: "And marchyng backe, they found a straunge Fish dead, that had been caste from the Sea on the shore, who had a Boane in his Head like an *Vnicorne*, which they brought awaye and presented to our Prince, whē thei came home" (*A Prayse, and Reporte of Maister Martyne Forbishers Voyage to Meta Incognita*, 1578, sigs. B5ᵛ–B6).

person of a King, reigning here vpon earth amõgst men,
hee is a liuely Embleme of the high and glorious Maiesty
of God in heauen." [106] George Gascoigne's *The Glasse of
Governement* (1575) contains typical evidence that the
patriotic Englishman felt that honor, obedience, and love
given to the king were necessarily rendered to God. This
soldier-poet repeatedly says that the king

> hath, (from God above) his grace,
> And is *viceroy*, on earth to beare the sway. [107]

He praises Elizabeth as on "earth the liuetenant of the
moste hygh God." [108] Elizabeth never made the stupid
Stuart mistake of dogmatizing about divine right. Tributes to her as God's "*viceroy*" have a tone of genuine
spontaneity. In appearing to Protestant fervor as the
preserver of "Pure Religion" she did seem to be chosen of
the English God for just that task. Her own miraculous
preservation from all plots against her life was not to be
explained apart from His particular care of her and His
people. Their enemies were silenced:

Your owne experience sheweth that no practize will preuaile to
harme one haire of hir head whom next God you hate most: for
the Lord of hostes doth kéepe hir, he hath set legions of Angels
about hir, they houer ouer hir, they marche with hir, they goe
before hir, and garde hir from all treasons: they make knowne
your wayes, they deliuer hir your drifts, and they discouer your
very thoughtes vnto hir. This you assuredly sée, that the whole
course of hir Maiesties life is myraculous. [109]

Such a widely current view of Elizabeth should not be
forgotten when one hears sophisticated poets join Spenser

---

[106] Thomas Heywood, *Englands Elizabeth: her life and troubles*, 1631, sig. C11ᵛ.
[107] *Works*, II, 57.   [108] II, 7.
[109] Henri Estienne, *The Stage of Popish toyes: . . . Compyled by G. N.* [George
North], 1581, sig. M4. See equally striking sentiment in Philip Stubbes, *The
intended treason, of Doctor Parrie: and his complices, against the Queenes moste
Excellent Maiestie*, [1584], sig. A3ᵛ.

to sing Eliza as "hevenly borne." Religious patriotism
— or patriotic religion — unites Deloney with Sir John
Davies in hymns to this queen who is preserved by God
to bring peace and to save "Pure Religion."

It is to this uniquely buoyant patriotism which mingles
inextricably with Protestant zeal, that one should look for
the final cause of the chivalric idealization of Elizabeth as
a "lady sovereign" like Emilia, as a "blessed virgin." It
sustains all her shrewd use of surviving medieval form and
ceremony in statecraft which was eminently practical.
Many of her subjects in their unconscious selves were in a
deep quandary about religious allegiances. The Blessed
Virgin Mary did not seem to them quite so lovely a lady
as she had been before Mary Tudor's tragic efforts to
establish the Virgin's church. This church had excommunicated their virgin Elizabeth. Out of their dilemma
about the technicalities of religious allegiances most Englishmen were finally led, half unconsciously, by the elemental instinct of loyalty to the soil that had produced
them. Love of native land found that land personified by
a brilliant virgin queen. It was inevitable that she should
be exalted in view of what she had done and in view of
what she was. It was equally inevitable that she should
be exalted in forms long consecrated to the expression of
man's admiration of perfection in sovereignty and womanhood. Her virginity was a fortunate distinction. It fitted
her to attract Christian sentiment and pagan fancy alike.
It made her "in earth the first, in heaven the second
Maid"; it made her the famous Renaissance Diana. The
virgin queen who had masculine intelligence and daring
evoked a loyalty and devotion that probably had its ancestry far behind a Christian knight's service to his over-
lord and his lady. One suspects that at Tilbury Elizabeth
even aroused instincts descended from Saxon thegns in
service to their comitatus, from the German tribesmen,

HYMNVS

COMITIALIS, in honorem VIRGINIS VICTRICIS, D. ELISA-BETHAE: per *Eduuardum Iohnfonem*, in *Muficis* bacchalaureum.

Quæst.   Vænam ea eſt, quæ ſceptra vbicunǫ mundi
Temperat, cœli decus invidendum:
Et Dei, & ſyncera hominum voluptas?
Reſp. Eccho.   ELISABETHA.

Chorus 1.   *Victrix virgo!* decus poli invidendum,
Et ſyncera hominum, & Dei voluptas.

Chorus 2.   Securam, ô Superum SANCTE, perenniter
Alarum ELISABET remigio tege.

Quæst.   Quænam ea eſt, quæ pace domi togatâ
Regnat, externas licet vndiǫue vrbes,
Civium crebræ exaniment querelæ?
Reſp.   ELISABETHA.

Chorus 1.   Cujus lambit imaginem aurea oliva,
Dum inteſtina foris vagantur arma.

Chorus 2.   Securam ô Superum &c.

Quæst.   Quænam ea eſt, quam nec dolus imprecantium,
Aut furor quoquàm potis eſt avito:
E throno (armatus licèt) amovere?
Reſp.   ELISABETHA.

Chorus 1.   *Victrix virgo!* dolus furorǫ; quam non
Armatus potis è throno movere eſt.

Chorus 2.   Securam ô Superum &c.

Quæst.   Quænam ea eſt, cui iam imperium, ter acta,
Et quater (nos ſi benè computemus)
Luſtra, tranquillum ſtetit integrumǫ;?
Reſp.   ELISABETHA.

Chorus 1.   Largitor, DEVS, hos precamur annos
Poſſe ipſam reparare duplicatos.

Chorus 2.   Et da, funera poſt, angelicâ frui
Luce, CHRISTO ibidem vivere cum ſuo.

Amen.

H. H. D. F.

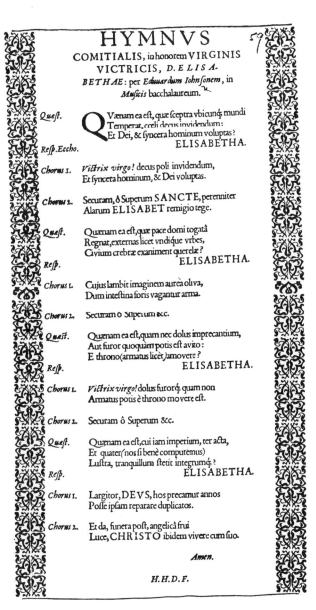

EDWARD JOHNSON, *Hymnus comitialis, in honorem virginis victricis, D. Elisabethæ* [1595?]

who, as Tacitus witnesses, venerated women, often followed them as brave leaders in battle, and even believed
that there was something sacred in the sex that gave them
power to divine the future.[110] Perpetual virginity had
been exalted among the ancient Celts, if Pomponius Mela
is to be trusted.[111] Profound patriotism is surely the greatest common denominator of the many and various celebrations of Elizabeth. The medieval knight had one
temporal lord and another spiritual. But the English
knights who repulsed the Armada had a virgin mistress
who personified with complete felicity for them both the
new state and the new church. The Elizabethan state was
not constructed without lessons from Greek concepts of
the city–state which the Italian Renaissance taught to
England. Devotion to an abstraction, the state, demands
a more ideal allegiance than the masses of Englishmen had
been able to summon and sustain for long until this Renaissance princess came to build a state upon a feudal corner-
stone which they understood, to personify that new
creation in familiar chivalric terms of loyal service rendered by a knight to his "lady sovereign." "Mediaeval
chivalric writers occupied themselves chiefly with the
relations of individuals to one another in cosmopolitan
fellowship. They exalted wise *self*-government, but
scarcely mentioned patriotism or politics. On the other
hand, courtiers of the Renaissance strongly urged young
men to contribute to the public weal of their various
lands." [112] Feudal society could never have sustained
national expansion overseas and defense at home. Elizabeth drew feudal loyalty due lord and lady and "Pure
Religion." In her person she could give compelling repre-

[110] See *Historical Works*, trans. Arthur Murphy, Everyman's Library ed.,
1928, II, 322–324, 316–317.
[111] W. J. Courthope, *A History of English Poetry*, 1926, I, 116, where the
passage in Pomponius Mela (iii. 6 [48]) is cited.
[112] Schofield, *Chivalry*, p. 240.

sentation of all these objects of chivalric veneration. That veneration obtained, she could turn such devotion into molding a commonwealth to rival that which she knew in Greek and Italian political writers. She used this chivalric heritage well. The civil war that rose when a wise ruler was no more did not ultimately destroy her structure.

Elizabeth built her state before the full decay of the aristocratic feudal order and the ascendancy of conscience and commons. The rich fruits of her age still prove that she effected a happy synthesis of the best in the old system and much of the good that grew with the new. The cozy spiritual economy of medieval Christendom was dissolving before expanding knowledge of the ancient world and exploration of the present. But in England, for a time, at least, knights who had learned in Italy to be courtiers in service to the state and its prince, felt that their own land might, inspired by ancient models in art and life, even outstrip them — and prove a fair road to the next world. Love of adventure and religious enthusiasm which animated the chivalry of the twelfth and thirteenth centuries had not wholly died; medieval romance was still read. In England of the sixteenth century it had particular cause to revive anew, even if around curiously changed objects. Courtiers like Ralegh, who sought fame and riches on the high seas in the name of a virgin lady at home, were animated by some of the crusading ardor of the Middle Ages. Did they not go "down to the sea in ships, and do business in great waters" in the name of the true God and his chosen princess? Chivalric energy that once carried English knights to Jerusalem for the glory of Christ and his mild mother Mary welled up again for the glory of the English God and His queen. Drake led Protestant sailors who saw Elizabeth as God's agent sent to protect "Pure Religion" against the Inquisition, the pope, and the

Spaniards. Both ages were shot through with many sordid
motives, but bright ideals were woven into the later as well
as into the earlier expeditions. During a brief term in
English life a virgin queen contrived to stimulate almost
all the old and the new ideals that animated her subjects,
and somehow to counter by her individual genius their in-
herent disruptive tendencies. The feudal order has been
well characterized as "sensitive but partial," as an example of "patriotism wholly submerged in loyalty." [113]
Elizabeth accepted the remnants of that decadent feudal
order, and summoned the chivalric idealism which had
been its sadly flying goal. Courtly servants for whom
various kinds of medieval romance still lived heard the
call to their submerged patriotism which she made in the
name of loyalty to herself as the symbol of the new English
state. She called to her knights as a Welsh princess sprung
of Arthur's line. She called as a lovely virgin lady who
was also the mother of their England. The chivalry which
John Addington Symonds defined as an "ideal binding
men together by participation in potent spiritual enthusiasms" came at her call. Its old and high ideal of loyal
service to *Dieu et les dames* was transmuted by the virgin
"lady sovereign" into one of devoted service to the new
state. Courtiers — all the people — for a moment found
in Diana a complete symbol for their deepest sentiment —
love of England. This queen with their chivalry made
England a nation.

[113] George Santayana, *The Life of Reason*, New York, 1924, II (*Reason in Society*), 178.

CHAPTER VI

Laura or Idea

Yf god wolde deigne to make, a *Petrarks* heire of me
the coomlyest Queene that ever was, my *Lawra* nedes must be.
— George Gascoigne [1]

THE royal English Laura might easily draw attention to the complex history of the sonnet mistress in Provence, in Italy, in France, and in England of the sixteenth century. But the salient fact is that she appears in English poetry when a various celebration of Elizabeth meets the sonnet vogue of the nineties. By her "mere English" blood Laura is kin to the lowly Judith and Deborah of broadside and progress verse, and to Eliza in the national drama. She is a sister of the pastoral Elisa and the courtly Diana who are now well known, and of Cynthia, Gloriana, and Belphœbe who will shortly appear. She and Idea are twins. The royal Laura is the queen and lady complimented as the first mistress of English sonneteers who emulate Petrarch.

More than a decade before the height of the sonnet craze in England, Spenser created "Elisa, queene of shepheardes all." At almost the same time that Colin sang his hymn to Elisa, Euphues lauded the queen in some of the most popular prose of the reign. The courtly portrait that Lyly early painted is a sound English base for the Italianate colorings that the sonneteers later apply. It must be carefully viewed.

Euphues. The Anatomy of Wyt, which appeared late in

[1] *Works*, II, 510.

1578, was hardly likely to please the queen and her ladies. Lucilla's old father argued against virginity in favor of matrimony.[2] Euphues's abuse of women as inconstant and his specious praise of them within a story whose burden was their falseness [3] were offenses hardly to be excused because he pertly apologized: "Whatsoeuer therfore I haue spoken of the spleene against yᵉ slights and subtilties of women, I hope ther is none wil mislike it if she be honest, neither care I if any doe if shee be an harlot."[4] But Livia's laments because her empress "gyueth ensample of vertue, and the Ladyes haue no leasure to followe hir," [5] if they shadowed the court, did seek to except the empress from blame. And Euphues in a letter "to his friend Liuia" gave promise of describing, when he had arrived in England, "a woman that in all quallyties excelleth any man." [6]

In the sequel to *The Anatomy of Wyt* Euphues shortly made ample amends for any offenses. The "Epistle Dedicatory" to *Euphues and his England* (1580) is followed by an address "To the Ladies and Gentlewoemen of England." Lyly "wisheth [them] what they would" and declares that his "*Euphues* had rather lye shut in a Ladyes casket, then open in a Schollers studie." Courtly flattery is in his very disavowal of an intent to flatter. Perhaps the restraining tastes of a virgin queen account in part for Lyly's promising that "there shall be nothing found, that may offend the chast minde with vnseemely tearmes, or vncleanly talke." [7] Philautus and Euphues, arrived in England, tell old Fidus that they have come solely to behold the great queen "the brute of the which

---

[2] *Works,* I, 229–230.
[3] I, 240–242, 252, 216–217. The misogynist's tirades may have come from Guevara and Pettie, but they were none the less offensive for that fact. See I, 142.

[4] I, 258.
[5] I, 320.

[6] I, 323.
[7] II, 8–10.

hath filled euery corner of the worlde." [8] Old Fidus, himself a courtier "in the dayes of that most noble King of
famous memorie *Henry* the eight, Father to our most
gratious Lady *Elizabeth*," has retired to the country, but
he is not forgetful of his king's glorious daughter. He has
full confidence in her noble mind; he is perhaps complimenting her rule when he praises the order in his hive of
bees.[9] Euphues now lauds all women extravagantly, and
especially English women.[10] Ultimate praise of Elizabeth
is redoubled by the fact that she is hailed as inexpressibly
superior to all ladies, even to Philautus's Camilla, who has
been declared matchless indeed. "But such a one she was,
as almost they all are y^t serue so noble a Prince, such virgins cary lights before such a *Vesta*, such Nymphes, arrowes w^t such a *Diana*." [11] Having penned such speeches,
Lyly has little need to let Philautus rebuke Euphues
severely [12] for the mean remarks about women in *The
Anatomy of Wyt*.

In *Euphues and his England* Lyly establishes a very influential pattern in courtly eulogy of Elizabeth, queen and
lady. At the outset of the eulogy Euphues laments that
his glass cannot show worthily such a princess. He knows
not "when to begin, nor where to ende." A "twoo hundred foote" frame was but little enough for Alexander's
picture, "when the whole worlde was to little for his personne." Yet Euphues will "manifest his faythfull heart"
toward his princess although he "presume not to paynt
hir" worthily. Almost with prescience that sonneteers
will gild his lily, he declares:

I will set downe this *Elizabeth*, as neere as I can: And it may
be, that as the *Venus* of *Apelles*, not finished, the *Tindarides* of
Nichomachus not ended, the *Medea* of *Timomachus* not perfected,

[8] II, 37.
[9] II, 45.
[10] II, 100–101, 91.

[11] II, 85.
[12] II, 92–93.

the table of *Parrhasius* not couloured, brought greater desire to
them, to consumate them, and to others to see them: so the
Elizabeth of *Euphues*, being but shadowed for others to vernish,
but begun for others to ende, but drawen with a blacke coale, for
others to blase with a bright coulour, may worke either a desire
in *Euphues* heereafter if he liue, to ende it, or a minde in those
that are better able to amende it, or in all (if none can worke it)
a wil to wish it.[13]

Euphues now summarizes English history since the
union of the "redde Rose and the white" to show England's emergence from the ruin that preceded the Tudors.
He speaks the sentiment of any balladist when he declares
that God has always had a tender care "of that *England*,
as of a new *Israel*, his chosen and peculier people." He
turns to Elizabetha Regina, sweetest flower of the happy
grafting that gave the Tudor rosebush, and recounts her
establishment of "Pure Religion," her clemency toward
her enemies upon her accession and always thereafter, and
her miraculous preservation. He exclaims:

O diuine nature, O heauenly nobilitie, what thing can there
more be required in a Prince, then in greatest power, to shewe
greatest patience, in chiefest glorye, to bring forth chiefest
grace, in abundaunce of all earthlye pompe, to manifest aboun-
daunce of all heauenlye pietie? O fortunate *England* that hath
such a Queene, vngratefull if thou praye not for hir, wicked if
thou do not loue hir, miserable, if thou loose hir.

Heere Ladies is a Glasse for all Princes to behold, that being called to dignitie, they vse moderation, not might, tempering
the seueritie of the lawes, with the mildnes of loue, not executing
al they wil, but shewing what they may. Happy are they, and
onely they that are vnder this glorious and gracious Souereign-
tie: in-somuch that I accompt all those abiects, that be not hir
subiectes.[14]

[13] II, 205.
[14] II, 208.

The notoriously ornate style need not finally obscure the patriotic sincerity that underlies such praise of Elizabeth's public virtues — her establishment of "Pure Religion," her justice and temperance, her mercy and moderation.

Euphues remembers that he has yet to praise the "most vertuous and beautifull lady." It is Elizabeth's virginity that most impresses the courtly imagination. Praise of her sacred virginity that eclipses that of ancient maidens leads to celebrating the blessings of her public achievements, however, especially of her peace. When Euphues would hold his glass up to the lady's personal beauty and talents, it reflects as well the achievements of the sovereign. I quote but parts of the eulogy.

As this noble Prince is endued with mercie, pacience and moderation, so is she adourned with singuler beautie and chastitie, excelling in the one *Venus*, in the other *Vesta*. Who knoweth not how rare a thing it is (Ladies) to match virginitie with beautie, a chast minde with an amiable face, diuine cogitations with a comelye countenaunce? But suche is the grace bestowed vppon this earthlye Goddesse, that hauing the beautie that myght allure all Princes, she hath the chastitie also to refuse all, accounting it no lesse praise to be called a Uirgin, then to be esteemed a *Venus*, thinking it as great honour to bee found chast, as thought amiable: . . . what hath this chast Uirgin *Elizabeth* don, who by the space of twenty and odde yeares with continuall peace against all policies, with sundry myracles, contrary to all hope, hath gouerned that noble Island. Against whome neyther forren force, nor ciuill fraude, neyther discorde at home, nor conspirices abroad, could preuaile. What greater· meruaile hath happened since the beginning of the world, then for a young and tender Maiden, to gouern strong and valiaunt menne, then for a Uirgin to make the whole worlde, if not to stand in awe of hir, yet to honour hir, yea and to liue in spight of all those that spight hir, with hir sword in the sheth, with hir armour in the Tower, with hir souldiers in their gownes, insomuch as hir peace may be called more blessed then the quiet raigne of *Numa Pom-*

pilius, in whose gouernment the Bees haue made their hiues in the soldiers helmettes. Now is the Temple of *Ianus* remoued from *Rome* to *England,* whose dore hath not bene opened this twentie yeares, more to be meruayled at, then the regiment of *Debora,* who ruled twentie yeares with religion, or *Semyramis* that gouerned long with power, or *Zenobia* that reigned six yeares in prosperitie.

.   .   .   .

O blessed peace, oh happy Prince, O fortunate people: The lyuing God is onely the Englysh God, wher he hath placed peace, which bryngeth all plentie, annoynted a Uirgin Queene, which with a wand ruleth hir owne subiects, and with hir worthinesse, winneth the good willes of straungers, so that she is no lesse gratious among hir own, then glorious to others, no lesse loued of hir people, then merualed at of other nations.

This is the blessing that Christ alwayes gaue to his people, peace: . . .

.   .   .   .

This peace hath the Lorde continued with great and vnspeake-able goodnesse amonge his chosen people of *England.* How much is that nation bounde to such a Prince, by whome they enioye all benefits of peace, hauing their barnes full, when others famish, their cofers stuffed with gold, when others haue no siluer, their wiues without daunger, when others are defamed, their daugh-ters chast, when others are defloured, theyr houses furnished, when others are fired, where they haue all thinges for superfluitie, others nothing to sustaine their neede. This peace hath God giuen for hir vertues, pittie, moderation, virginitie, which peace, the same God of peace continue for his names sake.

Touching the beautie of this Prince, hir countenaunce, hir personage, hir maiestie, I can-not thinke that it may be suffi-ciently commended, when it can-not be too much meruailed at: So that I am constrained to saye as *Praxitiles* did, when hee be-ganne to paynt *Venus* and hir Sonne, who doubted, whether the worlde could affoorde coulours good enough for two such fayre faces, and I whether our tongue canne yeelde wordes to blase that beautie, the perfection where-of none canne imagine, which seeing it is so, I must doe like those that want a cleere sight, who being not able to discerne the Sunne in the Skie are inforced to beholde it in the water. . . .

. . . .

In questioning not inferiour to *Nicaulia* the Queene of *Saba*, that did put so many hard doubts to *Salomon*, equall to *Nicostrata* in the *Greeke* tongue, who was thought to giue precepts for the better perfectiõ: more learned in the *Latine*, then *Amalasunta*: passing *Aspasia* in Philosophie, who taught *Pericles*: exceeding in iudgement *Themistoclea*, who instructed *Pithagoras*, adde to these qualyties, those, that none of these had, the *French* tongue, the *Spanish*, the *Italian*, not meane in euery one, but excellent in all, readyer to correct escapes in those languages, then to be controlled, fitter to teach others, then learne of anye, more able to adde new rules, then to erre in yᵉ olde: Insomuch as there is no Embassadour, that commeth into hir court, but she is willing & able both to vnderstand his message, & vtter hir minde, not lyke vnto yᵉ Kings of *Assiria*, who aunswere Embassades by messengers, while they thẽselues either dally in sinne, or snort in sleepe. Hir godly zeale to learning, with hir great skil, hath bene so manifestly approued, yᵗ I cannot tell whether she deserue more honour for hir knowledge, or admiration for hir curtesie, who in great pompe, hath twice directed hir Progresse vnto the Uniuersities, with no lesse ioye to the Students, then glory to hir State. Where, after long & solempne disputations in Law, Phisicke, & Diuinitie, not as one weried with Schollers arguments, but wedded to their orations, when euery one feared to offend in length, she in hir own person, with no lesse praise to hir Maiestie, then delight to hir subiects, with a wise & learned conclusion, both gaue them thankes, & put hir selfe to paines. . . . Hir wit so sharp, that if I should repeat the apt aunsweres, yᵉ subtil questions, yᵉ fine speaches, the pithie sentences, which on yᵉ soddain she hath vttered, they wold rather breed admiratiõ thẽ credit. But such are yᵉ gifts yᵗ the liuing God hath indued hir with-all, that looke in what Arte or Language, wit or learning, vertue or beautie, any one hath perticularly excelled most, she onely hath generally exceeded euery one in al, insomuch, that there is nothing to bee added that either mã would wish in a woman, or God doth giue to a creature.

I let passe hir skil in Musicke, hir knowledg in al yᵉ other sciences, whẽ as I feare least by my simplicity I shoulde make them lesse then they are, in seeking to shewe howe great they are, vnlesse I were praising hir in the gallerie of *Olympia*, where gyuing forth one worde, I might heare seuen.

But all these graces although they be to be wondered at, yet hir politique gouernement, hir prudent counsaile, hir zeale to religion, hir clemencie to those that submit, hir stoutnesse to those that threaten, so farre exceede all other vertues, that they are more easie to be meruailed at, then imitated.

Two and twentie yeares hath she borne the sword with such iustice, that neither offenders coulde complaine of rigour, not the innocent of wrong, yet so tempered wᵗ mercie, as malefactours haue beene sometimes pardoned vpon hope of grace, and the iniuried requited to ease their griefe, insomuch that in yᵉ whole course of hir glorious raigne, it coulde neuer be saide, that either the poore were oppressed without remedie, or the guiltie repressed without cause, bearing this engrauen in hir noble heart, that iustice without mercie were extreame iniurie, and pittie without equitie plaine partialitie, and that it is as great tyranny not to mitigate Laws, as iniquitie to breake them.

Hir care for the flourishing of the Gospell hath wel appeared, when as neither the curses of the Pope, (which are blessings to good people) nor the threatenings of kings, (which are perillous to a Prince) nor the perswasions of Papists, (which are Honny to the mouth) could either feare hir, or allure hir, to violate the holy league contracted with Christ, or to maculate the blood of the aunciente Lambe, whiche is Christ. . . .

. . . Next followeth the loue shee beareth to hir subiectes, who no lesse tendereth them, then the apple of hir owne eye, shewing hir selfe a mother to the aflicted, a Phisition to the sicke, a Souereigne and mylde Gouernesse to all.

Touchinge hir Magnanimitie, hir Maiestie, hir Estate royall, there was neyther *Alexander*, nor *Galba* the Emperour, nor any that might be compared with hir.

... This is that good Pelican that to feede hir people spareth not to rend hir owne personne: ...

.   .   .   .

Beholde Ladyes in this Glasse a Queene, a woeman, a Uirgin, in all giftes of the bodye, in all graces of the minde, in all perfection of eyther, so farre to excell all men, that I know not whether I may thinke the place too badde for hir to dwell amonge men.[15]

In *Euphues and his England* there is this full idealization of Elizabetha Regina and Elizabeth Tudor at the beginning of the most fruitful decades of the age. The praise of her peace and her saving of "Pure Religion" in this base for the sonnet idealization joins it to native broadside and progress verse. The praise of her virginity, her beauty, and her skill in the arts relates it to all the forms of cultivated Elizabethan lyricism that I am reviewing. The emphasis on her justice, wisdom, moderation, temperance, chastity, magnanimity, mercy, and service to "Pure Religion" is to be remembered in the study of Spenser's twofold compliment in *The Faerie Queene*. The glorification of the queen and woman during the remainder of the reign is rooted in Lyly's inclusive eulogy about 1580, and in Spenser's beautiful song to "Elisa, queene of shepheardes all," which immediately preceded it. Lyly exalts all the achievements and attributes of her public and private characters which Spenser during the eighties is giving their supreme idealization. Of course the sonneteers work with Lyly's eulogy in their consciousness, and that especially because its elaborate style has natural affinities for Petrarchan conceits which dominate in lyric fashions of the nineties. Laura is foreshadowed in the descriptions which have just been reviewed.[16]

[15] II, 209–216.
[16] The pattern of poems in which Olympian deities honor the royal Laura may be "Iouis Elizabeth" (II, 216–217) with which Lyly capped his eulogy in

QUEEN ELIZABETH ATTENDED BY PALLAS, MINERVA, AND VENUS

From the painting attributed to Hans Eworthe in Hampton Court Palace

The sonneteers of the nineties, who knew such eulogies and many others, repeatedly crowned Elizabeth queen of their songs. Her place in their imaginations may now be studied: first, by a review of some sonnets addressed to the queen and to the lady; next, by observing the happy ambiguity of many verses that might as appropriately compliment the queen as a conventional mistress; and then by a critical inquiry into the nature of the royal Laura.

Perhaps the finest quatorzain [17] ever to compliment Elizabeth was the following familiar one by Sir Walter Ralegh:

A VISION VPON THIS CONCEIPT OF THE FAERY QVEENE

Methought I saw the graue, where Laura lay,
Within that Temple, where the vestall flame
Was wont to burne, and passing by that way,
To see that buried dust of liuing fame,
Whose tumbe faire loue, and fairer vertue kept,
All suddeinly I saw the Faery Queene:
At whose approch the soule of Petrarke wept,

Euphues and his England. Juno, Pallas, and Venus would each claim the queen who excels in majesty, wisdom, and beauty. They refer their dispute to Jove — who settles it by declaring that Eliza shall be his only. See above, pp. 147-149. Bond (I, 23 n.; II, 535) argues that "this contest between Pallas, Juno, and Venus may have been suggested to Lyly by Lucas de Heere's painting of Elizabeth attended by these three goddesses." (This painting in Hampton Court Palace is now attributed to Hans Eworthe.)

Evidence of the imitation of Euphues's eulogy of Elizabeth by Lyly's followers is found in Anthony Munday's *Zelauto. The fountaine of Fame,* 1580, sigs. D4ᵛ-E4ᵛ, G1ᵛ-G2; in Brian Melbancke's *Philotimus,* 1583, sigs. Ff1ᵛ-Ff2; and in Barnaby Rich's *The Second Tome of the Trauailes and aduentures of Don Simonides,* 1584, sigs. O4ᵛ-P1. On sig. E1ᵛ of *Zelauto* is a picture of Elizabeth in a chariot of state with several courtiers and four knights on horseback. An angel blowing the trumpet of fame flies before the chariot, and verses above the queen honor her.

[17] I use the term sonnet to mean a "little song" of varying length and rhythm, for so it was usually understood by Elizabethans. I present some quatorzains first in this review.

And from thenceforth those graces were not seene.
For they this Queene attended, in whose steed
Obliuion laid him downe on Lauras herse:
Hereat the hardest stones were seene to bleed,
And grones of buried ghostes the heuens did perse.
　　Where Homers spright did tremble all for griefe,
　　And curst th' accesse of that celestiall theife.[18]

Ralegh is "*Petrarks* heire" quite clearly; but his admiration of Spenser's *The Faerie Queene* and his own devotion to "the coomlyest Queene that ever was" lift his conceits toward the realm of Dante's reverential adoration of Beatrice.

The following is the second of three sonnets addressed to Elizabeth by Henry Constable. His conceits seem stiff and stale by the side of Ralegh's; but they are typical of much verse that celebrates a mistress — or the queen.

To the Queene: touching the cruell effects of her perfections.

Most Sacred Prince! why should I thee thus prayse
　　Which both of sin and sorrow cause hast beene,
　　Proud hast thou made thy land of such a Queene.
Thy neighboures enviouse of thy happie dayes.
Who never saw the sunshine of thy rayes,
　　An everlasting night this life doth ween;
　　And he whose eyes thy eyes but once have seen
A thousand signes of burning thoughts bewrayes.
Thus sin thou caus'd, (envye, I meane, and pride),
　　Thus fire and darknesse doe proceed from thee.
The very paynes which men in hell abide:
　　Oh no; not hell but purgatorie this,
Whose soules some say by angells punish'd be,
　　For thou art shee from whom this torment is.[19]

---

[18] *Poems*, p. 32. See Ralegh's other prefatory sonnet (p. 31) to *The Faerie Queene* for further proof of his artistry in turning a twofold compliment to his friend and his sovereign.

[19] *Diana: The Sonnets and Other Poems of Henry Constable*, ed. W. C. Hazlitt, 1859, p. 32. Two other sonnets to Elizabeth (pp. 31–33) show farfetched, yet

Other sonnets were addressed to the queen,[20] but perhaps those that I have quoted will show fairly how the
conventional conceits were adapted to praise her. If sonneteers were often dazzled by the magnificence of the
sovereign, they were constantly charmed by the beauty
and accomplishments of the lady. In 1579 the author of
The Arte of English Poesie as a new year's gift offered the
queen a series of lyrics entitled *Partheniades*. The Muses
sing the glory of the queen and the beauty of the lady.
The following verses, bad though they are, anticipate
Spenser's description of Belphœbe.[21]

Parthe:7   A ryddle of the Princesse Paragon.
Euterpe

> I saw marche in a meadowe greene
> A fayrer wight then feirye Queene;
> And as I woulde approche her neere,
> Her head ys shone like Christall cleere;
> Of silver was her forehead hye,
> Her browes two bowes of Henevye;

---

typical, conceits. It is the "Queene of queenes," the "SOVEREIGNE of queenes"
— the blessed Queen of Heaven — who has the deepest allegiance of Catholic
Constable, as his sonnets to her prove. In them he begs her forgiveness if
"vayne ambition move" his "hart to seeke an earthly prynce's grace." The
conflict in loyalties to the two virgin queens is in itself significant. See above,
pp. 200 ff. Loyal Protestant poets are well represented by four songs that praise
Elizabeth in Gascoigne's *The Grief of Joye (Works,* II, 511–557).

[20] See the "Oracle from a Device made by the Earl of Essex for the Enter-
tainment of the Queen" (*Miscellanies of the Fuller Worthies' Library,* ed. A. B.
Grosart, IV (1876), 446. The courtier who wrote *The Arte of English Poesie*
illustrated his fanciest notions of figure poems with compliments to her. See
The Arte of English Poesie by George Puttenham, ed. Gladys D. Willcock and
Alice Walker, Cambridge, 1936, pp. 91 ff. Thomas Campion illustrated his
Observations in the Art of English Poesie with some lyrics to Elizabeth (*Works,*
ed. Percival Vivian, Oxford, 1909, pp. 43–44, 46, 50). His "Ad Pacem de au-
gustiss: Reg. Elizabetha" (p. 271) is notable, too. Much superior are two lyrics
which the queen heard at Elvetham in 1591: "How haps that now, when prime
is don" (Lyly, I, 443–444) and "O Come againe faire Natures treasure" (I,
451–452).

[21] See below, pp. 337–339.

Her tresses troust were to beholde,
Frizeld and fine as frenge of gold;
Her eyes, god wott what stuffe they arre,
I durst be sworne eche ys a starre:
As cleere and brighte as to guide
The pilot in his winter tide;
Twoo lippes wroughte out of rubye rocke,
Like leaues to shutt and to vnlocke,
As portall doore in princes chamber;
A golden toonge in mouth of amber,
That oft ys hard, but none yt seethe;
Without a garde of yvorye teethe,
Even arrayed, and richelye, all
In skarlett, or in fine corrall;
Her cheeke, her chinne, her neck, her nose,
This was a lillye, that was a rose;
Her hande so white as whales bone,
Her finger tipt with Cassidone;
Her bosome, sleeke as Paris plaster,
Held vpp twoo bowles of Alabaster;
Ech byas was a little cherrye,
Or as I thinke a strawberrye;
A slender greve, swifter than Roe,
A pretye foote to trippe and goe,
But of a solemne pace perdye,
And marchinge with a maiestye;
Her body shapte as strayghte as shafte,
Disclosed eche limbe with-outen craft;
Saue shadowed all, as I could gesse,
Vnder a vayle of silke Cypresse,
From toppe to toe yee mighte her see,
Timberd and tall as Cedar tree,
Whose statelye turfe exceedeth farre
All that in frithe and forrest arre.

.   .   .   .

Now reed aright, and do not mis,
What iolly dame this ladye is.

The assoile.

This fleshe and bloode, this head, members and harte,
These lively lookes, graces, and bewty sheene,
Make but one masse, by nature and by arte
Rare to the earth, rathe to the worlde seene:
Would yee faine knowe her name and see your parte?
Hye, and beholde a while the mayden Queene! [22]

Such barbarous conceits were of course authorized by the
orthodox Petrarchan tradition.

The famous auburn hair and dark eyes of Elizabeth
attracted all the stock conceits about "golden wires" and
"heavenly stars." One morning in the summer of 1591
when she was visiting Lord Montague at Cowdray, she
heard in the bower of a park a "Dittie," the first and last
stanzas of which I quote:

Behold her lockes like wiers of beaten gold,
     her eies like starres that twinkle in the skie,
Her heauenly face not framd of earthly molde,
     Her voice that sounds Apollos melodie,
The miracle of time, the ⟨whole⟩ worlds storie,
Fortunes Queen, Loues treasure, Natures glory.

.   .   .   .

Goddesse and Monarch of ⟨t⟩his happie Ile,
     vouchsafe this bow which is an huntresse part:
Your eies are arrows though they seeme to smile
     which neuer glanst but gald the stateliest hart,
Strike one, strike all, for none at all can flie,
They gaze you in the face although they die. [23]

---

[22] *Ballads from Manuscripts*, II, 77–79. All of the *Partheniades* are celebrations of the virtues of the queen and lady. Comparable to this "A ryddle of the
Princesse Paragon" is Nicholas Breton's acrostic poem on Elizabeth's name
(*Works*, I, *t*, 13) which begins "When nature fell to studie first to frame a daintie
peece." It tells of nature's lavishness in creating this paragon of princesses.
[23] Lyly, I, 423–424. Bond assigns the piece to Lyly on very slight evidence,

St. Ambrose and medieval devotees had allegorized the phœnix into a symbol of the resurrection; but a Renaissance sonneteer often compared his mistress to this glorious bird. There are countless specimens of the unique bird in Elizabethan poetry; [24] yet often the reader is assured that there is really "but one in these our daies" — the matchless Elizabeth. Loyal old Thomas Churchyard praised the royal phœnix directly in "A Few Plaine Verses of Truth Against the Flaterie of Time, Made when the Queens Majestie was last at Oxenford, 1592." His opening verses will illustrate the conceit:

Sith silent Poets all, that praise your Ladies so:
My Phenix makes their plumes to fall, that would like peacockes
    goe.
Some doe their Princes praise, and Synthia some doe like;
And some their Mistresse honour raise, as high as soldier's pike.
Come downe yee doe presmount, the warning bell it sounds,
That cals your Poets to account, for breaking of your bounds.
In giuing fame to those faire flowers that soone doth fade;
And cleane forget the white red rose, that God a Phenix made. [25]

---

as he does others which I quote from his edition. The following verses are attributed to Sir Philip Sidney (*Works*, II, 340):

Her inward worth all outward Show transcends,
Envy her Merits with Regrets Commends,
Like Sparkling Gems her Vertues draw the Sight,
And in her Conduct She is alwaies Bright;
When She imparts her thoughts her words have force,
And Sence and Wisdom flow in Sweet Discourse.

Grosart (*Complete Poems*, 1873, I, 224) has the following note on this conventional exercise of a courtier: "Found in a folio copy of Arcadia &c. at Wilton House. This Lock of Queen Elisabeth's owne Hair was presented to Sir Philip Sidney by Her Majesty's owne faire hands, on which He made these verses, and gaue them to the Queen, on his bended knee. Anno Domini 1573."

[24] See, for example, the phœnix verses the queen heard at Cowdray in 1591 (Lyly, I, 426). See, too, Petrarch, Desportes, and Ronsard, as noted by Professor Rollins in *The Phœnix Nest*, pp. ix-x, 152.

[25] Nichols, *Elizabeth*, III, 175. See Churchyard's "Verses of value, if Vertue bee seene, Made of a Phenix, a King and a Queen" that lament the flight of the

THE PHŒNIX JEWEL OF QUEEN ELIZABETH

From the original in gold and enamel in the British Museum

Incidental allusions to the queen or lady are numerous in the sonnets. They are important evidence of the way Elizabeth dominated the lyric imagination of the age. Typical is the opening quatrain of a sonnet which Barnabe Barnes addressed to Lady Bridget Manners:

> Rose of that Garland! fairest and sweetest
> Of all those sweet and fair flowers!
> Pride of chaste CYNTHIA's rich crown!
> Receive this Verse, thy matchless beauty meetest! [26]

Passing allusions drawn from sonnets or short lyrics of various types will suggest further how conscious any poet was of his first mistress:

> Toward *Auroras* Court a Nymph doth dwell,
> Rich in all beauties which mans eye can see. [27]

> These eighte now serve one noble Queene; —
> But if powre were in me,

royal phœnix from Hampton Court during the plague (Nichols, *Elizabeth*, III, 176–179). Cf. (no. 31 in *Fugitive Tracts*, first series) the same hack poet's *A handeful of gladsome verses, giuen to the Queenes Maiesty at Woodstocke this Prograce, 1592.* God "by power diuine" preserves "the *Phœnix* of our daies." He has "kept Phœnix safe and sound," and from her cage "brought her to the crowne." A devoted people "swarmes like Bees" to gaze "on *Phœnix* face" — "our faire red rose and white." This royal phœnix is again glorified in "Verse of variety to all those that honors [*sic*] the onely Phœnix of the worlde" (the same). There are many allusions to Elizabeth as a phœnix. See those in Richard Vennar's full and significant idealization, *The right way to heaven* (Nichols, *Elizabeth*, III, 532–543); in Henry Roberts's *Fames Trumpet soundinge* (no. 30 in *Fugitive Tracts*, first series); and in "An Epitaph vpon the death of Syr Edward Saunders" (*The Paradise of Dainty Devices (1576–1606)*, ed. H. E. Rollins, Cambridge, Mass., 1927, p. 104). Whatever else he intended, perhaps R. S., the compiler of *The Phœnix Nest*, did not forget that the royal phœnix could construe the name of his courtly anthology as a compliment to her and her singing court. See *The Phœnix Nest*, pp. xxxvi–xxxvii, where Sir Edmund Gosse's speculations on the anthology as a memorial to Sir Philip Sidney are presented.

[26] *Elizabethan Sonnets*, ed. Sidney Lee, 1904, I, 316.
[27] Sidney, II, 299.

For bewtise, prayse, and vertues sake,
   Eche one a *Quene* showld be.[28]

While of thy hart I was sole Soueraigne,
And thou didst sing none but MELLINAES name,
Whom for browne CLOE thou dost now disdaine,
[I] enuide not the Queene of Englands fame.[29]

But let her prayses yet be low and meane,
Fit for the handmayd of the Faery Queene.[30]

A A worthie Saint to serue a heauenly Queene,
M More faire then she that was the fame of youth,
E Except but one, the like was neuer seene.[31]

E Except but one, behold the onely ground,
L Loue such a ground, a Garden for a King:
L Looke in the world, the like is hardly found.[32]

H High of the honor of *Mineruaes* art:
E Except, excepted but one there is no more.[33]

Me thinkes I see a Queene come couered with a vaile.[34]

But for my selfe, God graunt me grace to craue,
   that he may thinke most meete for me to haue:
God saue our Queene, and God her Realme defend,
   confound her foes, and thus I make an end.[35]

---

[28] Richard Edwards, "The prayse of eight Ladyes of Queen Elizabeth's Court" (Sir John Harington, *Nugæ Antiquæ*, ed. Thomas Park, 1804, II, 394).

[29] "A Dialogue in Imitation of that betweene Horace, and Lidia" (*A Poetical Rhapsody*, I, 265).

[30] Spenser, *Amoretti*, no. 80. See *Amoretti*, no. 74, which praises the "three Elizabeths" — his mother, his queen, and his lady.

[31] Nicholas Breton, *Brittons Bowre of Delights 1591*, ed. H. E. Rollins, Cambridge, Mass., 1933, p. 17.

[32] Breton, *Works*, I, *d*, 8.

[33] The same.

[34] I, *d*, 13.

[35] Breton, *The vvorkes of a young wyt*, 1577, sig. C2ᵛ.

Oh let that Queene be truely angel-like,
  With Grace's scepter holdes the sword of peace;
And by her faith in Mercie's hande doth seeke,
  A ioyfull kingdome that shall neuer cease.[36]

And as those starres by PHOEBVS *lighte are seene,*
So, both these Earles haue honour, mighte, and power:
From PHOEBE *brighte, our moste renowmed Queene,*
Whose fame, no time, nor enuie can deuower:
  And vnder her, they showe to others lighte,
  And doe reioyce tenne thousand with their sighte.[37]

And pray the Lorde your honour to preserue,
Our noble Queene, and countrie long to serue.[38]

Yet famous *Sabrine* on thy banks doth rest
The fairest Maide that euer world admired:
Whose constant minde, with heauenly gifts possest
Makes her rare selfe of all the world desired.
  In whose chaste thoughts no vanitie doth enter;
  So pure a minde *Endymions* Love hath lent her.

Queene of my thoughts, but subiect of my verse,
(Divine *Eliza*) pardon my defect:
Whose artlesse pen so rudely doth reherse
Thy beauties worth; (for want of due respect)
  Oh pardon thou the follies of my youth;
  Pardon my faith, my loue, my zeale, my truth.

    .   .   .   .

Farre be it from my thought (diuinest Maid)
To haue relation to thy heauenly hew,
(In whose sweete voice the Muses are imbaid)
No pen can paint thy commendation due:
  Saue only that pen, which no pen can be,
  An Angels quill, to make a pen for thee.[39]

---

[36] Breton, *Works*, I, *j*, 8.

[37] Geoffrey Whitney, *A Choice of Emblemes*, ed. Henry Green, 1866, p. 106.

[38] Page 230. These verses end a concluding piece to Leicester, to whom Whitney's book was dedicated.

[39] Richard Barnfield, in "Cassandra," remembering to except Eliza when

When I did think to write of war,
And martial chiefdens of the field,
DIANA did enforce to yield
My Muse to praise the Western Star!
But PALLAS did my purpose bar,
My Muse as too weak, it to wield!

ELIZA's praises were too high!
Divinest Wits have done their best!
And yet the most have provèd least;
Such was her Sacred Majesty!
Love's Pride! Grace to Virginity!
O could my Muse, in her praise rest!

VENUS directed me to write
The praise of peerless Beauty's Wonder!
A theme more fit for voice of thunder!
PARTHENOPHE.⁴⁰

These wonders England breedes, the last remaines,
A Ladie in despite of nature chaste.
Of whome all love, in whom no love is plaste,
Where fairenesse yeelds to wisdomes shortest raines.

An humble pride, a skorne that favour staines:
A womans mould, but like an Angell graste,
An Angells mind, but in a woman caste:
A heaven on earth, or earth that heaven containes:
Now thus this wonder to myselfe I frame,
She is the cause that all the rest I am.⁴¹

Apollo would condemn the "inconstancie" of all women (*Poems*, pp. 73, 75).
Elizabeth is usually excepted whenever woman is condemned. One of numerous
examples is found in William Rankins, *The English ape, the Italian imitation,
the Footesteppes of Fraunce*, 1588, sig. Dıᵛ, after a vigorous condemnation of
English women. There she is "the Phœnix, endlesse in glory, and matchlesse in
mortall maiesty: At whose illustrate Lampe may our foolish virgins borrow oyle,
by her light direct the course of their life, thither where her name is already
eternized, to beare a light before the holy lambe." See Nashe, *Works*, I, 6.
   ⁴⁰ Barnabe Barnes, when praising Parthenophe (*An English Garner*, V
[1882], 452).
   ⁴¹ Sidney, concluding his "The 7. Wonders of England" (*Works*, II, 314).

The exhibit of such allusions might be extended far; but those that I have assembled make it clear that the royal Diana or Laura was omnipresent in the consciousness of all patriotic lyricists.

I approach now sonnets in which it is difficult to discern the exact rôle of Elizabeth. Lyrics of such courtier poets as Ralegh and Greville offer many puzzles of this sort. The vital part that the queen and lady played in Ralegh's life and poetry is best revealed by his *Cynthia*, as I shall later show.[42] Cynthia was the mistress of his imagination; and her lights and shadows fall bafflingly over more than one of his lyrics.[43] But to seek Cynthia in some of Ralegh's lyrics is to meet ambiguities that are abundantly illustrated by Fulke Greville's loose sequence of one hundred and ten short lyrics which he called *Caelica*. The "first

---

[42] See below, pp. 304 ff.

[43] See, especially, the verses beginning "Wrong not, deare Empresse of my Heart" (*Poems*, ed. Latham, pp. 104–105). I align this lyric with those that may be read as celebrating the conventional mistress or the queen even though in two manuscripts it appears as to Elizabeth. For a discussion of the poem, versions and attributions, see Miss Latham, *Poems*, pp. 187–190. Miss Latham (pp. 184–186) attributes to Ralegh the familiar "As You Came From the Holy Land," and observes with justice, I think, that "the theme of a lover deserted by his queenly mistress is like an echo of *Cynthia*." It well represents the puzzle of verse that may or may not shadow Elizabeth.

In *The Phœnix Nest* of 1593 (ed. Rollins, pp. 76–77) there appeared a Shakespearean sonnet beginning "Those eies which set my fancie on a fire" which Professor Rollins (p. 166) suggests may possibly praise Elizabeth. The piece, as he (pp. 182–183) notes, bears a close resemblance to another poem in *The Phœnix Nest* (pp. 82–83), "Those eies that holds the hand of euery hart," which also appeared with variants "in *Brittons Bowre of Delights*, 1591, C1ᵛ–C2, and again . . . in *The Arbor of amorous Deuises* (1594?, 1597, F1ᵛ–F2), two poetical miscellanies published under Breton's name by Richard Jones." The authors of these exercises would have hesitated to announce that any lady other than the royal Laura was the inspiration of such praise.

In "The Chesse Play" (*The Phœnix Nest*, pp. 36–38) occurs the command, "Loose not the *Queene*." Mr. Rollins (p. 144) writes: "The italics in *Queene* indicate that (as Park, editing *The Phœnix Nest*, p. 151, suggested) this is 'a delicate compliment to Q. Elizabeth.'" But Mr. Rollins notes passages in *Ludus Scacchiæ* which make it unnecessary so to construe the reference.

eighty express the love of the poet for a mistress whom he calls Caelica, Myra, or Cynthia, as his fancy directs." [44] Students have interpreted the sonnets very differently.[45] Tempting though it may be to say that "internal evidence strongly points to the fact that these poems afford one more proof of the power of Elizabeth," [46] it may be wise to follow a recent critic who writes:

The love-poems of the collection are exercises in the convention which flooded the later years of Elizabeth with sonnets to imaginary mistresses who all derived their existence ultimately from Petrarch's Laura. Whatever part personal experience may have played in giving an air of verisimilitude to the poet's fancies, there is no reason to suppose that Caelica or Myra stands for any real person; in fact, the only person certainly celebrated in the book is Queen Elizabeth, who is the subject of the eighty-second and probably of the third and seventeenth poems.[47]

The eighty-second sonnet is as follows:

> Vnder a throne I saw a virgin sit,
> The red and white rose quarter'd in her face;
> Starre of the North! and for true guards to it,
> Princes, Church, States, all pointing out her grace
> The homage done her was not borne of Wit;
> Wisdome admir'd, Zeale tooke ambition's place,

[44] Morris W. Croll, *The Works of Fulke Greville*, Philadelphia, 1903, p. 7.

[45] Sir Sidney Lee (*The Cambridge History of English Literature*, ed. A. W. Ward and A. R. Waller, Cambridge, III [1909], 267) found in *Caelica* no "sign of real passion," and thought Greville's Caelica and Myra mere "poetic figments of his brain." Contrast A. B. Grosart's effusions (*The Works in Verse and Prose Complete of the Right Honourable Fulke Greville, Lord Brooke*, 1870, I, xliii–xliv) about a "heart fired electrically with a real flesh-and-blood passion," "lips that had snatched burning kisses burningly," "truly pathetic love-verses" that are "plainly autobiographic."

[46] Professor Hugh de Sélincourt, in *The Cambridge History*, IV (1909), 160.

[47] The "Reviewer," "Fulke Greville, Lord Brooke" (*The [London] Times Literary Supplement*, August 30, 1928, p. 609). See Croll, p. 20. The late Professor Émile Legouis (*A History of English Literature*, p. 299) presented Greville as "a great admirer of Elizabeth, whose royal greatness he celebrated and whose personal praises he sang in his *Cælica.*"

State in her eyes taught Order how to fit,
And fixe Confusion's vnobseruing race.
Fortune can here claime nothing truly great,
But that this princely creature is her seat.[48]

But the other sonnets to Cynthia,[49] and those to Myra,
Myraphill, and Caelica, are more obviously "exercises in
the convention" than anything else. The significant point
is that such exercises by Greville and all courtly sonneteers
can often be read as actually descriptive of the recognized
character of the queen and woman more than of the
nature of any other living lady. The very first sonnet in
Greville's sequence is proof of this fact:

Loue, the delight of all well-thinking minds;
Delight, the fruit of vertue dearely lov'd;
Vertue, the highest good, that Reason finds;
Reason, the fire wherein men's thoughts bee prov'd;
    Are from the world by Nature's power bereft,
    And in one creature, for her glory, left.

Beautie, her couer is, the eyes' true pleasure;
In Honour's fame she liues; the eares' sweet musicke;
Excesse of wonder growes from her true measure;
Her worth is Passion's wound, and Passion's physicke;
    From her true heart, cleare springs of wisdome flow,
    Which imag'd in her words and deeds, men know.

Time faine would stay, that she might never leave her;
Place doth reioyce, that she must needs containe her;
Death craues of Heauen, that she may not bereaue her;
The heauens know their owne, and doe maintaine her;
    Delight, Loue, Reason, Vertue let it be,
    To set all women light, but only she.[50]

---

[48] *Works*, ed. Grosart, III, 103. The two sonnets which immediately precede
this one appear to be compliments to the virgin's government, especially by dint
of their position. My study of Elizabeth idealized as Cynthia (chapter vii,
below) gives a base for finding praise of Elizabeth in Greville's seventeenth
sonnet (III, 23–24), addressed to Cynthia.

[49] Nos. 46, 52, 53, 55, and 56.   [50] *Works*, III, 9–10.

All of the stock compliments to the mistress's hair and eyes, to her immutable and matchless worth, to her unfading beauty, to her command over all hearts and power over all lives — these and many others of old ancestry and new popularity were peculiarly fit in songs to "the coomlyest Queene that ever was." Greville lauds his ladies with them; his use of them to praise the actual royal lady in the midst of his "exercises" underscores the point, even if one hesitates to read the whole of *Caelica* as merely "one more proof of the power of Elizabeth."

Recalling some typical praise of the mistress by other sonneteers and carrying in mind the achievements and attributes and position of Elizabeth, one will be struck by the amusing ambiguity of many typical conceits that describe the royal Laura more faithfully than they do any actual mistress. It will appear inevitable that patriotic English sonneteers should exhaust on her their stock in trade in conceits.

> Consent to do true homage to your Queen!
> Lovely, fair, gentle, wise, virtuous, sober, sweet! [51]

> Sweet sovereign! since so many minds remain
> Obedient subjects at thy beauty's call!
> So many hearts bound in thy hairs as thrall!
> So many eyes die with one look's disdain!
> Go, seek the honour that doth thee pertain! [52]

> Mirror of Beauty! Nature's fairest Child!
> Empress of Love! my heart's high-prizèd jewel! [53]

> As burnished gold, such are my Sovereign's Hairs;
> A brace of stars divine, her blackish Eyes. [54]

---

[51] Bartholomew Griffin, Sonnet 31 of *Fidessa* (*An English Garner*, V, 606).
[52] Henry Constable, Sonnet 2 of Decade IV of *Diana* (*Elizabethan Sonnets*, II, 91).
[53] R. L[inche?], Sonnet 6 of *Diella* (*Elizabethan Sonnets*, II, 304).
[54] Robert Tofte, Sonnet 29 of Part I of *Laura* (*Elizabethan Sonnets*, II, 373).

Oh she is the heavnelie[st] Quene
That the worlde hathe euer seene.
Quene of suche powre
As sweeteth euery sowre;
Heavnelie perfeccon,
All perfect loves dyrection.[55]

Faire, fairer then the fairest!
   Oh hart how thow dispairest!
Yitt beawtie is not pitiles
   And therefore be not comfortles.

Oh eies that starres resemble!
   Oh sences, howe ye tremble!
Yitt neuer feare your blindnes,
   They are but lightes of kindnes.

Oh face of heavnely feature!
   Oh dye not wretched creature!
The comfort neuer dyeth
   That in her favor lyeth.

Oh gracious heavnely goddesse!
   Evne of thy heavnely goodnesse
Cast one good looke vppon me,
   That am thus wo begoñ me.

That I may saie and vowe itt,
   And reason may allow itt;
If anie helpe the helpeles
   It is mine only Princesse.[56]

"But if thou Love wilt paint with greatest skill;
A Love, a Maid, a goddess, and a Queen!
Wonder and view at Licia's picture still!
For other Love, the World hath never seen.
   For She alone, all hope, all comfort, gives:
   Men's hearts, souls all, led by her favour, live." [57]

---

[55] Breton, *Works*, I, *t*, 14.   [56] I, *t*, 16.
[57] Giles Fletcher, Sonnet 10 of *Licia* (*Elizabethan Sonnets*, II, 39).

She is the onely saint on earth, whom God and man doth
   loue.
Let this in summe suffice for my poore Muse and mee,
   She is the Goddesse of the earth, and there is none but
    she.[58]

The moning lines which weeping *I* haue written,
And writing red vnto my ruthfull sheepe,
And reading sent with teares that neuer fitten,
To my loues Queene, that hath my heart in keepe:
   Haue made my Lambkins, lay them downe and sigh:
But *Phillis* sittes, and reades, and cals them trifles:
Oh heauens why clime not happie lines so high,
To rent that ruthlesse heart, that all hearts rifles?
   None wrightes with truer faith, or greater loue,
   Yet out alas I haue no power to moue.

.   .   .   .

Since she who holdes my heart, and me in durance,
   Hath life, death, loue and all in hir procureance.[59]

My Cynthia hath the waters of mine eyes,
   The ready handmaids on her Grace attending,
   That never fall to ebb, nor ever die;
For to their flow she never grants an ending.
   The Ocean never doth attend more duly
Upon his sovereign, the night wand'ring Queen;
Nor ever hath his import paid more truly,
Than mine, to my soul's Queen hath ever been.
   Yet her hard rock, firm fixt for aye removing,
No comfort to my cares she ever giveth:
Yet had I rather languish in her loving,
Than to embrace the fairest she that liveth.
   I fear to find such pleasure in my reigning;
   As now I taste in compass of complaining.[60]

---

[58] Breton, *Works*, I, d, 15. The verses are the conclusion of "In the praise of
his Mistresse."
[59] Thomas Lodge, Sonnets 4 and 6 of *Phillis*, 1590 (pp. 10, 12, *Works*, vol. II).
[60] *Elizabethan Sonnets*, I, 95. This is one of the Daniel sonnets first printed
with *Astrophel and Stella* in 1591.

Sought by the world, and hath the world disdain'd,
Is she, my hart, for whom thou doost endure,
Vnto whose grace, sith Kings haue not obtaind,
Sweete is thy choise, though losse of life be sowre:
> Yet to the man, whose youth such pains must proue,
> No better end, than that which comes by Loue.

. . . .

Where many a Prince had perished before.[61]

But there are countless examples of such verse. The appropriateness that all such conceits would have if they did really celebrate the royal Laura is worth emphasis.

It is time to inquire into the genesis of the concept of this Laura, of the queen and lady as the popular sonnet mistress *par excellence.*

In their beautiful and complete mythology the ancients had acknowledged that human love may ultimately transcend the objects which evoke it. After a long age in which the spirit fell so in love with the Christian transcendence of this vain world that it disowned its fated home, it began to claim its full pagan heritage. Even so, it could not escape the imprint of medieval denials. The return bred many paradoxical loyalties, and only a profound upwelling of vital energy from beneath could have sustained simultaneous allegiance to the Virgin and to Venus in the Renaissance heart. Italians who read Plato and Plotinus with Christian eyes developed an oddly sensuous idealism, impact of the most spiritual pagan rationale of love upon the ascetic medieval soul, now wide awake to the disturbing presence of the natural world in its perennial beauty. Much French and English poetry of the sixteenth century is akin to Italian poetry in which the lady becomes, paradoxically enough, a refraction, now of Venus, now of Diana, and, for the most vaulting minds,

[61] *The Phœnix Nest*, p. 79.

an embodiment of the idea of the beautiful and the good. Elizabethan Englishmen had drunk a full cup of such Italian wine. Their reach after perfection of one sort or another is evident in minds as diverse as Marlowe's and Bacon's. Unless the best of all such love trope as I have been illustrating is seen as the quest of the spirit for the ideal, its true worth as poetry or as thought will go uncomprehended. But if such poetry is so viewed, the conventional and imitative nature of most of it will be distinct proof of the common spiritual quality in it all. The glorification of Elizabeth by her poets as the archetype of the good and beautiful in sovereignty and womanhood will appear as another, and a notable, effort of the human spirit to tell of the best that earth can reveal to it.

When one studies the idealization of Elizabeth as a part of the sonnet vogue in England, the question of the sincerity of conventionalized sonnets at once arises. It is hardly more reasonable to protest that the sonneteer's mistress was not real (not that it is sensible to identify her with some particular female creature), or to protest that Elizabeth was not Gloriana, Cynthia, and Astræa to her poets, than it is to insist that any Jack's Jill is not actually Venus — at least to Jack. If Venus or Gloriana is to be truly known, her being must be accepted at least for the lover's and the poet's eyes. The family quarrel of facts with fancies once pacified by reason, the understanding sympathy may begin to behold those ladies in their pristine beauty. The elaborate conceits in the sonnets do become insufferably stale and tedious in the hands of many servile imitators of Dante and Petrarch; but that fact is nothing against their worth if the genius of a Shakespeare orders the old, old words once more into the magic alignment of great poetry. All formal conventions have their taproots deep in the human mind; they need not die unless the emotions sustaining them fade or change. The tedious, stale, and forced diction of the sonnet can renew its poetic life at any moment — as in Ralegh's first sonnet on *The Faerie Queene*. Certainly one must grant as much potential sincerity to the elaborate conceits used in praising the queen and lady as is granted to the same conceits which celebrate "Delia," "Diana," and the numerous others. Sincerity in poetry comes by a masterly use of the old forms more often than by mere invention of new ones.

The sonnet vogue in England has striking relations to the actual lady and queen and to her court. How adequately Elizabeth embodied the "lady sovereign" of chivalric romance has been seen. The attributes of the royal Emilia are absorbed in the character of the royal Laura, just as the sonnet mistress was the immediate heir of the lady of courtly love. Yet Elizabeth's appearance and character as a Petrarchan sonnet mistress deserve special attention. Whatever one may now think of her looks, her courtiers found beauty in her according to their tastes, if many testimonies are to be trusted. Today one too often thinks of the withered old queen and forgets the accomplished young queen. Sir Robert Naunton's and Sir John Hayward's descriptions should stand beside Hentzner's famous portrait. Hayward writes:

Shee was a Lady, upon whom nature had bestowed, and well placed, many of her fayrest favores; of stature meane, slender, streight, and amiably composed; of such state in her carriage, as every motione of her seemed to beare majesty: her haire was inclined to pale yellow, her foreheade large and faire, a seemeing sete for princely grace; her eyes lively and sweete, but shortsighted; her nose somewhat rising in the middest; the whole compasse of her countenance somewhat long, but yet of admirable beauty, not so much in that which is tearmed the flower of youth, as in a most delightfull compositione of majesty and modesty in equall mixture.[62]

[62] *Annals of the First Four Years of the Reign of Queen Elizabeth*, ed. John

Even Hentzner's description in 1598 convinces one of her brilliance toward the end of the reign if not of her beauty; for Elizabeth was dazzling to the end. Renaissance taste, which often identified brilliance with beauty, idolized the bejeweled queen who shone with sunset glory after the Armada. Jewels, feathers, and fine fabrics came increasingly to her aid as her early good looks went the way of all beauty, regal or not. Her having a magnificent wardrobe and yet strictly regulating rich dress in others has often been wrongly dismissed as mere feminine vanity and jealousy. Of course she loved her finery, but she regarded her splendor as England's, and so did most of her subjects. When Bacon said that Elizabeth aimed to have the glitter of her jewels attract attention from the decay of her person he was divining the wise policy of a queen whose motto was *Semper Eadem*. Her carefully buttressed power was jeopardized when subjects affected more finery than became their states.[63] She was an expert in arranging all the fresh young beauties at court as background for herself; she was positive that they would best set off the royal virgin rose if they were not too intimate with the bachelor's buttons in the court garden. In seeing Helen's beauty in the Tudor brow, patriotic English sonneteers, who were certainly much in love with feminine beauty and queenly nobility, were no exception to Theseus's description of the lover.

I noted how the queen's hair fortunately matched the

Bruce, 1840, p. 7. See Naunton, *Fragmenta Regalia*, especially p. 4; and W. B. Rye, *England as Seen by Foreigners*, 1865, pp. 104–107, for Hentzner's description. The beautiful portrait of Elizabeth as a princess, now at Windsor Castle, reveals charm in the young woman.

[63] If she rebuked their excess by proclamations against inordinate apparel, she was following Castiglione's advice (*The Book of the Courtier*, Everyman's Library ed., [1928], p. 293): "Therefore it is reason that the Prince set a stint to the over sumptuous buildinges of private men, banquetings, unmeasurable dowries of women, their riotous excesse, their pompe in jewels and apparell, which is

hair of the conventional sonnet mistress.[64] Elizabeth's talents in the arts, her wit, and her unique position at court also made her an embodiment of the sonnet mistress supreme. Many testimonies to her accomplishments as a linguist culminate perhaps in the Gentleman Usher's speech before her at Theobalds in 1591. He declared that she spoke and understood "all the languages in the world which are worthy to be spoken or understood." [65] She

---

nothing els but a token of their follie." It is surprising how fully Elizabeth, both in her accomplishments and in her policies, met Castiglione's standards for the ideal prince.

[64] It would of course be absurd to assert that sonneteers carefully chose blonde heads to idealize. Yet it is perhaps worth remembering that if, as was often the case, they were celebrating their ideal, her hair was almost always like that of their royal mistress. It is at least amusing to note that the abused lady of Shakespeare's sonnets is "dark," but that the bride of Spenser's *Epithalamium* is described (ll. 154, 158) as follows:

> Her long loose yellow locks lyke golden wyre,
>
> . . . . '. .
>
> Seeme lyke some mayden queene.

See *Amoretti*, no. 37. Elizabeth's notorious red wig to which the years drove her may as well have been the inspiration of some of the countless "golden wyres" of her poets as any one lady's hair, even though Elizabeth's "wyres," ironically enough, were not her own. No actual lady's head of hair need limit a poet's fancy, but the chances are that had the queen's — God-given or man-made — been like the raven's wing there would have been less praise of golden locks by tactful sonneteers.

[65] Nichols, *Elizabeth*, III, 77. Tributes to the queen's learning are so numerous and laudatory that one is inclined to take the declaration at Theobalds as expressive of the contemporary English view — if not of the truth. There is representative praise of Elizabeth the linguist in John Florio, *A worlde of Wordes*, 1598, sig. b1[v]; and in John Eliot's *Ortho-epia Gallica*, 1593, sigs. K4[v]-L2[v]. This second work, parallel French and English dialogue designed to aid the traveler, declares that no tongue can adequately set forth the praises of a queen who "*in liberalitie, magnificence, clemencie, wisedome, mercie, beautie, nobilitie, knowledge, courtesie and sagesse*" is the "*onely Phœnix of the world.*" The question, "*Doth her maiestie speake many languages?*" is answered, "*She speaketh eight at the least: to wit: the Greeke tongue, the Latine, Italian, French, Spanish, Scottish, Flemmish, and English.*" Powerless to praise her other virtues, Eliot quotes verses by Saluste du Bartas lauding this "claire perle du Nort." See *Babilon, a part of the seconde weeke of Guillaume de Saluste Seigneur du Bartas, . . . Englished by*

was William Byrd's most distinguished student of the virginals, and her fondness for the instrument set an example for a great age in English music. She was proud of her skill, and when the Duke of Wirtemberg had an audience on August 18, 1592, she was so far prevailed upon "that she played very sweetly and skilfully on her instrument, the strings of which were of gold and silver." [66] "*Queen Elizabeth was not only a Lover of this Divine Science, but a good proficient herein . . . she did often recreate her self on an excellent Instrument call'd the* Polyphant, *not much unlike a* Lute, *but strung with Wire.*" [67] Her private patronage of the Chapel Royal does not illustrate her notorious parsimony.[68] One report even has it that "in the hour of her departure, [she] ordered her musicians into her chamber, and died hearing them." [69]

Elizabeth loved the dance. On June 4, 1565, Adam Zwetkovich wrote to the Emperor Maximilian: "I had also seen her dancing in her apartments, some Italian dances, half Pavane and half Galliard, and she also played very beautifully upon the clavichord and the lute." [70] On December 22, 1589, John Stanhope wrote from Richmond to Lord Talbot: "My Lo. the Q. is so well as I assure you six or seven gallyards in a mornynge, besydes musycke

---

William L'Isle, 1596, sigs. A2ᵛ–A4, H3–H3ᵛ, I4ᵛ. What Roger Ascham wrote of his royal pupil to Sturm when she was but a young princess is high praise from a sober scholar even in a century distinguished by learned noblewomen. See *The Whole Works of Roger Ascham*, ed. J. A. Giles, I (1865), lxii–lxiv, 191–192.

[66] Rye, p. 12.

[67] John Playford, *An Introduction to the Skill of Musick*, 19th ed., 1730, sig. A7ᵛ.

[68] See Nichols, *Elizabeth*, I, 487 n.

[69] Sir John Hawkins, *A General History of the Science and Practice of Music*, 1776, V, 201. The queen's taste for music (see Nichols, *Elizabeth*, I, 293, 487 n., 529) may have encouraged Spooner, Churchyard, and others to defend early in the reign music as a proper subject for young ladies to study.

[70] *Queen Elizabeth and Some Foreigners*, p. 228.

and syngynge, is her ordinary exercyse." [71] This "half Italian" [72] lady was yet a "mere English" queen who enjoyed jolly English country dances,[73] and they entertained her both at court and on her progresses. In 1571 she danced to prove her leg good enough for young Anjou.[74] In her sixty-seventh year she attended the nuptials of Lord Herbert at Blackfriars. "After Supper the Maske came in, . . . Mrs. *Fitton* leade, . . . Mrs. *Fitton* went to the Queen, and woed her to dawnce; her Majestie asked what she was; *Affection*, she said. *Affection!* said the Queen, *Affection* is false. Yet her Majestie rose and dawnced." [75] In the spring of 1602 she danced with the Duke of Nevers; on May Day she "went *a-maying*, to Sir Richard Buckley's at Lewisham, some three or four miles off Greenwich." [76]

This beautiful and learned princess was not only a musician and dancer; she was also a court poet *à la mode*. The courtly author of *The Arte of English Poesie* (1589) concludes his discourse "Of Poets and Poesie" with the

[71] Nichols, *Elizabeth*, III, 32.

[72] When a German envoy tactfully told the queen that his countrymen held with the Italians in manners, the royal Laura declared: "'That pleases me, . . . for I like the manners and customs of the Italians better than those of all the rest of the world, and I am, as it were, half Italian'" (*Queen Elizabeth and Some Foreigners*, p. 195).

[73] Nichols, *Elizabeth*, III, 597.

[74] A mean report was spread in France that Elizabeth's royal French suitor would do well to marry an old creature who had the evil in her leg, and who could quickly be made away with. To La Mothe Fénélon she declared in anger "que, nonobstant le mauvais raport qu'on avoit faict de sa jambe, elle n'avoit layssé de baller le dimanche précédant aulx nopces du marquis de Norampton, et qu'elle espéroit que Monsieur ne se trouveroit si trompé que d'avoir espousé une boyteuse au lieu d'une droicte, avec d'aultres bien gracieux deviz" (*Correspondance Diplomatique de Bertrand de Salignac de la Mothe Fénélon*, Paris, IV [1840], 94).

[75] *Letters and Memorials of State* (Sydney Papers), ed. Arthur Collins, 1746, II, 203. Sir John Davies's *Orchestra or a poeme on dauncing* (1596, although entered June 25, 1594) contains passages that make the poem seem designed to compliment the English queen of the dance. See *Poems*, I, 209, especially.

[76] Nichols, *Elizabeth*, III, 577.

following tribute, which, for all its flattery, is worth
quoting:

But last in recitall and first in degree is the Queene our soueraigne Lady, whose learned, delicate, noble Muse, easily sur-
mounteth all the rest that haue writtē before her time or since,
for sence, sweetnesse and subtillitie, be it in Ode, Elegie, Epi-
gram, or any other kinde of poeme Heroick or Lyricke, wherein
it shall please her Maiestie to employ her penne, euen by as
much oddes as her owne excellent estate and degree exceedeth
all the rest of her most humble vassalls.[77]

From her most sensational love affair "the Queene our
soueraigne Lady" gleaned the following poetic harvest:

> I greefe & dare not shewe my discontent
> I love & yet am forced to seeme to hate
> I doe, yet dare not say, I ever meant
> I seeme starke mute but inwardly doe prate
>   I am and not, I freese & yet am burnd
>   Since from my self, my other self I turnd.

> My Care is like my shaddowe in the Sune
> followes one fliinge, flies when I pursue it.
> Standes & lies by me doth what I have don
> His too familiar care doth make me rue it
>   Noe meanes I finde to rid him from my brest
>   Till by the end of thinges it be supprest

> Some gentler passions slide into my minde
> ffor I am softe & made of meltinge snowe
> or be more cruell love & soe be kynd
> Let mee or flote or sinke be high or lowe

---

[77] *The Arte of English Poesie,* p. 63. See Francis Meres in *Palladis Tamia*
(*Elizabethan Critical Essays,* II, 321). The printer of *The Arte of English Poesie,*
Richard Field, declared in his dedication to Lord Burghley that "*many expresse
passages in the same at large*" made him conclude "*that it was by the Authour
intended to our Soueraigne Lady the Queene, and for her recreation and seruice
chiefly deuised*" (p. 2). The work is full of such evidence. See below, pp. 449–450.
The author, whose identity has been in dispute, was most certainly a great
admirer of the queen.

or let me live w^t some more sweete Content.
or dye & soe forget what love ere meant.
F i n i s.
Eliza: Regina vpon mounzeurs departure.[78]

One may wonder where the "learned, delicate, noble Muse" was hiding when this lament was perpetrated. But it was authorized by Petrarch's Sonnet 102; Sir Thomas Wyatt had translated Petrarch; and Elizabeth was not the only other poet to echo it thereafter.[79] It was quite at home among the "pretie amourets in Court to entertaine their seruants and the time withall, their delicate wits requiring some commendable exercise to keepe them from idlenesse." [80]

It is, then, small wonder that this royal lady of many charms, talents, and achievements was idealized into the queen of English Lauras. The "coomlyest Queene that ever was" came close to embodying the complete sonnet mistress, supreme

> For glory, pleasure, and fair flourishing;
> Sweet singing, courtly dancing, curious love,
> A rich remembrance; virtue's nourishing;
> For sacred care of heavenly things;
> For voice's sweetness, music's notes above;
> When she divinely speaks or sings.[81]

---

[78] Printed as "Liebesklage" by Ewald Flügel in "Die Gedichte der Königin Elisabeth" (*Anglia*, XIV [1891–1892], 360). Flügel writes: "Die überschrift im Tanner Ms. lautet: 'relative to her passion for the Earl of Essex'; wir wollen hoffen, dass das Tanner Ms. recht hat, denn dem 'frosch' von Anjou sind die worte nicht zu gönnen, ebenso wenig wie der historische kuss (Froude ii, 205)." Equally in the mode was this royal Sappho's familiar love lament with the refrain "Importune me no more" (pp. 356–357). The verses which Flügel collected show that Elizabeth was a poetaster with wit enough to please the fancy of her age in more than one style of verse.

[79] See Sonnet 31 of *Parthenophil and Parthenophe* (*An English Garner*, V, 356). [80] *The Arte of English Poesie*, p. 91.

[81] Parthenophe is thus described in the first verses of Barnabe Barnes's

In very truth an unattainable lady for any poet; the actual royal mistress of every Englishman; perpetual "about-to-be-won" bride who favored handsome courtiers to the end of her days, yet remained "in earth the first . . . Maid" — she cast a spell over the lyric imagination. A sonneteer found it just a turn in sentiment, and hardly that in vocabulary, from celebrating the mistress of his heart, actual or ideal, to celebrating the mistress of his England, especially since England's Laura, as I have shown, had mastered the art of arousing all the latent chivalry in her noblemen, and of inspiring endless devotion. Such a transition is very apparent in Constable's *Diana*. "Diana," the name, might even be taken as a twofold compliment to his personal and to his royal "mistress"; "my divinitye," "miracle of the world," "servant," "tyrant," "favor," "grace," "Queen of my affections," and numerous other epithets were interchangeable terms. Every poem hymning the glory of "chastitee," no matter to whom addressed, was necessarily a compliment to the paragon of English virgins.[82] Courtier poets were surely not unconscious of the fortunate ambiguity of the sonnet language. Elizabeth's swift wits hardly missed it. In the new stream of sonnet literature that, fed by various ancient and medieval springs, eddies and flows around the queen and lady, the figures of many goddesses and heroines are reflected and blended with the image of Elizabeth. It is for such reasons as these that one may find any number of lyrics which would be very appropriate celebrations of this royal Laura — were they not celebrations either of some personal mistress or of no mortal in particular.

"Madrigal 9" (*An English Garner*, V, 369). Elizabeth's spell is felt in "What causes mooved so many forreigne Princes to bee sutours to her Maiestie for mariage, and what by coniecture hath hitherto mooved her to refuse them all" ("Parthe: 12," in *Ballads from Manuscripts*, II, 83).

[82] See above, pp. 159–160, where I have discussed "The Sheepheardes praise of his sacred Diana."

Such sonnets to the unknown Caelica — to the ideal lady who, as shown, resembles the actual queen more than any other creature — are one reason for viewing the entire courtly idealization of Elizabeth as an instance of Renaissance Platonizing. Colin's love of Elisa early inspired a rhapsodic hymn to the idea of perfect queen and lady.[83] The graceful music of Sir John Davies's *Hymnes of Astræa* (1599) is often suggestive of the song which poets from Dante down had raised to honor the idea of the perfect lady which they thought they saw more or less incarnate in some individual. Illustrations will show that the whole burden of the *Hymnes* is the beauty of the royal Idea.

HYMNE VII.

To the Rose.

E ye of the Garden, Queene of flowres,
L ove's cup wherein he nectar powres,
I ngendered first of nectar;
S weet nurse-child of the Spring's young howres,
A nd Beautie's faire character.

B est iewell that the Earth doth weare,
E uen when the braue young sunne draws neare,
T o her hot Loue pretending;
H imselfe likewise like forme doth beare,
A t rising and descending.

R ose of the Queene of Loue belou'd;
E ngland's great Kings diuinely mou'd,
G aue Roses in their banner;
I t shewed that Beautie's Rose indeed,
N ow in this age should them succeed,
A nd raigne in most sweet manner.

---

[83] See above, pp. 130–132.

HYMNE XIII.

Of her Minde.

E arth, now adiew, my rauisht thought
L ifted to Heau'n sets thee at nought;
I nfinite is my longing,
S ecrets of angels to be taught,
A nd things to Heau'n belonging.

B rought downe from heau'n of angels kind,
E uen now doe I admire her *mind*;
T his is my contemplation,
H er cleare sweet spirit, which is refin'd
A boue humane *creation*.

R ich sun-beame of th' Æternall light,
E xcellent *Soule*, how shall I wright?
G ood angels make me able;
I cannot see but by your eye,
N or, but by your tongue, signifie
A thing so admirable.

HYMNE XIIII.

Of the Sun-beames of her Mind.

E xceeding glorious is the starre,
L et vs behold her beames afarre
I n a side line reflected;
S ight bears them not, when neere they are,
A nd in right lines directed.

B ehold her in her vertues' beames,
E xtending sun-like to all realmes;
T he sunne none viewes too neerly:
H er well of goodness in these streames,
A ppeares right well and clearely.

R adiant vertues, if your light
E nfeeble the best iudgement's sight,
G reat splendor aboue measure

I s in the *mind* from whence you flow;
N o wit may haue accesse to know,
A nd view so bright a treasure.[84]

To Idea Fulke Greville most probably addressed the
third sonnet of *Caelica*:

More than most faire, full of that heauenly fire,
Kindled aboue to shew the Maker's glory;
Beautie's first-born, in whom all powers conspire
To write the Graces life and Muses storie:
    If in my heart all saints else be defaced,
    Honour the shrine, where you alone are placed.

Thou window of the skie, and pride of spirits,
True character of Honour in perfection;
Thou heauenly creature, iudge of earthly merits,
Thou glorious prison of man's pure affection;
    If in my heart all nymphs else be defaced,
    Honour the shrine, where you alone are placed.[85]

Idea is a most appropriate name for what courtly poets
like Sir John Davies, Fulke Greville, and Spenser made of
Elizabeth. Sensuous or sentimental love of some particular individual may pass into a celebration of the loveliness of the lady, and thence to reverential adoration of
the beautiful and the good seen in the lady as through a
glass not too darkly. Whatever be its date, that verse is
essentially Platonic in which love of the ideal and contemplation of the eternal overshadows personal passion.
However Ovidian courtly love was at bottom, its lady did
often lead the troubadour into the kingdom of ideal beauty.

[84] *Poems*, I, 135, 141, 142. The titles of some others of the twenty-six
"hymnes" will suggest how completely Elizabeth seemed to embody the idea
of the perfect queen and lady: "Of her Wit," "Of her Will," "Of her Memorie,"
"Of her Phantasie," "Of the Organs of her Minde," "Of the Passions of her
Heart," "Of the Innumerable Vertues of her Minde," "Of her Wisdome," "Of
her Justice," "Of her Magnanimitie," "Of her Moderation."
[85] *Works*, III, 11.

In Tuscany her influence flowered in Dante's Beatrice. Beatrice Portinari became for Dante the symbol of all grace and goodness in woman, a Platonic type of truth and beauty calling him to the loftiest good and highest blessedness. She appeared "as a manifestation of absolute beauty and as an avenue of divine grace. Dante merely added his humility and tenderness to the insight of the Pagan philosopher." [86] His Platonism was the "expression of his inner experience moulded by the chivalry and theology of his time." [87] Petrarch remained "lachrymose and sentimental at the end as at the beginning, and his best dream of heaven, expressed, it is true, in entrancing verse, is only to hold his lady's hand and hear her voice." [88] Yet he did repeat stock Platonic phrases which became the common property of his imitators.[89] The Italian Renaissance brought a revival of Neoplatonic thought that reached aristocratic England of the sixteenth century by various ways.[90] One need recall only a few, chiefly Castiglione's *Cortegiano*, which Sir Thomas Hoby translated in 1561, at the very outset of Elizabeth's reign. It popularized Neoplatonic conceptions of love and beauty. One may remember that Lord Julian exalts woman with Diotima as a witness of her supremacy, and be sure that his victory over Lord Gaspar was as pleasing at Elizabeth Tudor's court as at Lady Elizabeth Gonzaga's. Some of the noble English

[86] George Santayana, *Interpretations of Poetry and Religion*, New York, 1927, p. 129.

[87] Page 121.

[88] Page 130.

[89] "Platonic thought, especially as it helped them [sonneteers] to deify their mistress's beauty, make a virtue of their desire and assure eternal life at once to their verses and to the lady of their choice, made its way into all their minds" (Legouis and Cazamian, pp. 320–321).

[90] The queen herself wrote a comment on Plato. See *Queen Elizabeth's Englishings*, ed. Caroline Pemberton, Early English Text Society, 1899, for the queen's translations from Boethius, Plutarch, and Horace, and for criticism of her work.

readers of Castiglione visited Italian courts where Bembo's rhapsodies still echoed. Giordano Bruno, whose doctrines on love were Neoplatonic, came to Oxford and was warmly welcomed by Sir Philip Sidney, Fulke Greville, and their circle. Enthusiasts were, after all, reviving a fundamental base of Christian theology, Neoplatonic thought which had entered the western world in St. Augustine, Boethius, and Dionysius the Areopagite. One must remember, however, that Platonic idealism of the Renaissance inherited a chivalric exaltation of the lady and the Holy Virgin of which Plato and his early followers never dreamed. Yet Ficino's commentaries on the *Convivium* reconciled Renaissance love of beauty and medieval love of Christian virtue.

I have shown how completely the regal lady Elizabeth met Renaissance standards of beauty and virtue for the mistress of a sonneteer's fancy. How she seemed the embodiment of the full idea of perfect royal lady will appear clearly from a summary glance at her character and its fitness to evoke the eclectic Platonizing spirit with which her court was acquainted, and which I have just characterized. When a court poet, admiring the obvious beauty of the queen and lady, passes to the altar where she is the symbol of all that is beautiful and good in sovereignty and womanhood, he is best seen as praising Idea. Elizabeth was peculiarly well endowed for the rôle of Idea. Her attributes as a "lady sovereign" with a divine right to rule, her own knightly spirit, and her virginity drew all chivalric hearts to her. I have suggested how her continuous playing at love and her skill in the arts that the age admired led patriotic sonneteers to find in her all the charms of their Lauras. The royal Laura in her silks and jewels stimulated the amorous fancy of the sonneteer who usually sang in the vein of "Come live with me and be my love." Margaret of Navarre in her court at Nérac gave fashionable Renaissance Platonizing an emotional and sensuous setting that echoed Marlowe's very unplatonic song. In Sidney's *Arcadia* Zelmane pretends not to be able to imagine what Basilius's amorous words might "intend." The reply is amusingly illustrative of the Renaissance love that opposed ideal love — or begot it: "Intend? (said *Basilius*, proud that that was brought in question) what may they intend, but a refreshing of my soule, and a swaging of my heat, and enjoying those your excellencies, wherin my life is upheld, and my death threatned?" [91] Of course Laura and her poets understood as well as Zelmane the drift of such talk. But the English "sacred virgin" somehow remained not of the treacherous world of love even if always in it. A sonneteer who was inclined to distill the poetry of passion into that of reflection turned to her as the incarnation of the perfect idea of feminine majesty, beauty, and virtue. A lyric poet whose deepest devotion was to the ideal, whose imagination was still stirred by all in chivalric love that was congenial to the Christianized Platonism of the Renaissance, inevitably found his noblest Diana or Laura in the royal Idea. Any particular mistress was eclipsed by the glory of this Perfect Fair. She, more than any living thing, seemed to be a uniquely lovely copy of all the ineffable and heavenly patterns for queen and lady that a patriotic English poet of eclectic culture found adorable. He plundered ancient, medieval, and Renaissance literature for conceits and figures in which to catch reflections of her light. He needed to wait no longer

> Till that Divine
> *Idea*, [should] take a shrine
> Of Chrystall flesh, through which to shine.

This royal Idea was "that not impossible she."

[91] *Works*, I (1912), 254.

To Idea Sir John Davies dedicated the 1599 edition of the most successful philosophical poem of the reign, *Nosce Teipsum.*

TO MY MOST GRACIOVS DREAD SOVERAIGNE.

To that cleere maiestie which in the North
Doth, like another Sunne in glory rise;
Which standeth fixt, yet spreads her heauenly worth;
Loadstone to hearts, and loadstarre to all eyes.

Like Heau'n in all; like th' Earth in this alone,
   That though great States by her support doe stand,
   Yet she herselfe supported is of none,
   But by the finger of the Almightie's hand:

To the diuinest and the richest minde,
   Both by Art's purchase and by Nature's dowre,
   That euer was from Heau'n to Earth confin'd,
   To shew the vtmost of a creature's power:

To that great Spirit, which doth great kingdomes mooue,
   The sacred spring where right *and* honor *streames,*
   Distilling Vertue, *shedding* Peace *and* Loue,
   In euery place, as Cynthia *sheds her beames:*

I offer up some sparkles of that fire,
   Whereby wee reason, liue, *and moue, and be;*
   These sparkes by nature euermore aspire,
   Which makes them to so high *an* highnesse *flee.*

Faire Soule, *since to the fairest body knit,*
   You giue such liuely life, such quickning power,
   Such sweet celestiall influences to it,
   As keepes it still in youth's immortall flower:

(As where the sunne is present all the yeere,
   And neuer doth retire his golden ray,
   Needs must the Spring bee euerlasting there,
   And euery season like the month of May.)

O! many, many yeeres may you remaine,
A happy angell to this happy Land;
Long, long may you on Earth our empresse raigne,
Ere you in Heauen a glorious angell stand.

Stay long (sweet spirit) ere thou to Heauen depart,
Which mak'st each place a heauen wherein thou art.

Her Maiestie's least and vnworthiest Subiect

IOHN DAVIES.[92]

The royal Laura or Idea appeared to all English sonneteers as the archetype of the Petrarchan mistress. To
those with minds of Platonic mold she seemed a supreme
exception to the rule that the individual was at best no
more than a poor mutable copy of some full and lovely
idea. Euphues's empress was the perfect example of the
idea of woman toward which all profane mistresses might
strive but to which they could never attain. Idea was an
anointed queen and a gracious lady, *semper eadem,* who
towered in achievement and character far above all her
kind into a realm where, for robust imaginations which can
discover the ideal through the actual, the manifestation
and the idea seem at moments identical. Idea early appeared to Colin as Elisa; Cynthia was ultimately Idea for
Sir Walter Ralegh. The radiance of this "Divine Idea"
shines through the rich colors with which Spenser painted
Gloriana and Belphœbe.

[92] *Poems,* I, 9–11. There are passages in the poem (pp. 33–34, especially)
that are skilfully designed to compliment "*the diuinest and the richest minde.*"

CHAPTER VII

Cynthia, the Ladie of the Sea

In widest ocean she her throne does reare,
That over all the earth it may be seene.
                              — *The Faerie Queene* [1]

AFTER 1588 Queen Elizabeth was mistress of the seas as well as of an island. Perhaps the secret of the development of English maritime power from 1558 to 1603 is that throughout this period there was a "reasoned, coöperative effort which left no means untried" to bring sound economic health to a needy nation. Richard Hakluyt's epic may best be read as "no paean of victory but [as] a tribute to service and suffering." [2] The service of the voyagers was devoted. It was doubly so because Elizabeth happily personified their native land. For her they "labored all." As Elizabethan poets saw their domain widen to include the waves, they celebrated their queen as "Cynthia, the Ladie of the Sea."

Of course this new consciousness of empire renewed devotion to their "demi-paradise" "set in the silver sea." Songs to the "Ladie of the Sea," especially after 1588, harmonize into those to the Queene of Faery Land. Yet they have a fascinating genesis and individual beauty that may well absorb attention before it is concentrated on Gloriana.

This English Cynthia, like many concepts in Renaissance poetry, is begotten on ancient imaginative forms by

[1] II. ii. 40.
[2] See Dr. J. A. Williamson's introduction in G. B. Parks, *Richard Hakluyt and the English Voyages*, New York, 1928, p. xi.

the new energies and needs of Elizabethan Englishmen. One better appreciates her character after first looking at adaptations of native and classical water myth to compliment the queen before the great victory in 1588 gave special point to praise of her as "Cynthia, the Ladie of the Sea."

Indigenous water legend, colored by classical sea myth, was featured in devices which entertained Elizabeth when she paid her celebrated third visit to Kenilworth Castle. She arrived on July 9, 1575.

When her Majestie was entred the gate, and come into the base Court, there came unto her a Ladie attended with two Nimphes, who came all over the Poole, being so conveyed, that it seemed shee had gone upon the water. This Ladie named her selfe the Ladie of the Lake, who spake to her Highnesse as followeth,

. . . .

(most peereles Prince, the honor of your kinde)

. . . .

I am the Lady of this pleasant Lake,
who since the time of great king *Arthures* reigne
That here with royal Court aboade did make,
have led a lowring life in restles paine.
Til now that this your third arrivall here
doth cause me come abroad, and boldly thus appeare.

All the great of England since King Arthur's day have failed to call her from her waters. But now comes a greater than they, and she declares:

I wil attend while you lodge here,
(most peereles Queene) to Court to make resort,
And as my love to *Arthure* dyd appeere,
so shalt to you in earnest and in sport,

Passe on Madame, you neede no longer stand,
   the Lake, the Lodge, the Lord, are yours for to cõmande.[3]

Arthur's descendant, as all patriotic Englishmen believed
the Tudor Elizabeth to be, was thus fittingly welcomed to
Kenilworth Castle by this native water lady. When the
queen passed over a great bridge into the castle, she found
appropriate presents placed on the tops of the bridge-
posts by classical deities. The fifth pair of posts had "each
a fair large trey streawd a littl with fresh grass, and in
them, Coonger, Burt, Mullet, fresh Herring, Oisters,
Samon, Creuis, and such like, from Neptunus, God of the
Sea." [4] In fact, "thear waz no deintée that the sea coold
yéeld, but Neptune (thoough hiz reign at the néerest ly
well ny a hundred mile of) did dayly send in great plenty,
swéet and freash." [5]
    The lake about Kenilworth Castle and the gardens
joined to compliment the queen. In the center of the
"goodly Gardein" was a "very fayre Foountain" with
beautiful carvings "all heawen oout of rich & hard white
Marbl. A one syde, Neptune with his Tridental Fuskin
triumphing in hiz Throne, trayled into the déep by his
marine horsez. On another, Thetis in her chariot drawn
by her Dollphins. Then, Triton by hiz fyshez. Héer,
Protheus hearding hiz sea buls. Thear, Doris & her
dooughterz solacyng a sea & sandz. The wauez soourging
with froth & fome, entermengled in place with whalez,
whirlpoolz, sturgeonz, Tunneyz, Conchs, & wealks: all
engrauen by exquisit deuize and skill." [6] Most interesting
of the many devices designed to compliment Elizabeth in

---

[3] Gascoigne, II, 93–94. These verses were "*devised and penned by M. Ferrers,
sometime Lord of misrule in the Court.*"
    [4] *Robert Laneham's Letter: Describing a Part of the Entertainment unto Queen
Elizabeth at the Castle of Kenilworth in 1575*, ed. F. J. Furnivall, 1907, pp. 8–9.
    [5] Page 45. Cf. Neptune's gift at Norwich in 1578, above, p. 83.
    [6] Page 52.

terms of mingled water myth, native and classical, was the "deliverie of the Lady of the Lake." "*Tryton* in likenesse of a Mermaide, came towarde the Queenes Majestie as she passed over the bridge, returning from hunting." He addressed her as follows:

Muse not at all most mightie Prince,
   though on this lake you see:
Me *Triton* floate, that in salt seas,
   among the Gods should be.
For looke what *Neptune* doth commaund,
   of *Triton* is obeyde:
And nowe in charge I am to guyde,
   your poore distressed mayde.
Who when your highnesse hither came,
   dyd humbly yeeld her Lake:
And to attende upon your Court,
   did loyall promise make.
But parting hence that yrefull knight,
   syr *Bruce* had hyr in chase:
And sought by force, her virgins state,
   full fowlie to deface.
Yea, yet at hand about these bankes,
   his bands be often seene:
That neither can she come nor scape,
   but by your helpe, O Queene.
For though that *Neptune* hath so fenst,
   with floods her fortresse long.
Yet *Mars* her foe must needes prevaile,
   his battries are so strong.
Howe then can *Diane*, *Junos* force,
   and sharpe assaults abyde?
When all the crue of cheefest Gods,
   is bent on *Bruse* his side.
Yea, oracle and prophecie,
   say sure she can not stande:
Except a worthier maide than she,
   her cause do take in hand.

Loe, here therefore a worthy worke,
 most fit for you alone:
Her, to defend and set at large:
 (but you, O Queene) can none:
And Gods decree, and *Neptune* sues,
 this graunt O peereles Prince:
Your presence onely shall suffice,
 her enemies to convince.

Triton blows his "wreathed horn" and in Neptune's name commands the winds, waters, and fishes to be at bay

 Untill such time this puissaunt Prince,
  sir *Bruse* hath put to flight:
 And that the maide released be,
  by soveraigne maidens might.[7]

Of course her majesty has only to advance along the bridge to have the freed Lady of the Lake sail toward her "uppon heapes of Bulrushes" and sing her humble thanks for delivery from the cruel "tyrant *Bruce, Sans pittie*." Then comes "*Protheus* . . . sitting on a *Dolphyns* backe." He sings his "congratulation, aswell in the behalfe of the Lady distressed, as also in the behalfe of all the Nimphs and gods of the sea." [8] His "delectabl ditty" is "wel apted too a melodious noiz, compoounded of six seuerall instruments al coouert, casting soound from *the* Dolphin's belly within." [9] Master Hunnis, for he was the author of this device, "had also designed a preliminary night skirmish on the water between the Lady of the Lake's men and Sir Bruce's, all floating upon heapes of bulrushes; but this was not carried out." [10] Her majesty was then to have given formal succor to the Lady's champion so as to fulfill Merlin's prophecy that "she should never be delivered but by the presence of a better maide then her selfe." [11]

[7] Gascoigne, II, 102–104.
[8] II, 104.
[9] *Laneham's Letter*, p. 35.

[10] Page 71 (editor's note).
[11] Gascoigne, II, 106.

This association of the British Lady of the Lake and Greek water deities at Kenilworth Castle to do honor to the virgin Elizabeth is rather stiff in its effect. But it is a significant early use of native and foreign forms combined to praise a queen who is destined to become the English Cynthia.[12]

In September, 1575, Elizabeth at Woodstock heard some Latin verses by Laurence Humphrey. They show how naturally sea imagery, a virgin queen, classical mythology, and the Protestant God became associated in the mind of an English poet who rejoiced in the blessings which Elizabeth had brought to the island and sought in an heir assurance of their continuance. I quote illustrative verses:

O Deus altitonans Mundi Cœlique Monarcha,
　　Qui mare, qui terras, infera quique regis:
Prospice de cœlo, Regnum spectato Brytannum,
　　En nunc confligunt spesque metusque simul.
Quid non speremus, quid non timeamus amantes?
　　Spes, metus, huc illuc, hæc vocat, ille trahit.
Anglia cincta mari est, circumfluit undique pontus,
　　Est spes nonnullo concomitata metu.
Hactenus afflavit Zephyrus, fuit aura secunda,
　　Spes est: mox portum, qui bene solvit, habet.
At mare fluctisonum est, Syrtes, Pirata, Charybdis,
　　Saxa latent, scopulos nolle timere, furor.
Hæc, hæc vita mare est peramarum, navigat omnis,
　　Qui vivit, sperat plurima, multa timet.
Nunc mare sulcamus, mare nunc ingressa Carina est,
　　Flatibus aspires, o bone Jova, bonis.
Sis prora & puppis, nostræ sis ancora navis,
　　Et peregrinantis dirige vela ratis.

---

[12] Water carnivals complimented the queen on other progresses; at Norwich in 1578 bad weather interfered with the speeches of the water nymphs (Nichols, *Elizabeth*, II, 210).

Suffice nunc doctos qui clavum rite gubernent,
Ne ruat in tumidas naufagra puppis aquas.

. . . .

O virgo Elisabeth, Phœnix et gemma regentum,
O flos, o patrii stella decusque soli,
Heu cur non liceat semper producere filum?
Heu cur non semper vivere fata sinunt? [13]

In 1587, "John Wolf obtained a license to print 'The
Oration of Neptarne to Jupiter, in ye praise of Q. Elizabeth;' and 'A New Yeres Guifte, cõprehending apparition
against ye prognosticated daungers of the yere 1588,
cõpyled by Tho. Tymme, Minister, upon condicõn, &c.'"[14]
Clearly by this date the Greek god of the sea is recognizing
the ascendancy of Elizabeth over his domain. After she
had victoriously met the "daungers of the yere 1588"
there was no doubt as to her right to the title of "Cynthia,
the Ladie of the Sea." Before examining verse to Cynthia
one should remember the nurture which the concept of the
"Ladie of the Sea" drew from Tudor maritime expansion
that reached a climax in the Armada. Actual achievements synthesized the elements of fact and fancy which I
have illustrated into a fit symbol for the mature maritime
spirit of Elizabethan England. The English Cynthia became of age in 1588.

It is Hakluyt's *Principal Navigations*, first published in
1589, just after the great Armada triumph, that tells best
of the history and the spirit of Elizabethan voyaging.
What is Elizabeth's place in his work? Hakluyt was "one
of her majesties scholars" at Westminster when he first
dreamed of his great collection of narratives which "em-
balm and treasure up" Elizabethan voyaging. His
"Epistle Dedicatorie" to "Sir Francis Walsingham
Knight, Principall Secretarie to her Majestie," which
prefaces the first edition, has familiar sentences in which

[13] Nichols, *Elizabeth*, I, 583-584.   [14] II, 527.

there pulses the ardent patriotism that is to flow through the stories that follow. Hakluyt declares that

in this most famous and peerlesse governement of her most excellent Majesty, her subjects through the speciall assistance, and blessing of God, in searching the most opposite corners and quarters of the world, and to speake plainly, in compassing the vaste globe of the earth more then once, have excelled all the nations and people of the earth. For, which of the kings of this land before her Majesty, had theyr banners ever seene in the Caspian sea? which of them hath ever dealt with the Emperor of Persia, as her Majesty hath done, and obteined for her merchants large & loving privileges? who ever saw before this regiment, an English Ligier in the stately porch of the Grand Signor at Constantinople? who ever found English Consuls & Agents at Tripolis in Syria, at Aleppo, at Babylon, at Balsara, and which is more, who ever heard of Englishman at Goa before now? what English shippes did heeretofore ever anker in the mighty river of Plate? passe and repasse the unpassable (in former opinion) straight of Magellan, range along the coast of Chili, Peru, and all the backside of Nova Hispania, further then any Christian ever passed, travers the mighty bredth of the South sea, land upon the Luzones in despight of the enemy, enter into alliance, amity, and traffike with the princes of the Moluccaes, & the Isle of Java, double the famous Cape of Bona Speranza, arive at the Isle of Santa Helena, & last of al returne home most richly laden with the commodities of China, as the subjects of this now flourishing monarchy have done?

. . . But as the purpose of David the king to builde a house and temple to God was accepted, although Salomon performed it: so I make no question, but that the zeale in this matter of the aforesaid most renowmed prince [Henry VIII] may seeme no lesse worthy (in his kinde) of acceptation, although reserved for the person of our Salomon her gratious Majesty, whome I feare not to pronounce to have received the same Heroicall spirit, and most honorable disposition, as an inheritance from her famous father.[15]

[15] *The Principal Navigations*, I, 3–5.

Clearly in this dedication Elizabeth symbolizes the new commerce and exploration of the Tudor age. The *Navigations* opens with an account of King Arthur's voyages to establish his island kingdom. Implicitly, Hakluyt compliments Elizabeth as Arthur's descendant under whom English voyages come again to glory. All readers of his fascinating pages know how frequently the queen at home appears in the consciousness of her sailors. She does more than give important trade grants to merchants and send diplomatic letters to the monarchs of the East. She represents for the mind's eye all that is dear in the native land left behind. A glance at some of the references to her will show her place in the consciousness of seamen. Drake, on taking Nova Albion, sets up a monument with a plate carrying Elizabeth's name; and beneath the plate he puts a sixpenny piece that bears her picture and her arms.[16] Her title to "Newfound Lands" derives from Madock ap Owen Gwyneth, of the "blood royall, borne in Wales," "as appeareth in an ancient Welsh Chronicle."[17] Frobisher calls new territory "Queene Elizabeths Forland" or "Queene Elizabeths Cape."[18] His queen, who was a proud Latinist, named "Meta Incognita" herself.[19] When he landed far to the northwest on July 20, 1577, he did "chiefly thanke God for [his] safe arrival: secondly beseech him, that it would please his divine Majestie, long to continue [his] Queene, for whom he [Frobisher], and all the rest of [his] company in this order tooke possession of the Countrey."[20] He prays that the pagan natives may be reduced to the knowledge of true religion, and adds "other words very apt to signifie his willing mind, and affection toward his Prince and Countrey."[21] Her majesty's will is always to be supreme in actions at Cartagena

[16] VIII, 66–67.
[17] VI, 58.
[18] V, 195, 218.

[19] V, 229.
[20] V, 142.
[21] V, 143.

in 1585.[22] Drake on his famous voyage executes Thomas
Doughtie because of his treason to the queen, and that in
spite of a personal fondness for him; but the traitor ends
his life on the block "with prayer for the Queenes majestie
and our realme." [23] Sir Jerome Bowes, "her Majesties
ambassadour to Ivan Vasilivich the Emperour of Mus-
covia, in the yeere 1583," wins admiration and favor from
the emperor by a spirited defense of the queen's power as
equal to that of any prince, although at one moment he
had almost been thrown "out of the doores" by the Mus-
covites.[24] Elizabeth's "being but a woman" and yet very
mighty impresses the officials of Eastern cities that her
traders visit.[25] Her fame as a "mayden Queene" spreads
into Persia.[26] Some oriental flattery from "the most high
and mighty Empresse the wife of the Grand Signior Sultan
Murad Can" is interesting. She writes to "the most gracious and most glorious, the wisest among women, and
chosen among those which triumph under the standard of
Jesus Christ, the most mighty and most rich governour,
and most rare among womankinde in the world, the most
gracious Queene of England, which follow the steps of the
virgine Mary, whose end be prosperous and perfect, according to your hearts desire." [27] But such address hardly
seemed flattery to an English agent. When her sailors face
the Inquisition Elizabeth personifies the land for which
they suffer. She is the handmaid of the Lord set against
the Catholic Spaniards.[28] Drake on his expedition to the
West Indies in 1585–86 has an ordnance "shot off in
honour of the Queenes Majesties coronation day, being
the seventeenth of November, after the yeerely custome

---

[22] VII, 98.   [25] III, 354.
[23] VIII, 55.   [26] II, 182.
[24] II, 256.   [27] IV, 19.
[28] See J. A. Froude, *English Seamen in the Sixteenth Century*, New York,
1895, p. 25; Richard Hasleton's *Strange and Wonderful Things* (*An English
Garner*, VIII [1896], 367 ff.).

of England." [29] The Earl of Cumberland and his men, sailing back "meerily before the winde" from the Azores in 1589 "make accompt they would see what running at Tilt there should bee at Whitehall upon the Queenes day." [30] Ships were named for Elizabeth. On July 3, 1559, the queen went to Woolwich "to the launching of a fine ship newly built, and called by her own name ELIZABETH." [31] And narratives of voyages were dedicated to her. [32]

If the dust of Elizabeth's brave voyagers was fated to find rest in English soil, they could speak like Anthony Jenkinson, who crossed many foreign lands and seas for his queen, when he concluded a list of his travels: "And thus being weary and growing old, I am content to take my rest in mine owne house, chiefly comforting my selfe, in that my service hath bene honourably accepted and rewarded by her majestie and the rest by whom I have bene imploied." [33] If their dust was to mingle with the waves, they could wish to die breathing such words as these: "Here die I Richard Greenvil with a joyful & quiet mind, for that I have ended my life as a true souldier ought to do, that hath fought for his countrey, Queene, religion and honor, whereby my soule most joyfull departeth out of this body, & shal alwayes leave behind it an everlasting fame of a valiant & true souldier that hath done his dutie as he was bound to doe." [34]

Elizabeth as the adequate symbol for the ideals of the

[29] Hakluyt, VII, 83. See VIII, 113, 237. This holiday seems to have been regularly kept at sea as well as at home.

[30] IV, 372.

[31] Nichols, *Elizabeth*, I, 73. See Hakluyt, VIII, 87.

[32] See below, pp. 428, 435, 457.

[33] Hakluyt, II, 158.

[34] V, 37. Sir Humphrey Gilbert died at sea wearing the queen's jewel. Kingsley's Salvation Yeo, as a type of humble Elizabethan seaman, is more truth than fiction. In Cynthia's days the "sailor lads" were certainly the chief maintainers of the state. But the "martial men" also exalted Cynthia, as at Tilbury. See Lyly, I, 485–490; and Gascoigne, I (1907), 179.

seamen of her age, such as she is in Hakluyt's narratives, appears in a number of poems of the Armada decade.[35] But before I present this verse, it is important to note the direct encouragement which Elizabeth gave to the growth of the concept of Cynthia. As a Renaissance princess, she loved compliment dressed in ancient myth. Greek water myth and native lake legend were loosely attached to her at Kenilworth in 1575. After the victory of 1588, the facts about her rule of the ocean were potent enough to lead the court dramatist Lyly to adapt other Greek myth to praise of her as mistress of the seas. But between 1575 and 1588 the queen's own part in the maritime activity of the nation did much to nourish the Cynthia concept to its post-Armada maturity. John Cabot's explorations under Elizabeth's grandfather had marked the beginning of modern English sea power. When Henry VIII built up the royal navy he set a precedent for Elizabeth that she did not forget, even though England's navy had fallen on evil days during the confused reigns of her brother and sister. The full story of Elizabeth's development of the old Nordic maritime empire of Canute is a tremendous one. I need only recall some familiar incidents as they show Elizabeth's policy coöperating with the spirit of her seamen to form the concept of Cynthia. Above all, her government gave the consolidated state necessary for the new expansion over the seas. Feudal society could never have sustained it. In Elizabeth's state the "search for wealth, the desire for adventure, patriotism, hatred of Spain, and a restless energy, all combined to bring about the assertion of this new spirit." [36] The position and the temperament of Elizabeth identified her with all of these

---

[35] In Anthony Munday's *Zelauto* (sigs. E2ᵛ–E4) there is notable verse lauding Cynthia, some printed above the picture of a "ship . . . made with a gallant deuise, that in her presence . . . ran vpon a Rock, and was dispoyled."

[36] Lewis Einstein, *Tudor Ideals*, New York, 1921, p. 291.

elements in the new spirit; they made her a fortunate balance for centrifugal and centripetal forces in insular development. She took endless care to avoid entangling alliances and antagonisms in Continental politics, and she encouraged privateering by disclaiming responsibility for it. People and prince had joined to promote a unified effort in mercantile expansion, and the privateering it involved "suited Elizabeth's convenience, and suited her disposition." [37] By winking at privateering she could strike directly but unofficially at her Continental enemies, form a great navy for the destined clash, and have her own hand in needed booty. Her patronage of Drake and Hawkins well indicates her direct part in the maritime activity of the age, but any full history of it would introduce most of the prominent exploring, naval, and commercial ventures of many celebrated seamen.[38] Castiglione advised his prince to "shew favour to marchant men, and to helpe them also with stockes." [39] Elizabeth took shares in Hawkins's slave trade and lent a large ship of her own, the *Jesus*, for his second voyage in 1564. She gave him a farewell audience at Enfield, and she welcomed him when he returned. She sent him her physician when he was taken by mistake for Hatton and stabbed. She gave him high honor when Howard knighted him on July 26, 1588.[40] When

[37] Froude, p. 23.

[38] *The third voyage of Captaine Frobisher, pretended for the discoverie of Cataia, by Meta Incognita, Anno Do. 1578* has a notable account of the queen's reception of Frobisher upon his return to England after his second voyage, and of her interest in his next (Hakluyt, V, 228–231). It illustrates well how admirably Elizabeth stood by to inspire adventurous exploration.

[39] *The Book of the Courtier*, p. 293.

[40] I have drawn these facts from Mr. J. A. Williamson's study, *Sir John Hawkins The Time and the Man*, Oxford, 1927. For typical instances of the partnership of the queen and her merchants in treasure voyages, see Williamson, pp. 54–55. For instances of Hawkins's fine loyalty to a queen who could be a hard mistress, see pp. 135, 147–148, 452–453, 466–467, 489–490. Hawkins may

Globe-engirdling *Drake*, the Navall Palme that wonne,
Who strove in his long Course to emulate the Sunne,[41]

sailed back to England in November, 1580, he first of all
asked some fishermen if his queen was well. His "Queene
received him graciously, and layed up his wealth by way
of sequestration, that it might be forth comming if the
Spaniard should demand it. His Ship she caused to be
drawne up into a little creek neere *Depford* upon the
Thames, for a monument of his so lucky sayling round
about the world, . . . And in it being consecrated for a
memoriall with great ceremony, she was banquetted, and
honoured *Drake* with the dignity of Knighthood." [42] "In
a list of jewels given to the Queen at New-year's tide, 1589,
is 'A fanne of ffethers, white and redd, the handle of golde,
inamaled with a halfe moone of mother of perles, within
that a halfe moone garnished with sparks of dyamonds,
and a fewe seede perles on th'one side, having her Majestie's picture within it; and on the back-side a device with
a crowe over it. Geven by Sir Francis Drake.'" [43]   An
appropriate gift for Cynthia from a sea knight who had
circled the globe for her. This jeweled Cynthia was eager
for her share in the plunder worth £67,000 which this
knight brought home in 1585. She had six ships in the
fleet of twenty-seven that sailed in 1595 on the fatal
Hawkins-Drake voyage.[44] When Essex, Ralegh, the Lord
Admiral, and their companions returned in 1596 from
Cadiz, the queen "welcommed them very graciously, and

be visualized as a powerful "sea-dog," growing old in guarding the feet of his
royal mistress as she became the "Ladie of the Sea." Much of the time he stood
and waited, but his service to the "Ladie" is best seen when she is imagined
without such a watchdog.

[41] So wrote Drayton in Song 19 of *Poly-Olbion* (*Works*, IV [1933], 405).
[42] Camden, p. 224.
[43] Nichols, *Elizabeth*, II, 119 n. In 1578 at Yarmouth a "silver cup, in form
of a ship, . . . was made on purpose to be presented to her Majesty" (II, 275).
[44] Hakluyt, VII, 183.

gave singular thankes to every of them of better note,
especially to *Essex* and the Admirall, whom she extolled
with extraordinary praises." [45] Such instances as these,
which are typical of her dramatic association with her
seamen, show how nicely Elizabeth's character and policies were calculated to build up an admiration for her in
the voyage literature of her reign.

This admiration entered into the poetry of the last
decades of the age.

Henry Roberts's poem, *A Most Friendly Farewell to Sir
Francis Drake*,[46] was occasioned by Drake's great expedition to the West Indies in 1585. The "Lord" appears
side by side with Neptune in this awkward good-by to
Drake and his men. "God and S. Georg" are with the
"valiant Knights" who serve "in Princes cause."

What Drake and his "valiant Knights" did to Philip's
pride on this expedition led directly to the launching of
the Armada in 1588. Victory then effected a happy synthesis of native legend, classic myth, and maritime enthusiasm which, as I have shown, Elizabeth attracted long
before the event. With it, Cynthia became of age. The
power of the Armada victory to unify all sea trope that
had attached itself directly or indirectly to Elizabeth and
to transmute it into an adequate symbol for English maritime achievement was no doubt due to the decisive part
which the sea played in defeating the enemies of England.
The sea had indeed become a pathway to new worlds, but
it remained for Elizabethan Englishmen a "moat defensive
to a house," to their "dear, dear land." And the sea
fought against the Invincible Armada from the very first.
When Neptune's fury united finally with the skill and
courage of English seamen to wreck the proud fleet, there
could be little doubt that the sea sought the English

[45] Camden, p. 465.
[46] Reprint, ed. E. M. Blackie, Cambridge, Mass., 1924.

Cynthia for its mistress. By the same token, Protestant
zeal saw God's hand in the victory. Dr. Pierce, bishop of
Salisbury, preached a sermon before the queen on the day
that she celebrated in state at St. Paul's, and his text was
"Thou didst blow with thy winds, and they were scattered." [47] Had not the Spaniards advanced as upon a
religious crusade in the name of God? Had not the dons
fought under the patronage of Our Lady and the choir of
saints? "Both sides had appealed to Heaven, and Heaven
had spoken." [48] Heaven had spoken for our virgin "Ladie
of the Sea" — for English Elizabeth — for "Cynthia."
After the great victory that "Ladie" was almost deified
by the fervor of national pride and patriotism, inseparable
from Protestant zeal. Who would say that God had not
inspired his chosen queen? Had not "Queene ELIZABETHS
foresight prevented both his [the Prince of Parma's] dili-
gence, and the credulous hope of the *Spaniards*: for by her
commandement, the next day after the *Spaniards* had
cast anchor, the Lord Admirall made ready eight of his
worst ships, besmeared with wild-fire, pitch, and rosin,
and filled with brimstone and other combustible matter,
and sent them downe the wind in the dead of the night,
under the guiding of *Young* and *Prowse*, into the *Spanish*
Fleet." Coins "were stamped, some in memory thereof
with a fleet flying with full sayles, and this inscription,
Venit, Vidit, fugit, that is, It came it saw, it fled: others in
honour of the Queene, with incendiary ships and a fleet
confused, and inscribed, *Dux fœmina facti*, that is, A
woman was conductor of the fact." [49] The Lord "commandeth, and raiseth the stormy wind, which lifteth up
the waves." His "great waters" were on Cynthia's side.
Neptune's sea had fought for her. She herself had dis-

[47] Strickland, IV, p. 592.
[48] Froude, p. 228.
[49] Camden, pp. 369–371.

patched the fire ships. After the summer of 1588,
"Cynthia" was a rich and favored symbol for much that
animated the Elizabethan mind. The concept satisfied the
patriotic Englishman who looked backward, now to the
glory of Arthur's island empire, now to the beauty of
Greek mythology, and frequently at the naval achievement of his own day. The use that the poetic imagination
now made of Cynthia is the next concern.

Just after the Armada victory, when Elizabeth celebrated it in London in the midst of her adoring people,
"many verses were penned to the honour of her Majesty
by learned men," if Hakluyt is to be believed. He gives
the following verses on the repulsion of the Spaniard who
would have spoiled Cynthia's "Islands wealth, by peace
made great":

> But well have windes his proud blasts overblowen,
> And swelling waves alayd his swelling heart,
> Well hath the Sea with greedie gulfs unknowen
> Devoured the devourer to his smart:
> And made his ships a pray unto the sand,
> That meant to pray upon anothers land
> ... O Queene, above all others blest,
> For whom both windes and waves are prest to fight.[50]

---

[50] Hakluyt, II, 401. The verses are from Théodore de Bèze's *Ad serenissimam
Elizabetham Angliæ reginam*, 1588, a short poem which felicitates Cynthia on her
victory and, presented in Latin, Dutch, Spanish, Hebrew, Greek, Italian, and
French, as well as English, flatters her wits for languages. See, too, the rare
volume, *Triumphalia de victoriis Elisabethæ ... contra classem instructissimam
Philippi Hispaniarum regis potentissimi, ... CIƆ IƆ LXXXVIII. Iulio et
Augusto mensibus*, [1589]. It is a collection of Greek and Latin poems in which
N. Eleutherius (who signs the dedication) and others sing of Cynthia and her
victory. "*Pro patriâque mori, vel vincere certus, ELISA*" (sig. B1ᵛ) — catches
the spirit that animated Cynthia's sea knights. A prayer for the destruction of
the Armada signed "Rob. H." (Bodleian Library's Douce fragm. d.12[12]) had
pleaded for the navy of "thy chosen seruant Elizabeth": "let not furious
stormes, windes, or tempestes hurte them, nor surging Seas harme them." The
prayer is of striking interest in view of what the winds and waves did. The first

A curious version of the disaster that Neptune brought upon the Spaniard is found in Nicholas Breton's "A Conceipt Vpon an Eagle, and A Phœnix." It is a thinly veiled allegory in which Cynthia, appearing this time as a glorious phœnix, is victorious over Philip, a "foule olde birde." When he

> heard what was become
> Of all his flight, that flick'red here and there;
>   Some sicke, some hurt, some lame, and all and sūme
> Or farre from hope, or all too neere in feare.
>   He stoupt his traine, and hung his head so sore,
>   As if his heart had never burst before.[51]

John Lyly's allegory of Cynthia's victory certainly pleased court taste more than Breton's did. Lyly's *Midas* was printed as "'played before the Queenes Maiestie vpon Twelfe Day at Night. By the Children of Pavls'" — probably on January 6, 1590.[52] The allegory in the play, whatever may be its full scope, certainly satirizes Philip as a Midas, who would have seized England and had its gold even as he had taken the new world's. "Chast *Celia*"[53] and her "petty ilands" shall yield, declares greedy Midas. But after his great disaster at sea when Neptune decided that his pride should fall, Midas laments his defeat at the hands of a prince "protected by the Gods" and by "huge waues."[54] Apollo threatens that Midas shall find his ass's ears reaching to Lesbos (i.e., England) unless he withholds his grasping hand. Midas

---

edition of Hakluyt's *Principal Navigations* was nicely timed to meet public enthusiasm for voyage narratives, which must have run high after the voyage against Medina Sidonia.

[51] *Works*, I, *h*, 14.

[52] The date is Bond's (*Works*, III, 111). Bond thinks that "the play was composed between May and September, 1589."

[53] Bond (III, 522) thinks that this name may be an allusion to Philip's early proposal for the hand of Elizabeth.

[54] III. i. 46–60.

bemoans his disgrace and admits that the gods have defended the island.[55] This play is a sophisticated satire
designed to compliment the "Ladie of the Sea" at her
court by ridiculing the foe that Neptune has overcome
for her.

The expedition which was sent to Portugal under Drake
and Norris in 1589 was meant to bother Midas more than
by lengthening his ears. George Peele wrote *A Farewell.
Entituled to the famous and fortunate Generalls of our English forces: Sir Iohn Norris & Syr Frauncis Drake Knights,
and all of theyr braue and resolute followers.* On the back of
the title-page Elizabeth's arms appear with her motto,
Semper Eadem, and these verses:

> *Gallia victa dedit flores, inuicta Leones*
> *Anglia: ius belli in flore, leone suum:*
> *O sic O semper ferat Elizabetha triumphos,*
> *Inclyta Gallorum flore leone suo.*[56]

Seventy-six lines of patriotic blank verse culminate as
follows:

> You fight for Christ, and England's peerless queen,
> Elizabeth, the wonder of the world,
> Over whose throne the enemies of God
> Have thunder'd erst their vain successless braves.
> O, ten-times-treble happy men, that fight
> Under the cross of Christ and England's queen,
> And follow such as Drake and Norris are! [57]

More successful than the Lisbon expedition was the
voyage of Richard Ferris in 1590. An account of it was

---

[55] See V. iii. 52–54, 101–103. Actually, the Spaniards, unwilling "to allow
that the Upper Powers had been against them, . . . set it frankly down to the
superior fighting powers of the English" (Froude, p. 227). Truth often emerged
by curious ways from the tangle of patriotic fervor and religious prejudice which
was the nationalism of the sixteenth century.

[56] *Works,* II, 235.

[57] II, 240.

printed as *The most dangerous and memorable adventure of Richard Ferris, one of the five ordinary Messengers of Her Majesty's Chamber: who departed from Tower Wharf, on Midsummer Day last past, with Andrew Hill and William Thomas; who undertook, in a small wherry boat, to row, by sea, to the city of Bristow; and are now safely returned.*[58] Ferris's dedication to Sir Thomas Heneage closes with a prayer for her health and long life: "Her Majesty, my dread Sovereign and most gracious Mistress! peace to this land!" The wherry, its oars, and its sail were painted green; and it bore her majesty's arms and a red cross for England. When he passed the court gate at Greenwich Ferris fired a volley of shot. The seamen at Plymouth gave him great entertainment because he was "Her Majesty's Messenger." Of course the success of this voyage was "the handy work of Almighty GOD."

Gervase Markham's account of the last fight of the *Revenge* in *The Most Honorable Tragedie of Sir Richard Grinuile, Knight* (1595) presents the "Ladie of the Sea" in a more celebrated incident than that of which Ferris was the hero. The following quotations show the "Ladie" representing what Sir Richard Grenville died to serve:

> To flye from them that holds my God in hate,
> My Mistres, Countrey, me, and my sworne fayth,
> VVere to pull of the load from *Typhons* back,
> And crush my selfe, with shame and seruile wrack.
>
> .   .   .   .
>
> VVho ist that flies? *Grinuile?* Captayne no,
> T'is *England* flies, faire Ile of happines,
> And true diuine *Elizas* holynes.
>
> .   .   .   .

---

[58] Reprinted in *An English Garner*, VI (1883), 153–166. Included is a "new Sonnet" made upon the event; it prays for "our royal Rose."

The life I haue, I for my Mistris beare,
Curst were that life, should it her scepter wound,
   And trebble cursed be that damned thought,
   Which in my minde hath any fayntnes wrought.

.   .   .   .

Say if I perrish, t'was mine honours will,
   My Countries loue, religion, and my Queene,

.   .   .   .

And where thou sayst the *Spanyards* shall not braue,
   T' haue tane one ship due to our virgin Queene.[59]

Of much more value is Charles Fitzgeffrey's long poem,
*Sir Francis Drake, His Honorable lifes commendation, and
his Tragicall Deathes lamentations* (1596). The following
verses are significant:

Neptune encircled in his watry armes
His silver-shining darling *Albion*,

.   .   .   .

And like as *Perseus* kept his *Andromeda*,
So kept he her from monsters of the sea.

.   .   .   .

So DRAKE (divine ELISA's champion)
Ceazing upon a praie of *Indian* gold,
Meaning to ship it home to *Albion*,
Ballasts his barke with treasures manifold;
Which when the griev'd *Iberians* doe behold,
   They swarme in troupes to take his prize awaie,
   And to disrob him of his gained praie:

A thousand hel-mouth'd canons deadly shot,
A thousand ratling muskets hayle-stones flie,
Yet thousand deadlie canons hurt him not,

---

[59] *The Last Fight of the Revenge at Sea*, ed. Edward Arber, English Reprints,
no. 29, 1871, pp. 58-82. See verses on p. 43.

Nor thousand ratling muskets reckneth he,
But still rebeates them all as eagerlie;
   And, maugre all their beards, brings home the spoile,
   Ritching ELISA, and ELISA's soile.

.   .   .   .

A heavenly fury DRAKES minde did inflame,
To purchase glory to *Elysa's* name:

.   .   .   .

How that their loftie mindes could not be bounded
Within the cancels, that the world doe bound;
How that the deepest seas they search'd, and founded,
Beyonde all landes that ever have beene found,
Making the farmost seas our praise resounde:
   And nations, which not Fame her selfe had seene,
   To carrol *Englands* fame, and fames rare Queene.

.   .   .   .

Intending for to worke his countries pleasure,
O cruell chance! he wrought his countries paine:
And minding to augment faire *Englands* treasure,
(Alasse!) he drowned in the *Ocean* maine
The richest treasure *England* did containe,
   Save one rare iewell, whose rich price is such,
   As none can either prize, or praise too much.[60]

This poem in its retrospective summary of Tudor maritime achievement, is a kind of epitome of much Hakluyt.
Fitzgeffrey glorifies chiefly the explorations and naval
victories of Drake and his fellows, but he also recalls what
English seamen did under Cynthia's ancestors. Of Richard
the Lion-hearted, he writes:

[60] *The Poems of the Rev. Charles Fitzgeoffrey (1593–1636),* ed. A. B. Grosart,
[Manchester], 1881, Part I, pp. 43–102. Similar references to Cynthia occur in
A Golden Mirrour (1589) by Richard Robinson (ed. Thomas Courser, The
Chetham Society, vol. XXIII, [Manchester], 1851). See, especially, pp. 8–11.
Further praise by Fitzgeffrey appears in his *Affaniae: sive epigrammatum Libri
tres,* 1601, D2ᵛ, H4.

His hart was richest, that a lyons was,
Save her rich hart, whose hart all harts doth passe.[61]

Elizabeth personifies England for Drake and his associates in this verse narrative of Tudor achievement on the seas as much as she does in Hakluyt's prose. Drake is a great dragon, and "all the sea-sourges passage to him [give]." Many "peerless Peeres," the "sage attendants on ELISA's crowne," are eager to fight by his side. "All the sea-monsters [tremble] at his name." And

He, who alive to them a Dragon was,
Shalbe a Dragon unto them againe; [62]

for the dead "*Hyperborean* Dragon" shall become a "dreadfull Meteor" portending "*Englandes* successe." [63] Although the great English dragon is gone, Cumberland, Howard, Essex — "rampant Lions" — survive to destroy Philip. Furthermore,

ELISA lives, and while ELISA raignes
One *England* neede not feare an hundred *Spaines.*[64]

Fitzgeffrey makes elaborate and consistent use of classical mythology throughout his poem. He shows well how Elizabethan patriotism could celebrate its heroes and its queen in both pagan and Christian forms with no sense of incongruity.[65]

[61] *Poems*, p. 67.
[62] Page 105.
[63] The insular nature of the glorification of Drake and of the concept of Cynthia appears amusingly when one remembers that the same facts that Fitzgeffrey saw inspired Lope de Vega's *La Dragontea* (1598), in which this "Dragon" is a cursed monster preying on God's holy church and the domain of his Spanish prince.
[64] *Poems*, p. 105.
[65] Fitzgeffrey's poem was popular. A second edition was called for a few months after the first; and Meres in 1598 praised the author for the work. The poem (p. Oxford, 1596) was dedicated (sig. A2) in an Elizabethan sonnet: "TO THE BEAVTEOVS, AND vertuous Lady ELIZABETH, late wife unto the high-

Elizabeth's rôle in the poetry which I have been review-
ing is apparent again in Fulke Greville's *A Treatise of
Monarchy*, and in William Warner's *Albion's England*.
The loyal courtier Greville in "Of War" writes:

> Nay in the Indian's East and West again,
> What great things men may with sea-forces do,
> Not only in suppressing of the main,
> But in possessing land and cities too,
>   By undertakings of a maiden Queen,
>   May as in models to the world be seen.[66]

Warner's long patriotic recital of English legend and history is more than once developed so as to glorify Elizabeth,
but I shall present only verses which show her as the
"Ladie of the Sea." The Armada victory, he declares,
came because

> God
> Did patronize our Ile.[67]

His recital of the sea fight glorifies

> Our god-blest queene, palladium of
> Our happie publique weale.[68]

Before rehearsing the voyages of her reign, he writes:

> Her fleetes haue oftentimes
> Set prosprously her men on shore,
> Euen in the farthest climes:

> Whence have they brought, by fayr commerce,
> Great riches to our land,

.   .   .   .

lie renowmed Sir Francis Drake *deceased*." It is so reprinted in Grosart's
edition (p. 5) and (p. iii) in the privately printed edition at Kent in 1819. Bullen
in the *Dictionary of National Biography* (XIX [1889], 109) states that it "was
dedicated to Queen Elizabeth, and commendatory verses were prefixed."
    [66] *Works*, I, 204. Cf. Greville's references to the queen and her war by water
which appear in his *Life of Sir Philip Sidney*.
    [67] *The Works of the English Poets*, ed. Alexander Chalmers, 1810, IV, 613.
    [68] IV, 619.

The maiden empresse, and her Knights,
　　Their enterprises rare,
Which now haue pearst through euery pole,
　　Of all admired are.

　　.　　.　　.　　.　　.　　.　　.　　.　　.

Thy raigne also, Elizabeth,
　　Shall bound our pen in it,
Which to our theame inferreth texts,
　　No times yeeld more so fit.[69]

Warner tells proudly of the achievements of the sea
knights of the "maiden empresse" — of Drake, Hawkins,
Gilbert, Grenville, Frobisher, Fenton, Warde, Davis, and
others. His poem closes with praise and prayer for this
great island empress.

Thus far I have introduced poetry in which Elizabeth
as the "Ladie of the Sea" is a character almost identical
with Elizabeth as she appears in Hakluyt's narratives. In
the verse to which I now turn the "Ladie's" favored name
is Cynthia. In the realm of courtly poets Cynthia is a
paragon of perfection. Their patriotism is as genuine as
that which I have already shown centered upon the
queen.

Perhaps the vogue of Cynthia as a name for Elizabeth
as queen of the sea was fixed by John Lyly's *Endymion*
(1588).[70] Certainly the Armada victory gave the name
peculiar appositeness. In *Endymion* Cynthia is elaborately

---

[69] IV, 632–643. Cf. verses in Drayton's *Poly-Olbion* (*Works*, IV, 337–338),
which is steeped in Elizabethan patriotism, although it was printed under
James.

[70] There has been dispute about the date of this play. Bond (*Works*, III, 13)
places its composition between May and November, 1585. I give the production
date taken by Chambers. Most criticism sees Cynthia as shadowing Elizabeth,
however much dispute there may be about the place of her politics and amours
in the involved allegory.

glorified as an omnipotent goddess of the moon and the sea. Endymion defends her mutations:

> O faire *Cynthia*, why doe others terme thee vnconstant, whom I haue euer founde vnmoueable? . . . There is nothing thought more admirable or commendable in the sea, then the ebbing and flowing; and shall the Moone, from whom the Sea taketh this vertue, be accounted fickle for encreasing, & decreasing? . . . What thing (my Mistris excepted) being in the pride of her beauty, & latter minute of her age, that waxeth young againe? [71]

There is "nothing pleaseth her but the fairenesse of virginitie." She herself admits that she is "placed for light on earth," and is "protected by the powers of heauen." [72] Endymion, whose life has been saved by one kiss from Cynthia, declares that to her "hands the Ballance that weigheth time & fortune are committed." [73] At the end of the play, her patronage of learning and wisdom is praised by her philosophers. Pythagoras vows that he "had rather in *Cynthias* Court spende tenne yeeres, then in Greece one houre." [74] Lyly's Cynthia is the matchless sum of virtues. She is so characterized as to please the reigning tastes of the court. Nor has one of the most poetic of ancient myths about the moon goddess, whose gleaming arrows smote the sea, been robbed of all of its original grace. [75] It is such characterization of Elizabeth as an omnipotent Cynthia, supreme in graciousness and magnanimity, that inspires Spenser, Ralegh, and other courtly poets. Their portrayals of Cynthia are of interest now.

But before meeting Cynthia in the courtly verse of Spenser and Ralegh it may be well to see her in some occasional pieces spoken before her during the late years of the

---

[71] I. i. 30–50.   [72] V. iii. 27–28.

[73] V. iii. 190–191.

[74] V. iii. 290–291. Such extravagant compliment to Cynthia runs throughout the play.

[75] Legouis and Cazamian, p. 403.

reign. When this goddess visits Lord Montague at Cowdray
in August, 1591, an angler finds that her brilliance keeps
the fish from biting. He complains that "*the Sunne so
glisters, that the fish see my hooke through my bait.*" [76] This
fisherman's wit is excessive, yet to the taste of the age. It
plays of course to compliment the goddess of English fish-
ing. His song pledges the loyalty of "hearts as true as
steele." For her he nets all the fish in the pond.

When Cynthia came to Elvetham in September of the
same year to be the guest of the Earl of Hertford, there was
an elaborate water carnival on the second day of her visit.
It recalls the Kenilworth tributes of 1575, but the Armada
victory has now given life to devices turning on classic
water myth. The "Oration of Nereus to her Maiesty"
well shows the change:

> *Faire* Cinthia *the wide Oceans Empresse,*
> *I watry* Nereus *houered on the coast*
> *To greete your Maiesty with this my traine*
> *Of daucing* Tritons, *and shrill singing Nimphs.*
> *But all in vaine:* Elisa *was not there;*
> *For which our* Neptune *grieud, and blamd the star,*
> *Whose thwarting influence dasht our longing hope.*
> *Therefore impatient, that this worthles earth*
> *Should beare your* Highnes *weight, and we sea Gods,*
> *(Whose iealous waues haue swallowd vp your foes,*
> *And to your Realme are walles impregnable)*
> *With such large fauour seldome time are grac't:*
> *I from the deepes haue drawen this winding flud,*
> *Whose crescent forme figures the rich increase*
> *Of all that sweet* Elisa *holdeth deare.*
> *And with me came gould-brested* India,
> *Who daunted at your sight, leapt to the shoare,*
> *And sprinkling endlesse treasure on this Ile,*

---

[76] Lyly, I, 427. Bond (I, 404–409) claims for Lyly most of the late progress
materials from which I quote, but, it seems to me, without convincing evidence
for his authorship.

Left me this iewell to present your Grace,
For hym, that vnder you doth hold this place.
See where her ship remaines, whose silkewouen takling
Is turnde to twigs, and threefold mast to trees,
Receiuing life from verdure of your lookes;
(For what cannot your gracious looks effect?)
Yon vgly monster creeping from the South,
To spoyle these blessed fields of Albion,
By selfe same beames is chang'd into a Snaile,
Whose bulrush hornes are not of force to hurt.
As this snaile is, so be thine enemies,
And neuer yet did Nereus *wishe in vaine.*
That Fort did Neptune *raise, for your defence;*
And in this Barke, which gods hale neare the shore,
White footed Thetis *sends her Musicke maydes,*
To please Elisaes *eares with harmony.*
Hear them fair Queene: and when their Musick ends
My Triton *shall awake the Syluane Gods,*
To doe their hommage to your Maiesty.[77]

A feature of the celebrated *Gesta Grayorum* of 1594 was
an elaborate sea masque designed to compliment the royal
patroness. The "Dialogue between the Squire, Proteus,
Amphitrite, and Thamesis," with its marine setting, culminates in significant characterization of Cynthia. Proteus
has boasted loudly of his

Adamantine Rocks,
Which forceth iron, which all things else commands.

The Esquire soon shames him by describing Cynthia as
follows:

[77] I, 442–443. Speeches by Sylvanus and Neæra, and by the "poet" at
"her Maiesties departure" are notable for "sea pastoral" compliment. John
Sandford's *Apollinis et musarum* Εὐκτικὰ Εἰδύλλια, Oxford, [1592?], describes in
Latin verses the banquet given by the president and fellows of Magdalen to
Cynthia and her followers when she made her last visit to the university in
September, 1592. Notable praise of her as favored of Neptune appears on
sig. B2.

Excellent QUEEN, true Adamant of Hearts;

. . . .

Your Rock claims kindred of the Polar Star,
Because it draws the Needle to the North;
Yet even that Star gives place to Cynthia's rays,
Whose drawing virtues govern and direct
The flots and re-flots of the ocean.
But Cynthia, praised be your wat'ry reign,
Your Influence in Spirits have no place.
This Cynthia high doth rule those heavenly tides,
Whose sovereign grace, as it doth wax or wain,
Affections so, and Fortune's ebb and flow:
Sometimes their waves applauding on the Shore,
Sometimes retiring to their narrow depths,

. . . .

In the Protection of this mighty Rock,
In *Britain* land, whilst tempests beat abroad,
The lordly and the lowly shepherd both,
In plenteous peace have fed their happy flocks.
Upon the force of this inviolate Rock,
The giant-like attempts of Power unjust
Have suffer'd wreck. And, Proteus, for the Seas,
Whose Empire large your praised Rock assures:
Your gift is void, it is already here;
As *Russia*, *China*, and *Negellan*'s Strait
Can witness here, well may your presence be
Impressa apt thereof; but sure, not cause.
Fisher divine, congratulate yourself,
Your eyes hath won more than your State hath lost;
Yield Victory, and Liberty, and Thanks.

Of course after such revelation Proteus pays homage to
Cynthia:

Against the Truth, that's Lands and Seas above,
It fits no Proteus make a vain reply.
The shallop may not with small ships contend,

Nor windy bubble with a billow strive,
Nor earthly things compare with greatest Queen
That hath and shall a regal sceptre sway.
Bless'd be that Prince that forc'd me see this Grace,
Which worldly Monarchies, and Sea-Powers adore.
Take Thanks of Gift, and Liberty of Due.[78]

Classical myth in such speeches as these has been thoroughly adapted to the celebration of the English Cynthia. Since the time of the Kenilworth water shows, the sea has actually become her domain.

It is time to meet Spenser's Cynthia and Ralegh's. Spenser's portrait of her is in *Colin Clouts Come Home Againe*. Spenser's poem might be called a "marine pastoral" in official pattern.[79] In it Elisa suffers a sea change

---

[78] Nichols, *Elizabeth*, III, 315–318. One might think that a poet's ingenuity could hardly go farther in exalting Cynthia. However, when a carrack was taken in June, 1602, Sir John Davies knew how to turn the capture to the praise of the "true Adamant of Hearts." In his "A Lottery," which was presented before Cynthia at the Lord Chancellor's house in the same year, a "*Marriner with a Boxe vnder his arme, contayning . . . things . . . supposed to come from the Carrick, came into the Presence*," sang a pretty song to her, and offered lottery gifts to all. See *Poems*, II, 87–95.

[79] Campion's "Ad Thamesin" which appeared in *Poemata* (1595) might be called a "river pastoral." Verses "Ad Dianam" (*Works*, p. 329) open their praise of Elizabeth:

> Dij nemorum, et vati Thamesinæ adsistite nymphæ,
> Dum struit herbosum vestras altare Dianæ
> Propter aquas, iaculantis apros, vulpesque Dianæ.

"Ad Thamesin" concludes its celebration of the defeat of the Spaniards (pp. 334–335):

> At tu nympharum Thamesis pulcherrima limphis
> Alta tuis, procul vt vidisti hostilia signa,
> Tu dea flumineam spaciosa gurgite frontem
> Celata, æquoreas turbasti fluctibus vndas.
>
> .   .   .   .   .   .
>
> At te diua rosis ambit formosa iuuenta,
> Atque Heliconiacas aspergit floribus vndas,
> O diua, ô miseris spes Elisabetha Britannis
> Vna, senectutem superes, plusisque superstes
> Hostibus, innumeros gemines virtutibus annos.

into "Cynthia, the Ladie of the Sea." [80] The "furious insolence" that inspired Colin to a soaring Platonic paean of praise is in honor of the "Ladie of the Sea" as much as of the "queene of shepheardes all." But of course Cynthia and Elisa are only different names for the same Tudor rose. In singing of that sweet flower as "Cynthia, the Ladie of the Sea" Spenser is first paying a graceful compliment to Elizabeth's maritime glory, which, as has just been seen, plays a great part in verse idealizing her after the climactic year, 1588. By the use of this sea trope Colin compliments no less the "Shepheard of the Ocean," Cynthia's favorite "from the main-sea deepe," to whom he is indebted for his introduction to her glorious court in Faery Land. When Colin marvels at the mighty wonders of her sea over which the Shepheard escorts him to the court, that guide tells him

"that that same was the regiment
Of a great shepheardesse, that Cynthia hight,
His liege, his ladie, and his lifes regent.
'If then,' quoth I, 'a shepheardesse she bee,
Where be the flockes and heards, which she doth keep?
And where may I the hills and pastures see,
On which she useth for to feed her sheepe?'
'These be the hills,' quoth he, 'the surges hie,
On which faire Cynthia her heards doth feed:
Her heards be thousand fishes, with their frie,
Which in the bosome of the billowes breed.
Of them the shepheard which hath charge in chief

---

[80] The epithet was popular before and after Colin's use of it. When Elizabeth in 1582 showed Alençon all her ships at Rochester, the French lords "confessed that of good right the Queene of England was reported to be Ladie of the seas" (Nichols, *Elizabeth*, II, 346). Cf. "To conclude, her Maiestie had bene made such an absolute Queen of the Ocean, and her enemie so disarmed by sea, as she might either enforce him to any conditions of peace, or make warre to her infinite aduantage and his vtter ruine" (*An apologie of the Earle of Essex, . . . Penned by himselfe in anno 1598*, 1603, sig. B3ᵛ). See Einstein, *Tudor Ideals*, p. 292; and George Ballard, *Memoirs of British Ladies*, 1775, p. 148.

Is Triton blowing loud his wreathed horne:
At sound whereof, they all for their relief
Wend too and fro at evening and at morne.
And Proteus eke with him does drive his heard
Of stinking seales and porcpisces together,
With hoary head and deawy dropping beard,
Compelling them which way he list, and whether.
And I among the rest, of many least,
Have in the ocean charge to me assigned:
Where I will live or die at her beheast,
And serve and honour her with faithfull mind.
Besides, an hundred nymphs, all heavenly borne,
And of immortall race, doo still attend
To wash faire Cynthiaes sheep, when they be shorne,
And fold them up, when they have made an end.
Those be the shepheards which my Cynthia serve
At sea, beside a thousand moe at land:
For land and sea my Cynthia doth deserve
To have in her commandement at hand.'" [81]

It is to the poetry of Colin's intimate friend and benefactor, Ralegh, that one turns for what is perhaps the most
fascinating portrayal of Elizabeth as the "Ladie of the
Sea." In his *Cynthia* a great seaman and a true poet seems
to have effected an elaborate idealization of the queen who
played a vital part in his life and imagination. One longs
for the whole poem which Spenser and Harvey lauded.
But time has apparently spared only fragments, the date,
number, and meaning of which are disputed. In such circumstances, all allusions to the poem as Ralegh's contemporaries knew it are important for our knowledge of
his portrait of Cynthia.

"His song was all a lamentable lay,
Of great unkindnesse, and of usage hard,
Of Cynthia, the Ladie of the Sea,

---

[81] Lines 233–263. "Craik suggests that Triton is meant for Howard of
Effingham, Proteus . . . for Hawkins" (Dodge's note, *Poems*, p. 810).

Which from her presence faultlesse him debard.
And ever and anon, with singulfs rife,
He cryed out, to make his undersong:
'Ah! my loves queene, and goddesse of my life,
Who shall me pittie, when thou doest me wrong?'"
    Then gan a gentle bonylasse to speake,
That Marin hight: "Right well he sure did plaine,
That could great Cynthiaes sore displeasure breake,
And move to take him to her grace againe." [82]

Spenser again refers to *Cynthia* in a sonnet to Ralegh prefixed to the first three books of *The Faerie Queene*,[83] and in two stanzas in the introduction to the third book, which I shall quote when I turn to Gloriana.[84] Gabriel Harvey in notes made at the end of his copy of Speght's *Chaucer*, some time between 1598 and 1601, praised Ralegh's poem by name for its "fine & sweet inuentions." [85]

[82] Lines 164–175. Cf. ll. 56–79.
[83] *Works*, p. 142.
[84] See below, p. 341.
[85] *Poems*, ed. Latham, pp. 23–24. Miss Latham (the same) notes references to Ralegh as one of the "Courtly makers" in *The Arte of English Poesie*, and, in *Palladis Tamia*, as one among "the most passionate . . . to bewaile and bemoane the perplexities of Loue." In Book I, song 4, ll. 679–682, of William Browne's *Britannia's Pastorals* (*Poems*, ed. Gordon Goodwin, 1894, I, 129) occur the following lines in which, as the editor notes, Cynthia may be equated with Elizabeth and "Endymion" with Ralegh:

The first note that I heard I soon was won
To think the sighs of fair Endymion;
The subject of whose mounful heavy lay
Was his declining with fair Cynthia.

These appreciations of the original *Cynthia* one may perhaps supplement with the verses which Spenser lets his Shepheard speak in *Colin Clouts Come Home Againe* as descriptive of Cynthia's "regiment" of the sea. If Spenser is drawing Ralegh at all objectively, he may be letting him describe that "regiment" somewhat as Spenser knew him to have done in

that sweete verse, with nectar sprinckeled,
In which a gracious servaunt pictured
His Cynthia, his heavens fayrest light.

Lines 240–263 of *Colin Clouts Come Home Againe* may give Spenser's imaginative summary of Ralegh's original *Cynthia*, in so far as it was not a "lamentable lay."

What, however, is Cynthia like in the surviving fragments of the long poem that bore her name? It is in the
third fragment that the characterization of Cynthia, as it
is known directly, centers.[86] The opening verses of the

[86] Miss Latham, Ralegh's most recent editor, has summarized (*The Review
of English Studies*, IV [1928], 129) as follows part of the history of *Cynthia*: "In
Colin Clouts Come Home Againe, Spenser describes how Sir Walter Ralegh
visited him at Kilcolman in the autumn of 1589, heard him read some of *The
Faerie Queene*, and persuaded him to come back to England and publish it there.
To Spenser Ralegh read a poem of his own, which was never published, and was
long known only from Spenser's account, as the 'lost poem' of *Cynthia*. But in
the middle of the last century, when Mr. C. J. Stewart was cataloguing the Cecil
Papers at Hatfield House, he came upon a manuscript in Ralegh's hand, which
contained part of the lost poem." Miss Latham (*Poems*, p. 175) continues:
"The poem has been discussed by Hannah in his edition of 1870, by Sir Edmund
Gosse in *The Athenaeum* (Jan. 1886, pp. 32 and 66), and by Mr. Stebbing in his
Life of Ralegh published in 1891. Hannah believed the Hatfield fragments to be
a continuation of *Cynthia*, written some time between 1603 and 1612, when
Ralegh was in the Tower, but referring to his earlier disgrace of 1592. Sir
Edmund Gosse claimed the eleventh book as part of the original *Cynthia* written
in 1589, but denied that the other three fragments belong to the same poem, and
doubted whether the MS is autograph. Finally Mr. Stebbing, agreeing with
Hannah that the poem refers to the events of 1592, dates it between 1592 and
1595."
     Miss Latham, after a careful re-examination of the manuscript and of internal
and external evidence for the date and nature of the surviving *Cynthia*, has come
(*Poems*, pp. 172–179) to the following conclusions pertinent to my consideration
of the poem: (1) The manuscript is autograph. (2) The two short pieces which
are unnamed and which preface the other two fragments are likely not "completely irrelevant matter." (3) The "last two pieces must be accepted on
Ralegh's own testimony as the eleventh and twelfth books of *Cynthia*, and the
heading, 'the 11:th [evidently a misprint in Miss Latham for 11th: — which
does appear in the title of the fragment as printed on pp. 77 ff.] and last booke,'
which led Sir Edmund to declare that the eleventh was the last book, must be
understood as a general heading meaning 'the eleventh book and (the twelfth
or) last book.'" (The manuscript figures, until Miss Latham studied them, had
been read "21" and "22." She is convinced that the initial figure in each instance is actually a "1" with a backward flourish on it that accounts for the
readings "21" and "22" in the transcript which Hannah used and which Sir
Edmund followed via him. She thinks that "Ralegh finished according to
classical precedent with the twelfth book." Her belief seems to me particularly
likely because Spenser, Ralegh's close associate, was composing a twelve-book
epic — at least so in immediate plan — to glorify the queen at the same time
that Ralegh was writing his *Cynthia*.) (4) *Cynthia*, on Spenser's evidence in
Colin Clouts Come Home Againe, was at least begun in 1589. The poem which

eleventh book expand with ingenuity and feeling Ralegh's
conceit that Cynthia is dead since for him her favor is no
more.[87] A mariner conceived the ninth quatrain:

> no pleasinge streames fast to the ocean wendinge
> the messengers svmetymes of my great woe
> but all onn yearth as from the colde stormes bendinge
> shrinck from my thoughts in hygh heauens and below.[88]

This imagery introduces a very significant remembrance
of the devotion which Cynthia has inspired:

> To seeke new worlds, for golde, for prayse, for glory,
> to try desire, to try loue seuered farr
> when I was gonn shee sent her memory
> more stronge then weare ten thowsand shipps of warr
>
> to call me back, to leue great honors thought
> to leue my frinds, my fortune, my attempte
> to leue the purpose I so longe had sought
> and holde both cares, and cumforts in contempt.

Within the conventional love conceits of the age Ralegh
achieves, at least in these two quatrains, an eloquent expression of the queen's command over the heart and action
of a favorite courtier and voyager.[89]

---

we have was written "some time during or not long after 1592." I accept these
conclusions in the main in studying the fragments of *Cynthia* for their portrait
of the queen.

[87] Hannah's view (*The Poems of Sir Walter Raleigh*, 1892, p. xvi) that Ralegh
wrote of an actually dead queen seems to me quite wrong.

[88] *Poems* (ed. Latham), p. 78. Further quotations are from Miss Latham's
editing of the manuscript (*Poems*, pp. 75–95). The verse numbers appear in my
quotations for convenience of reference. The stops within my quotations are exactly after Miss Latham's reproduction of the manuscript. She (p. 173) suggests
that Ralegh employed them usually "to indicate some abrupt turn in the sense."

[89] Sir Edmund Gosse (*The Athenaeum*, January 9, 1886, p. 66) sees in these
lines a reference to the Virginian expedition which Elizabeth would not permit
Ralegh to join. Hannah (*Poems*, p. xvii) and Stebbing (*Sir Walter Ralegh A
Biography*, Oxford, 1891, p. 75) think that they refer to the recall of Ralegh from
the Panama expedition of 1592. Miss Latham (p. 178) adduces the lines in
arguing for 1592 as the date of composition of *Cynthia* as it survives.

Then several figures lament the falling off of the poet's fortunes. Thereafter the following is a notable passage:

My weery lymes, her memory imbalmed,
my darkest wayes her eyes make clear as day
what stormes so great but Cinthias beames apeased.
what rage so feirce that loue could not allay.

Twelue yeares intire I wasted in this warr 120
twelue yeares of my most happy younger dayes,
butt I in them, and they now wasted ar
of all which past the sorrow only stayes,

So wrate I once and my mishapp fortolde 124
my minde still feelinge sorrowfull success
yeven as before a storme the marbell colde
douth by moyste teares tempestious tymes express.

So fealt my hevy minde my harmes att hande
which my vayne thought in vayne sought to recure
att middell day my soonn seemde vnder land
When any littell cloude did it obscure.[90] 131

The forty-one verses which follow these develop this presage of the greater woe that was to come, and at times lament that sorrow with poignant power. Ralegh then asserts the sovereignty of sweet memories in engendering love, although "strong reason" warns the lover of the hollowness of all "flames that rize from formes externall."

---

[90] Of ll. 120–131, especially l. 124, Miss Latham (p. 177) writes: "This seems to be a reference to an earlier poem, possibly the *Cynthia* that Spenser knew, as distinct from the *Cynthia* that has survived. Ralegh is saying that his excessive distress at a slight disgrace (1589) was prophetic of more serious trouble to come (1592)." Of ll. 120, 121 she writes (pp. 177–178): "The reference here is to Ralegh's struggle for the Queen's favour. Sir Edmund Gosse counts twelve years from the entry in the Middlesex registers in 1578 of 'Walter Rawley, Esq. de Curia.' He believes Ralegh was reminding the Queen of the devotion he showed her when he was campaigning in Ireland. Mr. Stebbing reckons, I think with greater probability, twelve years from Ralegh's sudden rise to favour in 1582, which brings the date of the poem to the eve of his Guianian expedition in 1594."

His description of this deceitful base of love, "formes externall," merges subtly into another celebration of Cynthia's "marvelous perfections." He then tells with imaginative power of sadly changed times:

> thos thoughts so full of pleasure and content
> that in our absence weare affections foode
> ar rased out and from the fancy rent
> in highest grace and harts deere care that stood
>
> ar cast for pray to hatred, and to scorne
> our deerest treasors and our harts trew ioyes
> the tokens hunge onn brest, and kyndly worne
> ar now elcewhere disposde, or helde for toyes [91]
>
> and thos which then our Ielosye removed
> and others for our sakes then valued deere
> the on forgot the rest ar deere beloved
> when all of ours douth strange or vilde apeere
>
> Thos streames seeme standinge puddells which before,
> Wee saw our bewties in, so weare the cleere
> Bellphebes course is now obserude no more   271
>
> that faire resemblance weareth out of date
> our Ocean seas are but tempestius waves
> and all things base that blessed wear of late . . .

In these last four verses Ralegh mourns that the queen in her private character as Belphœbe, as his virtuous and adored lady, smiles on him no more. The sea imagery is notable, too.

Again vigorous metaphors reveal his grief. He is powerless to uproot his love. After twenty-five verses, come

[91] Hannah (*Poems*, pp. xvii–xviii) suggests that these last verses "may refer to the interchange of toys between the queen and her courtiers; as when she sent to Sir H. Gilbert 'a token from her Majesty, an anchor guided by a lady,' with a request for his picture in return." Hannah also notes that a "'ring with a diamond which he weareth on his finger, given him by the late Queen,' was among the jewels found on Raleigh's person after his execution." Cf. below, p. 347.

lines in which he sees his love as beyond time and self-seeking desire:

> I pourless was to alter my desire
> my love is not of tyme, or bound to date
> my harts internall heat, and livinge fier
>
> would not, or could be quencht, with suddayn shoures
> my bound respect was not confinde to dayes
> my vowed fayth not sett to ended houres.

Yet sorrow returns:

> But love was gonn, So would I, my life weare.
>
> a Queen shee was to mee, no more Belphebe [92]
> a Lion then, no more a milke white Dove,
> a prissoner in her brest I could not bee
> shee did vntye the gentell chaynes of love
>
> Love was no more the love of hydinge
> all trespase, and mischance, for her own glorye
> It had bynn such, it was still for th'ellect
> but I must bee th'exampell in loves storye
> this was of all forpast the sadd effect . . .
>
> But thow my weery sowle and hevy thought
> made by her love a burden to my beinge
> dust know my error never was forthought
> or ever could proceed from sence of lovinge.[93]

327

The next quatrain but one begins a passage in which Cynthia is a magnet for Platonic idealism:

---

[92] Cf. the reference to Belphœbe in l. 271, and with this careful distinction between the queen as an imperious sovereign, as Cynthia and Gloriana, and as the chaste and beloved lady, "Belphebe," compare Spenser's careful distinctions in his letter to Ralegh that prefaces *The Faerie Queene*.

[93] Miss Latham (p. 178) notes that these four lines (and l. 3) seem "to suggest in veiled language that a love affair was the cause of the Queen's displeasure." So do the five verses that precede the quatrain.

This did that natures wounder, Vertues choyse
the only parragonn of tymes begettinge
Devin in wordes angellicall in voyse
that springe of ioyes, that floure of loves own settinge

Th'Idea remayninge of thos golden ages
that bewtye bravinge heavens, and yearth imbaulminge
which after worthless worlds but play onn stages,
such didsst thow her longe since discribe, yet sythinge.[94]

that thy vnabell spirrit could not fynde ought
in heavens bewties, or in yearths delighte
for likeness, fitt to satisfy thy thought.

But Ralegh's is tortured Platonizing. Although he
would glean some abiding peace in having loved the
"Idea" of Cynthia well if not wisely, the "sorrow suckinge
bees" remain at his heart. The next twenty-one verses
lament the vanity of his present plea, which is a tale that
is "tolde out of tyme." Cynthia's "harde hart" and
"estranged minde" have forgotten all his "past deserv-
inge," and now remember only his offence. But his pride
would still seek some sweet consolation within the bitterness of her lack of pity. Finally bitterness gives way to a
sense of the futility of "waylings":

On highest mountaynes wher thos Sedars grew
agaynst whose bancks, the trobled ocean bett

and weare the markes to finde thy hoped port
into a soyle farr of them sealves remove
on Sestus shore Leanders late resorte
Hero hath left no lampe to Guyde her love[95]

---

[94] This verse suggests that the earlier books of *Cynthia* contained more idealization in Platonic style.
[95] This line and the preceding, in the opinion of Sir Edmund Gosse (*Athenaeum*, pp. 32–33), refer to the narrow Irish channel, which divided Ralegh and
the queen in 1589.

Thow lookest for light in vayne, and stormes arise
Shee sleaps thy death that erst thy danger syth-ed
strive then no more bow down thy weery eyes
eyes, which to all thes woes thy hart have guided.

Ralegh the voyager ploughs on through his sea of troubles to a poignant close.

I have quoted at length from this third fragment of *Cynthia* for two reasons: first, because I wish Ralegh's complex and often obscure adoration of Elizabeth to speak for itself; and second, because I think it the best specimen extant of the intricate fusion of varied forms and sentiments into amorous eulogy of her. Elizabeth evoked pastoral, Petrarchan, medieval, and Platonic types of idealization from courtier poets who were inspired in varying degrees by love of the queen and woman and by burning ambition to reach high place at her court. But nowhere is there such a subtle blending of all these types of idealization and motives for praise as this fragment of Ralegh's *Cynthia* reveals. It is her "Shepheard" who sings, and he sounds pastoral notes. His lamentation fuses Petrarchan conceits and the inherited courtly love ideal of a knight's faithful service to his lady, however hopelessly she withhold her favor. At times an "essentiall love" brings him to contemplation of Cynthia as "th'Idea remayninge of thos golden ages." However, his Platonic moments are submerged in the tide of sorrow and regret which flows through all of his verses — through the very last, in which he gives to God the "sowles sole love" that Cynthia has "returnd agayne," disdained. But the embracing conceit of the eleventh book of *Cynthia* is that of Elizabeth as an omnipotent "Ladie of the Sea," who sends her servants over the waves "to seeke new worlds, for golde, for prayse, for glory" — or who commands them back to serve at her court. The most glamorous of Cynthia's courtly poets is no less her daring sea captain. When his imagination

fetches up "consaytes" from his memories, they often
suggest his voyages over the deep in her name. The eleventh book of *Cynthia* harmonizes almost all of the elements
in the courtly idealization of Elizabeth.[96]

[96] The fragment of the twelfth book and the two pieces which preface the
eleventh in the Hatfield manuscript are best studied with the eleventh in mind.
The first of the prefatory pieces Miss Latham (p. 75) prints as follows:

> If Synthia be a Queene, a princes, and supreame,
> keipe thes amonge the rest, or say it was a dreame,
> for thos that like, expound, and those that louth express,
> meanings accordinge as their minds, ar moued more or less,
> for writinge what thow art, or shewinge what thow weare,
> adds to the on dysdayne, to th' other butt dyspaire,
>   Thy minde of neather needs, in both seinge it exceeds.

The meaning of these lines is certainly not obvious. Yet if one grants that this
and the other prefatory piece are not "completely irrelevant material," do not
these lines appear as an appropriately cryptic apology for the final books of
Cynthia in which "bitter constraint" fills with censure Ralegh's eulogy of the
"lion"? Cannot the "riddling nature" of the lines, which Miss Latham modestly confesses "completely baffles" her, be resolved as follows: "If Cynthia be
a supreme queen and princess (as contrasted with a merciful 'Belphebe' and
'Dove'; cf. ll. 271, 327–328, pp. 309, 310, above) keep (i.e., hide or conceal)
these verses (pleading ones) among the rest (i.e., the preceding books, which
were presumably not so sorrowful and critical as the two that he is about to
write); or say my complaining sorrow was but a dream. For those that approve
(will) interpret, and those that condemn (will) express (find) such meanings (in
my complaining eleventh and twelfth books) as their minds are more or less
moved to. (My) writing of what Cynthia is but increases her disdain toward me.
Writing of what she was to me (i.e., gracious) but increases my despair (because
of my present banishment from her favor). Her mind needs neither my present
nor my past praise, seeing that it is of exceeding worth in both cases." If the
lines are so construed, their "riddling nature" fits them for an introduction to
books in which complaining criticism is heard through all the "language of a
lover-like devotion" (as Hannah [p. xv] characterizes the diction of *Cynthia*).
The concluding compliment in the last three lines is then the part of tactful
circumspection.
The second of the prefacing pieces Miss Latham (p. 76) prints as follows:

> My boddy in the walls captived
> feels not the wounds of spightfull envy.
> butt my thralde minde, of liberty deprived,
> fast fettered in her auntient memory,
> douth nought beholde butt sorrowes diinge face,
> such prison earst was so delightfull

It is always dangerous to seek in an artist's creations his personal character and biography. The heavy drapery of convention and imitation hides the individual in most Elizabethan lyric poems. Yet Ralegh's "poetry was no

> as it desirde no other dwellinge place,
> Butt tymes effects, and destines dispightfull
> haue changed both my keeper and my fare,
> loves fire, and bewtes light I then had store,
> butt now close keipt, as captives wounted are
> that food, that heat, that light I finde no more,
> Dyspaire bolts vp my dores, and I alone
> speake to dead walls, butt thos heare not my mone.

This sonnet is admirably expressive of the despair of an actually imprisoned favorite, who remembers with envy the time when he was prisoner only to his memory of his mistress. Then he enjoyed the fire of her love and the light of her beauty. Now, a captive within prison walls, he cares not for his body's plight; but he longs for the heat and light of love which formerly he enjoyed, and he despairs because only the dead walls now hear his moans. This sonnet might well have been written by Ralegh when he was captive in the Tower in 1592 because of his marriage disgrace. Its conceited compliment, which is after the sonnet vogue of the moment, would have made it a good further preface to the last books of *Cynthia* in which he meant to complain of the queen's treatment of him in hopes that she in her personal character of "Belphebe" would show him mercy.

The last fragment is headed "The End of the Boockes, of the Oceans Love to Scinthia, and the Beginninge of the 12 Boock, Entreatinge of Sorrow." Miss Latham (p. 95) prints it as follows:

> My dayes delights, my springetyme ioies fordvnn,
> which in the dawne, and risinge soonn of youth
> had their creation, and weare first begvnn,
>
> do in the yeveninge, and the winter sadd
> present my minde, which takes my tymes accompt
> the greif remayninge of the ioy it had.
>
> my tymes that then rann ore them sealves in thes
> and now runn out in others happines
> bringe vnto thos new ioyes, and new borne dayes,
>
> so could she not, if shee weare not the soonn,
> which sees the birth, and buriall, of all elce,
> and holds that poure, with which shee first begvnn,
>
> levinge each withered boddy to be torne
> by fortune, and by tymes tempestius,
> which by her vertu, once faire frute have borne,

part of his public character, but something essentially
intimate and private." [97] His eleventh book of *Cynthia*
does raise the question of the sincerity of his idealization
of Elizabeth. [98] It would certainly appear that Ralegh, in
writing *Cynthia*, aimed first to advance himself at a treacherous court after some passing difficulty there, and then to
reinstate himself at that court when he had exchanged it
for the Tower. But if one comprehends the mind of the
age, the fact that he had such ends need not belie his sincerity when he renders Elizabeth "stately homage" in all
of his writings

from the time when he made her the standard of virtue and
beauty . . . in whom was "virtue's perfect image cast" . . .
for whose "defence we labour all" . . . to the time when he
offered his touching petition to Queen Anne of Denmark just
before his death . . . : —

> "That I and mine may never mourn the miss
> Of Her we had, but praise our living Queen." [99]

I find it easier to harbor the paradox in Ralegh's aims and
ideals than to believe that his praise of Elizabeth came of
no more than "his ambition and desire to get on which
made him put no limit to his exaggeration, in scornful

---

knowinge shee cann renew, and cann create
green from the grovnde, and floures, yeven out of stonn,
by vertu lastinge over tyme and date,

levinge vs only woe, which like the moss,
havinge cumpassion of vnburied bones,
cleaves to mischance, and vnrepayred loss

for tender stalkes.

These verses, which break suddenly off, seem to continue the sad complaining of
the preceding eleventh book. Perhaps the description of the sun is meant as a
covered rebuke to omnipotent Cynthia.

[97] Miss Latham, *Poems*, p. 12.
[98] In this connection, see above, pp. 256–257; and below, pp. 394–396.
[99] Hannah, *Poems*, p. xv.

contempt of the vanity that could be pleased by such language." [100]   Cynthia was a happy symbol of English glory by sea and land. The many-sided mind of Sir Walter Ralegh — soldier, courtier, man of science, historian, politician, statesman, poet, and voyager had need of that symbol in its imaginative life. [101]

[100] Louise Creighton, in *The Cambridge History of English Literature*, IV (1909), 52.

[101] The queen as the "Ladie of the Sea" is in Ralegh's consciousness when he writes of the *Revenge* and of the Guiana voyage of 1595. See Hakluyt, V, 14; VII, 285, 336, 343, 350. Interesting in this connection are verses, "De Guiana, carmen Epicum," by George Chapman, which were prefixed to Lawrence Keymis's *A Relation of the second Voyage to Guiana* (1596). I quote a few of the most striking (*The Works of George Chapman*, ed. R. H. Shepherd, 1874–1875, II [*Poems and Minor Translations*, Introd. by A. C. Swinburne, 1875], 50):

> Riches, and conquest, and renown I sing,
> Riches with honour, conquest without blood,
> Enough to seat the monarchy of earth,
> Like to Jove's eagle, on Eliza's hand.
> Guiana, whose rich feet are mines of gold,
> Whose forehead knocks against the roof of stars,
> Stands on her tip-toes at fair England looking,
> Kissing her hand, bowing her mighty breast,
> And every sign of all submission making,
> To be her sister, and the daughter both
> Of our most sacred maid.

As everyone knows, Ralegh's Virginia was named "in honour of Queene ELIZABETH a Virgin" (Camden, p. 285). She so christened it and was regarded as its godmother (Hakluyt, VI, 229). It was fitting that the first child born there should be named to honor both the new land and its queen (VI, 205). Thomas Harriot tells of a certain "faire chaine" of pearls from Virginia which was intended for her majesty but was unfortunately lost "through extremity of a storme" (VI, 171–172). Froude (*English Seamen*, p. 147) declares that Ralegh "imagined, or had been led by others to believe, that there was an Indian Court there [in Virginia] brilliant as Montezuma's, an enlightened nation crying to be admitted within the charmed circle of Gloriana's subjects."

The "Ladie of the Sea" figures notably in the following places: Stephanus Parmenius Budeius, *De nauigatione illustris et magnanimi Equitis Aurati Humfredi Gilberti, ad deducendam in novum orbem coloniam susceptâ, carmen*, 1582, sigs. B3ᵛ–B4 (Sir Humphrey Gilbert's *Queene Elizabethes Achademy*, setting out a scheme for the education of the queen's wards, has much praise of her); Thomas Greepe, *The true and perfecte Newes of the woorthy and valiaunt exploytes, performed and doone by that valiant Knight Syr Frauncis Drake*, [1587], sigs. A4,

Ralegh's *Cynthia*, which is extant in fragments darkly stained with sorrowful regret, was probably in its earlier books which Spenser admired, the supreme expression of what the queen was to the imaginations of her courtly knights of the sea, whatever else it may have been. Ralegh was the seaman and poet who most brilliantly transmuted fact and fancy into Cynthia.

I suspect that the censure and sadness of Ralegh's *Cynthia* as we have it was not the usual mood in songs to the "Ladie of the Sea." It is well to hear last one that was sung on May Day in 1600 "*before her sacred Maiestie at a shew on horsebacke, wherwith the right Honorable the Earle of Cumberland presented her Highnesse.*" In it the concept of Cynthia appears in its final beauty:

ODE.

Of Cynthia.

Th' Ancient Readers of Heauens Booke,
Which with curious eye did looke
    Into Natures story;
All things vnder *Cynthia* tooke
    To bee transitory.

This the learned only knew,
But now all men finde it true,
    Cynthia is descended;

C3; Francisco Lopez de Gomara, *The Pleasant Historie of the Conquest of the VVeast India*, . . . Translated . . . *by T. N.*, [1578], sig. a2ᵛ; Albertus Meierus, *Certaine briefe, and speciall Instructions for Gentlemen, merchants, students, souldiers, marriners, &c.*, 1589, sig. A4; *A true Report of the . . . Imbarrement of all English Shippes*, 1585, sig. B4ᵛ; Humphrey Mote, *The Primrose of London with her valiant aduenture on the Spanish coast*, 1585, sig. A4ᵛ. Sea trope plays a large part in the longish complimentary poem which Pierre de Ronsard addressed to Elizabeth in *Le Bocage Royal* (*Œuvres Complètes*, ed. Prosper Blanchemain, III [1858], 323–337). Oliver de la Marche's *The resolued Gentleman. Translated out of Spanishe into Englyshe, by Lewes Lewkenor*, 1594, contains (sigs. N1–N3, V2ᵛ–V3) very full praise of "that excellent & matchlesse Empresse of the Ocean," even though "this Treatise was first written in French, By Sir *Olyuer de la Marche*, in the yeere of our Lord. 1483"!

With bright beames, and heauenly hew,
    And lesser starres attended.

Landes and Seas shee rules below,
Where things change, and ebbe, and flowe,
    Spring, waxe olde, and perish;
Only Time which all doth mowe,
    Her alone doth cherish.

Times yong howres attend her still,
And her Eyes and Cheekes do fill,
    With fresh youth and beautie:
All her louers olde do grow,
But their hartes, they do not so
    In their Loue and duty.[102]

It was inevitable that the captain of the Elizabethan
ship of state should be idealized as the "Ladie of the Sea"
by poets who spoke for a nation imbued with the voyaging
spirit. The part of the queen in the growth of this spirit is
always to be remembered. The poets of the voyages served
a mistress who was in her statecraft the shrewdest mariner
of all. If the story of her coming to the throne was that of
a passage perilous worthy of the applause of the hardiest
buccaneer, that of her reign showed a supreme skill in
piloting the ship of state through the most precarious
straits with the aid of God's own winds. Her statecraft
knew with unerring intuition how to tack and veer with
the storms of circumstance. It exacted an admiration not
unlike that given by her subjects to the great voyagers
who were active during her peace. The idealization of her
by seamen and poets grew as they came more and more to
rely on her mastery of that ship which sailed securely over
the dangerous political sea where, as for her captains on
the Spanish Main, the good of England as an end justified
means which the international ethics of the age scarcely

[102] *A Poetical Rhapsody*, I, 236. The "Ode" appeared as the last poem in the
1602 edition of the *Rhapsody*.

rebuked. The fact that her ship made port drew attention from the piracy of some of her seamanship. Elizabeth knew well the secret of the successful leadership that characterized her great sea captains. She worked with her men as much as she worked them. Yet no one in her council chamber aboard ship doubted who the captain was. Captain and crew of the ship of state sailed for the greater glory of England with a spirit not unlike that which brought Drake and his sailors round the world aboard the *Golden Hind*.

I have shown how ancient forms, native and classical, fused with the facts about Elizabeth and the seas which she ruled to develop the concept of Cynthia. The English Cynthia was a child of both the new and the antique world. Like Lodge's *Rosalynde*, she was "*hatcht in the stormes of the Ocean, and feathered in the surges of many perillous seas.*" The returning voyagers told such stories as gave new life to the inherited fund of fable, superstition, and myth in spite of the developing rationalism of the century. If the poets, "voyaging through strange seas of thought," lent a "willing suspension of disbelief" to the strange stories from distant new lands and to revived myths from the old, their public lent some actual belief. All could unite to believe in this Cynthia. The character that they created for her was the happy adaptation of old fancy to the new world. When they celebrated Cynthia they honored the virgin empress who made their England mistress of the waves. Cynthia proves the idealization of Elizabeth to be inseparable from the imaginative life of her age in its looking back to "the glory that was Greece" and ahead to the days when "Britannia rules the waves." Cynthia is witness to the profoundly national quality of the idealization of Elizabeth. As such she is of greater significance than any of the more exclusively court ladies — Elisa, Diana, Laura, and Idea. She really stands beside Judith and

Deborah of broadside and progress verse; but her poetic beauty is infinitely superior to that of those humble country cousins, if second to that of Gloriana. She is the fit symbol for the most impressive fact of Elizabethan political evolution — the development of an isolated island into a great ocean power.

AN ELIZABETHAN RIAL
From an example in the British Museum

CHAPTER VIII

Gloriana and Belphœbe

G LORIANA and Belphœbe epitomize the familiar Judith, Deborah, Eliza, Elisa, Diana, Laura, Idea, and Cynthia.

Spenser meant *The Faerie Queene* to be read as the greatest of many poems idealizing Elizabeth as a national heroine, various types of which have now been examined. One should remember that his readers knew the queen as the center of other poems more or less epic in scope.[1] The Elizabethan approach to his epic is by way of Christopher Ocland's *Anglorum prælia* and Είρηναρχία *Siue Elizabetha* and William Alabaster's *Elisæis*.

[1] Many writers told of Elizabeth as the bringer of epic achievements in war and peace. Edward Hake's *A Commemoration of the most prosperous and peaceable Raigne of our gratious and deere Soueraigne Lady Elizabeth*, which was "newly set foorth" in the eighteenth year of the reign, foreshadows some of Gloriana's virtues (sigs. A8ᵛ, B2ᵛ, B4). *Albion's England* poetizes English history from the time of Brutus and Arthur so as to make their glory a setting for the Tudor queen's. Her victories are strikingly lauded in Book IX, chapters 48–49 (Chalmers, IV, 612–614). Surely the crudest attempt to poetize the epic events of Elizabeth's reign was James Aske's *Elizabetha Triumphans* (Nichols, *Elizabeth*, II, 545–582). Written just after the Armada, when national feeling ran most fiercely, this cumbersome and violent narrative of Elizabeth's victories before 1588 culminates in a burst of praise for the routing of the papal wolves and Spanish devils by God's anointed queen in 1588. This "maiden Queene" of "courage stoot" has beaten the "raging Panther" (the pope) and trapped the "cubbes" (Jesuits) sent to eat the English chickens. The thing hardly deserves to be called poetry, but it does show the furious surge of national and religious feeling which ebbed and flowed around Elizabeth at the time of the Armada. *The Faerie Queene* was an Armada poem; Spenser was in the surging tide when he told of the trial of Duessa. See below, pp. 352–353.

In 1586 George Whetstone brought out *The English Myrror*, with a dedicatory preface (sigs. ¶2–¶2ᵛ) to Elizabeth, and on the verso of the title-page beneath her arms an acrostic poem on her name, the second part of which I quote:

Christopher Ocland's *Anglorum prælia, Ab Anno Domini. 1327. Anno nimirùm primo inclytiss. Principis Eduardi eius nominis tertij, vsque ad annum Do. 1558,* appeared in 1580. It was dedicated to Elizabeth in the following verses:

Regia Nympha, soli moderatrix alma Britanni,
    Quæ pace & vera relligione nites,
Quæ vitæ meritis, morum & candore coruscans,
    Zenobiam vincis, siqua vel antè fuit:
Iunonem sceptris, Venerem vultu, arte Mineruam
    Quæ exprimis, & plusquàm fœmina, mente sapis:
Lenis ades, fœlixque meis illabere cœptis:
    Vultus (Diua) tuus numinis instar erit.
Grande opus est, impar tanto succumbo labori,
    Ni fausto nobis sydere Diua mices.
Diua mica, proauosque tuos & auita trophæa
    Qualia, quæ fuerint, per tria sæcla, vide.
Quorum cùm teneas solium, diadema, vicesqúe,
    Illorum bellis gloria parta, tua est.
Nec sanè insipidum est, describere bella puellæ,
    Vt pax, sic doctæ Palladi bella placent.

R enowne our Queene her diademe doth giue,
E lizabeth alone in peace doth liue:
G lory of God, most blessed Prince aliue.
I mage of grace, in whome all vertues thriue.
N o death vpon her memorie may feede,
A Phenix right, but one, yet neuer dead.

This prose work is offered as "A REGARD Wherein al estates may behold the *Conquests of Enuy:* Containing ruine of common weales, *murther of Princes, cause of heresies, and* in all ages, spoile of deuine and humane blessings, vnto which is adioyned, *Enuy conquered by vertues.* Publishing the peaceable victories obtained by the Queenes most excellent Maiesty, against this mortall enimie of publike peace and prosperitie, and lastly *A Fortris against Enuy, Builded vpon the counsels of sacred Scrip*ture, Lawes of sage Philosophers, and pollicies of well gouerned common weales: wherein euery estate may see the dignities, the true office and cause of disgrace of his vocation. *A worke safely, and necessarie to be read of euerie good subiect.*" The long sub-title tells the tale: familiar praise of the virtues of Elizabeth and her epic reign is woven into all three books of *The English Myrror.*

CORONO

EXHILER

ELIZA, TRIVMPHANS

AN ENGRAVING OF QUEEN ELIZABETH BY WILLIAM ROGERS
From an original in the British Museum

Hoc opus ergò precor Princeps, lege fronte serena:
    En ego iudicio stóue cadóue tuo.
Abijciant omnes, conculcent, nil moror omnes:
    Vni (si possim) posse placere sat est.
Det Deus, vt semper geniali pace fruaris,
    Et superes proauos gloria, honore, tuos.[2]

Ocland's survey of English battles ends as follows:

Regali extemplò solio Regina locatur
ELISABETA *potens, magni altera filia Regis,*
Elisabeta pijs primos imbuta per annos
Moribus, & sophiæ studijs, instructa sacrata
Doctrina, & linguæ Latiæ Graiæque perita.
Linguas Europæ celebres intelligit omnes,
Quid Teuto, Hispanus, Gallúsue, Italúsue loquatur:
Plusquam credibile est, iuris rerumque perita,
Ore verecundo, vultu facieque venusta.
Vis animi talis, qualem (vix credo) videre est
Fœmineo in sexu: diuinum lucet in illa
Ingenium: sæcli laus ô laus vnica nostri.
Reuera è cœlo demissa ad sceptra gerenda,
Virgo pacis amans, quæ stat contraria bellis.
Cui vitam studiumque Deus regnique coronam
Fœlicem, sanctum, cuncto splendore repletam
Perpetuet, beet, & tranquillo prosperet vsu:
Póstque hanc exactam vitam, studium, atq; coronam,
Cœlesti vita, solio, diademate donet.[3]

When *Anglorum prælia* appeared again in 1582 it was
accompanied by Εἰρηναρχία *Siue Elizabetha.* This work
was popular enough to be translated by John Sharrock in
1585 as *Elizabeth queene. Or a short and compendious
declaration of the peaceable state of England, vnder the gouernment of the most mighty and vertuous Princesse Elizabeth.*
In verses "To the gentle Reader" Sharrock writes:

[2] Sig. A2.
[3] Sig. S2ᵛ.

I worthie her confesse, whome *Homer* should in sugred verse,
   Or with the Notes, of warbling Lute *Apollo* great rehearse.
I am no Poet, you pardon must me, since I pardon pray,
   If that a bourden ouer vast, do downe my shoulders way.
My arte vnto the vertue yeeldes, of her a Prince so great,
    VVhich shuld be sounded by a trompe more shril, with winds
      repleat.
If others lye in silence shrinde, why should my Muse not sing?
    But when her laud, in fluent phrase, from one more learnd
      shal spring
Then will I these my papers voyde the fiery flames to feed,
    Meane time the honour of her Grace, let these my verses
      breede.

Since "sugred verse" from an English Homer singing
Elizabeth — from Spenser — is still "in silence shrinde,"
Sharrock renders Ocland's work, but in ludicrously un-
Homeric style. He unconsciously burlesques praise of the
feats of an epic hero when he sings of Elizabeth's precocious
childhood:

A Virgin doth her mothers blisse, her fathers ioy increase,
In time to come this Virgine shall procure the Britaines peace.
  .   .   .   .

She at her prudent sayinges, made astoinisht men to stand,
And bookes desirous to be taught, would alway haue in hand.
She scarse the letters with her eyes intentiue did behold,
Their seuerall names, but thrise before by her instructor told:
But perfect them at fingers end, as two monthes taught, she bare,
Their figures diuerse made, deciphering well, by iudgement rare.
Yea in few dayes (a marueile great it is to speake no dout)
The Princely impe by industrie, such sap had sucked out:
That without councell to assist, she any thing could reed,
So nothing intricate is found, nor difficult in deed,
To willing mindes, deceauing toyles the loue of vertue true.
  .   .   .   .

Now silken vesture holdeth she,
In lilly handes, and sitting fine, with pliant fingers small:
With needle worke imbrodereth rich, and ouerspreadeth all.
Mineruaes pretious webbe, the vewers would haue voucht it sure,
The hemmes distinguisht with a gard, of glistering mettall pure.
Now doth she exercise her selfe, of solempne Lute to play,
On warbling stringes, now more, now lesse, sad dumpes to
    driue away.
The Nightingale her chirping voyce, so diuers scarce could make,
Diuided into sondry tunes: as she most sweetly strake,
with quauering fingers small, and gentle touching of the strings.
All men admiring much, whence that celestiall Musicke springs.[4]

And there is throughout the work familiar celebration of her services to "Pure Religion," of her unique peace maintained in spite of turmoil abroad, and of her many mercies.[5]

By 1589 great events evoked Ocland's *Elizabetheis. Siue de pacatissimo et florentissimo Angliæ statu, sub fœlicissimo augustissimæ Reginæ Elizabethæ imperio, Liber secundus. In quo, præter cætera, Hispanicæ classis profligatio, Papisticarúmque molitionum & consiliorum hostilium mira subuersio, bona fide explicantur.* The following verses in the dedicatory address to the queen's advisors will, with their echo of epic style, suggest the content of the song:

> *Augustæ cecini pacem almam Principis olim:*
> *Diuæ victricis nunc fera bella cano,*
> *Pacis amans, solióque sedens quæ fœmina gessit,*
> *Fœmina magnanimi fregit vt arma viri.*

---

[4] Sigs. A3ᵛ, B2, B3, C2–C2ᵛ. With the first two verses quoted, compare James Sandford in dedicating to Elizabeth *Certayne poemes* (in Ludovico Guicciardini, *Houres of recreation . . . Done . . . into Englishe by Iames Sandford*, 1576, sig. Q2; see below, p. 452):

> Your vertues are so great, that they be thought,
>   Worthy of *Homers* and of *Maroes* stile.

[5] See sigs. C2ᵛ, D4ᵛ, E1–E1ᵛ.

Totius annales oculis percurrite mundi,
Non habet in terris Elisabeta parem.[6]

About 1595 the epic acts of Elizabeth's reign inspired one William Wodwall, once a schoolmaster of the Free Grammar School, Birmingham, Warwickshire, to a particularly bad long poem that is yet of interest.

The original title of the work was simply "The Acts of Queen Elizabeth," to which "allegorized" was added àt some subsequent period. That addition indicates the nature of the author's design. The leading facts in the reign of the celebrated Queen, and more especially those which relate to the active contest carried on throughout it between Roman Catholics and Protestants, are represented under the disguise of a war between the Devil, the World, and the Flesh on the one side, and Conscience on the other. The object of the assailants is to dispossess Conscience from Castle Coeur [i.e., England], and the actions of these opposing parties, the attack and defense in this great contest, are divided into Six Assaults or Conflicts, each of which forms the subject of a separate canto of the poem.[7]

The climactic "Sixth Conflict" treats the victory over the Invincible Armada in great detail. But the significant

---

[6] Sig. [A2]. Significant passages appear on sigs. B1, C1, G1^v, G2^v–G3. Cf. epistles by Théodore de Bèze (sig. G3^v) and Thomas Newton (sig. G4). One 1582 edition of *Anglorum prælia* contains after the title-page "A Copie of the Letters directed by hir Maiesties High Commissioners in causes Ecclesiasticall, to all the Byshoppes thorowout hir Highnesse dominions of *Englande* and *Wales*, by especiall order from the Lords of the priuie Councel, for the publike reading & teaching of this Booke in all Grammer and Free scholes within their Dioceses." Ocland's *The Fountaine and VVelspring of Variance, Sedition, and deadlie Hate* (1589; sigs. B1, D3^v, E3–E4, F3–F4^v) has praise of Elizabeth's achievements.

[7] The poem survives in the original manuscript, which was described in some detail by John Bruce in *Notes and Queries*, fourth series, III (1869), 305–307, when it was in the library of Lord Foley. It was offered for sale in the Maggs Brothers *Catalogue 636* (1936), no. 45, where the date which I take was given. The manuscript of 225 small quarto pages is adorned with curious pen and ink drawings. I have not seen it. I quote from the communication in *Notes and Queries*.

point about the poem is its evidence that poets other than Spenser appreciated the invitation to allegorical treatment given by the epic achievements of the reign.

Samuel Daniel in an epistle "To her sacred Maiestie" that prefaces his *Works* (1601) and introduces six books of his *Civil Wars* shows at once the spirit in which Ocland, Wodwall, and all Elizabethans recounted their past and looked upon their epic present:

> *Heere sacred Soueraigne, glorious Queene of Peace,*
> *The tumults of disordred times I sing,*
> *To glorifie thy Raigne, and to increase*
> *The wonder of those blessings thou doost bring*
> *Vpon thy Land, which ioyes th' intire release*
> *From bloud and sorrowes by thy gouerning,*
> *That through affliction we may see our ioyes,*
> *And blesse the glory of* Elizaes *dayes.*

> *Happier then all thy great Progenitors*
> *That euer sate vpon that powrefull Throne;*
> *Of all thy mightiest neighbour-Gouernors,*
> *Which wonder at the blessings of thy Crowne,*
> *VVhose Peace more glorious farre than all their warres,*
> *Haue greater powres of admiration showne;*
> *Receiue these humble fruites of mine increase,*
> *Offred on th' Altare of thy sacred Peace.*

> *I, who by that most blessed hand sustain'd,*
> *In quietnes, do eate the bread of rest:*
> *And by that all-reuiuing powre obtain'd*
> *That comfort which my Muse and me hath blest,*
> *Bring here this worke of Warre, whereby was gain'd*
> *This blessed Vnion which these wounds redrest,*
> *That sacred Concord which prepar'd the way*
> *Of glory for thee onely to enioy.*

> *Whereto if these my Labors shall attaine,*
> *And which, if Fortune giue me leaue to end,*

It will not be the least worke of thy Raigne,
Nor that which least thy glory shall commend,
Nor shall I hereby vainely entertaine
Thy Land, with ydle shadowes to no end;
But by thy Peace, teach what thy blessings are,
The more t' abhorre this execrable warre.[8]

Clearly the materials are at hand — and the spirit is most willing — for the creation of a formal epic poem about Elizabeth. At least one was composed in Latin hexameters in faithful imitation of Virgil. William Alabaster's unpublished *Elisæis* is a more significant portrayal of Elizabeth as a national heroine of epic stature than Ocland's effort. *Elisæis: apotheosis poetica, sive de florentissimo imperio et rebus gestis augustissimæ et invictissimæ principis Elizabethæ, Dei gratia Angliæ, Franciæ et Hiberniæ Reginæ, poematis in duodecem libros tribuendi liber primus,*[9] is dedicated in ornate prose "Potentissimæ et Serenissimæ Principi Elizabethæ." The opening verses announce the familiar themes. The movement is painfully slow; there are many epic similes and echoes from Greek and Latin poets, especially Virgil.

Virgineum mundi decus, augustamq₃ Britannæ
Regnatricem aulæ, et lætis digesta tot annos
Imperijs, pacisq₃ artes, belliq₃ triumphos,
Ordior æternæ rerum transcribere Famæ.

---

[8] *The works of Samuel Daniel Newly augmented,* 1601, sigs. A2–A2ᵛ. In the third and fourth stanzas of Book I in the 1601 edition (sig. B1ᵛ) the "sacred Goddesse," "ELIZA," is the muse invoked to "giue peace to my life, life to my Verse." These two stanzas, with certain differences in phrasing, appear in *The poeticall essayes,* 1599, sig. B1ᵛ; but the preface "To her sacred Maiestie" does not.

[9] I draw the full title from the Bodleian Library's description of its manuscript copy of the poem (MS. Rawlinson D. 293); but my quotations are from a photostat of the manuscript in the Newberry Library (MS. Y 682.A 3). I have not seen the manuscript in the library of Emmanuel College, Cambridge.

argumentum ingens magnis fæcundaq₃ curis
copia, præsentem primis deducere pompam
Auspitijs: qvas illa vices? quæ nubila rerum
Et consangvineum tulit orsa injuria, sævi
Dæmonis insidijs, atq₃ atro turbine, donec
Vivida lassavit rigidam constantia sortem
Multa qvoq₃ et regno passa est furialibus ausis
pontificum: dum Romuleris erepta ruinis
fragmina, victura pietatis condidit arce.

.   .   .   .

Hic, Regina, tuum genus, . . .
. . . et raptos de sorte triumphos
Justituam, castamq₃ deo tutante salutem
Et meritam sartâ de religione coronam.
Addam urbes *Scotiæ* domitas, Gallumq₃ repulsum
Et conjuratas vano conamine, turmas.
Atq₃ hic ferventem bello, vatisq₃ latentem
Cædibus oceanum, et magnâ de classe ruinas
Atq₃ nicæstatos *Hispano* sanguine fluctus.[10]

Satan and his daughter Rome conspire to create discord
between Mary and Elizabeth, happy sisters. Gardiner is
a ready tool. Soon the "pia virgo" is seized and thrown
into the Tower. Then the poem as we have it ends —
clearly but a fragment of what Alabaster planned as an
ambitious epic to celebrate the queen who had led England
to triumph over all God's enemies. The following portrait
of Eliza just before her enemies seize her is notable:

Et jam flammifero Phæbei lampadis haustu
Territa cæruleo latuerunt sidera velo;
Sola venus magno vultum submissa pudore
Substitit vt rutili præsentia numina patris
Ore salutaret niveo, lumenq₃ referret
Cum teneros Henricæis discussa sopores
Extulit os sacrum et cælo radiavit Elisa.

.   .   .   .

10 Fol. 3.

Magnanimi proceres reverentia major Elisæ
Qvos habuit sacram expectant ad limina divam
Tandem lacteolo Nimpharū sydere fulta
Progreditur thalamo, flavos cui gemea crines
Vitta insignibat, fulvoq₃ incanduit auro
Qvam supra nivei fluitabant cærula veli
Carbasa: sed rutilæ tereti sub tegmine gemmæ
Purpureum fudere jubar: mixtoq₃ nitore
Aureolæ sacro crispabant vertice sqvammæ
vndabat toto viridans Bombicina tergo
Vestis et Æois horrebat sqvallida conchis
Qvalis Amasoniæ ductrix fortissima gentis
Hippolite qvoties peltatæ armata cohortis
Turbine Sarmaticis populatrix intonat arvis
Aureus á tergo corytus pendet & auro
Thermodoonticæ radiant problemata peltæ
Regia sic animos sic ora ferebat Elisa.[11]

Elisæis shows that *The Faerie Queene* is the perfection of a type of national epic poem built about the reign of Elizabeth.[12]

In turning now to Spenser's epic as a compliment to Queen Elizabeth, to the Faery Queene as in particular "the most excellent and glorious person of our soveraine the Queene," I would recall the declaration, "And yet, in some places els, I doe otherwise shadow her." Nor is Belphœbe, that portrait of the "most vertuous and beautifull lady," the only other shadow of Elizabeth. Gloriana and Belphœbe are of first importance, but other reflections will arrest attention.

A key to the pervasiveness of the compliment intended for Elizabeth in *The Faerie Queene* is given at once by

---

[11] Fols. 13, 13–14.

[12] But it certainly does not arouse such enthusiasm as it drew from Colin (*Colin Clouts Come Home Againe*, ll. 400–415), who praised extravagantly his friend's unfinished "heroick song" of the "mightie princesse." Perhaps Spenser felt spurred by Alabaster's epic of Elizabeth in creating his own.

Spenser's noble dedication, especially in its third adjective: —

TO

THE MOST HIGH,

MIGHTIE

And

MAGNIFICENT

EMPRESSE RENOVV-

MED FOR PIETIE, VER-

TVE, AND ALL GRATIOVS

GOVERNMENT ELIZABETH BY

THE GRACE OF GOD QVEENE

OF ENGLAND FRAVNCE AND

IRELAND AND OF VIRGI-

NIA, DEFENDOVR OF THE

FAITH, &C. HER MOST

HVMBLE SERVAVNT

EDMVND SPENSER

DOTH IN ALL HV-

MILITIE DEDI-

CATE, PRE-

SENT

AND CONSECRATE THESE

HIS LABOVRS TO LIVE

VVITH THE ETERNI-

TIE OF HER

FAME.[13]

She is inseparable from the "continued" moral allegory of the poem.

The introductory stanzas to Book I link Elizabeth to the first of the "twelve private morall vertues." She, even before Prince Arthur, embodies magnificence (magnanimity), the virtue which "is the perfection of all the rest, and

---

[13] So reads the dedication (sig. A1ᵛ) in the edition of 1596, but the varying one in the edition of 1590 (sig. A1ᵛ) also has the significant epithet "MAGNIFICENT."

conteineth in it them all." Gloriana is also glory, the proper end of this supreme virtue. Spenser begs the help of Clio and the gods as he sets about the story of Arthur in his search for "fayrest Tanaquill," but he then prays:

> And with them eke, O Goddesse heavenly bright,
> Mirrour of grace and majestie divine,
> Great Ladie of the greatest Isle, whose light
> Like Phœbus lampe throughout the world doth shine,
> Shed thy faire beames into my feeble eyne,
> And raise my thoughts, too humble and too vile,
> To thinke of that true glorious type of thine,
> The argument of mine afflicted stile:
> The which to heare vouchsafe, O dearest dread, a while.[14]

One must bear in mind, too, that the books of *The Faerie Queene* which were written celebrate the "private morall virtues"; hence Gloriana, the shadow of the public character of Elizabeth, naturally remains in the background. In Book I there are a number of passing references to her or to her court.[15] At least twice she comes forward — in Arthur's account of his dream of her,[16] and in the holy aged man's praise of Cleopolis and its queen:

> "Till now," said then the knight, "I weened well,
> That great Cleopolis, where I have beene,
> In which that fairest Fary Queene doth dwell,
> The fairest citty was, that might be seene;
> And that bright towre all built of christall clene,
> Panthea, seemd the brightest thing that was:
> But now by proofe all otherwise I weene;
> For this great citty that does far surpas,
> And this bright angels towre quite dims that towre of glas."

> "Most trew," then said the holy aged man;
> "Yet is Cleopolis, for earthly frame,
> The fairest peece that eie beholden can:
> And well beseemes all knights of noble name,

---

[14] Stanza 4.   [15] See i, 3; vii, 36, 46; xi, 7; xii, 18, 41.   [16] ix, 13–17.

That covett in th' immortall booke of fame
To be eternized, that same to haunt,
And doen their service to that soveraigne dame,
That glory does to them for guerdon graunt:
For she is hevenly borne, and heaven may justly vaunt." [17]

Una may be a compliment to the first achievement of the "most royall queene or empresse" — the establishment of Protestantism.[18] In this "flowre of faith and chastity," in this "virgin borne of heavenly brood," [19] in this "royall virgin" or "mayd" [20] who when adorned seems "such as she was, a goodly maiden queene," [21] patri-

[17] x, 58–59.

[18] Dr. Ray Heffner (*Studies in Philology*, Chapel Hill, N. C., XXVII [1930], 161) has drawn the following conclusions from a study of the allegory in Book I as it is illuminated by pageants at Elizabeth's coronation:

1. Spenser seems to have got from the pageants at Elizabeth's coronation a suggestion for his Una (Truth) and his allegorical method in Book I.

2. Spenser chose Religion as the subject for Book I because he viewed it not only as the first problem to confront the Queen, but also as the first of her virtues.

3. Spenser's contemporaries read Book I as the allegory of Elizabeth and her relation to the establishment of Pure Religion.

These conclusions are justified by the materials which Mr. Heffner has assembled; they are reinforced, I think, by the preceding chapters of this study, especially by all that has been shown of Judith or Deborah as God's chosen leader for fixing England in "Pure Religion." Direct support for this point appears also in Whitney, *A Choice of Emblemes*, p. 1 (cf. p. 61); Drayton, *Works*, II, 300–301; Matthew Sutcliffe, *A briefe replie to a certaine odious and slanderous libel*, 1600, sigs. B1–B4ᵛ; Peter Viret, *An Epistle to the Faithfull, . . . englished by F. H.*, 1582, sigs. ¶3ᵛ–¶4; T. T., *A booke, containing the true portraiture of the countenances and attires of the kings of England, from William Conqueror, vnto our Soueraigne Lady Queene Elizabeth now raigning*, 1597, sig. F3ᵛ; *De ecclesia Dei ab Antichristo per eius excidium liberanda*, [1590?], sigs. E2ᵛ, M2–M4 (very striking passages in an apparently unique tract in the British Museum); and in Alexander Neville, *Alexandri Neuylli ad VValliæ proceres apologia*, 1576, sig. B4 ("hinc ELIZABETHA, non *ANGLIÆ* modò lumẽ, sed totius terrarum orbis stella. Hinc denique pax, pietas, relligio").

[19] iii, 8. Cf. vi, 5; x, 8, 9.   [20] ii, 7; iii, 5; vi, 47; viii, 26; xii, 33.

[21] xii, 8. Spenser follows the diction of the century in his frequent designation of a young unmarried woman as a virgin or maid; but the words probably acquired a stricter connotation of chastity with the ascendancy of the English Diana.

otic readers easily found both a reflection of the virginity
of the goodliest of maiden queens, Gloriana, and a lovely
personification of her "Pure Religion."

If Book I brings Elizabeth into intimate association with
holiness and truth, Book II binds her directly and indirectly to the second private virtue, temperance. The introductory stanzas are addressed to the "most mighty
Soveraine":

> And thou, O fayrest Princesse under sky,
> In this fayre mirrhour maist behold thy face,
> And thine owne realmes in lond of Faery,
> And in this antique ymage thy great auncestry.

> The which O pardon me thus to enfold
> In covert vele, and wrap in shadowes light,
> That feeble eyes your glory may behold,
> Which ells could not endure those beames bright,
> But would bee dazled with exceeding light.
> O pardon! and vouchsafe with patient eare
> The brave adventures of this Faery knight,
> The good Sir Guyon, gratiously to heare;
> In whom great rule of Temp'raunce goodly doth appeare.[22]

Passing references to Gloriana keep one mindful of whom
Sir Guyon, knight of temperance, serves.[23] When Medina
asks him to tell of his home and of his quests, he replies:

> "This thy demaund, O lady, doth revive
> Fresh memory in me of that great Queene,
> Great and most glorious virgin Queene alive,
> That with her soveraine powre, and scepter shene,
> All Faery Lond does peaceably sustene.
> In widest ocean she her throne does reare,
> That over all the earth it may be seene;
> As morning sunne her beames dispredden cleare,
> And in her face faire peace and mercy doth appeare.

---

[22] Stanzas 4-5.
[23] i, 1; ix, 38.

"In her the richesse of all heavenly grace
In chiefe degree are heaped up on hye:
And all, that els this worlds enclosure bace
Hath great or glorious in mortall eye,
Adornes the person of her Majestye;
That men beholding so great excellence,
And rare perfection in mortalitye,
Doe her adore with sacred reverence,
As th' idole of her Makers great magnificence." [24]

The "fayre ymage of that heavenly mayd" which Sir Guyon bears on his shield attracts attention three times [25] before Guyon, asked why he carries this lifelike semblance, exclaims:

"Fayre sir," sayd he, "if in that picture dead
Such life ye read, and vertue in vaine shew,
What mote ye weene, if the trew livelyhead
Of that most glorious visage ye did vew?
But yf the beauty of her mind ye knew,
That is, her bounty and imperiall powre,
Thousand times fairer then her mortal hew,
O how great wonder would your thoughts devoure,
And infinite desire into your spirite poure!

"Shee is the mighty Queene of Faery,
Whose faire retraitt I in my shield doe beare;
Shee is the flowre of grace and chastity,
Throughout the world renowmed far and neare,
My liefe, my liege, my soveraine, my deare,
Whose glory shineth as the morning starre,
And with her light the earth enlumines cleare:
Far reach her mercies, and her praises farre,
As well in state of peace, as puissaunce in warre." [26]

---

[24] ii, 40–41. In stanza 43 she is a sovereign
        "Whose glory is in gracious deeds, and joyes
        Throughout the world her mercy to maintaine."

[25] i, 28; v, 11; viii, 43.

[26] ix, 3–4. See the next three stanzas of this canto for the glory of knightly service under this "mighty Queene of Faery."

In a volume that "hight *Antiquitee of Faery Lond*" Guyon reads the great ancestry of his queen. Spenser devotes canto x to a genealogy of Gloriana that certainly delighted Elizabethan patriotism as much as it astonishes our historical sense. His patriotic prejudice is clear in his second stanza:

> Ne under sunne, that shines so wide and faire,
> Whence all that lives does borrow life and light,
> Lives ought that to her linage may compaire,
> Which, though from earth it be derived right,
> Yet doth it selfe stretch forth to hevens hight,
> And all the world with wonder overspred;
> A labor huge, exceeding far my might:
> How shall fraile pen, with feare disparaged,
> Conceive such soveraine glory, and great bountyhed?

He misses no chance to exalt all women members of the family tree. Perhaps even the musical skill of "fayre Helena," daughter of "King Coyll," is emphasized to please Gloriana at her virginals.[27] Sir Guyon,

> At last, quite ravisht with delight, to heare
> The royall ofspring of his native land,
> Cryde out: "Deare countrey! O how dearely deare
> Ought thy remembraunce and perpetual band
> Be to thy foster childe, that from thy hand
> Did commun breath and nouriture receave!
> How brutish is it not to understand
> How much to her we owe, that all us gave,
> That gave unto us all, what ever good we have!"[28]

Such ardent patriotism, of a piece with John of Gaunt's speech, identifies queen with "deare countrey." It hardly saw the amusing understatement we find in the announcement that Oberon (Henry VIII) "doubly supplide, in spousall and dominion" the "emptie place" which the death of his elder brother left. Oberon

[27] Stanza 59.   [28] Stanza 69.

dying left the fairest Tanaquill,
Him to succeede therein, by his last will:
Fairer and nobler liveth none this howre,
Ne like in grace, ne like in learned skill;
Therefore they Glorian call that glorious flowre:
Long mayst thou, Glorian, live, in glory and great powre! [29]

In canto iii "vaine Braggadocchio" is "of fayre Belphœbe fowle forlorne." The lavish description of the "most vertuous and beautifull lady" surpasses even the account of the origin of Gloriana, "most excellent and glorious . . . soveraine." As the richest idealization of the royal Laura, the familiar stanzas demand quotation:

Eftsoone there stepped foorth
A goodly ladie clad in hunters weed,
That seemd to be a woman of great worth,
And, by her stately portance, borne of heavenly birth.

Her face so faire as flesh it seemed not,
But hevenly pourtraict of bright angels hew,
Cleare as the skye, withouten blame or blot,
Through goodly mixture of complexions dew;
And in her cheekes the vermeill red did shew
Like roses in a bed of lillies shed,
The which ambrosiall odours from them threw,
And gazers sence with double pleasure fed,
Hable to heale the sicke, and to revive the ded.

In her faire eyes two living lamps did flame,
Kindled above at th' Hevenly Makers light,
And darted fyrie beames out of the same,
So passing persant, and so wondrous bright,
That quite bereav'd the rash beholders sight:
In them the blinded god his lustfull fyre
To kindle oft assayd, but had no might;
For with dredd majestie and awfull yre
She broke his wanton darts, and quenched bace desyre.

---

[29] Stanza 76.

Her yvorie forhead, full of bountie brave,
Like a broad table did it selfe dispred,
For Love his loftie triumphes to engrave,
And write the battailes of his great godhed:
All good and honour might therein be red:
For there their dwelling was. And when she spake,
Sweete wordes, like dropping honny, she did shed,
And twixt the perles and rubins softly brake
A silver sound, that heavenly musicke seemd to make.

Upon her eyelids many Graces sate,
Under the shadow of her even browes,
Working belgardes and amorous retrate,
And everie one her with a grace endowes,
And everie one with meekenesse to her bowes,
So glorious mirrhour of celestiall grace,
And soveraine moniment of mortall vowes,
How shall frayle pen descrive her heavenly face,
For feare, through want of skill, her beauty to disgrace?

So faire, and thousand thousand times more faire,
She seemd, when she presented was to sight;
And was yclad, for heat of scorching aire,
All in a silken camus lylly whight,
Purfled upon with many a folded plight,
Which all above besprinckled was throughout
With golden aygulets, that glistred bright,
Like twinckling starres, and all the skirt about
Was hemd with golden fringe.

Below her ham her weed did somewhat trayne,
And her streight legs most bravely were embayld
In gilden buskins of costly cordwayne,
All bard with golden bendes, which were entayld
With curious antickes, and full fayre aumayld:
Before, they fastned were under her knee
In a rich jewell, and therein entrayld
The ends of all their knots, that none might see
How they within their fouldings close enwrapped bee.

Like two faire marble pillours they were seene,
Which doe the temple of the gods support,
Whom all the people decke with girlands greene,
And honour in their festivall resort;
Those same with stately grace and princely port
She taught to tread, when she her selfe would grace,
But with the woody nymphes when she did sport,
Or when the flying libbard she did chace,
She could them nimbly move, and after fly apace.

And in her hand a sharpe bore-speare she held,
And at her backe a bow and quiver gay,
Stuft with steele-headed dartes, wherewith she queld
The salvage beastes in her victorious play,
Knit with a golden bauldricke, which forelay
Athwart her snowy brest, and did divide
Her daintie paps; which, like young fruit in May,
Now little gan to swell, and being tide,
Through her thin weed their places only signifide.

Her yellow lockes, crisped like golden wyre,
About her shoulders weren loosely shed,
And when the winde emongst them did inspyre,
They waved like a penon wyde dispred,
And low behinde her backe were scattered:
And whether art it were, or heedelesse hap,
As through the flouring forrest rash she fled,
In her rude heares sweet flowres themselves did lap,
And flourishing fresh leaves and blossomes did enwrap.

Such as Diana by the sandy shore
Of swift Eurotas, or on Cynthus greene,
Where all the nymphes have her unwares forlore,
Wandreth alone with bow and arrowes keene,
To seeke her game: or as that famous queene
Of Amazons, whom Pyrrhus did destroy,
The day that first of Priame she was seene,
Did shew her selfe in great triumphant joy,
To succour the weake state of sad afflicted Troy.[30]

[30] Stanzas 21–31. See the remainder of the canto.

Belphœbe emphasizes the moral of Book II when she speaks of winning honor by renouncing Acrasia's world in the name of temperance.[31] Book II is perhaps best read as a compliment to Elizabeth's temperate *via media* in government.[32]

Book III, "contayning the Legend of Britomartis or of Chastity," is definitely inspired by the chaste Elizabeth — Ralegh's Cynthia — as the introductory stanzas show:

It falls me here to write of Chastity,
That fayrest vertue, far above the rest;
For which what needes me fetch from Faery
Forreine ensamples, it to have exprest?
Sith it is shrined in my Soveraines brest,
And formd so lively in each perfect part,
That to all ladies, which have it profest,
Neede but behold the pourtraict of her hart,
If pourtrayd it might bee by any living art.

But living art may not least part expresse,
Nor life-resembling pencill it can paynt,
All were it Zeuxis or Praxiteles:
His dædale hand would faile, and greatly faynt,
And her perfections with his error taynt:
Ne poets witt, that passeth painter farre
In picturing the parts of beauty daynt,
So hard a workemanship adventure darre,
For fear through want of words her excellence to marre.

How then shall I, apprentice of the skill
That whilome in divinest wits did rayne,
Presume so high to stretch mine humble quill?
Yet now my luckelesse lott doth me constrayne

---

[32] Cf. Edwin Greenlaw (*Studies in Spenser's Historical Allegory*, Baltimore, 1932, p. 100): "The first achievement of the queen was the restoration of religion; the next was the establishment of a settled government by routing Discord, Guile, Zeal and all fanaticisms, the lure of the irrational and intemperate. These basal idealisms, themes treated in a large body of Elizabethan writings, Spenser built into his poem."

Hereto perforce. But, O dredd Soverayne,
Thus far forth pardon, sith that choicest witt
Cannot your glorious pourtraict figure playne,
That I in colourd showes may shadow itt,
And antique praises unto present persons fitt.

But if in living colours, and right hew,
Your selfe you covet to see pictured,
Who can it doe more lively, or more trew,
Then that sweete verse, with nectar sprinckeled,
In which a gracious servaunt pictured
His Cynthia, his heavens fayrest light?
That with his melting sweetnes ravished,
And with the wonder of her beames bright,
My sences lulled are in slomber of delight.

But let that same delitious poet lend
A little leave unto a rusticke Muse
To sing his mistresse prayse, and let him mend,
If ought amis her liking may abuse:
Ne let his fayrest Cynthia refuse,
In mirrours more then one her selfe to see,
But either Gloriana let her chuse,
Or in Belphœbe fashioned to bee:
In th' one her rule, in th' other her rare chastitee.[33]

Again the reader is told that Elizabeth is to be seen in
more mirrors than one. The noble character of Britomart
appealed even more to Elizabethans than it does to us because for them her chastity was embodied in their queen.
I cannot trace the full development of Britomart; but
direct association of her character with Elizabeth's is frequent and notable. Numerous scattered epithets commend Britomart's chastity. Canto ii opens with a defense
of the skill of women in "warres," in "artes and pollicy,"
which must have had quick meaning at a time when the
"regiment of women" was ardently defended by apolo-

[33] Stanzas 1-5.

gists for the rule of the warrior maiden who vanquished
the Armada.[34]   The queen is the "precedent" of this
"faire martiall mayd":

> Of warlike puissaunce in ages spent,
> Be thou, faire Britomart, whose prayse I wryte;
> But of all wisedom bee thou precedent,
> O soveraine Queene, whose prayse I would endyte,
> Endite I would as dewtie doth excyte;
> But ah! my rymes to rude and rugged arre,
> When in so high an object they doe lyte,
> And, striving fit to make, I feare doe marre:
> Thy selfe thy prayses tell, and make them knowen farre.[35]

Again genealogy begins and ends by lauding Elizabeth:

> Begin then, O my dearest sacred dame,
> Daughter of Phœbus and of Memorye,
> That doest ennoble with immortall name
> The warlike worthies, from antiquitye,
> In thy great volume of eternitye:
> Begin, O Clio, and recount from hence
> My glorious Soveraines goodly auncestrye,
> Till that by dew degrees and long protense,
> Thou have it lastly brought unto her Excellence.

> .   .   .   .

> "Tho, when the terme is full accomplishid,
> There shall a sparke of fire, which hath long-while
> Bene in his ashes raked up and hid,
> Bee freshly kindled in the fruitfull ile
> Of Mona, where it lurked in exile;
> Which shall breake forth into bright burning flame,
> And reach into the house that beares the stile
> Of roiall majesty and soveraine name:
> So shall the Briton blood their crowne agayn reclame.

---

[34] See the Earl of Northampton's *A Dutifull defense of the lawfull regiment
of Woemen*, described below, p. 435.
[35] Stanza 3.

"Thenceforth eternall union shall be made
Betweene the nations different afore,
And sacred Peace shall lovingly persuade
The warlike minds to learne her goodly lore,
And civile armes to exercise no more:
Then shall a royall Virgin raine, which shall
Stretch her white rod over the Belgicke shore,
And the great Castle smite so sore with all,
That it shall make him shake, and shortly learne to fall." [36]

Women rulers and their chastity are exalted at every opportunity.[37]

Spenser bravely seeks to resolve his idealization of the past into praise of the Tudor present:

But when I reade, how stout Debora strake
Proud Sisera, and how Camill' hath slaine
The huge Orsilochus, I swell with great disdaine.

Yet these, and all that els had puissaunce,
Cannot with noble Britomart compare,
Aswell for glorie of great valiaunce,
As for pure chastitie and vertue rare,
That all her goodly deedes do well declare.
Well worthie stock, from which the branches sprong
That in late yeares so faire a blossome bare
As thee, O queene, the matter of my song,
Whose lignage from this lady I derive along.[38]

With Belphœbe's reappearance in canto v and her rescue of Timias, Spenser redoubles his praise of the "most vertuous and beautifull lady" by portraying this "heavenly mayd" as the source of all grace to that poor knight (usually taken to figure Sir Walter Ralegh). His service is wholly to "her, . . . whom the hevens doe serve and sew. . . . [her] hevenly borne, and of celestiall hew." [39] This

[36] iii, 4, 48–49.
[37] See, especially, stanzas 54 ff.
[38] iv, 2–3.
[39] Stanza 47.

canto closes with a Platonic hymn to feminine virtue —
which Belphœbe best embodies:

> Fayre ympes of beautie, whose bright shining beames
> Adorne the world with like to heavenly light,
> And to your willes both royalties and reames
> Subdew, through conquest of your wondrous might,
> With this fayre flowre your goodly girlonds dight
> Of chastity and vertue virginall,
> That shall embellish more your beautie bright,
> And crowne your heades with heavenly coronall,
> Such as the angels weare before Gods tribunall.

> To youre faire selves a faire ensample frame
> Of this faire virgin, this Belphebe fayre,
> To whom, in perfect love and spotlesse fame
> Of chastitie, none living may compayre:
> Ne poysnous envy justly can empayre
> The prayse of her fresh flowring maydenhead;
> Forthy she standeth on the highest stayre
> Of th' honorable stage of womanhead,
> That ladies all may follow her ensample dead.

> In so great prayse of stedfast chastity
> Nathlesse she was so courteous and kynde,
> Tempred with grace and goodly modesty,
> That seemed those two vertues strove to fynd
> The higher place in her heroick mynd:
> So striving each did other more augment,
> And both encrease the prayse of woman kynde,
> And both encrease her beautie excellent;
> So all did make in her a perfect complement.[40]

Canto vi tells of the parentage and birth of "fayre Belphœbe" in an idealization of Elizabeth which can hardly
be understood without realizing that this "most vertuous
and beautifull lady" enshrined the idea of all feminine
worth and beauty for a patriotic and Platonic mind.

[40] Stanzas 53-55.

But to this faire Belphœbe in her berth
The hevens so favorable were and free,
Looking with myld aspect upon the earth
In th' horoscope of her nativitee,
That all the gifts of grace and chastitee
On her they poured forth of plenteous horne;
Jove laught on Venus from his soverayne see,
And Phœbus with faire beames did her adorne,
And all the Graces rockt her cradle being borne.

Her berth was of the wombe of morning dew,
And her conception of the joyous prime,
And all her whole creation did her shew
Pure and unspotted from all loathly crime,
That is ingenerate in fleshly slime.
So was this virgin borne, so was she bred,
So was she trayned up from time to time
In all chaste vertue and true bounti-hed,
Till to her dew perfection she was ripened.[41]

At the outset of canto ix Spenser takes care to ask that
his portrayal of a "wanton lady" cast no cloud on the
"shyning glory" of "honorable dames." Soon Britomart
appears as "lineally extract" from "noble Britons"
"sprong from Trojans bold." [42] Troynovant is praised in
stanzas that are not to be disassociated from Elizabeth as
descended from Brutus and Arthur. In canto xi Britomart, "the flowre of chastity," is a model for all lovers:

And ye, faire ladies, that your kingdomes make
In th' harts of men, them governe wisely well,
And of faire Britomart ensample take,
That was as trew in love as turtle to her make.[43]

Book III in its celebration of chastity does varied homage to the most distinctive virtue of the lady Elizabeth.

[41] Stanzas 2–3. See the stanzas which follow on.
[42] Stanza 38.
[43] Stanza 2.

Britomart and Belphœbe are beautiful shadows of her virginity.

If the "empresse" recedes in Book III before the "most vertuous and beautifull lady," [44] in the introductory stanzas of Book IV, which celebrates friendship, she is addressed immediately. Yet as soon as Spenser has denounced those who abuse love, he seeks, not the cold regal virgin, but the woman who long toyed with love. He addresses

> that sacred saint my soveraigne Queene,
> In whose chast breast all bountie naturall
> And treasures of true love enlocked beene,
> Bove all her sexe that ever yet was seene:
> To her I sing of love, that loveth best
> And best is lov'd of all alive, I weene;
> To her this song most fitly is addrest,
> The queene of love, and prince of peace from heaven blest.

> Which that she may the better deigne to heare,
> Do thou, dred infant, Venus dearling dove,
> From her high spirit chase imperious feare,
> And use of awfull majestie remove:
> In sted thereof with drops of melting love,
> Deawd with ambrosiall kisses, by thee gotten
> From thy sweete smyling mother from above,
> Sprinckle her heart, and haughtie courage soften,
> That she may hearke to love, and reade this lesson often. [45]

It is Ralegh's Belphœbe whose ear he would have, and for that friend's sake. [46] Whatever the exact interpretation given to cantos vii–viii, one must find in their characterization of Belphœbe a reflection of the "vertuous lady's" exaction of the utmost loyalty from one of her favored

[44] But formal references appear, as in i, 2; iv, 54.
[45] Stanzas 4–5.
[46] See above, pp. 309, 310, where Ralegh in *Cynthia* makes the same distinction between the stern queen and the loving lady.

servants. I think that Belphœbe's stinging rebuke to Timias's divided affection points unmistakably to all that Ralegh's *Cynthia* shadows at about the time that Spenser wrote these cantos.[47]

When Britomart, that other image of the "most vertuous and beautifull lady," appears in the rôle of peacemaker, perhaps one may see a suggestion of Elizabeth's mediation at court between her captious knights. In canto vi Britomart, who must of course never be equated with Elizabeth Tudor in any absolute way, inspires the poet to some beautiful descriptive verses when she unloosens her golden braids.[48] The victories of this "faire ladie knight" reflect glory on those of the maiden knight of Tilbury; so, too, the praise of warlike women.[49] Perhaps the high dignity of Britomart in love [50] comes because she often reflects the exalted and imperious Elizabeth. Britomart's part in sustaining the motif of Book IV [51] brings Elizabeth into association with the fourth private virtue. The celebration of friendship cannot possibly be made so appropriate a compliment to the queen as the celebration of chastity was.[52] Yet if the story of Timias and Belphœbe is read as one of broken friendship healed by the grace of the offended friend, the "most vertuous . . . lady" does appear as the heroine of a major episode of the book.

[47] What I have written of *Cynthia*, if brought into association with the episode of Timias and Belphœbe, gives new occasion for finding in Spenser's story a representation of the Throckmorton affair. Compare Ralegh's "toyes" with the ruby "shap'd like a heart yet bleeding of the wound" (viii, 6 ff.). Dr. Kathrine Koller (*English Literary History*, I [1934], 47–48) has written effectively of the Timias-Belphœbe story as figuring the Throckmorton episode.

[48] See III, ix, 20 ff., where Britomart's appearance again improves the quality of the poetry.

[49] xi, 22.

[50] See vi, 44 ff.

[51] See vi, 46.

[52] One should remember how many late morality plays and interludes had linked Elizabeth with the various virtues — for example, Richard Edwards's play about a classic friendship, *Damon and Pythias* (1565). See above, p. 98.

Book V very obviously compliments Elizabeth.[53] Justice has its home in her breast.[54] As Mercilla she is a chief figure. However much Spenser laments the passing of a golden age when justice was everywhere, he ends his introduction as follows:

> Dread soverayne goddesse, that doest highest sit
> In seate of judgement, in th' Almighties stead,
> And with magnificke might and wondrous wit
> Doest to thy people righteous doome aread,
> That furthest nations filles with awfull dread,
> Pardon the boldnesse of thy basest thrall,
> That dare discourse of so divine a read,
> As thy great justice praysed over all:
> The instrument whereof, loe! here thy Artegall.[55]

When in canto i distressed Eirena complains to Gloriana of her sad state,

> That soveraine queene, that mightie emperesse,
> Whose glorie is to aide all suppliants pore,
> And of weake princes to be patronesse,
> Chose Artegall to right her to restore;
> For that to her he seem'd best skild in righteous lore.[56]

Radigund may be seen as illustrative of "th' insolent commaund of womens will";[57] judgment is passed on her kind when Britomart slays her in the name of true justice —

> The skill whereof to princes hearts he [Jove] doth reveale.[58]

---

[53] Greenlaw (*Spenser's Historical Allegory*, p. 142) even found in the incident of the two brothers who quarrel over the treasure chest on the seashore (canto iv) a treatment of Cynthia's rule of the sea.

[54] The classic personification of justice as Astræa, virgin goddess of the golden age to whom stanza 11 of canto i is devoted, lends itself admirably, of course, to the celebration of the just virgin queen of an English golden age. Witness Sir John Davies's *Hymnes of Astræa.*

[55] Stanza 11.   [56] Stanza 4.

[57] Radigund is the condemned type of feminist. Surely no satirical thrust at Elizabeth's rule is intended; Elizabeth is clearly Mercilla. If criticism of the queen is intended in Radigund, it is too covert to be found now.   [58] vii, 1.

Stanzas descriptive of Britomart,[59] the admired woman warrior, would please Elizabeth, more or less mirrored in this "magnificke virgin."

Just after his portrait of an unjust regiment of woman Spenser places that of Mercilla, who of course represents Elizabeth as an exponent of merciful justice. Artegall, again about

suite of his avowed quest,
Which he had undertane to Gloriane,[60]

comes upon a damsel in flight. She explains:

> "I
> Doe serve a queene, that not far hence doth wone,
> A princesse of great powre and majestie,
> Famous through all the world, and honor'd far and nie.
>
> "Her name Mercilla most men use to call;
> That is a mayden queene of high renowne,
> For her great bounty knowen over all,
> And soveraine grace, with which her royall crowne
> She doth support, and strongly beateth downe
> The malice of her foes, which her envy,
> And at her happinesse do fret and frowne:
> Yet she her selfe the more doth magnify,
> And even to her foes her mercies multiply.
>
> "Mongst many which maligne her happy state,
> There is a mighty man, which wonnes here by,
> That with most fell despight and deadly hate
> Seekes to subvert her crowne and dignity,
> And all his powre doth thereunto apply:
> And her good knights, of which so brave a band
> Serves her as any princesse under sky,
> He either spoiles, if they against him stand,
> Or to his part allures, and bribeth under hand." [61]

---

[59] See especially stanzas 21 and 42.

[60] viii, 3. As in the other books, so in Book V passing allusions or references to Gloriana keep the reader conscious of her dominant place in the design of the poem.   [61] viii, 16-18.

The rest of canto viii gives the familiar English view of the Armada victory in 1588. It was by God's favor — his power over the storms, which raged for Mercilla's cause. "Justice that day of wrong her selfe had wroken." [62]

In canto ix the maiden prevails on Arthur and Artegall to visit the palace of her lady by declaring:

> "There shall ye see my soverayne Lady Queene,
> Most sacred wight, most debonayre and free,
> That ever yet upon this earth was seene,
> Or that with diademe hath ever crowned beene." [63]

The verses which follow describe the beauty of Mercilla's palace — its freedom from Guile, Malice and Despight, its rule by Order to secure "joyous peace" and "just judgements," its intolerance of "wicked sclaunders." Then

> They, passing by, were guyded by degree
> Unto the presence of that gratious queene:
> Who sate on high, that she might all men see,
> And might of all men royally be seene,
> Upon a throne of gold full bright and sheene,
> Adorned all with gemmes of endlesse price,
> As either might for wealth have gotten bene,
> Or could be fram'd by workmans rare device;
> And all embost with lyons and with flourdelice.

> All over her a cloth of state was spred,
> Not of rich tissew, nor of cloth of gold,
> Nor of ought else that may be richest red,
> But like a cloud, as likest may be told,
> That her brode spreading wings did wyde unfold;
> Whose skirts were bordred with bright sunny beams,
> Glistring like gold, amongst the plights enrold,
> And here and there shooting forth silver streames,
> Mongst which crept litle angels through the glittering gleames.

---

[62] Stanza 44.
[63] Stanza 20.

Seemed those litle angels did uphold
The cloth of state, and on their purpled wings
Did beare the pendants, through their nimblesse bold:
Besides, a thousand more of such as sings
Hymnes to High God, and carols heavenly things,
Encompassed the throne on which she sate:
She angel-like, the heyre of ancient kings
And mightie conquerors, in royall state,
Whylest kings and kesars at her feet did them prostrate.

Thus did she sit in soverayne majestie,
Holding a scepter in her royall hand,
The sacred pledge of peace and clemencie,
With which High God had blest her happie land,
Maugre so many foes which did withstand.
But at her feet her sword was likewise layde,
Whose long rest rusted the bright steely brand;
Yet when as foes enforst, or friends sought ayde,
She could it sternely draw, that all the world dismayde.

And round about, before her feet there sate
A bevie of faire virgins clad in white,
That goodly seem'd t' adorne her royall state,
All lovely daughters of high Jove, that hight
Litæ, by him begot in loves delight
Upon the righteous Themis: those they say
Upon Joves judgement seat wayt day and night,
And when in wrath he threats the worlds decay,
They doe his anger calme, and cruell vengeance stay.

They also doe by his divine permission
Upon the thrones of mortall princes tend,
And often treat for pardon and remission
To suppliants, through frayltie which offend.
Those did upon Mercillaes throne attend:
Just Dice, wise Eunomie, myld Eirene;
And them amongst, her glorie to commend,
Sate goodly Temperance in garments clene,
And sacred Reverence, yborne of heavenly strene.

Thus did she sit in royall rich estate,
Admyr'd of many, honoured of all,
Whylest underneath her feete, there as she sate,
An huge great lyon lay, that mote appall
An hardie courage, like captived thrall,
With a strong yron chaine and coller bound,
That once he could not move, nor quich at all;
Yet did he murmure with rebellious sound,
And softly royne, when salvage choler gan redound.[64]

Then the famous trial of Mary Stuart is vividly allegorized
with all the bias of a zealous English patriot to whom
Elizabeth is "Mercilla myld," who, instead of "just vengeance," would rather let fall

> Few perling drops from her faire lampes of light.[65]

Canto x opens so as to make Mercilla all but identical
with Divine Mercy itself:

Some clarkes doe doubt in their devicefull art,
Whether this heavenly thing whereof I treat,
To weeten Mercie, be of Justice part,
Or drawne forth from her by divine extreate.
This well I wote, that sure she is as great,
And meriteth to have as high a place,
Sith in th' Almighties everlasting seat
She first was bred, and borne of heavenly race;
From thence pour'd down on men, by influence of grace.

For if that vertue be of so great might,
Which from just verdict will for nothing start,
But, to preserve inviolated right,
Oft spilles the principall, to save the part;
So much more then is that of powre and art,
That seekes to save the subject of her skill,
Yet never doth from doome of right depart:
As it is greater prayse to save then spill,
And better to reforme then to cut off the ill.

---

[64] Stanzas 27–33.   [65] Stanza 50.

Who then can thee, Mercilla, throughly prayse,
That herein doest all earthly princes pas?
What heavenly muse shall thy great honour rayse
Up to the skies, whence first deriv'd it was,
And now on earth it selfe enlarged has
From th' utmost brinke of the Americke shore
Unto the margent of the Molucas?
Those nations farre thy justice doe adore:
But thine owne people do thy mercy prayse much more.[66]

Mercilla, reluctantly drawn to punish false Duessa, thereafter continues to show to the two knights

Royall examples of her mercies rare,
And worthie paterns of her clemencies;
Which till this day mongst many living are,
Who them to their posterities doe still declare.[67]

Most illustrative is her relief of Belgæ through Arthur, which is told in the rest of canto x and in canto xi. Artegall, having left Mercilla, goes about "Irenaes franchisement," "Sir Burbon's aide," and "Grantortoes worthy punishment" — all for the glory of his just "empresse." [68]

When Spenser introduces his treatment of courtesy in Book VI he caps his praise of the past and disparagement of the present as an age of courtesy with the following stanzas:

But where shall I in all antiquity
So faire a patterne finde, where may be seene
The goodly praise of princely Curtesie,
As in your selfe, O soveraine Lady Queene?
In whose pure minde, as in a mirrour sheene,
It showes, and with her brightnesse doth inflame

---

[66] Stanzas 1–3.
[67] Stanza 5.
[68] His service to "that mightie Faerie prince, Great Gloriane" is kept before the reader by reference to her and her court in xi, 37; xii, 3, 43 (the last stanza of the book).

The eyes of all which thereon fixed beene;
But meriteth indeede an higher name:
Yet so from low to high uplifted is your fame.

Then pardon me, most dreaded Soveraine,
That from your selfe I doe this vertue bring,
And to your selfe doe it returne againe:
So from the ocean all rivers spring,
And tribute backe repay as to their king:
Right so from you all goodly vertues well
Into the rest which round about you ring,
Faire lords and ladies, which about you dwell,
And doe adorne your court, where courtesies excell.[69]

Canto i opens by continuing the association of the queen's
court with courtesy:

Of Court, it seemes, men Courtesie doe call,
For that it there most useth to abound;
And well beseemeth that in princes hall
That vertue should be plentifully found,
Which of all goodly manners is the ground,
And roote of civill conversation.
Right so in Faery court it did redound,
Where curteous knights and ladies most did won
Of all on earth, and made a matchlesse paragon.[70]

But the book on courtesy does not celebrate that virtue in
Elizabeth so precisely as Book V exalted her justice and
mercy.[71] Spenser does not sing of the Graces and of
Pastorella, whom Sir Calidore

worthy deemed
To be a princes paragone esteemed,[72]

---

[69] Stanzas 6–7.

[70] Stanza 1.

[71] Incidental allusions or references to Gloriana or Belphœbe do appear in ii,
37; v, 12; x, 1. Back in Book III the reader has learned (vi, 1) that the "court
and royal citadell" is "the great schoolmaistresse of all courtesy."

[72] ix, 11.

without straightway subordinating all beauty to

Glorianaes heavenly hew,
To which what can compare? [73]

He inserts a stanza to "faire Elisa, queene of shepheardes all" to temper Meliboe's expressed disillusion with the court and to balance the song to Colin's lovely lass:

"Sunne of the world, great glory of the sky,
That all the earth doest lighten with thy rayes,
Great Gloriana, greatest Majesty,
Pardon thy shepheard, mongst so many layes
As he hath sung of thee in all his dayes,
To make one minime of thy poore handmayd,
And underneath thy feete to place her prayse,
That, when thy glory shall be farre displayd
To future age, of her this mention may be made." [74]

The "Two Cantos of Mutabilitie" contain no allusions to the queen, but one doubts if Spenser would have developed a celebration of constancy without full tribute to a sovereign whose motto was *Semper Eadem*.

So much for a survey of the text of *The Faerie Queene* to see something of how all the shadows of Elizabeth from Judith to Idea are woven into it. It can hardly be gainsaid that these shadows of Elizabeth are deep in the warp and woof of the moral allegory of the poem.[75] They show the inclusiveness of Spenser's idealization — the fullest and richest of all. Gloriana, Una, Mercilla, Belphœbe, and Britomart incorporate all the types of praise which have been studied. The queen's victorious war, her fertile peace and plenty, her preservation of "Pure Religion" by God's

[73] x, 4.
[74] x, 28.
[75] I have not sought to follow in detail the queen's part in the political allegory as such. See Greenlaw, *Spenser's Historical Allegory*, pp. 197–199. I recognize that political and moral allegories fused inextricably for patriotic readers.

guidance, her patronage of the arts, her conquest of "widest ocean," her temperate, just, and merciful government, her courteous court — all the achievements of Judith, Deborah, Eliza, and Cynthia are Gloriana's, Una's, Mercilla's. Belphœbe and Britomart in their beauty and virginity, their talents and graces, sum up and transcend the attributes of Elisa, Diana, Laura, and Idea. Spenser weaves all types of praise and almost every poetic device into the moral and political epic of a great age in English life.

This gathering of Laura, Diana, and Idea into Spenser's chief heroines is worth direct attention.

The commendatory verses and dedicatory sonnets [76] show the translation of Laura into the Faery Queene. Hobynoll writes:

> And faire befall that Faery Queene of thine,
>   In whose faire eyes Love linckt with Vertue sittes:
> Enfusing, by those bewties fyers devyne,
>   Such high conceites into thy humble wittes,
> As raised hath poore pastors oaten reede,
> From rustick tunes, to chaunt heroique deedes.
>
> So mought thy Redcrosse Knight with happy hand
>   Victorious be in that faire Ilands right,
> Which thou dost vayle in type of Faery Land,
>   Elizas blessed field, that Albion hight:
> That shieldes her friendes, and warres her mightie foes,
> Yet still with people, peace, and plentie flowes.
>
> But (jolly shepheard) though with pleasing style
>   Thou feast the humour of the courtly trayne,
> Let not conceipt thy setled sence beguile,
>   Ne daunted be through envy or disdaine.
> Subject thy dome to her empyring spright,
> From whence thy Muse, and all the world, takes light.[77]

---

[76] See Ralegh's two notable sonnets, one of which is quoted above, pp. 239–240. [77] *Works*, p. 139.

For R. S. she is

that sacred Crowne,
Whose hand strowes palme and never-dying bayes.[78]

H. B. would help his friend to reward for singing the praises of the royal Laura:

Grave Muses, march in triumph and with prayses;
Our Goddesse here hath given you leave to land,
And biddes this rare dispenser of your graces
Bow downe his brow unto her sacred hand.
Desertes findes dew in that most princely doome,
In whose sweete brest are all the Muses bredde:
So did that great Augustus erst in Roome
With leaves of fame adorne his poets heede.
Faire be the guerdon of your *Faery Queene*,
Even of the fairest that the world hath seene.[79]

W. L. tends to see the worthy praise of her as beyond even Spenser's power. Spenser, addressing a sonnet to Lord Hunsdon, is conscious of his favor with

'that Empresse,
The worlds sole glory and her sexes grace.[80]

In another to Lord Buckhurst he evidences his first intention — to laud his queen:

In vaine I thinke, right honourable Lord,
By this rude rime to memorize thy name,
Whose learned Muse hath writ her owne record
In golden verse, worthy immortal fame:
Thou much more fit (were leasure to the same)
Thy gracious Soverains praises to compile,
And her imperiall majestie to frame
In loftie numbers and heroicke stile.[81]

---

[78] The same.
[79] The same.
[80] Page 142.
[81] Pages 142–143.

In his last sonnet it is this peerless Laura who is the "worlds sole wonderment":

TO ALL THE GRATIOUS AND BEAUTIFULL
LADIES IN THE COURT

The Chian peincter, when he was requirde
  To pourtraict Venus in her perfect hew,
  To make his worke more absolute, desird
  Of all the fairest maides to have the vew.
Much more me needs, to draw the semblant trew
  Of Beauties Queene, the worlds sole wonderment,
  To sharpe my sence with sundry beauties vew,
  And steale from each some part of ornament.
If all the world to seeke I overwent,
  A fairer crew yet no where could I see
  Then that brave court doth to mine eie present,
  That the worlds pride seemes gathered there to bee.
Of each a part I stole by cunning thefte:
Forgive it me, faire Dames, sith lesse ye have not lefte. [82]

These commendatory verses show how generally the poem was read as one to laud Elizabeth; [83] and the "Beauties Queene" in them prepares one to recognize in the extravagant description of Belphœbe the supreme example of the beautiful sonnet mistress anatomized. The enthusiasm in this lavish description of Belphœbe appears again in the

[82] Page 144.

[83] The influence of such a reading is perhaps seen in the entertainment for Elizabeth on the fourth day of her visit to Elvetham in 1591 (Lyly, I, 449–450). There "the Fayery Queene came into the garden, dauncing with her maides about her. Shee brought with her a garland made in fourme of an imperiall Crowne; within the sight of her Maiestie, shee fixed <it> vpon a siluer staffe, and sticking the staffe into the ground," spoke her praises, crowned her, and with her maids danced around the garland and sang to Elizabeth a pretty song beginning:

Elisa is the fairest Queene
That euer trod vpon this greene.
Elisaes eyes are blessed starres,
Inducing peace, subduing warres.

account of her birth. In his portrait of the "most vertuous and beautifull lady" Spenser catches some of the rapturous ecstasy before beauty that marks a Platonic imagination.

For "Beauties Queene" is also the ultimate portrait of the royal Diana and the royal Idea. The Faery Queene in her milieu of chivalric idealism inherits all the medieval devotion to the virgin lady which in chapter v appeared drawn to "Eliza [with] her sort of goodly knights." The literary cult of the English Diana, as has been seen, is inseparable from medieval adoration of the virgin Queen of Heaven. Yet Spenser, in an age which was neither naïvely pietistic nor naïvely patriotic, created Britomart and hymned Gloriana's chastity only after having known virgin lady knights in Italian epic poetry. Clorinda and Bradamante are antecedents of Britomart, and Britomart is a final name for the virgin knight Elizabeth.[84]

As was Colin's Cynthia, so is "Beauties Queene" a creation of Spenser's Platonizing imagination. Spenser "saw earthly beauty, and especially the beauty of woman, which inspires love, as the reflection and index of divine beauty, virtue rendered visible, the beam from on high lodged in a body and fashioning its fleshly habitation into a marvellous palace."[85] "Faire dames," unless their "goodly Beautie" which is "heavenly borne" is "foule abused," remain "lively images of heavens light." The "shadow" of their "first informed grace" yet shines in their "beauteous face."[86] Before his eyes from his youth was the great queen and brilliant virgin, personifying his beloved England. She seemed nothing less than an "abiding image of

---

[84] Edward Fairfax dedicated to Elizabeth in twenty-four verses his *Godfrey of Bulloigne, or The Recouerie of Ierusalem* (1600). She is a "Towre *of goodnes, vertue, bewtie*" (sig. A2).

[85] Legouis and Cazamian, p. 283.

[86] The phrases are from "An Hymne in Honour of Beautie."

heavens light" sent to reveal all regal and feminine loveliness. "T' adore thing so divine as beauty were but right."

> And he himselfe long gazing thereupon,
> At last fell humbly downe upon his knee,
> And of his wonder made religion,
> Weening some heavenly goddesse he did see,
> Or else unweeting what it else might bee;
>
> .   .   .   .
>
> And drawing nigh, when as he plaine describe
> That peerelesse paterne of Dame Natures pride,
> And heavenly image of perfection,
> He blest himselfe, as one sore terrifide,
> And turning feare to faint devotion,
> Did worship her as some celestiall vision.[87]

The queen and lady seemed to embrace all the virtues
which the poet planned to represent in the character of
"a gentleman or noble person [of] vertuous and gentle
discipline." "In hir [was] vertues perfect image cast."
Her magnificence was a living and visible model for that
of his Arthur. Hence the variously sustained adoration of
her in *The Faerie Queene.* In idealizing the mundane
Elizabeth, Spenser is but a consistent Platonist, not attending to the mortal biding place of magnificent royalty
and virtuous womanhood, but to the perfect form, the
revealed idea which is most true and apparent to an indomitable Platonist, whose grip on mixed actuality is as
intermittent [88] as his dedication to the ideal is complete.

[87] These verses describe the effect of Britomart on Artegall and Scudamore
(IV, vi, 22, 24).

[88] One hesitates to say "limited," because Spenser in his *A Veue of the
Present State of Ireland* has left as cold a Machiavellian appraisal of facts as his
sovereign, who ruled not without "pollicie," could have asked. But perhaps
Professor Legouis (*Spenser*, 1926, p. 23) was right in pointing out that "even
here the idealist may still be detected. He betrays himself by his very pitiless-
ness; are not often idealists, when they have to deal with human problems, the
most unfeeling of men? With their eyes lifted up to the glorious vision that

When the idealizing cast of Spenser's imagination has been comprehended, the question of his sincerity is less perplexing. For a Platonist, things become symbols, and symbols enfold the ideal. Historical facts about the queen and lady do reveal a distinguished person. But Spenser was probably often no more blind to the faded face and worldly diplomacy of Elizabeth than he was to his actual wives as compared with the glorious bride he beholds in his *Epithalamion*. Spenser's affinity as artist and lover was with the best he saw in these ladies. That was enough to inspire noble hymns to regal magnificence and feminine beauty.

To see Spenser as enamoured of "goodly formes and faire aspects" helps one to read aright the moral allegory in *The Faerie Queene*. It is a "continued allegory" — the most continued allegorical element.[89] As a Platonist he

---

shines in the distance they will run towards it, never caring if they must cut their way through poor suffering flesh." This brilliant scholar seems to me less penetrating when, in attempting (pp. 19–23) to divine what "the poet thought of his sovereign in the secret of his heart" after painting her as complete perfection, he writes: "He did not paint the queen as he knew she was, but as she liked to be painted, and he justified the enormous lie to himself by considering her as a mere figure-head of an ideal England, an ideal femininity." And to say that Spenser "obviously used his panegyrics to cover his assaults" is to assume a designing intent on his part at odds with the Platonic nature of his imagination. As Professor A. C. Sprague reminds me, the belief that the king can do no wrong was potent in Spenser's time. The picture of the queen which I have just exhibited is executed with too much enthusiasm for one not to believe that Spenser painted Elizabeth as he liked to paint her. To see him as needing deliberately to justify to himself his portrait as an "enormous lie" is to forget that Elizabeth, whatever else she was, was a final symbol for the "glorious vision" of nationality and perfect womanhood that shone before Spenser's Platonic imagination — half blinded him, if you please. The vision was one that the age shared. It was the vision of England's full glory. Elizabeth was not merely the "figure-head of an ideal England"; she was its present glory. She was Gloriana.

[89] "There is political and contemporary allusion aplenty, and persons and events in contemporary affairs appear often enough. For it is the essence of Spenser's Platonism that the perfect idea, the ideal virtue, should be incarnated now in one and now in another person belonging to that brilliant court" (Greenlaw, *Spenser's Historical Allegory*, pp. 100–101).

has his eye fixed on the "goodly formes," the moral virtues, and all his characters are created to illustrate them as fully and variously as possible. Hence the moral beauty of the queen and lady is in Gloriana, Una, Mercilla, Belphœbe, and Britomart — in fact, in every admirable portrayal of womankind. Holiness, temperance, chastity, friendship, justice, courtesy, constancy — all the private virtues are united in the shadows of the "high, mightie and magnificent empresse," in her glory and magnanimity even before they shine in the magnificence of Prince Arthur and in his knights. If Spenser could so constantly and variously fit his "twelve private morall virtues" to the lady, one wonders how "continued" the allegory would have been in the books in which he planned to set forth the twelve "polliticke vertues," of which Elizabeth was of course the embodiment *par excellence.*[90]

[90] Dr. Heffner (*Studies in Philology*, XXVII, 152) notes in Peele's *Speeches to Queen Elizabeth at Theobalds* (1591) a reference to her twelve virtues: "The Gardener says to her Majesty: 'All the Virtues, all the Graces, all the Muses winding and reathing about your Majesty, each contending to be chief . . . the virtues were done in roses, flowers fit for the *twelve* Virtues.'" See the verso of the title-page of John Case's *Sphæra Civitatis* (1588) and the title-page of *The holi bible* (1569) for further evidence of the constant association of the queen with admired virtues. Note, too, the following quotations: "Queene Elizabeth . . . sole Princesse of Peace, and second to no annointed kyng, in the exercise of all the Capitol Vertues" (George Whetstone, *The enemie to Vnthryftinesse*, [1586], sig. G4); "that sacred virgine pure: [Eliza] . . . O perfect magnanimitie" (John Derricke, *The image of Ireland*, 1581, sigs. B1v–B2); "Fortie whole yeares that this magnanimious and most prudent Queene hath reigned" (Cipriano de Valero, *Two treatises: . . . translated . . . by Iohn Golburne*, 1600, sig. M5); "a Queene, that of iustice is not only the very perfect image & paterne; but also of mercie & clemencie (vnder God) the meere fountaine & bodie itselfe" (Reginald Scott, *The discouerie of witchcraft*, 1584, sig. A2v); and "*her Maiesties proceedings vvith the Spaniard* (*she hauing liued in greater temperance then any Prince of her time*)" (Edward Daunce, *A briefe discourse dialoguevvise*, 1590, sig. A2). Richard Vennar's *The right way to heaven* (1601) celebrates Elizabeth's beauty, wisdom, mercy, grace, constancy, love of God, gracious speech, zeal for "Pure Religion," patience, justice, and magnanimity (Nichols, *Elizabeth*, III, 532–543). It is dedicated to the queen; see below, p. 456. It is notable that virtues in which she excels — prudence, justice, magnanimity, and moderation or temperance — are

PHILOSOPHORVM ROGATO ÆSCVLAPIO SVO.

Vluere cui vires & robora sana dedisti,
Scribere mi vellem, nec robore durior essem.
Ergo mihi (quæ privato pertingere multi
CASE dabis) communi satis & satis Astra mereris.

QVAM bene CŒLESTI CIVILIS machina formæ
Congruat, & quàm sit paribus distincta figuris,
Vinca pro multis Reipublica nostra loquetur.
Aspicis alterno circum gyrantia curfu
Sidera, & æquali causa quæ pondere librat
IVSTITIAM, nostri centrum invariabile mundi?
Aspicis emensos SEPTEM spatia ampla PLANETAS,
Quorum quisque suo studiose præsidet orbi?
VBERTAS RERVM, Lunæ & FACVNDIA, Regni
Mercurius: Venus esse potest CLEMENTIA Regis.
Par soli PIETAS medijs diffunditur Astris.
VIS ANIMI iustis Mauortem spirat in armis.
Nata Iovem simulat PRVDENTIA prouida patrem:
Saturnum'q; graui MAIESTAS plena timore.
Hæ sunt quæ nostras collustrant Lampades oras
Præcipuæ:verùm his Octauam apponere Sphæram
Luminibus fixis, claris, varijs'q; micantem
Iam libet, vt olim STELLATVM dicere CŒLVM.
Cœlum Stellatum CAMERA est STELLATA Britannis,
Consilijs munita pijs, Procerumq; frequenti
Nobilium stipata manu, qui munia Regni
Ardua procurant, & magna negotia versant,
Omnibus impedet globus is, cui MOBILE PRIMVM
Nomen, & amplex nexus qui continet omnes.
Tu VIRGO, REGINA Potens, tu MOBILE PRIMVM
ELISABETHA, rapis tecum molimina Gentis.
Inde reluctantes animos, mentesq; rebelles
Debilitas, MOTVque trahis Suprema DIVRNO.
Hic ordo, sic conspirat status ORBIS, & VRBIS:
Hæc tamen hoc tantum discrimine distat ab ILLO,
Quòd non perpetuò firmari possit vt ILLE.
Ergò diu SPHÆRÆ SVMMA MOTRICE feruntur,
Ergò diu SPHÆRAS & MOTRIX SVMMA gubernet.

RICHARDVS LATE—WAR, Collegij
D. Iohannis Præcursoris Socius.

SPHÆRA CIVITATIS

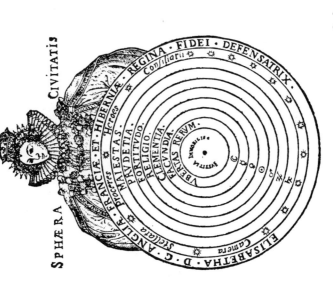

JOHN CASE, Sphera civitatis, 1588

Undoubtedly, then, all the virtues celebrated appear first in Gloriana and Belphœbe and their sisters, no matter what knights and ladies may illustrate them. Britomart officially exemplifies chastity, but Spenser quickly wonders why he need

> fetch from Faery
> Forreine ensamples, it to have exprest . . .
> Sith it is shrined in my Soveraines brest.

All "forreine ensamples" are indirectly tributes to its enshrinement in Gloriana. Even the portrait of Acrasia can be read as an indirect compliment to her opposite, the temperate queen. Chastity or virginity seems to have been for Spenser the "fayrest vertue, far above the rest." Over and over again "virgin" or "maiden" is the epithet given to a noble character.[91] Diffused throughout the poem is this admiration of virginity; and so, equally diffused is his compliment to the English Diana. Britomart, a name denoting a martial Britoness, is really one of the names of Diana. Belphœbe, declared compliment to the "most vertuous and beautifull lady" is preëminently a shadow of the virgin huntress and warrior, Elizabeth. Furthermore, if one remembers that Spenser's imagination seeks to illustrate as richly as possible lovely ideas, not to tell perfect stories that can be neatly and exhaustively allegorized,

---

the "foure Cardinal Vertues" treated in Dominicus Mancinus, *The Mirrour of Good Maners . . . translated . . . by Alexander Barclay*, [1570].

[91] "Virgin queen" was an indispensable symbol for Spenser. Alma (II, xi, 2) is "like a virgin queene most bright." Even in "An Hymn in Honour of Beautie" one reads (*Works*, p. 748):

> Thereof it comes that these faire soules, which have
> The most resemblance of that heavenly light,
> Frame to themselves most beautifull and brave
> This fleshly bowre, most fit for their delight,
> And the grosse matter by a soveraine might
> Tempers so trim, that it may well be seene
> A pallace fit for such a virgin queene.

there will be no perplexing biography in Amoret as Belphœbe's sister or Artegall as Britomart's mate. A chaste
queen who indulged a liberal love of Renaissance beauty,
who for many years symbolized virginity's promise of renewed life, impressed profoundly a Platonizing temperament that harbored both a love of "maidenliness" and of
rich sensuousness. His own taste, his heritage of medieval
symbolism, and the virginity of a dominant queen combined to make chastity the fairest idea for Spenser. In
The Faerie Queene the virginity of Elizabeth is constantly
idealized.

But it is her intimate association with all the virtues
that is to be emphasized, for then the fullness of Spenser's
idealization is clear.[92] Then one suspects that his readers

[92] Such association in a forerunner of *The Faerie Queene* is strikingly seen in
Maurice Kyffin's *The Blessednes of Brytaine* (1587), written to celebrate the
thirtieth year of the reign. In it Elizabeth, "who came from *Arthurs* rase and
lyne" (Thomas Churchyard, *The Worthines of Wales*, 1587, sig. D3), incarnates
all virtues, as the following verses (*Fugitive Tracts*, first series, no. 29) suggest:

> Two things make blisfull Realmes, *Religion* pure and *Peace*:
>   Which *Two* our England hath enioyd, long time with large increase.

.   .   .   .

> A Monarch Mayden Queene adorned rare,
> With Regall Heauenly dowres, of diuers kinde;
> In whome, who list dame Natures Workes compare,
> With those rich Thewes, & Vertues of her Minde,
>   Shall much admire, at such a Myrrour sheene,
>   At such a Prince, at such a Peereles Queene.

.   .   .   .

> Elizabeth, Large Light of Sov'raigne Seat,
> Whose Iustice, Prudence, Temprance, Fortitude,
> Ingrafted yong, are grown foorth spreading Great,
> Throughout the world, mong Nations wise & rude:
>   No land, but laudes this right Resplendant Rose,
>   Tutor to Frends, and Terror vnto Foes.

.   .   .   .

> Lib'rall Rewarder of Heroicall Acts;
> Ritch in Reward, large giuing Gwerdons great;
> Prone eke to pardon, many offending facts,

did not quarrel so much about the unity and true beauty of his epic as critics have since his day. Elizabethans, who were direct descendants of ages that were very fond of moral allegory and symbolism, and who were also alert to the varied appeal of a renewed national life, read *The Faerie Queene* for neither its moral nor its esthetic worth exclusively. They read the poem for everything that was in it — description, story, allegory, and all. They saw the

---

Yea though the same, concern her Regall Seat;
   Rigor of Iustice, in Reuenging Lawes,
   Mylde by her Mercy, wreaks not eche Cause.

A Blessed Branch of Brutus Royall Race;
To Brytish wightes a Blisfull worldly ioy,
Puissant Princesse of Their Natiue place,
To shield their Earthly liues from all annoy:
   And to their Sickly Soules, a Sov'raigne Leche,
   Graunting Christs Gospel, in their Country Speche.

.   .   .   .

Ye Bryttish Poets, Repeat in Royall Song,
(With waightie woords, vsde in King Arthurs daies)
Th' Imperiall Stock, from whence your Queene hath sprong;
Enstall in verse your Princesse lasting prayes:
   Pencerddiad, play on Auncient Harpe, and Crowde:
   Atceiniaid, sing her prayses pearcing lowd.

Sir George Buc expressed the dominant view of Elizabeth as Arthur's descendant: "& now king Artur is com agayn for this is that prince & that heroicall lady that did not onely affect & desire to doo good to hir kingdom & to procure & advanc the flourishing stat therof as king Artur did but also she fully accomplished it." To honor "the Returned K. Artur" Sir George wrote a Latin elegy lauding the virtues and achievements of Elizabeth as the "Parens Patriæ, Mater nutriciæ ecclesiæ Dei, Ciuiũ deliciẹ, sexus sui Phẹnis, regũ exemplar." See R. C. Bald, "A Manuscript Work by Sir George Buc," in *The Modern Language Review*, XXX (1935), 8–9. (I am indebted to the author for drawing my attention to this article.) Elizabeth, "indued with many heroicall vertues, who is lineally descended from ancient *Brutus* to the vnspeakable comfort of al true hearted Brytaines" (Thomas Salisbury in an epistle to the reader in a Welsh version of the Psalms, *Psalmæ y brenhinol brophvvyd Dafydh, gwedi i cynghanedhu mewn mesurau cymreig*, 1603, sig. ¶2ᵛ), is celebrated in numerous Welsh poems that survive in manuscript. She appears in several that have been printed in *Canu Rhydd Cynnar*, ed. T. H. Parry-Williams, Caerdydd, 1932; and *Cerddi Rhydd Cynnar*, ed. D. Lloyd-Jenkins, Llandysul, [1931].

full significance of its name, the dedication, and the author's avowed intentions in his letter to Ralegh. They felt no need to divorce its poetic beauty from its moral burden. Its beauty and its moral interest were one. They were aided in so reading the poem by finding deep in its fabric the public and private virtues of their magnificent queen. In her was magnanimity, the

goodly golden chayne! wherewith yfere
The vertues linked are in lovely wize.[93]

Her constant presence in various charming disguises gave a certain unity of interest to the poem which one, aware of the wide idealization of Elizabeth which is its proper background, can recapture. She first gave English nationalism a completely adequate center and symbol. Inevitably she inspired epic poetry. King Arthur had not been, in spite of all efforts to make him so, such a full embodiment of English nationality. Naturally the two figures were constantly associated; rightly Spenser's Prince Arthur pursued Gloriana. The queen's achievements and her virtues had been evident in actual life. They had been sung in hundreds of poems of every type.[94]

[93] I. ix. I.

[94] From many of these poems that show familiar themes I have not had space to quote; but I should like at least to introduce some of them because to do so will give final emphasis to the epic reach of the idealization of Queen Elizabeth in the poetry of her reign.

I note first some works which turn on the idealization of Elizabeth or are capped by praise of her epic achievements. Striking is John Norden's *A pensiue soules delight* (1603). The title-page concisely describes its one hundred and three stanzas: "The Contents whereof, is shewen in these Verses following. 1. *The Pensiue soule recounteth in this place*, Elizaes *troubles, and* Elizaes *grace*. 2. *Here are expressed the stratagems of foes*, Elizaes *conquests, and their falls that rose*. 3. *Here is set forth* Elizaes *lenitie, And* Locust Catholickes *superbitie*." An ardent prayer for Eliza at the end makes it clear that she was alive when the poem appeared. At the end of *The massacre of Money* (1602; dedication signed "T. A.") Virtue gains Eliza's aid in a combat with Vice and Fortune, and is hence certain of triumph. The allegory ends with ardent praise of Eliza. Another effete allegorical poem, *A fig for Fortune* (1596), has its climax in a shower

THE TITLE-PAGE OF *The holi bible*, 1569

All "antique praises" — classical, Biblical, and medieval — had been fitted to this very present person. Now they were harmonized within a great national epic rightly dedicated to her, to Gloriana, that is "[a]live with the eternitie of her fame."

---

of "virgin-Roses" both white and red from the "virgin-lap" of Eliza. England is figured as "Eliza's Elizium." At the end of Lodowick Lloyd's *The pilgrimage of Princes* [1573] are verses (sigs. Iii3–Kkk2) that bid all famous princesses to retire before Elizabeth. *In Catilinarias proditiones, ac proditores domesticos, Odæ 6* (Oxford, 1586; another edition in the same year contains nine odes) is a collection of poems in which the "*Diuina virgo*," saved from traitors, is celebrated. Cf. similar celebration in three other pieces from the Oxford press of Joseph Barnes in 1585 and 1586: *Pareus, In Guil. Parry proditorem Odæ & Epigrammata*, and *Anglia Querens*. Richard Rowlands's *England's Ioy* [1601?] is a rare laudatory poem on Elizabeth, with introductory acrostics on her name, which was occasioned by Lord Mountjoy's defeat of the Irish rebels under Tyrone. *Verses Of Prayse and Ioye, Written vpon her Maiesties preseruation* (1586; reprinted in *Fugitive Tracts*, first series, no. 26) carries a phœnix and crown upon its title-page, and rejoices in the life of the "*maiden & a Queene*" who brings a "*Roselike Royal peace.*" Roger Cotton's *A Spiritual Song: conteining an Historicall Discourse from the infancie of the world, vntill this present time* (1596) has as its sixth and culminating part "*a thanksgiuing to God for the preseruation of her Maiestie, and of his Church.*" George Gascoigne's *The fruites of Warre, written uppon this Theame, Dulce Bellum inexpertis* (1575) is inspired by the contrast which Eliza's peace offers with the turmoil of the Continent (*Works*, I, 139–184). George Carleton addressed an extended *Carmen Panegyricum* (British Museum MS. Royal 12. A. XLIII; printed in Nichols, *Elizabeth*, III, 180–189) to Elizabeth in which he lauded her many virtues and achievements. To the name "Elizabeth" are devoted thirty of the two hundred pages (sigs. R2–V4ᵛ) of William Patten's *The Calender of Scripture. VVhearin the Hebru, Challdian, Arabian, Phenician, Syrian, Persian, Greek and Latin names, of Nations, Cuntreys, Men, Weemen, Idols, Cities, Hils, Riuers, & of oother places in the holly Byble mentioned, by order of letters ar set, and turned into oour English toong* (1575). The Hebrew meanings of the name, "The fulness of my God. The oth of my God. The Seauenth of my God," are analyzed and applied in amazing fashion. The running title shortly changes to "ELIZABETH." Rich praise abounds when the etymologist turns to Elizabeth the queen, who, born on the seventh day of the seventh month, speaks seven languages, rules seven lands, and embodies the seven moral virtues (faith, hope, charity, prudence, justice, fortitude, and temperance). "Hæc est Diua Dei summum Septemmia Donum." All culminates in an eight-page Latin poem (on four unsigned leaves following fol. V4) celebrating her and her counselors.

Perhaps the epic range of the idealization of Queen Elizabeth is suggested even more effectively by verse or prose in the variety of places which I cite below: G. B., *A fig for the Spaniard*, 1591, sig. A4; Dominicus Baudius, *Poemata*, Amsterdam, 1640, pp. 91–93, 493–495, 544–550; Ralph Birchensha, *A discourse occasioned vpon the late defeat, giuen to the Arch-rebels, Tyrone and Odonnell*, 1602, sigs. C2, E1; William Baldwin, *The Funeralles of King Edward the sixt*, 1560, sigs. C1–C2ᵛ; Joannes Brunsuerdus, *Ioannis Brunsuerdi, Maclesfeldensis Gymnasiarchæ Progymnasmata quædam Poetica*, 1590, sig. D2; George Buchanan, *Georgii Buchanani Scoti. Franciscanus et fratres. Elegiarum liber I. Sylvarum liber I. Hendecasyllabωn lib. I. Epigrammatωn libri III*, sigs. B3ᵛ–B4, F12ᵛ, G3ᵛ–G4, in *Poemata omnia in numeris penè locis, ex ipsius autographo castigata & aucta*, Edinburgh, 1615; Heinrich Bullinger, *A confutation Of the Popes Bull . . . against Elizabeth the most gracious Quéene of England*, 1572, sig. A1; *Academiæ Cantabrigiensis lachrymæ tumulo Noblissimi Equitis, D. Philippi Sidenij Sacratæ per Alexandrum Nevillum*, 1587, sigs. ²B3, ²C3ᵛ, ²D3; John Carpenter, *A preparatiue to Contentation*, 1597, sig. Dd1ᵛ; Sir Thomas Chaloner, *De Rep. Anglorum instauranda libri decem, . . . Huc accessit in laudem Henrici Octaui . . . carmen Panegyricum. Item, de illustrium quorundam encomiis miscellanea, cum epigrammatis, ac Epitaphijs nonnullis*, 1579, sigs. S7–T4ᵛ (the *Carmen* is dedicated to Elizabeth; see below, p. 423); Thomas Churchyard, *A Description and playne discourse of paper* (Nichols, *Elizabeth*, II, 597–600); his *A pleasaunte Laborinth called Churchyardes Chance*, 1580, sigs. G3ᵛ–G4, H3ᵛ; and his *A wished reformacion of wicked Rebellion*, 1598, sig. A2; George Colclough, *The Spectacle to Repentance*, 1571, sig. E2ᵛ; Roger Cotton, *An Armor of Proofe*, 1596, sigs. D3–D3ᵛ; John Donne, "Satyre V" (*Poems*, ed. H. J. C. Grierson, 1912, Oxford, I, 169; but in *The Progresse of the Soule* [1601] Donne, then Catholic in sympathy, seems to have intended a satirical reflection of Elizabeth as a heretic); Anne Dowriche, *The French Historie*, 1589, sig. L1ᵛ; Thomas Edwards, *Cephalus and Procris*, ed. W. E. Buckley, Roxburghe Club, 1882, p. 4; Ulpian Fulwell, *The Flower of Fame*, 1575, sigs. C2, O3ᵛ; C. G., *A Watch-worde for Warre*, Cambridge, 1596, sig. A2; Scipione Gentile, *Paraphrasis aliquot Psalmorum Dauidis, carmine heroico*, 1581, sig. *4; William Gager, [Latin verses to Queen Elizabeth], British Museum Additional MS. 22583, fols. 46ᵛ, 54ᵛ–55, 79ᵛ–80ᵛ, 80ᵛ–81, 83–83ᵛ, and (in English) 84ᵛ–85; Charles Gibbon, *Not so new, as True. Being a verie necessarie Caueat for all Christians to consider of*, 1590, sig. A4ᵛ; Humfrey Gifford, *A posie of Gilloflowers*, 1580, sig. K2ᵛ (in "A commendation of Peace"); Dionis Gray, *The store-house of Breuitie in vvorkes of Arithemetike*, 1577, sigs. A6ᵛ–A7; Antonio de Guevara, *A looking Glasse for the Court . . . into Englishe by Sir Fraunces Briant*, 1575, sig. A3ᵛ; Walter Haddon, *Poematum . . . libri duo*, 1576, sigs. A3ᵛ, G2–G2ᵛ, H4ᵛ–H7, I1; *De caede et in teritu Gallorum regis, Henrici tertii valesiorum vltimi, epigrammata*, Oxford, 1589, sig. A2ᵛ; Quintus Horatius Flaccus, *A Medicinable Morall, that is, the two Bookes of Horace his Satyres, Englyshed . . . Also Epigrammes. T. Drant*, 1566, sigs. L4ᵛ–L5; David Hume, *Davidis Humii theagrii lusus poetici, in tres partes distincti*, 1605, sigs. F1ᵛ–F2; W. I., *The VVhipping of the Satyre*, 1601, sigs. E1, E4; Thomas Kempe, [Latin and Greek poems in praise of Queen Elizabeth], Bodleian Library MS. Rawlinson poet. 63; Timothy Kendall, *Flovvers of epigrammes*, 1577, sigs. M4ᵛ, R1ᵛ; John Leland,

Principum, Ac illustrium aliquot & eruditorum in Anglia vivorum, Encomia, Trophœa, Genethliaca, Epithalamia, 1589, sigs. H1v–H2 (on sigs. Q1v– Q2 are sixteen verses "Ad Chr. Oclandum, de Elizabetheide sua"); John Lyster, *A rule how to bring vp Children,* 1588, sig. S7v; Paulus Melissus, *Melissi Mele sive odæ ad Noribergam et septemviros Reipub. Norib.,* Nuremberg, 1580, sigs. F1v, F4, G1, H7, I1, I4 (notable celebration as a *rosa*), I4v; and his *Melissi Schediasmatum Reliquiæ,* Frankfurt am Main, 1575, sig. K4; Robert Moore, *Diarium historico poeticum,* Oxford, 1595, sigs. K4, M3; Bishop John Parkhurst, *Iohannis Parkhursti Ludicra siue Epigrammata Iuuenilia,* 1573, sigs. H3v–H4 (verses addressed to the princess in 1547 in praise of her virtues and her skill in languages); Genenuefue Petau-Maulette, *Deuoreux. Vertues teares . . . translated into English. Ieruis Markham,* 1597, sigs. D3v–D4, E2v–E3v, K3v, M3v; John Phillip, *A commemoration of the Right Noble and vertuous Ladye, Margrit Duglasis,* [1578], sigs. C3–C3v; John Ross (of Reed, near Bury St. Edmunds), *Parerga,* Folger Shakespeare Library MS. 800.1, pp. 3–4, 43, 50, 59, 60; Robert Chester, "Præcatio" (*Poems by Sir John Salusbury and Robert Chester,* ed. Carleton Brown, Early English Text Society, 1914, p. 19); Cyril Tourneur, *The Transformed Metamorphosis* (*Works,* ed. Allardyce Nicoll, [1930], p. 74); *Funebria nobilissimi ac præstantissimi equitis, D. Henrici Vnton à Musis Oxoniensibus Apparata,* Oxford, 1596, sig. E2; John Weever, *Epigrammes in the oldest cut, and newest fashion,* 1599, sig. B1v; George Whetstone, *A mirror of treue honnour and Christian nobilitie, exposing: The life, death, and deuine vertues, of the . . . Earle of Bedford,* 1585, sigs. C4, D1; Whetstone's *A Remembraunce of the Life, Death, and Vertues, of the . . . Erle of Sussex,* 1583, sig. A4v; and his *A remembraunce of the wel imployed life, . . . of George Gaskoigne,* [1578?], sigs. B2v–B3; Edward Wilkinson, *E. W. his Thameseidos,* 1600, sigs. D1v–D2; Richard Willes, *Ricardi Willeii Poematum Liber,* 1573, sig. C4; James Yates, *The Castell of Courtesie, Whereunto is adioyned The Holde of Humilitie With the Chariot of Chastitie thereunto annexed,* 1582, sigs. ²L4–²M1; [Poems by Wykehamists on the intended visit of Queen Elizabeth to Winchester, chiefly in Latin, *ca.* 1600], Bodleian Library MS. Lat. misc. e. 23; [An acrostic hexameter poem on Queen Elizabeth], Bodleian Library MS. Brasenose College 48, fols. 34v–35; [Verses for a thanksgiving for Elizabeth's peaceable reign, at Berwick, 1586], British Museum MS. Egerton 2877, fols. 104v–105; and [A poem in praise of Henry VIII and Queen Elizabeth], Bodleian Library MS. Ashmolean 208, fols. 250–260.

CHAPTER IX

In Memoriam — Judith, Deborah, Eliza, Elisa, Diana, Laura, Idea, Cynthia, Gloriana, and Belphœbe — 1603

POPULAR and courtly poets wept together for
England's Eliza when she died on March 24, 1603.

Gone is our Queene, whose like cannot be found,
  gone is our Queene which alwayes lou'd vs deare,
Gone is our Queene whose vertues did abound,
  as by her care it often did appeare.
    Gone is our ioy, our stay, our life, our loue,
    Gone is our Load-starre vnto heauen aboue.[1]

A sorrowfull Epitaph on the death
of Queene ELIZABETH.

Shee was the Souldiers captaine, the law's life,
The Churches deerest spouse, the Churchmans wife,
Learnings greene Lawrell, vertues chiefe refector:
Peaces maintainer, onely Truths protector.
The Orphants parents, and the ritchmans stay:
The poore mans comfort, and the nights cleere day.
The tradsman fauorer, and the marchants gaine;
The sea mans night starre, and the lyers staine,
The pride of all her sex, all womens boast:
The worlds wonder, that they wondred most;

---

[1] *The Poores Lamentation for the Death of our Late dread Soueraigne the High
and Mightie Princesse Elizabeth, late Queene of England, France and Ireland,*
1603, sig. B2. A strict ordering of illustrations by type in this chapter is not
possible, and hardly desirable.

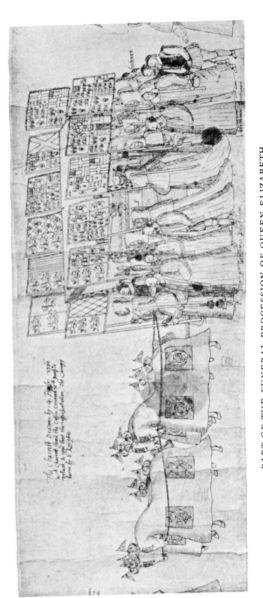

PART OF THE FUNERAL PROCESSION OF QUEEN ELIZABETH

From a drawing in MS. Additional 5408 in the British Museum

The Courtiers glory, entertaining all
Louers of truth young, old, in generall.
She dy'de bewayld, she iustly liu'd admir'd,
Her body sunke her spotlesse soule aspir'd.[2]

Her insight saw, all outward flawes of winde,
Her iudgement crept, into our cunning Age,
No practize could, surpasse her Princely minde,
Her calmie wordes, could swelling Sea asswage,
Religion burnd, like Lampe in her bare brest,
And for her faith, shee still set vp her rest,
Shee gaue great things to thousands, world well knowes,
As at well head, and Fountaine Water flowes.
Cæsars, sharpe Spirit, her speeches vttr'ed oft,
Cyrus great power, and wealth she wanted not,
Shee pluc't downe Pride, to set meeke hearts aloft,
Her matchles deedes, great Fame and Glorie got,
Opened her bagges, to such as suffered wrong,
Much money lent, but felt the losse to long,
Escap't bad men, that sought to shed her blood,
Forgaue great faultes, to winne worldes loue and zeale:
But when most safe, in health we thought shee stood,
Her Ghost past hence, (from Crowne & Common-weale)
To GODS high Throne, like Torch and Candle blaze,
(Lost earthly light) and left vs in a maze.[3]

---

[2] John Fenton, *King Iames his welcome to London. With Elizaes Tombe and Epitaph,* 1603, sigs. B2–B2ᵛ. Cf. Charles Best, "An Epitaph on Queene Elizabeth" (*A Poetical Rhapsody 1602–1621,* I, 299).

[3] Thomas Churchyard, *Sorrowfull Verses made on [the] death of our most Soueraigne Lady Queene Elizabeth, my Gracious Mistresse* (Collmann, p. 96). It is fitting that the last publication of old Churchyard, who often spoke to the queen for her loving people throughout her reign, should be these *Sorrowfull Verses.* Their sentiment is echoed more or less in the following pieces: (1) *A mourneful ditty entituled Elizabeths losse, together with a Welcome for King James* (folio broadside in the Huntington Library); (2) *An excellent new ballad, shewing the petigree of our royal King Iames, the first of that name in England* (*Shirburn Ballads,* pp. 316–320); (3) *Englands vvelcome to Iames by the grace of God, King of England, Scotland, France and Ireland, defender of the faith* (*Fugitive Tracts,* second series, 1600–1700, ed. W. C. Hazlitt, 1875, no. 3); and (4) *On Queene Elizabeth Queene of England* (*Ballads from Manuscripts,* II, 101). I have not seen Lemon, no. 108 — *A Lamentation for the losse of our late Soueraigne Lady*

Death came vnto her hauing Gods Commission,
That she to heauen her progresse must commence:

.   .   .   .

Giue honour to the Queene *of good-desartes:*
The reuerent Lady, Nurse of all our Land,
That sway'd a Sword like Judeth's, *in her hand.*
The Debora *that iudged Israell:*
Whose blessed actions God did prosper well:

.   .   .   .

She that with Mercyes *winges adorn'd her Throne,*
And yet with Justice *ballance sate thereon.*

.   .   .   .

Yea let the very Stones where shee shall lie,
Tell ages following, this of ours gone by:
Within our marble armes we do enclose
The virgin Queene, *the White and Red-crown'd Rose,*
That rul'd this Realme so happy, fourtie fowre,
As neuer Prince did raigne the like before
From Men, with Sainctes shee liues in high esteeme,
Seated in blisse, which best doth her esteeme.[4]

The "theatres were probably closed from Elizabeth's
death to March 1604."[5] Shepherds sang funeral songs
during those months.

Queene Elizabeth, with joy and exultation for our High and Mightie Prince King James, her lineall and lawfull Successor.

[4] *Aue Caesar.... The ioyfull Ecchoes of loyall English hartes, entertayning his Maiesties late ariuall in England. With an Epitaph vpon the death of her Maiestie our late Queene (Fugitive Tracts,* second series, no. 4).

[5] Chambers, *Elizabethan Stage,* III, 367. Soon, however, Eliza appeared as the heroine of two idealizing plays by Thomas Heywood. Part I of *If You Know not Me, You Know Nobody* (1605) treats of "the troubles of Queene Elizabeth"; Part II, of "the famous Victorie of Queene Elizabeth, in the Yeare 1588." Of Thomas Dekker's *The Whore of Babylon* (not earlier than 1605 or later than 1607) Chambers (*Elizabethan Stage,* III, 296) writes: "Truth and Time, but not Candlelight, are characters in the play, which deals with Catholic intrigues against Elizabeth, represented as Titania, and her suitors." Dr. Ray Heffner

The Funeral Song between Collin and Thenot, Dryope and
Chloris, upon the Death of the sacred Virgin Elizabeth.

Collin.

Ye sacred Muses, dwelling
Where art is ever swelling;
    Your learned fount forsake,
    Help funeral songs to make;
    Hang them about her hearse,
    That ever loved verse.
Clio, write down her story,
That was the Muses' glory.

Dryope.

And, ye soft-footed Hours,
Make ready cypress bowers;
    Instead of roses sweet
    (For pleasant spring-time meet)
    Strew all the paths with yew,
    Night-shade and bitter rue.
Bid Flora hide her treasure;
Say, 'tis no time of pleasure.

Thenot.

And, you divinest Graces,
Veil all your sacred faces,
    With your bright shining hair,
    Shew every sign of care.
    The heart, that was your fane,
    The cruel Fates have slain:
From earth no power can raise her,
Only our hymns may praise her.

(*Studies in Philology*, XXVII, 142–161) shows *The Faerie Queene* to be the base
of the idealization of Elizabeth in Dekker's play, which he thinks was written
before 1603. Shakespeare's belated tribute came with Cranmer's familiar
prophecy in *Henry VIII*. Jacobean drama and subsequent drama is rich in
idealization of Elizabeth, but Eliza, not the tradition of good Queen Bess, is the
subject of my study.

Chloris.

Muses, and Hours, and Graces,
Let all the hallow'd places,
 Which the clear moon did view,
 Look like a sable hue:
 Let not the sun be seen,
 But weeping for the Queen,
That grace and muse did cherish;
O that such worth should perish!

Collin.

So turn our verse, and on this lofty pine
Each one engrave for her some funeral line:

Thus I begin.

COLLIN's Epitaph.

 Eliza, maiden mirror of this age,
Earth's true Astræa, while she liv'd and reign'd,
 Is thrown by death from her triumphant stage;
But by that fall hath endless glory gain'd;
 And foolish death would fain, if he could, weep
 For killing her, he had no power to keep.

THENOT's Epitaph.

Eliza, rich and royal, fair and just,
Gives heaven her soul, and leaves her flesh to dust.

DRYOPE's Epitaph.

There is no beauty but it fades;
No glory, but is veil'd with shades:
So is Eliza, queen of maids,
  Stoop'd to her fate.
Yet death, in this, hath little thriv'd,
For thus her virtues have achiev'd,
She shall, by verse, live still reviv'd,
  In spite of hate.

Chloris's Epitaph.

Eliza, that astonished her foes,
Stoop'd her rebellious subjects at her feet:
  Whose mind was still the same in joy, in woes;
  Whose frown was fearful, and her favours sweet:
    Sway'd all this land, but most herself she sway'd,
    Liv'd a chaste queen, and died a royal maid.[6]

Lament the Lady of the *Faiery*-land.

  .   .   .   .

For siluer *Cynthia* has eclipst her light,
And with her absence makes eternall night.
She that so gallantly your daunces led,
That could so sweetly sing, so softly tread,
And with her musicke make your Consorts euen:
In scorne of earth, is gone away to heauen:

  .   .   .   .

And eke you Virgins chast, lament her fall:
The Goddesse of your sports is lapt in lead,
And faire *Virginia's* fairest Queene is dead,
Oh, come, and do her corse with flowres embraue,
And play some solemne musicke by her graue,
Then sing her Requiem in some dolefull Verse
Or do the songs of *Colin Clout* rehearse.

  .   .   .   .

---

[6] Henry Chettle, *England's Mourning Garment; worn here by plain Shepherds, in Memory of their sacred Mistress, Elizabeth; Queen of Virtue, while she lived; and Theme of Sorrow, being dead. . . . Dedicated to all that loved the deceased Queen, and honour the living King* (*Harleian Miscellany*, III [1809], 539–540). Sad shepherds review in prose the glories of Elisa's reign. Some verses summoning poets to lament her fittingly, rebuke those silent, especially "silver-tongued Melicert" and the "sweet singer Corydon" (Shakespeare and Drayton). Cf. "A true Subiects sorowe, for the losse of his late Soueraigne," following *Epicedium. A Funerall Oration Vpon the death of the late deceased Princesse (of famous memorye), Elizabeth . . . Written: by Infelice Academico Ignoto* (Lyly, I, 514–516), attributed in the *Dictionary of National Biography* to Richard Niccols. In 1603, Elisa's godson, Sir John Harington, wrote (*Nugæ Antiquæ*, I, 180): "Here now wyll I reste my troublede mynde, and tende my sheepe like an Arcadian swayne, that hathe loste his faire mistresse; for in soothe, I have loste the beste and faireste love that ever shepherde knew, even my gracious Queene; and sith my goode mistresse is gone, I shall not hastily put forthe for a new master."

For loe, the Flower which was so fresh and gay,
And made Nouember like another May,
How daintily so ere it did compose
The beautie of the white and crimson Rose,
The Flower is parcht, the silken leafe is blasted,
The Roote decay'd, and all the glory wasted.
Let *Israel* weepe, the house of *Iacob* mourne,
Syon is fallne, and *Iudah* left forlorne,
The Hill of *Hermon* drops no precious oyle,
Nor fruitfull *Bashan*, from his fattest soile,
But *Dauids* throne has all his beautie lost,
So farre admir'd through euery forreine coast.
The Paradice and *Eden* of our Land
Planted and kept by GODS Almightie Hand:
Where milke and honie *Canaan*-like did flow,
And Flowers of peace, and fruites of plentie grow;
Where Vines and Oliues, euer more were seene,
Vines euer Fresh, and Oliues euer greene:
With Brambles now and Briers is ouer-cast,
And like a desert desolate and wast.
The royall daughter of that royall King,
To whom all nations did their presents bring,
So bright of late, and glorious to behold,
Shining in garments of embroydered gold,
Esther our *Queene*, whose fame (with triumph crownd)
Haman of *Spaine* had neuer force to wound,
In spight of whom although he dar'd to striue
She has preserude her people all aliue;
This royall *Queene*, the heauens bright reflexe;
This foe of pride, this pride of all her sexe,
This *Phœnix* of the world, the worthiest *Dame*
That euer acted on the Stage of Fame:
(Hers be the ioy,) to our eternall sorrow
Has payd to death the life that she did borow.

.   .   .   .

Spaine, clap thy hands, and laugh while we lament,
Our Staffe is broken, and our treasure spent,

The Staffe of ioy, the treasure of our ease,
The Life, the Crowne, the glory of our Peace:
Righteous *Astræa* from the earth is banish't.

.   .   .   .

Beta is dead, the honour of her race,
That has so long vp-held the royall Mace,
Whose Predecessours all haue princes beene,
And she her selfe a Princely *Mayden-Queene*.
Farewell (sweet Prince) where euer thou do bide,
Whether in earth, or by some angels side:
Farewell (great *Queene*) that art of God y-blest,
Well may thy buried bones securely rest:
Beta, farewell, and let thy purest spirit
(Where euer fled the purest place inherite.
Goe blessed soule, and vp to heauen climbe,
Among the Angels seate thee there betime,
Shine like an Angell with thy starrie crowne,
And milke-white Robes descending fayrely downe,
Wash't in the blood of the vnspotted Lambe,
That slew the Beast, and made the Dragon tame.
There let thy sacred life (most sacred Dame)
Thy famous vertue, and thy vertuous Fame;
Whereof so many Pens haue writ the Story
Receiue the crowne of euerlasting glory.
Feast euer there and feed on sweetest ioy,
Without the tast of any sharpe anoy:
Liue euer there, in that Cœlestiall skie,
Where (spight of death) thou neuermore shalt die;
Raine euer there on that *Elyzian* greene:
Eliza, well may be *Elyziums Queene*.[7]

Bright Maiestie hath dimm'd her brightest parts,
Since Glorie's sunshine left the Royal Throne:
In mournefull blacke sit the more mournefull arts
Viewing their life-protecting Empresse gone.

.   .   .   .

---

[7] John Lane, *An Elegie vpon the death of the high and renowned Princesse, our late Soueraigne Elizabeth* (*Fugitive Tracts*, second series, no. 2).

O soule-deare countrie, thou aboue the rest
　　Liest in deepe floudes of bitter Sorrow drown'd:
Woe's mortall arrowes pierce each mortal brest,
　　But thy lost heart receives no common wound;
Wounded thou art with woe aboue all other,
Losing thy virgin scepter-swaying Mother.

　　　　　·　　·　　·　　·　　·　　·　　·　　·　　·

Oh, whither shall the Arts for succour flie?
　　Since Art's perfection, Nature's chiefe delight;
Jove's dearest darling, Fates have done to die,
　　The Earth's bright glorie, and the World's cleare light.
　　Weepe, Muses, weepe, lament your wofull plight.

　　·　　·　　·　　·　　·　　·　　·　　·　　·

Peace did her raigne begin, peace it maintain'd;
　　Peace gave her leave in peace hence to depart;
Peace shee hath left behind; which, no way stain'd
　　With bloody warre, reioyceth England's heart:
Though we a King of Peace haue in her stead,
Yet let vs mourne, — the Queene of Peace is dead.

　　·　　·　　·　　·　　·　　·　　·　　·　　·

An Epitaph upon our late Souveraigne.

Here in this earthen pot lies withered,
　　Which grew on hie, the white rose and the red.

　　·　　·　　·　　·　　·　　·　　·　　·　　·

Since that to death is gone that Royall maide,
　　That Pellican, who for her people's good
(O loue, o vertue, which too soone doeth fade!)
　　Stickt not to spill, alas! her owne deare blood;
　　　That maide, that Pellican, England's sole power
　　　Thus soone, too soone hath breath'd her latest houre.

Since that to death is gone that Princely Dame,
　　Whilome to whose admired deitie
Vesta, Minerva, Pallas, Venus came,
　　Yielding as captiues to her Maiestie;

Let's now poure forth our willing teares and cries,
Since that so soone such rare perfection dies.

.   .   .   .

A STAY–GRIEFE FOR ENGLISHMEN,
WITH A MOTION TO THE POPE,
AND ENGLISH PAPISTS.

Elizabeth our English Queene,
The like to whome was never seene,
Is gone from Earth to Christ aboue
To dwell with him her onely loue.

.   .   .   .

Sleepe, dearest Queene, your vertue never sleepeth;
    Rest in your bed of earth, your honour waketh;
Slumber securely, for your glorie keepeth
    Continuall guard; and liuing ioy partaketh:
Dearest of deare, a rising doth remaine,
For sunnes that sleeping set, must rise againe.

The blessed morne 'fore blessed Marie's day,
    On Angel's wings our Queene to Heaven flieth;
To sing a part of that celestiall lay,
    Which Alleluiah, Alleluiah crieth.
In heauen's chorus so at once are seene,
A Virgin Mother and a Maiden Queene.[8]

The universities lamented their loss in Latin anthologies. The following verses are representative of various
pieces in the Oxford volume:

Morte cadit Regina potens, clarissima stella,
    Cura dei, mundi gloria, Gentis honos.[9]

---

[8] *Sorrowes Ioy; or, A Lamentation for our late deceased Soveraigne Elizabeth,
with a Triumph for the prosperous Succession of our gratious King Iames* (Nichols,
James, I, 2–15).

[9] *Oxoniensis academiæ Funebre Officium in memoriam honoratissimam serenissimæ et beatissimæ Elisabethæ, nuper Angliæ, Franciæ, & Hiberniæ Reginæ*,
Oxford, 1603, sig. A1. The anthology has a few Greek and Hebrew pieces with
its numerous Latin ones.

Felix illa parens patriæ, pietatis asylum,
    Virtutis specimen, virginitatis honos.
Quæ tot quæsitis sine labe excelsa trophæis,
    Victrix virgo virum, cœlica regna tenet.[10]

Filia pacis erat viuens, Anglisque Columbæ
Persimilis, quam olim Patriarcha admisit in Arcam,
Gestantem rostro folium viridantis oliuæ.
Rettulit imperio Deboram, pietate Dauidem.[11]

Elisabetha vale, pia, prudens, iusta, pudica.[12]

Debora, Alexander rari, rariq; Camilli
    Rara avis & Cæsar, rarior ista fuit.[13]

Regina in terris nuper, nunc Cælica Civis,
    Pro fragili, æterno gaudet Eliza throno.
Anglica, dum vixit, Princeps: sed morte perempta
    Angelica est sancto Virgo recepta choro.[14]

    Qui mortem celebrabo tuam dignissima Phœnix! [15]

Elisa, cedri æternitatem præferens,
    Regina virgo, regiarum virginum,
Regum, Imperantium perennis gloria;
Prior tuum quæ posteris tradet decus,
Pallas, Salus, Relligio, Pax, Victoria?
Mandare, diffundere, volunt omnes simul.[16]

Sic quæ mater erat, iam Diva vocabitur Anglûm.[17]

Digna *Rosa* imperio (flos præstans,) nobilis herba
    Occidit, atq; horti gloria sola tui.

Ni foret exortus novus alter *Flos benedictus*
    Perdideram omne meum terra misella decus.[18]

Debora vincebat Sisaren, Iuditha Holophernen:
    Hos regina duos vicit Elisa simul.
Hispanum Sisaren, sævum Romæq; Holophernen,
    Dum procul à regno monstra tremenda fugat.

---

[10] Sig. A1ᵛ.
[11] Sig. A2ᵛ.
[12] Sig. B2.

[13] Sig. B4ᵛ.
[14] Sig. C1.
[15] Sig. C4.

[16] Sig. I1.
[17] Sig. I2.
[18] Sig. I2ᵛ.

Quòd Regina, dolor: dolor est, quòd virgo peribat:
    Quòd pia virgo, dolor: quòdq; parens patrię.
Cum virgo, regina, pia hæc, patriæq; parens sit,
    Proh, dolor est superans tristitiam & lachrymas.[19]

Virgo puella, senex: Regina, & subdita, Virgo:
    Vt sata, sic etiam mortua, Virgo fuit.
Bis septena senex Virgo. fœliciter egit,
    Lustraq́; regnavit, Regia Virgo, novem.
Quippè futura polo quod erat, priùs Angelus esse
    Cæpit: & humanæ nescia sortis erat.[20]

Pollicita es (princeps) temet fore *semper eandem*:
    Sed memorem dicti mors vetat esse tui:
Nunc et enim, nuper quæ regna Britanna tenebas,
    Non eadem, at *melior*, cœlica regna tenes.[21]

    Ceres, defunctam Elisabetham queritur,
      pacis suæ nutricis parentem optimam.

Mater Eliza, meæ, dum vixerat alma, parentis,
    Dives eram, placidæ Pacis alumna, Ceres.[22]

Lux ea quæ divæ festum natale Mariæ
Iuncta præit, fuit illa dies natalis Elizæ,
Quaq; salutatum venit Iove missus ad ipsam
Seraphico è numero celer, alatusq; minister,
Ista diem anticipans animam expiravit in auras:
Hoc ego vaticinor, sociam se velle Iosephi
Coniugis esse, parem proavis, divisq; secundam.[23]

Dum fugit ardentis Daphne connubia Phœbi,
    Perpetuæ frondes Virginitatis habet.
Sic Regina potens tædas exosa iugales,
    Perpetuæ laudes Virginitatis habet.
Frondes inter, aves concentibus æthera mulcent,
    Musa inter laudes cantet Eliza tuas.[24]

---

[19] Sig. I3ᵛ.
[20] Sigs. O4ᵛ–P1.
[21] Sig. S4.

[22] Sig. S4ᵛ.
[23] Sig. T1.
[24] Sig. T2ᵛ.

Scire cupis causam pridiè cur, sacra, diei
    Virginis, ad superas scandit *Elisa* domus?
Disce brevi: moritura diem sibi legerat istum,
    Cætera quòd paribus, par sit vtrisq; dies.
Virgo *Maria* fuit, fuit *illa*: beata *Maria*,
    Inter fœmineum *Beta* beata genus.
Hæres *huic* princeps fuit, *altera* principis hæres,
    Hæc vtero gessit, corde sed *illa* Deum.
Cætera cùm similes, cùm cætera pœme gemellæ,
    Hoc vno parilem non habuere statum:
In terris *hæc* vixit inops, nunc regnat in astris,
    Illa solo, superis *illa* beata polis.

Esse quid hoc dicam? cecidit *Rosa* tempore veris,
    Frigore quam nequijt lædere bruma suo.
Quid dixi demens, potuit non lædere bruma?
    Ver fuit æternum, dum *Rosa* nostra fuit.[25]

Cambridge, too, mourned in many verses for "Virgo."
The pervasive celebration of Elizabeth as a virgin mother
is again notable:

Vna fuit semper qui contigit vna potestas,
    Vna fides, & eò recta quòd vna fuit.
Vna fuit servire deo, servare popellum
    Cura; licèt cura hæc vna, nec vna, fuit.
Vna fuit virgo semper, placidissima semper;
    Mira cano, mulier quæ fuit, vna fuit.

    Vna fuit moriens, quæ vixerat vnica, princeps;
        Vna fuit nobis, nunc erit vna deo.[26]

---

[25] Sigs. P2–P2ᵛ. Elizabeth's name is etymologized (sigs. M3–M3ᵛ); and there
is a figure poem (sig. O1). "Phœnix," "stella," "Astræa," "mater," "lilia
casta," "dea," and "diva" are favorite epithets. Similar idealization appears in
In Mortem Serenissimæ Reginæ Elizabethæ, Nænia consolans, 1603, by Richard
Mulcaster; also in *Post Nubilia Sudum*, Oxford, 1603. This last piece (sig. B4)
shows the queen's motto treated as follows:

    Semper eras *eadem*, pietatis sedula nutrix:
        Ac eadem famæ munere semper eris.
    Semper eris musæ post funera munere sospes,
        Sospes, & invito verme superstes eris.

[26] *Threno-thriambeuticon. Academiæ Cantabrigiensis ob damnum lucrosum, &
infælicitatem fælicissimam, luctuosus triumphus*, Cambridge, 1603, sigs. A2ᵛ–A3.

Virgo secunda Deæ; nam littera Beta secunda est:
Virgo Deæ compar; nam par sonat isa pelasgis:
Virgo Dea in terris; namq̃; El dat numen Hebræis:
ELISABETA, sonant vnà tria nexa retrorsum.[27]

Hic tumulus Divæ, Reginæ, Virginis: illa est;
   Hæc fuit, & nunc est, (hæc vt) &, ista, fuit.
Diva est. sic superest: Virgo fuit. integra virgo est;
   Et Regina fuit. Regia virgo manet.
Quæ fuit in terris Dea, Virgo, Regia virgo
   Nunc est in cœlis Regia, Virgo, Dea.
Hanc quis defunctam dicet, quæ tota superstes,
   Vivit & in cœlo, regnat & in solio?
Regnat & in solio, quod dum successor habebit
   Hic novus, in solio regnat Elisa suo.[28]

The lamentations that I now present laud especially the
virtues of the Faery Queene — "our late Soverigne Ladye
Elizabeth (who maye without offence be paralleled with
the moste renowned and famous Kinges of all Christendome
for sacrednes of Relligion, hir wisdome, justice, governement, magnificence of estate, hir love and clemencye to hir
subjectes, hir generall skill and knowledge in all good
letters; finally, beinge a most rare, singular, and pierelesse
patterne of all heroicall and princely virtues)." [29] The
descendants of Welsh bards mourned their loss of Gloriana,
sprung of Brutus and Arthur. My first quotation is from
an elegy in the form of a *cywydd* written by Richard Philip.

      mwya rhann am yr hen waed
      fu ran hon o frenhinwaed

      .   .   .   .   .   .

      henwaed Mon oedd goronawg
      huned yr hen waed y rhawg.

      .   .   .   .   .   .

---

[27] Sig. A4.
[28] Sig. D1.
[29] Nichols, *Elizabeth*, III, 614 (as from a manuscript in the Cathedral Library
at Lichfield). Cf. a similar declaration in *Epicedium* (Lyly, I, 511–512).

burwaed dwys had Brutus hên

.   .   .   .   .

gwreichionen brenhinbren had
galwyd haul goleuad hedd
goronog wawr o Wynedd
Elsbeth ymhôb pêth fu'n parch
Elizabeth lwys hybarch.[30]

The chast *Belphœbe* is of life depriu'de,
Merrour of Chastetie, when shee suruiu'de:
Shee like a Rose mong'st many weedes was placed,

.   .   .   .

Prudence, and Constancie possest her minde;
A rare memoriall for all women-kinde:

.   .   .   .

O Virgin chast, O Phenix of thy kind,
Which being gone, leaues not thy like behind.
O Lampe of light, O Starre celestiall,
Thy matchlesse beautie was Angelicall,
With thee did die the worldes felicitie:
With thee decay'd all antique dignitie.[31]

---

[30] National Library of Wales MS. 3061 D (= Mostyn MS. 165), p. 129. I am indebted to Mr. Evan D. Jones for the following translation of these verses: "The greater share of kingly blood, in respect of the old blood, was the share of this one . . . the old blood of Mon [= Anglesey] was crowned [or crown-bearing], let the old blood sleep for a long time . . . the thick pure-blood of the seed of old Brutus . . . spark of a regal-tree seed, the sun, the luminary of peace was called, the crowned dawn from Gwynedd [= North Wales], Elizabeth in every thing was our reverence, Elizabeth fair, (holy, pure), venerable." Cf. a similar elegy in the National Library of Wales MS. Peniarth 184, pp. 13–15.

[31] T. W., *The Lamentation of Melpomene, for the death of Belphœbe our late Queene*, 1603, sigs. A3ᵛ–B1ᵛ. With the kind permission of the Huntington Library, I quote from its apparently unique copy of this tract. Belphœbe is also lamented in Henry Petowe, *Englands Cæsar. His Maiesties most Royall Coronation. . . . Eliza. her Coronation in Heauen*, 1603.

Shee kept her selfe a *Virgin* for the Lord,
With whom she longed daily for to be,
That onely he alwaies she did accord,
Should haue the prime of her virginitie;
Who hath aduanc'd her to his heau'nly throne,
Where she enioyes the perfect vnion.[32]

Her *Scepter* was the rule of righteousnes.
Her *Subiects* more for loue then feare obei'd.
Her *Gouernment* seem'd perfect blessednes.
Her *Mercie* with her *Iustice* euer swai'd.
Her *Bountie, Grace,* and *Magnanimitie,*
Her princely minde did plainely signifie.

She was the goldẽ *Pipe* through which great *Ioue*
Deriu'd to vs his blessings manifolde.
She was the token of his tender loue,
Chearing the hearts of all both yoong and olde.
She hath extinguisht all the mistie daies,
And brought a light more bright thẽ *Phœbus* raies.

Where first I do account that chiefest good,
Among so many blessings that are rife,
Gods sacred word surpassing Angels food,
That feeds the soule vnto eternall life.
Not mingle mangle mixt with Popish custome,
But sincere milk deriu'd frõ Gods owne bosome.

.   .   .   .

The second head whereto I do reduce,
The seuerall blessings of her Highnesse raigne,
Is long and quiet peace, whose pleasant iuice
Distilleth like the first and latter raine.

---

[32] Cf. *Sorrowes Ioy* (Nichols, *Elizabeth*, III, 652):

> She had espoused her selfe to th' Lord of Life,
> So still shee liues, a maiden, and a wife.
> He bought her deare; and it was reason good
> He should her wedd, who bought her with his blood.
> So now shee's crown'd with blisse, amongst those spirits,
> Which ransomd are, by Christ's all-saving merits.

For such a peace before was neuer seene,
As we enioy'd vnder a Virgin-Queene.

What *Age*, what *Nation*, or what *Country* can
Example bring of such a time of peace,
At any time since first the world began,
As God hath graunted in her *Highnesse* daies?
For he hath filled all his foes with shame,
And by her weaknesse magnifide his name.

He tooke her from the greedie-gaping iawes
Of them that sought to take her life away:
He did preserue her from the greedie clawes
Of *Tigers* fell, that sought her to betray.
He still protected her, and made her name
Extold in all the earth by *Trump* of fame.

He did defend her from the trecheries
Of *Antichrist* and all his hirelings;
Frõ *Spaniards* proud, her vowed enemies,
Vnder the shadow of his mightie wings:
And then did set her on a princely throne,
Which maintaind truth and true Religion.

He did her heart replenish eke with graces
Fit for her dignitie and royall calling,
To censure and to iudge all doubtfull cases
VVith wisedome, equitie, and vnderstanding.
In learning eke her vertues were so rare,
That for her Sex none might with her compare.

.   .   .   .

Bellona fierce long since had tooke her flight,
Sterne *Mars* his weapons then were laid away,
Peace crown'd this lãd with *Plenties* garlãd bright
Farre more resplendent then the *Lawrell* Bay.
Maugre the *Pope*, *Turke*, *Italy* and *Spaine*.
This famous Ile in honor did remaine.

From long-bred peace great plentie did proceed,
Euen as the chiefest off-spring of the same:

Of peace our plentie naturallie did breed,
Euen as the yong engender of the dame.
Destroy the Dam, the yong ones are not bred,
Take peace away, plenti's not gendered.

.   .   .   .

So that our Land an other *Canaan*
Did plentiously with milke and honey flow:
Eliza was our Iesus to withstand
Our enemies that sought to worke our woe;
And to destroy the Popish Cananites,
That would allure vs to their Idolrites.

.   .   .   .

All future ages shall admire her raigne,
When they shall heare her princely gouernment:
Vntill the liquid teares distill amaine,
Their owne vntimely birth they shall lament,
That they might not behold her golden daies,
So sweetly graced with immortall praise.

This Virgin-Queene did rule faire *Albion*
Twise two & twentie yeares, with great encrease
Of peace, ioy, wealth, much honour & renowne,
And then resigned vp her soule in peace,
To him that gaue it an immortall crowne,
In spite of thousands ten conspiracies
Which Antichrist against her did deuise.[33]

---

[33] Anthony Nixon, *Elizaes memoriall. King Iames his arriuall. And Romes downefall*, 1603, sigs. A3v–C1. See similar eulogies in Richard Johnson, *Anglorum Lacrimæ: In a sad passion complayning the death of our late Soueraigne Lady Queene Elizabeth: Yet comforted againe by the vertuous hopes of our most Royall and Renowned King Iames* (*Fugitive Tracts*, second series, no. 1). Eight quatorzains in Henry Petowe's *Elizabetha quasi viuens, Eliza's Funerall. A fewe Aprill drops, showred on the Hearse of dead Eliza. Or The Funerall teares of a true hearted Subiect* (1603) show the use of Petrarchan conceits to mourn the royal Laura. Cf. *Epicedium* (Lyly, I, 512): "Alas what should I say? if *Petrarch* knew not in what Sphere of Planets to lodge his *Lawra*, how shold I guesse in what order of Angels I should plãt our *Elizabeth*?"

There is inclusive praise of the virtues of the Faery Queene in *A Chaine of Pearle; or, a Memoriall of the Peerles Graces and heroick vertues of Queene Elizabeth, of glorious memory*, which was composed by "the Noble Lady DIANA PRIMROSE."

THE FIRST PEARLE. — RELIGION.

The goodliest Pearle in faire Eliza's Chaine
Is true Religion, which did chiefly gaine
A royall lustre to the rest, and ti'de
The hearts of all to her when Mary di'de.

.   .   .   .

THE SECOND PEARLE. — CHASTITY.[34]

The next faire Perle that comes in order heere
Is Chastity, wherein Shee had no peere,
Mongst all the noble Princesses which then
In Europe wore the Royall Anadem.
And though for beauty shee an Angell was,
And all our sex did therein far surpasse;
Yet did pure unspotted Chastitie
Her heavenly beautie rarely beautifie.

.   .   .   .

Thus her impregnable Virginity,
Throughout the world her fame did dignify.

.   .   .   .

THE THIRD PEARLE. — PRUDENCE.

How prudent was her government appear'd
By her wise counsels, by the which shee steer'd
In the most dangerous times that ever were,
Since King or Queene did crowne in England weare.

.   .   .   .

---

[34] Cf. the laments of Castitas in *Atropoïon Delion, or the Death of Delia: With the Teares of her Funerall. A Poetical Excursive Discourse of our late Eliza* (Nichols, *Elizabeth*, III, 630–636), in which the Fates, Mundus, Fama, Natura, Angeli, and so on praise and lament Eliza.

For though her wit and spirit were divine,
Counsels (shee knew) were best, where more combine:
That for experience and deepe policy
Are well approved; whose fidelity
Retaines them in the bonds of loyall love,
And no great pensions from their Prince can move.

. . . .

THE FOURTH PEARLE. — TEMPERANCE.

. . . .

This Pearle in her was so conspicuous,
As that the King her Brother still did use,
To stile her His sweete Sister Temperance;
By which her much admir'd selfe-governance,
Her passions still shee checkt, and still shee made
The world astonisht, that so undismaid
Shee did with equall tenor still proceede
In one faire course, not shaken as a reed,
But built upon the rocke of Temperance;
Not daz'd with Feare not maz'd with any chance;
Not with vaine Hope (as with an emptie spoone)
Fed or allur'd to cast beyond the Moone;
Nor with rash anger too precipitate,
Not fond to love, nor too, too prone to hate;
Not charm'd with Parasites, or Syrens songs,
Whose hearts are poison'd, though their sugred tongues
Sweare, vow, and promise all fidelity,
When they are bruing deepest villainy.
Not led to vaine or too profuse expence,
Pretending thereby State Magnificence:
Not spending on these momentary pleasures
Her precious time; but deeming her best treasures
Her subjects Love, which she so well preserv'd,
By sweet and milde demeanor, as it serv'd
To guard her surer than an Armie Royall;
So true their Loves were to her and so loyall:
O Golden Age! O blest and happie yeares!

O Musicke sweeter than that of the Spheares:
When Prince and People mutually agree
In sacred concord, and sweet symphonie!

THE FIFT PEARLE. — CLEMENCY.

Her Royall Clemency comes next in view,
The Vertue which in Her did most renew
The image of Her Maker, who in that
Exceeds himselfe, and doth commiserate
His very rebells, lending them the light
Of Sunne and Moone, and all those diamonds bright.
So did Eliza cast Her golden rayes
Of Clemency on those which many wayes
Transgrest Her lawes, and sought to undermine
The Church and State, and did with Spaine combine.

.   .   .   .

THE SIXT PEARLE. — JUSTICE.

Her Justice next appeares, which did support
Her Crowne, and was her Kingdomes strongest Fort.

.   .   .   .

THE SEVENTH PEARLE. — FORTITUDE.

This goodly Pearle is that rare Fortitude,
Wherewith this sacred Princesse was endu'd;
Witnesse her brave undaunted looke, when Parry
Was fully bent Shee should by him miscarry:
The wretch confest, that Her great Majestie
With strange amazement did him terrifie.
So Heavenly-gracefull, and so full of awe,
Was that Majesticke Queene, which when some saw,
They thought an Angell did appeare: Shee shon
So bright, as none else could her Paragon.
But that which doth beyond all admiration
Illustrate Her, and in Her this whole nation;

Is that heroicke march of Her's and speech
At *Tilbury*, where shee did all beseech
Bravely to fight for England; telling them
That what their fortune was, should Hers be then.
And that with full resolve Shee thither came
Ready to win, or quite to lose the Game.
Which words, deliver'd in most Princely sort,
Did animate the army, and report
To all the world her magnanimity,
Whose haughtie courage nought could terrify.

. . . .

The Eight Pearle. — Science.

Among the vertues intellectuall,
The Van is lead by that we Science call:

. . . .

How many Arts and Sciences did decke
This Heroina? who still had at becke
The Muses and the Graces, when that Shee
Gave Audience in State and Majestie.
Then did the Goddesse Eloquence inspire
Her Royall breast; Apollo with his lyre,
Ne're made such musicke; on her Sacred lips
Angells enthron'd most Heavenly Manna sips.

. . . .

Her Speeches to our Academians,
Well shew'd Shee knew, among *Athenians*,
How to deliver such well tuned words,
As with such places punctually accords.
But with what Oratory ravishments,
Did Shee imparadise Her Parliaments?
Her last most Princely Speech doth verify
How highly Shee did England dignify.
Her loyall Commons how did Shee embrace,
And entertaine with a most Royall Grace?

The Ninth Pearle. — Patience.

Now come we Her rare Patience to display:
Which, as with purest Gold, did pave her way
To England's Crowne; for, when her Sister rul'd,
Shee was with many great afflictions school'd;
Yet all the while Her mot was Tanquam Ovis,
Nor could her Enemies prove ought amisse
In her, although they thirsted for her bloud,
Reputing it once shed, their soveraigne good.

.　　.　　.　　.　　.　　.　　.　　.　　.

The Tenth Pearle. — Bounty.

As Rose and Lillie challenge cheefest place,
For milke-white lustre, and for purple grace;
So England's Rose and Lillie had no Peere,
For Princely bounty shining every-where;
This made her Fame with golden wings to fly
About the world, above the starry sky.
Witnesse France, Portugall, Virginia,
Germany, Scotland, Ireland, Belgia;
Whose Provinces and Princes found her aid
On all occasions, which sore dismaid
Spaine's King, whose European Monarchy
Could never thrive during her Soveraignty.
So did shee beate him with her distaffe; so
By Sea and Land Shee him did overthrow;
Yea, so that the Tyrant on his knees Shee brought,
That of brave England Peace he beg'd, and thought
Himselfe most happie, that by begging so
Preserv'd all Spaine from beggery and woe.
　　Here all amaz'd my Muse sets up her rest,
　　Adoring Her who's so divinely blest.[35]

To report of her death (like a thunder-clap) was able to kill
thousands, it tooke away hearts from millions: for hauing
brought vp (euen vnder her wing) a nation that was almost be-

[35] Nichols, *Elizabeth*, III, 642–650.

gotten and borne vnder her; that neuer shouted any other *Aue* than for her name, neuer sawe the face of any Prince but her selfe, neuer vnderstoode what that strange out-landish word *Change* signified: how was it possible, but that her sicknes should throw abroad an vniuersall feare, and her death an astonishment? She was the Courtiers treasure, therefore he had cause to mourne: the Lawyers sword of iustice, he might well faint: the Merchants patronesse, he had reason to looke pale: the Citizens mother, he might best lament: the Shepheards Goddesse, and should not he droope? . . .

.   .   .   .

Thus you see that both in her life and her death shee was appointed to bee the mirror of her time.[36]

[36] Dekker, *The VVonderfull Yeare*, pp. 18–19, 27. The titles of thirty-three of the pieces that mourned Eliza and welcomed James, from some of which I quote, are listed in Nichols, *James*, I, xxxvii–xli. Notable elegies appear, too, in the following: Thomas Bell, *The anatomie of popish tyrannie*, 1603, sigs. A2–A2ᵛ; George Carleton, *Heroici characteres. Ad illustrissimum equitem Henricum Nevillum*, Oxford, 1603, sigs. A4–B4, C1 ("Elizabetha parens, regni sanctissima nutrix"); Robert Fletcher, *A briefe and familiar epistle sheuuing his maiesties most lawfull, honourable and iust title to all his kingdomes*, 1603, sigs. B1–B2ᵛ; John Gordon, *A panegyrique of congratulation*, 1603, sigs. E3–E4; *The True Narration of the Entertainment of his Royall Maiestie*, 1603, sig. B1; *Quenne El'zabeths losse, and King Iames his vvelcome*, 1603 (chiefly about Elizabeth; James is rather slighted). Typical lamentation and praise in sermons at the time of her death are to be found in John Hayward, *Gods vniuersal right proclaimed*, 1603, sigs. C7–C7ᵛ, D2ᵛ–D3, especially; and Miles Mosse, *Scotlands welcome*, 1603, sigs. D4ᵛ–E1ᵛ, especially.

CHAPTER X

Retrospect

A CRITIC who dismisses the poet's celebration of Queen Elizabeth as flattery for advancement, or as exacted by a woman's vanity, has failed to grasp its true rationale and its poetic significance. I have sought to show that the idealization of Elizabeth expressed the imaginative life of her age, which made of her a complete symbol for the good and beautiful in sovereignty and womanhood. Eliza is one creation of the idealizing energy that marks European literature from Dante's intense dream of heaven and hell to Shakespeare's human pageant of infinite variety. In patriotic England poets wove for this "gorgeous dame" various gowns — Judith's, Diana's, Gloriana's — all inspired by the actual model, even if spun of far more radiant stuff than the finery the woman actually wore. "Seuerall names . . . expresse seuerall loues: Yet all those names make but one celestiall body, as all those loues meete to create but one soule."

Of course some of the poetry that celebrates Elizabeth can be paralleled in the formal compliment of other court poets before, during, and after her time. Much of the Latin and occasional verse is of this sort. One must, however, remember to take superlatives and hyperboles as of a piece with the style of an age that spoke in extravagant metaphor. If the queen was to be complimented above other royalty, excesses in excess were inevitable. One must remember, too, that figurative and conventional diction, as I insisted in the study of the royal Laura, may express

deep and sincere emotion. Free and vigorous imagination
likes to move in patterns, even old ones, where the personal
is sublimated in the impersonal. Part of the poetry lauding
Elizabeth is obviously clever or stupid flattery. The
Elizabethan gentleman who did not aim at high place was
a *rara avis* among the brilliant and motley flock at court.
One can hardly understand now how much the favor of the
monarch counted then for a man in any career. But a
queen who secured her throne after troubles that made her
aware of the ugly truth about power in a possessive world
as few rulers have learned it was the last person to mistake
the honeyed words of courtiers for more than they were
actually worth to her — mere verbal music that scarcely
irritated a woman forever burdened with the cares of state.
No astute ear is needed to tell the ring of true praise from
that of "fals flatours" as surely as the queen did. If she
was vain, she was nothing of a fool. She did not mistake
lip-service for the simple song of devotion with which her
people welcomed her when she pledged them her life and
love, and which was always audible. For their song she
kept a sensitive ear, and failed not to detect and to applaud
it whether it sounded in the crude ballads of the masses or
was transposed into Platonic music. With her quick wit,
keen temper, and uncanny ability to divine another's
motives while dissembling her own, she exacted and received skilful work even in flattery if the suitor won her
smile. To insist that the poets sang to Elizabeth merely
for pensions is to suggest that they, brilliant poets, were
stupid men. There was no widespread notion that this
Tudor queen rewarded anything save solid ability and devotion to the death. If a poet came to see that he might
expect richer words than gifts, he often kept up the song
out of delight in the service; for his was an age when men,
unlike Browning's hero, did think there was "cause in love
of power, high fame, pure loyalty" to wear out their lives

"chasing such shades." Elizabeth could give her poets no bed of roses, yet they were unusually good poets, however hard some called their bed. She was forced to finance her government on astonishingly limited funds;[1] and poets were not the only children she had to nurture. The full record of her direct patronage of literary men is not the mean one some students[2] would make it. Yet if she be unjustly blamed for not playing Maecenas to all her poets, she must be credited with a rule that brought a comparatively prosperous country in which to house them, and a court that was brilliant enough to lead some to sing of more abiding and beautiful things, however much others satirized abuses. Elizabeth gave to the really gifted something even more vital than money. She gave the light of her personality, her love of achievement and a splendid example in it, her smile of discerning approval wherever worth appeared. One may attribute some of the compliment lavished on Elizabeth to the timeworn custom of poets to address pretty speeches to the reigning monarch as a matter of state form, and more, to deliberate effort to obtain a powerful ruler's favor. But still more of the praise can only be explained as evoked by admiration for the achievement and character of the queen and of the woman. It cannot be reasonably dismissed as perfunctory flattery offered in exchange for easy pensions and unmerited honors.

If the critic is prone to feel that another sovereign might have won such a genuine and complete idealization as Elizabeth did, he should recall the reign of Mary Tudor and what she failed sadly to give and to receive; he should imagine her continuing on the throne. Mary Stuart, beau-

---

[1] See Neale, *Elizabeth*, pp. 282–289, especially.

[2] See, for example, the superficial argument by B. B. Gamzue, "Elizabeth and Literary Patronage," in *Publications of the Modern Language Association of America*, XLIX (1934), 1041–1049.

tiful and accomplished, has been idealized as a classic
queen of high romance by poets who did not live in her
turbulent Scotland. There are some French sonnets to her,
but there is no Scottish song to parallel England's to Eliza.
Mary, perhaps under an evil star, made a conspicuous
failure at the task fate set her. She did not reconcile her
personal desires with her country's good. Her task was no
harder than that which Elizabeth faced in 1558. When
James unwisely used the great heritage left him by Elizabeth, who had sacrificed much to rule well, he heard no
such hymns as those Sir John Davies raised to Astræa.
Thunder rumbled, and the music of court masques did not
resolve the ugly discord. One may profitably try to imagine Queen Victoria in the multiple rôle that Elizabeth
played. Although the later great queen came to symbolize
the empire for some of her poets, their song to her is not so
symphonic as that to Gloriana. On occasions when the
proper Victoria would have protested "We are not
amused," Elizabeth cried "On with the play!" to the
motley cast with which she acted the rôle of master come-
dienne in a drama of vast variety. "If in loftiness of aim
her temper fell below many of the tempers of her time, in
the breadth of its range, in the universality of its sympathy
it stood far above them all." [3] After every due subtrac-
tion has been made, the literature idealizing Elizabeth
keeps an admiration about as deep as one human being
can draw from others — a singularly full celebration of
an English ruler.

Further meaning in that hymn of devotion will appear
by lingering a moment on the range of Elizabeth's temper.
So many facets did it have that it reflected almost every
admiration of her people. Even in her grief for Essex,
the people's favorite and her own, Elizabeth expressed

[3] J. R. Green, *A Short History of the English People*, New York, 1916, 373-374.

the heart of all. She sorrowed still more deeply than the
people, for she also had loved him too well, yet more wisely
than a many-headed multitude could. But the range of
her temper is perhaps best revealed in the way it harbored
virtues of both Reformation and Renaissance as they developed in England. Elizabeth saw the practical value of
Protestant energy, directness, self-reliance, and trust in the
Lord as a personal ally against all enemies. But she saw
the danger of unrestrained individualism in religion and
politics, especially when it took itself with unrelieved seriousness. She was bent on such tolerance of individualism
as would not undermine her benevolent Tudor autocracy.
National harmony with its full fruition was her goal. By
refusing to follow Puritan counsel she postponed civil war
until the house was sound enough to survive it. She sought
a harmony in which neither body nor soul would deny the
other. By her own example she encouraged her people not
only to labor ardently and to respect the English establishment in religion; she encouraged them to merry-making,
and that even on the Sabbath, which she remembered was
made for man. Accomplished lady of the new learning,
delighting in all the arts and sports that Englishmen loved,
she shared their hearty enjoyment of the good things of
life. The "intellectual paganism of humanism" that
marked her temperament but "rested on the broad basis
of an instinctive paganism scattered wide among the
people." [4] Her constant playing with love and her robust
tastes pleased the new naturalism. Her chaste marriage
to duty satisfied a rising Puritan ideal even while her
sacred virginity stirred medieval devotion. She seemed
all that men could admire in woman save a mother, and
she skilfully made them feel that she was a nobler sort of
mother, the natural mother of their country, as she told

---

[4] Adapted to Elizabeth from Legouis and Cazamian, p. 261.

her Commons. Her invincible wit that mastered any scene where mere male sense strutted, her personal courage that matched any man's, her force, energy, and self-confidence drew Renaissance admiration of masculine virtues even while her feminine charms aroused chivalric adoration of the lady. The contrasts that the age liked were combined in its queen, full of fineness and coarseness, humor and anger, work and play, delicacy and roughness. Her character epitomized it — its ambition and daring, its love of adventure, its love of the new with the old in art and religion, its love of bright life within embosoming darkness, its surpassing love of England.

Inevitably Elizabeth came to symbolize England in all its new fullness. Perhaps the very lack of much expression in plastic and pictorial art in England of the sixteenth century encouraged the imagination to seize on this actual woman who seemed to embody for England's good all the best of the past and the present. A symbol can easily take the place of its object and become an idol.[5] Elizabeth was idolized, but not disastrously; for thinking of her time one might write: "The art of free society consists first in the maintenance of the symbolic code; and secondly in the fearlessness of revision, to secure that the code serves those purposes which satisfy an enlightened reason." [6] I have shown in some detail how truly Elizabeth became an adequate symbol for her people. Their poets maintained or revised all inherited symbols of the good to create Eliza, and that with double ease, perhaps, because man has al-

George Santayana, *The Life of Reason*, II (*Reason in Society*), 177.

[6] A. N. Whitehead, *Symbolism Its Meaning and Effect*, Cambridge, 1928, p. 103. Cf. Santayana's statement (*Reason in Society*, p. 178) that "a symbol needs to remain transparent and to become adequate; failing in either respect, it misses its function." All that Santayana writes of the king as "really the state's hinge and centre of gravity, the point where all private and party ambitions meet and, in a sense, are neutralized," may be strikingly associated with Elizabeth's successful reign.

ways personified as feminine the fructifying elements that
condition his life.

> Mother of *England*, and sweete nurse of all,
>   Thy countries good which all depends on thee,
> Looke not that countries father I thee call,
> A name of great and kingly dignitie;
>   Thou dost not onely match olde kings, but rather,
>   In thy sweet loue to vs, excell a father.[7]

So if one understands the full life of England when the
goddess Eliza is worshipped, some sweet reasonableness
may appear even in the most excessive adoration.

Such a symbol as Elizabeth was for a term gave a radical
stimulus to all forms of poetry, one may be sure. She was
a human representation of loved ideals otherwise bloodless.
Had the queen's taste and temperament not been what
they were over two generations, very different would be
the work by which we know Lyly, Ralegh, Spenser, and
various others. But one speculates idly about what the
age would have said of the good in sovereignty and womanhood had it had a king or a different queen. It would have
been a different age, for more than any other person Elizabeth kindled its spirit, and expressed it. One will not deny
her profound part in what it did say if the setting of lyrics
like "Queen and Huntress" is remembered. Even the
most perfunctory songs to the queen's virtue exercised
the idealizing imagination for such flights as it took in the
sonnets of Shakespeare. Before it stood an incarnation of
almost every ideal beauty that patriotic eyes desired to
behold.

Nor should the paradox of a worldly woman idealized as
the paragon of all virtues confuse one. It can be compre-

---

[7] *The Poems English and Latin of the Rev. Thomas Bastard, M.A.*, ed. A. B.
Grosart, Manchester, 1880, p. 37. Other epigrams lauding Elizabeth are on
pp. 26–27, 37, 48, 78, 87–88.

hended if the age and the complete woman are not forgotten. Ages of great freedom and vigor like the Renaissance in Italy and England are full of paradoxes in belief and behavior. At such times free imagination can transmute the facts of animal existence into abiding ideal beauty. The facts may be ugly from certain points of view. Yet often when they but irritate a moralist's eye, to a student of the ways of the creative imagination they are appealing in their power to inspire robust minds to rise on them to the realm of the ideal. So in England of the late sixteenth century the facts about Elizabeth and her England are full of astonishing contrasts. There was never a less idealistic or romantic woman in the loose sense of those abused words than the actual queen. Yet she became in patriotic verse a chaste goddess sent by heaven to lead her people into the land of milk and honey. The age was robust enough to behold the clay feet of its idol without ceasing to adore the head. Elizabeth's feet were most certainly clay, but in her head was rare sense and in her heart, rare love. Everything she did was done on the world's terms. She never spent the royal energy in seeking to save or to purify the world. Yet because she understood what happiness is possible in the world as few men or women have, she could rule a good part of it. A saint would have understood the world and spurned it. Elizabeth was neither saint nor the daughter of saints. She was the last of Tudor dynasts, and she accepted her rôle in the worldly drama of power just as circumstances wrote it and with a readiness to use any tricks in the mundane play. In so doing she showed wisdom which reformers have seldom learned — knowledge that the kingdom of this world is never to be made the kingdom of heaven. She saw that only some sure control of the world, however painfully or ignobly bought by someone, can make for those moments of security which give leisure for glimpses of that other kingdom, most rationally revealed in art. In idealizing her the poets let their devotion to ideal beauty rest on pagan sagacity about the unalterable nature of things. For England it was a fortunate moment in history. Ancient wisdom was quieting the medieval quarrel of spirit with body, and Protestant zeal was only beginning to aggravate the old family misunderstanding. Elizabeth so loved her country's varied good that she did not deny the tangle of good and evil by which men live on earth. If she had "the Body but of a week and feeble Woman," in it beat "the Heart . . . of a King, and of a King of *England* too," ready "to lay down for my God, and for my Kingdom, and for my People, my Honor, and my Blood, even in the Dust." Poets who were enabled to contemplate the beautiful and the good beneath the shadow of her throne did not fail to sing only the good in her. They were more gracious than many critics have been. They were more just, too, because more respectful of the dark mysteries of nature that enclose for us eternal beauty.

What seems to have been the attitude of Elizabeth herself toward the legend? One must remember her position as queen, her objectives, and the means available for attaining them. The sovereign personified the state in Europe of the sixteenth century. The state, truly the great mother of the Greeks and the Romans, had been displaced by Holy Church during the Middle Ages as the dominant authority in society. The Renaissance restored to the state much of its ancient prestige and exalted the prince. Elizabeth, a paradoxical virgin mother of her state at a time when many men were questioning the authority of a holy Virgin Mother, focused in her broad temper for all patriotic Englishmen that love of country which was now burning brightly. Even in her girlhood fate threw her into a Continental political web wherein she would eventually be either spider or fly. Her wits only could decide which. It was a web intricately woven by her predecessors, by Francis, and by Charles, and constantly tangled by others. It was one in which means were justified or forgotten if ends were achieved. Of course you fought the devil's agents with the devil's weapons, if you won. Obviously, her first need was a house not divided against itself if she was to succeed in her labor at home and abroad — the patient nursing of the nation into full health and self-expression. The clear intelligence of a master politician with a great statesman's goal must quickly have seen that the idealization was a secure buttress to power at home, especially since it sprang, for all the hollow flattery which was easily recognized and discounted, from the deep love of a grateful people. Her father had known the value of royal magnificence for stamping the public mind with the grandeur of the prince. As Deborah the daughter carried forward such work. As Judith, Eliza, Elisa, Diana, Laura, Idea, Cynthia, Gloriana, and Belphœbe she held the varied fancy of her own age. She did not forget that her fame as Judith would also strengthen her abroad. She trusted in God, of course, but she remembered who it is that heaven most helps. She knew that she was helping herself to meet the self-styled "Christ's Vicar" and Philip "his prince" when she nurtured the popular legend with its belief in God's guidance for a virgin queen. All the while the halo of divine right blended admirably with the crown of Gloriana. "We whose training is so different must remember that to many in those days kingship was a divine institution, just as was the Church. It gathered up and symbolized the requirements of orderly beauty in things secular, as the Church did in things spiritual, and the two at times might seem to a mind steeped in symbolism almost to flow together." [8] Symbolism seems to be at the

---

[8] P. E. More, *Shelburne Essays*, fourth series, New York, 1906, p. 82.

root of all religion. Elizabethan minds were still steeped in it, as the popularity of emblems, *imprese*, and heraldic devices shows. It was wholly natural to adore the princess who brought such blessings as only God could send, and to praise her in Biblical terms. Surely Elizabeth was quick to realize that the legend spread a radiant nimbus around a queen already winning and holding the affection and loyalty of her people by tangible services to them. Her ends made it expedient that she lend herself to the deification. She was hardly averse. And she did love England abidingly. She was too wise a governor and too sane a spirit not to give God or the grace of circumstances above her power the final credit for her success. Many may wish that Elizabeth had been a finer woman, but no one can evaluate justly all the diverse achievements in art and life that came when she integrated England and still honestly insist that she should have been a better governor. In her garden, and not without her gardening, the English Renaissance matured.

It is interesting to guess what the woman beneath the queen's crown thought of the idealization. Of course much of the praise was very sweet, especially when she heard sincerity in it, and little of it actually irritated. When she detected the voice of a grateful people she must have felt less lonely than her renunciations for England's sake made her early and late in life. As "creeping time" overtook her, and she saw that she must soon retreat to the grave to make way for another order, her quick intelligence surely perceived the irony when a withered and weary old woman was hailed as the paragon of goddesses. But a Tudor ego animated by a love of the drama of power as vital as life itself was kept sane by a fine sense of comedy, and by a proud resolve to live and die every inch a queen of England in every royal rôle. That love, and sense, and resolve sustained her through the restless last decade of the reign and during her own mortal decay to the last hour when she declared that her "*Throne hath beene the Throne of Kings*," and that none but a king should succeed her.[9] To think thus of the fading queen rather than to see her as a vain old shrew demanding flattery with her last breath is to do more than merely to imitate the chivalry of her age.

What was the attitude of practical intelligence toward the legend? What, for example, did Francis Bacon think of Gloriana? Bacon first of all revered a secure state as a solid base for the social order which would condition his great schemes for "the relief of man's estate." He drew away from Essex as that friend rebelled against Elizabeth's fruitful autocracy. Bacon saw the idealization as a support to her government. In *Mr. Bacon's Discourse in the Praise of his Sovereign* (1590-1592) [10] a man as little touched by poetic madness as any in an infected age lauds the queen for nearly every quality, royal and personal, which the poets sing; in fact, his eloquence almost takes him into their realm. Even if Bacon is shrewdly burning his part of the incense, the fact that he was conscious of the genuine political worth and essential truth of the legend is still evident. Bacon was too canny a politician to support a legend not inspired by true worth in its subject, one that was all sounding brass.

But during the nineties there was growing unrest about the inevitable new order that would succeed the queen's; and there was dissatisfaction, especially among the younger men, with Elizabeth's autocracy. Moralists had all along inveighed against one thing or another, and satirists were now speaking out. Elizabeth's own generation stood by her faithfully and no doubt saw her decline through a

---

[9] Camden, p. 584.
[10] *The Works of Francis Bacon*, ed. James Spedding, R. L. Ellis, and D. D. Heath, VIII (1890), 126–143. Cf. *In Felicem Memoriam Elizabethæ*, VI (1878), 281–318.

transfiguring veil, spun in part from memories of their youth together. Lord North seems to speak for servants like Burghley when he writes to the Bishop of Ely: "She is oure God in earth; if ther be perfection in flesh and blood, undoughtedlye it is in her Majestye." [11] But many young bloods bucked in the traces. They saw only the faded, sharp-tongued, and autocratic old woman. Foreigners at court had all along rent the insular veils. Seldom had they failed to admire Elizabeth's abilities, but they gave no willing suspension of disbelief to the divine epithets of patriotic poets. The legend was opposed by interests which I have consciously not emphasized in this study. For enemies the English Judith was the "Jezebel of the North."

> The Bee and Spider by a diuerse power,
> Sucke Hony & Poyson from the selfe same flower! [12]

Fin de siècle disillusion and the rising scientific temper fated the legend ultimately for the realm of the merest poetic fiction. For a few years England's living glory and Gloriana had seemed actually one. But the unanimity of spirit and action in 1588 soon passed. Rumblings of discord to come and the pressure of opposition increased. The idealizing energy long vital in Europe declined with the end of the sixteenth century. Growing doubt of the traditional in all spheres, the rising passion for facts, the attitude toward convention in poetry that Donne best represents — even the realistic statecraft of Bacon, Burghley, and the queen herself — scarcely nourished the legend. Patriotic fervor and Protestant zeal coalescing

---

[11] Quoted in L. F. Salzman, *England in Tudor Times*, 1926, p. 3.

[12] This couplet, a popular conceit in Elizabethan verse, is quoted from the title-page of *A Poetical Rhapsody*. The enemy's damnation of Elizabeth appears in a "sonet," "Les vertus de Iesabel Angloise" (Adam Blackwood, *Martyre de la royne d'Escosse*, Edinburgh, 1588, sig. A9); and in *De Iezabelis Angliæ parricidio varii generis poemata Latina et Gallica*, [Brussels, 1587?].

from beneath had done that. After the queen's death a very different prince ruled. Politics and religion divided the house against itself. The afterglow of "Virgo" lighted the skies, and the resplendent tradition of "good Queen Bess" and her golden age straightway arose, long to do service for political and religious partisans, and forever to evoke best her great times. But the times and their great queen were gone. A legend which in medieval days might have grown into a cycle of romance comparable to what developed around Alexander, Arthur, and Charlemagne, comes nowadays to be viewed as an antique political weapon by historians of the scientific temper, or as a poetic figment of the Renaissance mind.

Today some may almost wonder whether the poet's portrait of his sovereign within her mortal lifetime indicates that men of her age had puerile illusions about mortality, about the truth of the actual English scene around them. No one can wonder long. Not often have men been so aware that "night walks at the heeles of the day, and sorrow enters (like a tauernebill) at the taile of our pleasures." [13] Seldom or never has the grim specter death stalked more ominously in the background of the banquet, or horror and disease mingled more with beauty and health. All met every day the skeleton in the closet, but they were not modern enough to let their awareness of it spoil the music and the feasting in their "extant moment." Fortunatus declared: "If that leane tawnie face Tobacconist death, that turnes all into smoke, must turne me so quickly into ashes, yet I will not mourne in ashes, but in Musicke, hey old lad be merrie." [14] One day at dinner the "Queen asked what that covered dish was." Lord North, who was carving, lifted up the cover and replied, "*Madam, it is a Coffin*; a word which moved the Queen to

[13] Dekker, *The VVonderfull Yeare*, p. 35.
[14] Dekker, *Works*, I, 97.

anger: *And are you such a fool*, said she, *to give a Pie such a name?*" [15] There was a rare physical vitality and a thirst to drink fully of all the wines of life, a belief in the eternal world of art into which worthy achievement admitted a man, and, what must have made a vast difference, a sustaining faith in a stage far better than the poor one on which they strutted to which the best actors might make their exits. Because death, ugliness, and pain were constantly before the Elizabethan's actual eye, he summoned before his mind's eye the bright masque of poetry and song which can hide the meanness of the world for an interval. If life aims at and approaches a comfortable mediocrity, the extremes of beauty and happiness are not evoked by their opposites — which lay just beneath Gloriana's finery. One may, of course, smile at the extravagant idealization of the actual that marks much Elizabethan literature as no more than an elaborate defense mechanism to escape from the actualities of existence. Yet it held meaning and happiness for robust men of action who were not blind to the rest of the truth. Nor is it certain that later poets have achieved a nobler idealization from a more inclusive consciousness of the truth of things. Haunted by the mystery of time and sad mortality, the age found in Elizabeth something it thought *semper eadem*. She appeared to give gross mortality the lie where all most wanted it denied. [16]

[15] Sir Edward Peyton, *The Divine Catastrophe of the Kingly Family of the House of Stuarts*, 1652, p. 25 (quoted in Nichols, *Elizabeth*, III, 610 n.). The story, although I have not found it in a more reliable authority than Sir Edward, agrees with the tradition that Elizabeth hated deformity and ugliness in her presence and whatever bluntly reminded her of death and the uncertainty of life. Yet she was conscious of it all, and fearless before personal danger.

[16] When Elizabeth was sixty she heard the Hermit at Theobalds declare that that which most amazed his experienced eyes was: "I behold you the self-same Queene, in the same esteate of person, strength, and beautie, in which soe many yeares past I beheld yow, finding noe alteration but in admiration, in soe much as I am perswaded, when I looke aboute me on your trayne, that Time, which catcheth everye body, leaves only you untouched" (Nichols, *Elizabeth*, III, 243).

Repeatedly the poets sang her defiance of time and decay.
Age seemed not to wither Elizabeth.

> Only time which all doth mowe,
> Her alone doth cherish.

When the queen contrived the semblance of youth long
after the reality was no more she was but expressing and
satisfying the taste of her age, which demanded the show
of youth and beauty before its eyes, however unremittingly
the mind might face both ways, as in Marlowe's famous
song and Ralegh's reply.

For cunning Renaissance politicians, of whom Elizabeth
was truly queen, the idealization of her was a good device
for strengthening the place of the prince who is to rule.
But for the Renaissance poet the illusion was a dynamic
one of which the mortal Elizabeth was the *sine qua non.*
Gloriana was the actual queen exactly in so far as facts are
always the base metals of poetic alchemy. Poets and
people transmuted rich metal into a golden ideal of beauty,
virtue, and magnanimity. The actual Elizabeth epitomized her time. Her poets made her the mirror of its soul.
They live "with the eternitie of her fame." She lives with
the "eternitie" of theirs.

APPENDIX

A Short-title List of Books and Manuscripts Dedicated, Inscribed, or Presented to Queen Elizabeth*

M ANY and various books and manuscripts were dedicated to Queen Elizabeth. I think that I have discovered most of them. That the idealization of the queen was inclusive and sustained throughout the reign is confirmed by the variety, distribution, and number — toward two hundred and fifty — of the titles which I list. Elizabeth received some dedications while she was still a princess, many during the decade just after her accession, as many during the decade before the Armada victory, and a great many during the years that followed. There are a dozen Biblical entries in my list. Some authors dedicated several times to Elizabeth. Foreign authors and editors paid tribute. I cannot often give excerpts from the dedications, but I try to present them so as to suggest that they are rich in all the themes which I have traced in the poetry

* In this list of books and manuscripts dedicated, inscribed, or presented to Queen Elizabeth with a clear intent to compliment her I have respected the spelling and punctuation of the original titles when I have been able to see them. I have then reduced running capitals and ignored italics. Usually the edition cited is the first in which a dedication to the queen appeared; and most of the books dedicated to her were first editions. A dedication was seldom or never shifted from her to another until after her death. Unless otherwise noted, conjectured dates and attributions, as in my text and notes, are after A. W. Pollard and G. R. Redgrave, *A Short-Title Catalogue of Books Printed . . . 1475–1640*, 1926, or from library catalogues of books and manuscripts. Dr. C. S. Brown, Jr., and Dr. F. B. Williams, Jr., kindly drew my attention to several books that appear in my list.

of the reign. Verses and decorative devices, particularly the queen's arms, often accompany the dedications.

Acontius, Jacobus. Vna essortatione al timor di Dio. Con alcune rime Italiane, nouamente messe in luce. . . . [1580?]. The dedication (sigs. A2–A3ᵛ) is signed by G. B. Castiglione. On sigs. C4–C6 is a canzone in praise of Elizabeth.

—— Stratagematum Satanæ Libri octo: . . . Basileæ, . . . 1565. A complimentary Latin inscription to Elizabeth is on the verso of the title-page.

Alabaster, William. Elisæis, [1591?]. Newberry Library MS. Y 682.A 3. The dedication of this unfinished epic about Elizabeth is on fol. 1, and presentation verses follow on the next folio. See above, pp. 328–330.

Alvetanus, Cornelius. Epistola Cornelii Aluetani de conficiendo Divino Elixire, sive Lapide Philosophico. Deo optimo maximo Trino & uni Sacrum. Serenissimæ ac Clementissimæ Elizabethæ, . . . Principi in omni fortuna moderatissimæ, fortissimæque, humilimè ascripta & consecrata. The treatise, dated "Londini Anno 1565. 14. Julii," appears in *Theatrum Chemicum*, Strassburg, VI (1661), 501–507. See J. B. Black, *The Reign of Elizabeth 1558–1603*, Oxford, 1936, p. 264.

Andrewes, Roger. Advice of Roger Andrews to Queen Elizabeth, [n.d.]. Bodleian Library MS. Rawlinson D. 718, fols. 39–79. In his dedication (fols. 39–39ᵛ) of his work, which is chiefly in regard to the succession to the throne, and includes a short survey of sovereigns from the Conquest on, Andrewes pleads his zeal for the welfare of queen and state as excuse for his forwardness.

[Anonymous.] The first booke of the preseruation of King Henry the vij. when he was but Earle of Richmond, Grandfather to the Queenes maiesty; Compiled in english rythmicall Hexameters. . . . 1599. The "Dedication of the booke to the Queenes Maiestie" (sigs. D2–D2ᵛ) is preceded and followed by praise of her. Celebration of her is interwoven with the "rythmicall Hexameters" which the author champions. Toward the end of the book (sigs. N4–N4ᵛ) "Certain Latine

verses, that were made long since by one Doctor Buste a
phisitian, in commendation of the Queenes Maiesty, when she
came to Oxford" are turned into "English Hexameters, and
Pentameters, verse for verse." The book concludes with
praise of the queen in the author's own English Sapphics.

—— [Prayers in various languages — Greek, Latin, English,
French, Italian, Spanish, German, Dutch, and Hebrew —
beautifully written in inks of various colors, with illuminated
titles and initials, for presentation to Queen Elizabeth, 1578.]
British Museum MS. Stowe 30. The prayers are preceded
(fols. 2ᵛ–3ᵛ) by a short poem about Elizabeth in Latin elegiacs.

—— A preparation to the due consideration and reverent com-
ming to the holy Communion of the Body and Blood of our
Lorde.... 1580. The dedication (sigs. A2–A4ᵛ) of this very
rare book, which was in the library of the late Sir Leicester
Harmsworth, lauds her *by whom, as the onely meane from
God, we reape all these good things.*

Ariosto, Ludovico. Orlando Furioso in English heroical verse,
by Iohn Haringtō Esquire.... [1591]. In his dedication
(sig. ¶2) Harington declares: "I desire to be briefe, because I
loue to be plaine. VVhatsoeuer I am or can, is your Maiesties."

Arnold ab Haersolte. Aduersaria de actionibus omnibus,
tam civilibus quam criminalibus;... Antuerpiæ,... M.D.
LXXXIII. The Latin dedication (sigs. A2–A8ᵛ) praises
Elizabeth's peaceful rule. (I was led to this item and to several
other dedications of foreign books by entries in W. D. Macray,
"Early Dedications to Englishmen by Foreign Authors and
Editors," in *Bibliographica*, I [1895], 324–347, 455–473.)

Ascham, Roger. Disertissimi viri Rogeri Aschami, Angli, regiae
maiestati non ita pridem a Latinis epistolis, familiarium
epistolarum libri tres, magna orationis elegantia conscripti.
... [1576]. Twenty verses, "Liber de se ad illustrissimam Reginam Elizabetham," are on the verso of the
title-page. An "Epistola Dedicatoria" signed by "Ed.
Grant" follows (sigs. ¶2–¶4ᵛ). On sigs. X6ᵛ–X9ᵛ Latin
verses laud the "most illustrious virgin" for the blessings
which she brings the state.

Ascham, Roger. The scholemaster. . . . 1570. All copies of the early editions of this book which I have examined are dedicated to Cecil by Margaret Ascham; but Giles (*Works*, III [1864], 65–75) prints as "Ascham's Dedication" one "DIVÆ ELIZ-ABETHÆ." In *The English Works of Roger Ascham* (ed. James Bennett, 1761) this dedication appears (pp. 179–186) as a "letter to Queen *Elizabeth* . . . now first published from a manuscript." It is dated October 30, 1566, and signed by Ascham as "Your Majesties Most bounden, and Faithfull Servante."

B., J. F. L. P. Le merueilleux exploict, & oeuvre de la main de Dieu advenu l'an 1588 sur l'Armee navale de Philippe d'Austrice Roy d'Espagne, pensant envahayr le Royausme d'Angleterre. A La Serenissime Regne Elizabeth Reyne d'Angleterre France & Irlande. . . . [1597]. British Museum MS. Sloane 1603. The manuscript contains French poems of various meters and lengths, some of which celebrate the Armada victory. Elizabeth is frequently lauded, especially in a "Cantique pour la serenissime Reyne Elizabeth d'Angleterre d'Action de graces au Seigneur Dieu pour sa deliurance, & deffaicte de ses Ennemys" (fols. 43–50ᵛ).

Bacon, Francis, *Viscount St. Albans*. A collection of some principall rules and maximes of the Common Lawes of England, . . . CIƆ. IƆ. C. XXX (= Part I of *The elements of the common lawes of England*, 1630). In the undated dedication (sigs. *A2–A4*ᵛ) Elizabeth is the "*life of our lawes*" and the "*life of our peace, without which lawes are put to silence*." Her reign "*hath beene as a goodly seasonable spring-weather to the aduancing of all excellent arts of peace*."

Bale, John, *Bishop of Ossory*. Scriptorum illustriũ maioris Brytanniẹ, quam nunc Angliam & Scotiam uocant: Catalogus: à Iapheto per 3618 annos, usq₃ ad annũ hunc Domini 1557. . . . Basileæ, . . . 1559. Two years after the 1557 edition of this book, the printer at Basel inserted four preliminary leaves (duplicate signature a2–a5ᵛ) containing a dedication to Elizabeth and some Latin verses lauding her for bringing peace and "Pure Religion."

Barckley, Sir Richard. A discourse of the felicitie of man: or his Summum bonum.... 1598. The dedication (sigs. *3–A2ᵛ) lauds Elizabeth as Virgo "truly representing Iustice, and effectually executing it."

Barnaud, Nicolaus. Le réueille-matin des François, et de leurs voisins. Composé par Eusebe Philadelphe Cosmopolite,... à Edinbourg, 1574. A dedication of the earlier Latin version "aux Polonois" is on sigs. a3ᵛ–b3, but a French dedication to Elizabeth is on sigs. a2ᵛ–a3.

Basil, St., *Archbishop of Caesarea*. [Epistle to St. Gregory of Nazianzen on the eremitic life. Translated from Greek into French by Jan Bellemain, *ca.* 1550.] British Museum MS. Royal 16 E. 1. The dedication to the princess (fols. 1–5ᵛ) compliments especially her learning and her ability as a linguist.

Beacon, Richard. Solon his follie, or a politique discourse, touching the Reformation of common-weales conquered, declined or corrupted.... Oxford ... 1594. The dedication (sigs. ¶3–¶4ᵛ) is full of praise of the queen's reforms in Ireland.

Becon, Thomas. The Iewel of Ioye [1553], in *The worckes of T. Becon, whiche he hath hytherto made and published,*... 1564, 1560, 1563. The dedication (sigs. AAa1ᵛ–AAa4) is to "the moste excellente Pryncesse and Vertuous Ladye Elyzabeth her grace, Sister to the Kyng his Maiestye."

Beda, *the Venerable*. The history of the church of Englande. Compiled by Venerable Bede, Englishman. Translated out of Latin in to English by Thomas Stapleton ... Antwerp ... 1565. The dedication (sigs. *2– ▷ 3) compliments Elizabeth's learning and declares it fitting that "the generall history of the realms off England shoulde first be commended to the princely head and Souuerain gouuernour of the same."

Bell, James. British Museum MS. 17 C. XXIX. This manuscript has been edited (1926) by Miss Ethel Seaton as *Queen Elizabeth and a Swedish Princess*. It is an account of the visit of Princess Cecilia of Sweden to England in 1565. The dedication (pp. 35–38) declares that Elizabeth draws Cecilia as Solomon drew Sheba.

Bellehachius, Ogerius. Ogerii Bellehachii sacrosancta bucolica Elizabeth Britanniæ, Franciæ, et Hiberniæ reginæ dicata. . . . 1583. In thirteen Latin verses (sig. A2) the author presents his pastoral Bible-dialogues with a paraphrase of the Song of Songs.

Bellot, Jacques. Le iardin de vertu, et bonnes moeurs plain de plusiers belles fleurs, & riches sentences auec le sens d'icelles, recueillies de plusieurs autheurs, & mises en lumiere par, I. B. gen. Cadomois. . . . 1581. The dedication (sigs. *2ᵛ-*5) is in both French and English on opposite pages. The text is preceded by a poem of six stanzas celebrating the English "*Vierge au Dieu vif sacrèe*" and rededicating the *Iardin* to her.

Bentley, Thomas. The monument of matrones: . . . 1582. The prose dedication (sigs. [A3–A4]) is followed by dedicatory verses, part of which I have quoted above, p. 220.

Bercher, William. A Dyssputacōn off the Nobylytye off wymen . . . 1559. This work was edited from the manuscript in the possession of Charles Brinsley Marlay, Esq., by R. W. Bond, Roxburghe Club, 1904–1905. It is an abridged translation of *La Nobilità delle Donne* by Lodovico Domenichi, who based his version on a treatise by Cornelius Agrippa. The dedication (I [1904], 87–89) shows the author eager to compliment Elizabeth's mother, whose scholar he had been at Cambridge, and to win some sort of service with the daughter.

Bèze, Théodore de. Iobus, Theodori Bezæ partim Commentarijs partim Paraphrasi illustratus. Cui etiam additus est Ecclesiastes, Solomonis Concio de summo bono, ab eodem Th. B. paraphrasticè explicata. . . . 1589. The dedication (sigs. A2–A5ᵛ) of this book, which was soon translated into English, concludes with fourteen Latin verses which celebrate the victory that God's winds and waves brought to Elizabeth in 1588.

Bible. The bible and holy scriptures conteyned in the olde and newe Testament. . . . Geneva. M. D. LX. The dedication (sigs. *₊*₊2-*₊*₊3ᵛ) reveals an ardent reforming zeal that would draw the new queen to its courses.

—— The bible Translated according to the Ebrew and Greeke, and conferred with the best translations in diuers languages. ... 1583. The dedication (sigs. A3–A3ᵛ) sees Elizabeth as made by God a "builder of his spirituall Temple." A Bodleian Library copy (Douce Bib. Eng. 1583.b.1) of this Bible made a handsome new year's gift to the queen — "a large Byble in englysshe couered wᵗ crymson vellat alouer enbradered wythe venys golde and seade perle." See the *British Museum Quarterly*, VI, no. 4, March, 1932, pp. 95–96.

—— Y beibl cyssegr-lan. Sef yr hen destament, a'r newydd. ... 1588. The Latin dedication (sigs. *2–*3ᵛ), which is signed by William Morgan, praises Elizabeth's erudition, her peace, and her preservation "veræ religionis."

—— The Boke of Psalmes, where in are conteined praiers, meditatiõs, praises & thankesgiuĩg to God for his benefites toward his church: trãslated faithfully according to the Ebrewe. ... Geneva ... M.D.LIX. The dedication is on sigs. *2–*8ᵛ.

—— Liber Sapientiæ carmen redditur, 1559. British Museum MS. Royal 2 D. II. The dedication (fols. 2–10) of this Latin verse translation of the Wisdom of Solomon praises Elizabeth as the bringer of "veræ religionis." The translator is James Calfhill.

—— [The Book of Daniel, translated into Greek by Hugh Broughton, n.d. (before 1589).] British Museum MS. Royal 1 A. IX. The short and conventional dedication in Greek is on fol. 2.

—— ῾Η Καινὴ Διαθήκη. Testamentum Nouum. [*sic*] רַ֫דְּתָא הֲדַתָּא Est autem interpretatio Syriaca Noui Testamenti, Hebræis typis descripta, plerisque etiam locis emendata. ... Autore Immanuele Tremellio, ... [Geneva] M. D. LXIX. Tremellius dates his dedication of the Syriac New Testament (sigs. *2–*6): "Heidelbergę ad Kal. Martias, Anno M. D. LXVIII."

—— Testamentum Nouum, siue Nouum Fœdus Iesu Christi, D. N. Cuius Græco contextui respondent interpretationes duæ: vna, vetus: altera, Theodori Bezæ, nunc quartò diligenter ab eo recognita. ... Quarta editio, ... M.D.

LXXXIX. Bèze's dedication (sigs. ¶2–¶5ᵛ), dated from Geneva, "M.D. LXIIII, Decembr. xix," declares that Elizabeth, next after God, gives England peace and "Pure Religion."

—— [New Testament, in English, of the revised Wycliffite version, presented as a new year's gift by Elizabeth's chaplain, John Bridges.] British Museum MS. Royal I A. XII. The address (fols. 2–3ᵛ) in which Bridges presents his queen with this early manuscript is undated.

—— The text of the new testament of Iesus Christ, translated out of the vulgar Latine by the Papists of the traiterous Seminarie at Rhemes. With Arguments of Bookes, Chapters, and Annotations, pretending to discouer the corruptions of diuers translations, and to cleare the controuersies of these dayes. . . . By William Fulke, . . . 1589. Fulke opens his dedication (sigs. *2–*3) with a reference to a "defense of our English translations of the holie Scriptures, against the malicious cauils of *Gregorie Martine*," which had been offered "vnto your Maiesties moste honourable protection." He now comes forward again to defend the true religion from papist renderings of scripture, and to honor its protector who has been preserved in peace by "the miraculous prouidence of Almighty God."

—— Testament Newydd ein Arglwydd Iesu Christ. . . . 1567. In his English dedication (sigs. a1–a2ᵛ) of this Welsh translation of the New Testament William Salesbury lauds Elizabeth as surpassing heroines of the ancient Britons, and blesses her for the "Halcyons and quiet dayes" which she has brought.

—— The gospels of the fower Euangelistes translated in the olde Saxons tyme out of Latin into the vulgare toung of the Saxons, newly collected out of Auncient Monumentes of the sayd Saxons, and now published for testimonie of the same. . . . 1571. John Foxe, who signs the dedication (sigs. A2–A4ᵛ, ¶1–¶2ᵛ) lauds Elizabeth's "goldẽ peace."

Bilson, Thomas, *Bishop*. The true difference betweene Christian subiection and vnchristian rebellion: wherein the princes lawfull power to commaund for trueth, and indepriuable right to beare the sword are defended against the Popes censures and the Iesuits sophismes vttered in their apologie and defence of English Catholikes: . . . Oxford, . . . CIƆ IƆ XXCV. The dedication (sigs. A2–A6ᵛ) stresses the fact that "Princes are placed by God."

Bizzari, Pietro. De optimo principe, in *Petri Bizzari varia opuscula*, . . . Venetiis, MDLXV. Bizzari, a Protestant refugee from Perugia, dedicated to Elizabeth (sigs. A2–A2ᵛ) this first of six pieces in his volume. Latin and Greek verses by others (sigs. A3–A3ᵛ) praise Elizabeth. The work is dated at Venice, June, 1565; but British Museum MS. Royal 12 A. XLVIII shows a somewhat different dedication dated from London, December 25, 1561. An address to Elizabeth in the printed version (sigs. A4–D1ᵛ) asks her to see her virtues in the tract as "*in lucidissimo speculo.*"

Boaistuau, Pierre. Histoires tragiques, extraictes de quelques fameux autheurs, Italiẽs & Latins, mises en françois, par Pierre du Boystuau, surnommé Launay, gentilhomme François. Dediées à Tresillustre, & Treschrestienne, Elizabet de Lenclastre, par la grace de Dieu Royne d'Angleterre. . . . Paris. 1559. The laudatory dedication (sigs. a2–a3), dated from Paris, "*ce 20. d'Octobre 1559,*" is followed by a French sonnet to Elizabeth.

Bonjeu, Jaques de. [Eighteen short poems on "Dames illustres qui ont esté Roynes."] British Museum MS. Royal 20 A. XX. In a dedicatory letter (fols. 1–1ᵛ) dated Paris, June 15, 1575, de Bonjeu states that the poems were composed for the queen-mother (Catherine), and that she, on hearing them read, commanded him to send a copy to Elizabeth. He pays tribute to Elizabeth's "heureuse paix & concorde." On fol. 16 twelve French verses praise the "bel example" which the wise rule of Elizabeth gives to all princes.

Bridges, John, *Bishop*. The Supremacie of Christian Princes, ouer all persons throughout their dominions, in all causes so wel Ecclesiastical as temporall, both against the Counteblast of Thomas Stapleton, replying to the Reuerend father in Christe, Robert Bishop of VVinchester: and also Against

Nicholas Sanders his Visible Monarchie of the Romaine Church, touching this controuersie of the Princes Supremacie. Ansvvred by Iohn Bridges. . . . 1573. This defense of Elizabeth's supremacy in church and state, which runs to 1114 pages, is dedicated on sigs. ¶2–¶4ᵛ.

Bright, Timothy. Characterie an arte of shorte, swifte, and secrete writing by Character. . . . 1588. This early book on shorthand (reprint of the copy in the Bodleian Library, ed. J. H. Ford, 1888) is dedicated to Elizabeth on sigs. A2–A6.

Broughton, Hugh. A Concent of Scripture, . . . [1588, on the basis of unpublished bibliographical data assembled by Dr. E. E. Willoughby]. The dedication is on sigs. 1–1ᵛ.

—— An explication of the article κατῆλθεν εἰς ᾅδου, of our Lordes soules going from his body to Paradise; touched by the Greek, generally ᾅδου, the vvorld of Soules; termed Hel by the old Saxon, & by all our translations: vvith a defense of the Q. of Englands religion: To, & against the Archb. of Canterbury: vvho is blamed for turning the Q aucturity against her ovvne faith. . . . The second edition, vvherein the Typographicall falts of the former are emended. . . . 1605. The dedication is on sigs. (2)–A2.

—— Sundry workes, defending the certayntie of the holy Chronicle: dedicated togeather vnto her Maiestie: with request, that authoritie might stablysh the trueth vnto publique agreement. . . . [1591?]. The dedication is on sigs. ⚹2–A1.

Buckley, William. [Treatise on the nature and use of horary rings, in Latin.] British Museum MS. Royal 12 A. XXV. Buckley, who had an horary ring made for the princess, dates his dedication (fols. 2–2ᵛ) from King's College, Cambridge, "16° Calendas Aprilis 1546."

Butler, Thomas. [Rhetorical exercises, in Latin, on the judgment of Solomon (I Kings iii), 1603 (?).] British Museum MS. Royal 12 A. LI. The author dedicates (fols. 1–1ᵛ) his work as a new year's gift, and speaks of his gratitude for a "predium quod in multos annos toti nostrae genti ac familiae victum vestitumque prebet." At the end (fols. 15ᵛ–16) are five Latin stanzas in which the queen is complimented.

Calvin, John. Commentiares sur le Prophete Isaie. . . . Geneue, . . . 1572. The dedication (sigs. *2-*3) hails Elizabeth as the deliverer of the true church, and bids for her continued favor of it. It is dated from Geneva, "*l'an 1559. le 15. de Ianuier.*" The book had formerly been dedicated to Edward VI.

Camden, William. Britannia siue florentissimorum regnorum, Angliæ, Scotiæ, Hiberniæ, et Insularum adiacentium ex intima antiquitate Chorographica descriptio. . . . 1600. On sigs. *A2–A2*ᵛ is a dedication to Elizabeth replacing that to Burghley in the editions of 1586, 1587, 1590, and 1594.

Castiglione, Baldassare, *Count.* Balthasaris Castiglionis Comitis De Curiali siue Aulico Libri quatuor ex Italico sermone in Latinum conuersi. Bartholomæo Clerke Anglo Cantabrigiensi Interprete. . . . 1571. Clerke signs the dedication (sigs. A2–A4).

Chaloner, *Sir* Thomas, *the elder.* In laudem Henrici Octaui, regis Angliæ præstantiss. carmen Panegiricum. . . . 1560. This extended Latin poem, issued anonymously, is dedicated (sigs. A2–A2ᵛ) to Elizabeth in twenty Latin verses. It ends comparing her to classical deities.

Chambers, Robert. Palestina written by Mʳ· C[hambers]. P[riest]. and Bachelor of Diuinitie . . . Florence [London, John Wolfe?] . . . 1600. The dedication (sigs. ¶3–¶3ᵛ) is signed, "Your Maiesties humble seruant not worth the naming."

Charles V, *Emperor.* A copie of the last enstructions which yᵉ Emperoure Charles the fiueth gaue to his sonne Philippe before his death, translated oute of Spanishe, [n.d.]. British Museum MS. King's 166 (also in Stowe 95 and Stowe 161). The letter presenting the translation to Elizabeth (fols. 2–9) is signed by the translator, Lord Henry Howard, created Earl of Northampton in 1604.

Charnock, Thomas. [The *Dictionary of National Biography* states that this Somerset alchemist dedicated an inedited tract, "A Booke of Philosophie," to Queen Elizabeth in 1566. See Anthony à Wood, *Athenæ Oxonienses,* ed. Philip Bliss, III (1817), 1235. I have not seen the tract.]

Chelidonius, *Tigurinus*. A most excellent Hystorie, Of the Institution and firste beginning of Christian Princes, and the Originall of Kingdomes: . . . 1571. On the verso of the title-page are the royal arms and four English verses that declare God's protection for Elizabeth. The translator, James Chillester, who has worked from Pierre Boaistuau's French version of the Latin of Chelidonius, signs the dedication (sigs. A2–A4ᵛ).

Churchyard, Thomas. A handeful of gladsome verses, giuen to the Queenes Maiesty at Woodstocke this Prograce, 1592 . . . Oxforde, . . . 1592 (reprinted in *Fugitive Tracts*, first series, 1493–1600, ed. W. C. Hazlitt, 1875, no. 31 [no pagination]). A presentation address follows the title-page. See above, p. 245.

—— The miserie of Flaunders, calamitie of Fraunce, Misfortune of Portugall, Vnquietnes of Ireland, Troubles of Scotlande: And the blessed State of Englande. . . . 1579. In the dedication (sigs. A1–A1ᵛ) Churchyard writes: "*In whiche worke I compare*, Flaunders, Fraūce, Portugall, Irelande, and Scotlande, *to bee the shell of a precious Nutte, the sweete Kirnell whereof is the blessed state of* ENGLANDE." The work of course contains much praise of Elizabeth's peace.

—— A Pleasant conceite penned in verse. Collourably sette out, and humblie presented on New-yeeres day last, to the Queenes Maiestie at Hampton Courte. . . . 1593. The presentation speech (sigs. A3–A3ᵛ) thanks the queen for "your gracious goodnesse towardes me oftentimes (and cheefely now for my pencyon)."

—— A rebuke to rebellion. British Museum MS. Royal 17 B. VII. This poem of thirty-four nine-line stanzas is undated in the manuscript, but it is printed in Nichols, *The Progresses and Public Processions of Queen Elizabeth*, 2d ed., 1823, II, 603–612, and dated 1588. The new year's dedication (fols. 1–1ᵛ) declares that "the stable raigne and strong maintenance of a iust Prince" is the best rebuke to rebels and traitors.

—— The Worthines of Wales: VVherin are more then a thousand seuerall things rehearsed: . . . All the which labour and deuice is drawne forth and set out by Thomas Churchyard, to the glorie of God, and honour of his Prince and Countrey . . . 1587. The dedication (sigs. *2–*4ᵛ) testifies to the loyalty of the land of Elizabeth's ancestors. Churchyard (sig. A2) asks, "And doth not she daily deserue to haue books dedicated in the highest degree of honor to her Highnesse?"

Clayton, Giles. The Approued order of Martiall discipline, with euery particuler Offycer his offyce and dutie: with many other stratagemes adioyning to the same. . . . 1591. On the verso of the title-page is an engraving of the queen in a wreath of Tudor roses. Beneath it twelve Latin verses celebrate her virtues. In the dedication (sigs. A2–A3) a veteran in Ireland and the Low Countries for sixteen years praises the queen's military strength that shields the peace of England.

Conway, *Sir* John. Meditations and Praiers, gathered out of the Sacred Letters, and Vertuous Writers: Disposed in fourme of the Alphabet of the Queene her moste excellent Maiesties Name. . . . 1571. Acrostic verses lauding Elizabeth are on the verso of the title-page, and the dedication, on sigs. A2–B4ᵛ. The letters of the queen's name are moralized on sig. E4; and prayers are made upon them on sigs. E4ᵛ–I3, K1–L5ᵛ, and O1–P1ᵛ.

Cooke, Robert. A Coppie of the English Barons Booke from the Conquest to this yeare An°. 1592. Dedicated to the Queenes Maᵗʸ by Clarencieulx King of Armes and by her Highnes most graciously accepted and Princely rewarded, [*ca.* 1592]. Folger Shakespeare Library MS. 298.1. I quote the original title-page of this manuscript of colored coats of arms. According to a note in the autograph of Peter Le Neve this manuscript is a continuation of Cooke's work by Richard Ley.

Corro, Antonio de. Diuinorum operum Tabula, [London? or Norwich? 1570?]. This folio broadside in the Cambridge University Library (Broadside XVI) has a laudatory Latin dedication to Elizabeth which concludes: "offert hanc Tabulam, pro xeniolo huius noui Anni. 1570."

Cradock, Benjamin. Auriferæ artis Alchimiæ magisteriũ et mysteriũ. Quod oculis vidi et manib' tetigi, certificam possum. British Museum MS. Sloane 479. On fols. 2–2^v is a Latin prose dedication signed "Beniamin Cradock," and at the end (fol. 27), "Scripsi Londini, primo Februarij, anno 1595."

Cradock, Edward. [Tractatus de Lapide Philosophico, Latinis versibus conscriptus, adjectis ad marginem annotationibus quæ rem totam illustrant. . . . Reginæ Elizabethæ, carmen elegiacum dedicatum. MS. Ashmolean 1415, fols. 33–40. I have not seen this manuscript; I take the title from W. H. Black's *Catalogue of the Ashmolean Manuscripts*, Oxford, 1845, p. 1127.]

—— A treatise touchinge ẙ philosopher stone . . . [late sixteenth century]. Bodleian Library MS. Rawl. poet. 182 (also in MS. Ashmolean 1445, no. 6). The dedication of this English treatise (fols. 37–38) by the Oxford alchemist and divine is in rhyming couplets that praise Elizabeth's "godly quiet raigne."

Cyril, *Saint*. [The *Dictionary of National Biography* lists among Laurence Humphrey's works, "St. Cyril's Commentaries upon Isaiah, translated into Latin; dedicated to Queen Elizabeth." I have not seen the work.]

Daniel, Samuel. The Works of Samuel Daniel Newly augmented. . . . 1601. For the verse dedication (sigs. A2–A2^v), see above, pp. 327–328.

Daunce, Edward. A briefe discourse of the Spanish state, vvith a Dialogue annexed intituled Philobasilis. . . . 1590. Daunce's dedication (sigs. A2–A2^v) compliments Elizabeth's government "vnder the wing of God," and announces an intention to "display some *Spanish* colours, whereby the brightnesse of your glorie issued from your qualified gouernment may the sooner appeare to all men."

Davies, *Sir* John. Nosce teipsum. . . . 1599. For the verse dedication (sigs. A3–A3^v) see above, pp. 271–272.

Dee, John. The Brytish Queene Elizabeth, her tables gubernautik. The work is described (but not dated) in Dee's *General and rare memorials pertayning to the Perfect Arte of nauigation*, 1577, sig. ε.*3, as a "strange Monument, Dedicated to the Æternall, and Heroical Renown of our Queene her most Excellent Maiestie."

—— De Imperatoris Nomine, Authoritate: & Potentia: dedicated to her Maiesty . . . 1579. Dee thus lists the work in *A letter, Containing a most briefe Discourse Apologeticall*, 1599, sig. A4ᵛ.

—— De modo Euangelij Iesu Christi publicandi, propagandi, stabiliendique, inter Infideles Atlanticos: volumen magnum, libris distinctum quatuor: quorũ primus ad Serenissimam nostram Potentissimamque Reginam Elizabetham inscribitur: Secundus, ad summos priuati suæ sacræ Maiestatis consilij senatores: Tertius, ad Hispaniarum Regem, Philippum: Quartus, ad Pontificem Romanum — anno. 1581. Dee thus lists the work in *A letter*, sig. B1ᵛ.

Delahay, Jeremy. [An album of ornamental writing, in gilt and colors, with roughly illuminated initials, n.d. (end of sixteenth century).] British Museum MS. Royal 17 A. XXVIII. The manuscript is presented (to Elizabeth?) at the end (fol. 25) by "your graces most humble and obedient servant during life Ieremy delahay dwelling by the Artillirie yard neere bishopsgate streete."

Dering, Edward. M. Derings workes. More at large then euer hath heere-to-fore been printed in any one Volume. . . . 1597. "M. Derings owne Preface to her Maiestie" (sigs. *1–*3ᵛ) presents the six works in the volume to Elizabeth in hope, apparently, of overcoming disfavor that has prohibited his preaching. A notable prayer for her appears on sigs. F1–F2ᵛ of the last work in the volume.

Desainliens, Claude (=Claudius Holyband). Claudii a Sancto Vinculo, de pronuntiatione linguæ Gallicæ libri duo: Ad illustrissimam, simulq̃; Doctissiman Elizabetham Anglorum Reginam. . . . 1580. The dedication (sigs. A2–A4ᵛ) compliments the queen as a linguist.

Dethick, *Sir* William. Insignia Armorum Augustissimæ Supremæ, et Commilitonum prænobilissimi Ordinis Garterij, secundum eorum Sedes in Ecclesiâ Collegiatâ Regalis Castri

Windesorensis, quorum septem loca vacua conspiciuntur. 1602. British Museum MS. King's 417. Folio 1, which bears the title that I quote, continues: "Sacræ Ma^tatis vestræ Servus observantissimus Garterus principalis Rex Armorum dedicat, consecratque." Colored arms of Knights of the Garter are introduced (fol. 2) by the queen's.

Dodoens, Rembert. A nievve herball, or historie of plantes: . . . First set foorth in the Doutche or Almaigne tongue, by . . . D Rembert Dodoens . . . And nowe first translated out of French into English, by Henry Lyte . . . 1578. Lyte is moved to dedicate (sigs. 1*2–1*2^v) by his queen's "most cleare, amiable and chearefull countenaunce towardes all learning and vertue," and his "earnest zeale, and feruent desire" to show himself "a thankeful subiect to so vertuous a Soueraigne."

Dousa, James. Iani Dousæ a Noortwiick odarum Britannicarum liber, Ad D. Elisabetham Britanniarum Franciæ Hiberniæ que Reginam. . . . Lugduni Batauorum, . . . CIƆ. IƆ. LXXXVI. A dedicatory ode to Elizabeth appears on sig. *a. Geoffrey Whitney contributes commendatory verses (sigs. *3–*4) in which he declares Elizabeth's due praises are beyond the muse even of Homer and Virgil. Very laudatory birthday odes appear on sigs. A1–A3^v, G2; and an elegy in her honor, on sigs. G1–G1^v.

Drake, *Sir* Francis. Sir Francis Drake Reuiued: Calling vpon this Dull or Effeminate Age to folowe his Noble Steps for Golde & Siluer, By this Memorable Relation, of the Rare Occurances (neuer yet declared to the World) in a Third Voyage, made by him into the West-Indies, in the Yeares 72. & 73. . . . Faithfully taken out of the Reporte of M^r· Christofer Ceely, Ellis Hixon, and others, who were in the same Voyage with him. By Philip Nichols, Preacher. Reviewed also by S^r· Francis Drake himself before his Death, & Much holpen and enlarged by diuers Notes, with his owne hand here and there Inserted. Set forth by S^r· Francis Drake Baronet (his Nephew) now liuing. . . . 1626. The nephew's dedication to Charles I is followed by his famous uncle's "To the Queenes most excellent Maiestie, my Most dread Soueraigne" (sigs. *A3–A3^v*). It is signed, and dated "*Ian.* I. 1592."

Drant, Thomas, *poet and divine.* Thomæ Drantæ Angli Aduor-
dingamii Præsul. Eiusdem Sylua. . . . [1578?]. The "Nun-
cupatoria" of this book is addressed to Archbishop Grindal;
but British Museum's C.45.d.8 is a presentation copy from the
author to Elizabeth with, on the leaf before the title-page,
some MS. English verses addressed to her by way of a dedication. Three poems to her appear on sigs. E4–E4ᵛ.

Edwardes, Roger. Remembrances of Instrucciones necessarie
to be embraised for the policie of this and the time to comme.
British Museum Additional MS. 36705. The signed dedication
(fols. 3–3ᵛ) is dated "March : 8. *1568.*" The original draft
with many corrections and long passages erased is in MS.
Lansdowne 95, fols. 5–30.

Epictetus. The Manuell of Epictetus, Translated out of Greeke
into French, and now into English, conferred with two Latine
Translations. . . . By Ia. Sanford. . . . 1567. Latin verses to
Elizabeth on the verso of the title-page are followed (sigs. A2–
A3ᵛ) by Sandford's dedication extolling her virtues and
achievements, especially her abilities as a linguist.

Ethredge, George. [Panegyric upon Henry VIII, Ἐγκώμιον τῶν
πράξεων καὶ τῶν στρατηγημάτων τοῦ Ἑνρίκου ὀγδόου ἐμφανεστάτου
βασιλέως, in Greek elegiac verse (316 couplets), 1566?] British
Museum MS. Royal 16 C. X. Ethredge was deprived of his
regius professorship of Greek at Oxford soon after Elizabeth's
accession. His Greek prose dedication (fols. 1–4) to Elizabeth,
on the occasion of her visit to Oxford (1566?), is clearly an
effort to get reinstated in her favor.

Eton Scholars. Annales, qui historiam viginti et octo annorum
regni Elisabethæ complectuntur, totidem libris comprehensi,
[in or soon after 1586]. Bodleian Library MS. Rawlinson
G. 174. These poetical annals of public events, 1558–1586,
are preceded (fols. 1–1ᵛ) by twenty-six Latin dedicatory
verses, signed "Schola Ætonensis." Striking tributes to
Elizabeth appear throughout the work.

—— [Complimentary Verses, in Latin, as a new year's gift to
Queen Elizabeth, by forty-five members of Eton College,
evidently in 1559–60.] British Museum MS. Royal 12 A.

LXV. A Latin dedicatory inscription appears on fol. 2. The poems, in various meters, celebrate Elizabeth as a "Mulier sancta, pia, ac altera Iudith" (fol. 10ᵛ), as a "Virgo prępotens Britannis salus" (fol. 10ᵛ).

Eton Scholars. De aduentu gratissimo ac maximé exoptato Elisabethæ . . . suas Ætonensium scholarum maximé triumphans ouatio. British Museum MS. Royal 12 A. XXX. This manuscript contains complimentary Latin verses by twenty-three Eton boys presented to Elizabeth when she came to Windsor to escape the plague, and is dated September 19, 1563. A dedicatory Greek quatrain (fol. 1ᵛ) is followed by a Latin prose address (fols. 2–5). See above, p. 68.

Eunapius. The lyues, Of Philosophers and Oratours . . . now set foorth in English. . . . [1579]. In an epistle that dedicates this translation to Sir Thomas Bromley (sigs. *A2–A3*), one learns that the book "*laye hid in* Hungarie, *tyll* Hadrianus Iunius, *a great learned man, did cause it to be Printed in Greeke, and Translated it into Latine: and a eleuen yeares since, Dedicated it to the Queenes most excellent* Maiestie, *our Soueraigne Lady* Elizabeth." Junius's dedication (sigs. *A3ᵛ–A1*) is dated "From *Harlem*, the Kal. of March. 1568." Acrostic verses to Elizabeth appear on sigs. A1ᵛ–A2.

Euripides. Phœnissæ Euripidis tragœdia Latino metro versa à M. Georgio Calamino Silesio. . . . Argentorati . . . M, D. LXXVII. Twelve Latin verses (sig. A2) present this tragedy to Elizabeth. See above, p. 123.

Evans, Lewis. The Castle of Christianitie, detecting the long erring estate, asvvell of the Romaine Church, as of the Byshop of Rome: together with the defence of the Catholique Faith: Set forth, by Lewys Euans. . . . 1568. Below the queen's arms on the verso of the title-page are Latin lines to her. The dedication is on sigs. A2–A5.

Fenice da Ferrara, Giouan' Antonio. Stanze et Oratione di Giouan' Antonio Fenice da Ferrara a la Regina d' Angleterra, [late sixteenth century]. Bodleian Library MS. Bodl. 882. A sonnet (fol. 1ᵛ) presents the twenty-five eight-line stanzas and the prose oration.

Ferrarius, Joannes. A vvoorke of Ioannes Ferrarius Montanus, touchynge the good orderynge of a common weale: . . . Englished by William Bauande. 1559. The dedication is on sigs. ¶2–¶4.

Fletcher, Giles, *the elder*. Of the Russe Common Wealth. Or maner of gouernement by the Russe Emperour, . . . 1591. The dedication (sigs. A3–A4) presents a book that contrasts Russian tyranny with the benevolent rule of Elizabeth, a "Prince of subiectes, not of slaues, that are kept within duetie by loue, not by feare." Fletcher planned to write an extensive Latin history of the reign of Elizabeth.

Foxe, John, *the martyrologist*. Actes and Monuments of these latter and perillous dayes, . . . 1563. After a dedication to Christ, this notorious book is presented (sigs. B1–B2ᵛ) to Elizabeth as "*next vnder the Lorde, as well in causes ecclesiasticall, as also to the temporall state appertaining.*" She surpasses Constantine in her services to the true church. The initial letter of his name that opens the dedication to the queen encloses a decorative picture of her seated on her throne.

Frégeville, Jean de. Palma Christiana, seu, Speculum veri status Ecclesiastici, sub lege Naturæ, & lege Mosis, & institutione Christi, & traditione Apostolorum, & vivorum Apostolicorum, & consuetudine Primitiuæ Ecclesiæ ab Apostolis ad Patres Nicenos, & inde apud Aphricanos respuentes iugum Antichristi tempore Aureli Carthaginensis, & Augustini Hipponensis. . . . Ad serenissimam Reginam Angliæ. . . . 1593. Frégeville presents (sigs. A2–A3ᵛ) his book declaring: "*Tribuat Paris pomum Veneri precium formæ, Frigeuillæus Elizabethæ palmam in premiũ virtutis consecrabit.*"

Fulke, William. A Defense of the sincere and true Translations of the holie Scriptures into the English tong, against the manifolde cauils, friuolous quarels, and impudent slaunders of Gregorie Martin, one of the readers of Popish diuinitie in the trayterous Seminarie of Rhemes. . . . 1583. The copy of this book which is in the Huntington Library is dedicated (sigs. ¶1–¶2ᵛ) to Elizabeth, but copies in the British Museum and the Folger Shakespeare Library do not show the dedication.

Gaebelkhover, Oswald. The Boock of Physicke ... nuelye translatede out of Low-duche into Englishe by A. M. .... Dorte ... 1599. Isaac Canine, "Bibliopola at Dorte," dedicates (sigs. †1–†1^v) the translation to Elizabeth in gratitude for her aid to "these our vnitede Provinces."

Gascoigne, George. The Grief of Joye. Certeyne Elegies: wherein the doubtfull delightes of manes lyfe, are displaied. Written to the Queenes moste excellent Ma$^{tie.}$ ... 1576. Printed from photographs of British Museum MS. Royal 18 A. LXI in *Complete Works*, ed. J. W. Cunliffe, II (1910), 511–557. The dedication (pp. 513–515), offering the work as a new year's gift, is dated "this first of January, 1577." A verse preface (p. 516) to Elizabeth follows.

—— [Translations of] The Tale of Hemetes the Heremyte. Printed from photographs of British Museum MS. Royal 18 A. XLVIII in *Complete Works*, II, 473–510. The manuscript, which lacks a title-page, begins with a drawing of the poet presenting the book to the queen. The dedication (pp. 474–478), preceded by verses to her, is dated "this first of January 1576." Elizabeth heard the *Tale* (by an unidentified author) at Woodstock in 1575. Gascoigne shortly rendered it into Latin, Italian, and French to compliment his learned queen. See comment in Sir Edmund Chambers's *Sir Henry Lee* (Oxford, 1936).

Gemini, Thomas. Compendiosa totius Anatomię delineatio, ... 1559. On the title-page of this English compendium of Vesalius is an engraving of the young queen with her scepter (more probably, one of Mary Tudor quickly adapted; see *The Library*, XIII [1933], 367–394, for a relevant article by Dr. Sanford V. Larkey, to whom I am indebted for drawing the paper to my attention). Victory is above her, and Justice and Prudence are on either side; an angel above holds a rose. The dedication (sigs. *1–*2^v), concerned largely with vindicating the study of the human body as God's creation, lauds Elizabeth as one who has from "infancie most relygiously with trewe religion, godlyzele, and puritie of life, sowght the honoure of almightie God."

Gesner, Conradus. Icones animalium quadrupedum viuiparo-
rum et ouiparorum, quæ in historiæ animalium Conradi
Gesneri libro I. et II. describuntur, . . . Editio secunda, . . .
Tiguri . . . M. D. LX. Following the dedication (sigs. A2–
A3ᵛ), which praises Elizabeth's learning, are twenty-eight
laudatory Greek verses.

Goldingham, Henry. [The Garden Plot, An Allegorical Poem,
Inscribed to Queen Elizabeth, n.d.] Edited by Francis
Wrangham, 1825, from the unfinished and unpublished manuscript (British Museum Harleian MS. 6902). The dedication
is on pp. 1–2 of this edition. See above, pp. 134–135.

Guevara, Antonio de, *Bishop*. A Chronicle, conteyning the
liues of tenne Emperours of Rome. . . . translated out of
Spanish into English, by Edward Hellowes, Groome of her
Maiesties Leashe. . . . 1577. Hellowes dedicates to his mistress (sigs. ¶2–¶4) his translation of "*this historie* [which]
hath beene dedicated by Syr Antonie of Gueuara, & *accepted of*
Charles the fifth."

Guicciardini, Francesco. The historie of Guicciardin, conteining
the vvarres of Italie and other partes, . . . Reduced into
English by Geffray Fenton . . . 1579. Fenton's dedication
(sigs. *3–*4ᵛ) lauds the wisdom in government shown by the
"sacred and fixed Starre, whose light God will not Haue
put out."

Guillemeau, Jacques. The Frenche Chirurgerye, or all the
manualle operations of Chirurgerye, . . . Through Iaques
Guillemeau, of Orleans ordinarye Chirurgiane to the Kinge,
and sworen in the Citye of Paris. And novv truelye translated
out of Dutch into Englishe by A. M. . . . At Dort . . . M. D.
xcvij. On the verso of the title-page is an elaborate engraving
of the queen's arms with a Tudor rose beneath it and angels
of peace on either side. The dedication to Elizabeth (sigs.
†2–†2ᵛ) is signed by "*Maxmiliane Bouman Chirurgian at
Dort*," who has caused the book to be translated into English
to instruct English students and to honor Elizabeth — "seeing that there is noe King, nor Prince on earth, vvhich vvith
such fervent desire, and fidelitye endevoureth by all meanes

possible, to maytayne, and protecte, the health and vvealth, both of bodye and soule of theire subiectes, and peoples, as your (most Illustriouse M^{tye.}) doth for your peculiare inhabitantes, beinge of God thervnto constitutede, and ordaynede."

Gwyn, David. Certaine English verses . . . Presented to the Queenes most excellent Maiestie in the Parke at Saint Iames on Sunday the xviii. of August 1588. . . . 1588. There is no formal dedication, but caption titles on sigs. A3, A5, A6 describe the several poems as gifts to Elizabeth.

H., W. Ad Campianum Iesuitam eiusq̃ Decem rationes responsio. . . . 1581. Bodleian Library MS. Rawlinson D. 1096. The Latin prose dedication is on fols. 4–5ᵛ. On fol. 21 there is a complimentary "device" that lauds Elizabeth and dates the manuscript.

Hakluyt, Richard. Analysis, seu resolutio perpetua in octo libros Politicorum Aristotelis. British Museum MS. Royal 12 G. XIII. The Latin dedicatory address (fol. 2), dated at Oxford, September 1, 1583, compliments Elizabeth's rule as the admiration of all peoples.

Hanapus, Nicholas. The ensamples of Vertue and vice, gathered oute of holye scripture. By Nicholas Hanape patriarch of Ierusalem. . . . Englyshed by Thomas Paynell. . . . 1561. The translator's dedication (sigs. ¶4–¶6ᵛ) offers the work "as . . . an anker, or a staffe to stay you by, and fermely to stablyshe your grace, least that your grace should (that God forbid) wauer or slide from the Catholike and true faith of God."

Harding, Thomas. A confutation of a booke intituled an apologie of the church of England, by Thomas Harding doctor of diuinitie. . . . Antwerpe, . . . 1565. In the dedication (sigs. *2–*6ᵛ) to Elizabeth the Catholic author seeks to secure her favorable judgment for his attack on Bishop Jewel's *Apologie*. He notes her personal taste for Catholic form and ceremony — "the reuerent vse of the crosse in your priuate chappell."

Harvey, Gabriel. Gabrielis Harueij Gratulationum Valdinensium Liber Quatuor. Ad Illustriss. Augustissimámque Principem, Elizabetham, Angliæ, Franciæ, Hiberniæq̃ Reginam longè serenissimam atq̃ optatissimam. . . . CIↃ. IↃ.

LXXVIII. On the verso of the title-page is an engraving of Elizabeth enthroned. Fifty-two Latin verses present the numerous Latin and Greek pieces in her honor. See above, p. 78.

Holland, Hugh. Pancharis: The first Booke. The Preparation of the Loue betweene Ovven Tudyr, and the Queene, Long since intended to her Maiden Maiestie: And now dedicated to the inuincible Iames, . . . CIↃ IↃCIII. On sig. D5ᵛ of this volume in the Bodleian Library (Arch. Bodl. B.1.165) Holland declares that for Elizabeth "as by the Preface may appeare I had once intended this first booke of the Præparation or Præludium of the loue betweene *Owen Tudyr* and the Queene Which Præface notwithstanding I will haue printed [sigs. A10ᵛ–A12ᵛ] with the rest, that I doe so much right to that dead Lady, sometimes our Soueraigne Queene and Mistresse."

Hortop, Job. The rare Trauailes of Iob Hortop, an Englishman who was not heard of in three and twentie yeeres space. . . . 1591. The dedication (sigs. A2–A2ᵛ) asks acceptance of the "trauelles" even "as our Sauior Christ accepted the poore widdowes mite."

Howard, Henry, *Earl of Northampton* (1604). A Dutifull defense of the lawfull regiment of Woemen, [*ca.* 1590]. Newberry Library MS. C 19175. The elaborate dedicatory address occupies fols. 2–25. The manuscript is an interesting document in the controversy launched by John Knox's illtimed *The first blast of the trumpet against the monstruous regiment of women* in 1558.

—— Regina Fortunata, [*ca.* 1576]. British Museum MS. Egerton 944. This original presentation copy of a Latin prose treatise with a full-length colored portrait of Elizabeth prefixed is dedicated on fol. 1. Its elaborate praise runs through seventy-four folios.

Hozyusz, Stanislaus, *Cardinal*. A most excellent treatise of the begynnyng of heresyes in oure tyme, compyled by the Reuerend Father in God Stanislaus Hosius Byshop of Wormes in Prussia. . . . Translated out of Laten in to Englyshe by Richard Shacklock . . . and intituled by hym: The hatchet of heresies. . . . Antwerp . . . 1565. The dedication (sigs. a3–a8) is an attempt to place under Elizabeth's wing this translation of an attack on heresies, the Latin original of which was dedicated to the Catholic king of Poland.

Huicke, Robert. [Complimentary poems, in Latin, *ca.* 1559.] British Museum MS. Royal 12 A. XXXVIII, fols. 1–31ᵛ. These poems by Elizabeth's physician are preceded by the following inscription: "Ad Elizabetham Parentem patriȩ, virtutis & sapientiæ ergo, vere magnã, . . . reginam semper Augustam omnisq3 apud suos ordinis hominum gubernatricem dignissiman" (fol. 1).

Humphrey, Laurence. The Nobles or of Nobilitye. The original nature, dutyes, right, and Christian Institucion thereof three Bookes. Fyrste eloquentlye writtẽ in Latine by Lawrence Humfrey . . . and . . . late englished. . . . 1563. An extended dedication (sigs. A2–B2ᵛ) lauds Elizabeth's restoration of "Pure Religion" under God's guidance.

Hunnis, William. The Poore Widowes Mite, *in* Seuen Sobs of a Sorrowfull Soule for Sinne. . . . Wherevnto are also annexed his Handfull of Honisuckles; the Poore Widowes Mite; a Dialog betweene Christ and a sinner; diuers godlie and pithie ditties; with a Christian confession of and to the Trinitie; newlie printed and augmented. 1583. Acrostic verses (sig. F3) present *The Poore Widowes Mite* as a new year's gift. Prayers for the queen appear (sigs. G10, H4–H5) in *Comfortable Dialogs betweene Christ and a sinner.*

Jewel, John, *Bishop.* Apologie de l eglise d Angleterre tournee de latin en francois. British Museum MS. Royal 19 B. III. This translation of Jewel's *Apologia pro ecclesia Anglicana* (first printed in 1562) is dedicated (fol. 1ᵛ) in a short unsigned letter dated London, April 25, 1564.

—— A Defence of the Apologie of the Church of Englande, Conteininge an Answeare to a certaine Booke lately set foorthe by M. Hardinge, and Entituled, A Confutation of &c. . . . 1567. Jewel's dedication (sigs. A2–A4ᵛ) laments Harding's addressing his popish *Confutation* to the "*onely* Nource, *and* Mother *of the Churche of God within these your*

Maiesties moste Noble Dominions," and hopes she may *"liue an Olde* Mother *in* Israel."

Jones, John, *M. D.* The Arte and Science of preseruing Bodie and Soule in Healthe, Wisedome, and Catholike Religion: Phisically, Philosophically, and Diuinely deuised: . . . 1579. The verso of the title-page has the arms of the queen, and the dedication which follows (sigs. A2–a2) is full of praise of her virtues. On sig. N3 her "complexion of bodye" is praised.

Kett, Francis. The glorious and beautifull garland of Mans glorification. . . . 1585. Opposite the title-page are the queen's arms. The dedication (sigs. A3–A4^v) lauds Elizabeth as a "true branch of Christ" in elaborate scriptural terms. On sigs. Q4–Q4^v she figures prominently in "A Prayer of Thankesgiuing."

Kimhi, David, *Rabbi.* [Commentary on the minor prophets, from Hosea to Zephaniah, translated into Latin by Thomas Nele (*al.* Neale), regius professor of Hebrew at Oxford, 1559–1569.] British Museum MS. Royal 2 D. XXI. The work, presented to Elizabeth on her visit to Oxford in 1566, is dedicated to her on fols. 2–3.

Kingesmell, Henry. [A collection of eighty-eight instances of ways or "invencõns" for raising money for state purposes, gathered chiefly from ancient history, n.d.] Bodleian Library MS. Rawlinson D. 168. Kingesmell, just returned from ten years in France, Italy, Spain, Portugal, the Fortunate Islands, and the Great Turk's dominions, offers (fols. 1–4) Elizabeth the "firste frutes of my labour."

Kirchmeyer, Thomas. The Popish Kingdome, or reigne of Antichrist, written in Latine verse by Thomas Naogeorgus, and englyshed by Barnabe Googe. . . . 1570. The dedication (sigs. [A1^v–A2]) is to Elizabeth as "next vnder God the supreme gouernour" of "the Church of England and Ireland."

Lee, Thomas. A briefe declaration of the Gouerment of Ireland, opening many Corruptions in ẙ same: discouering ẙ discontentments of the Irishery, and the causes moving theis expected troubles: And Shewing meanes how to establish quietnes in that Kingdome honorably: to your Ma:^{ties} profit without any encrease of charge . . . 1594. British Museum MS. Royal 17 B. XLV. There is no dedicatory letter, but on fol. 2 the text is headed by "TO THE QVEENES MOST EXCELLENT MAIESTY," and she is addressed throughout. The British Museum catalogue, in which this manuscript is entered as dedicated to Elizabeth, notes that it is evidently the copy presented to her.

Leius, Matthias. Certamen Elegiacum nouem musarum, Apolline duce, contra Barbariem susceptum: & Serenissimæ, Potentissimæq́ Principi, ac Dominæ, D. Elizabethæ, Angliæ, Franciæ, & Hiberniæ Reginæ, &c. Barbariæ victrici: Dominæ clementissimæ, D. D. D. . . . 1600. Latin verses (sig. A1ᵛ) dedicate the work.

Lewis, Geoffrey. [Complimentary verses, in Latin and Greek, and a Greek address on the occasion of Elizabeth's visit to Oxford (probably in 1566).] British Museum MS. Royal 12 A. XXIII. There is no formal dedication, but Greek elegiac verses (fol. 2ᵛ) felicitate Elizabeth, express the university's delight in her visit, pray for her, and introduce an extended Greek laudatory address.

Livius, Titus. The Romane historie vvritten by T. Liuius of Padua. . . . Translated out of Latine into English, by Philemon Holland . . . 1600. On the verso of the title-page is an engraving of Elizabeth. The initial letter of the gracious dedication (sig. A3) is adorned with Tudor roses, cupids, the queen's motto, and the letters "E R."

Lloyd, Lodowick. A briefe conference of diuers lawes: Diuided into certaine Regiments. . . . 1602. The dedication (sigs. A2–A2ᵛ) is a flourish of scriptural and historical allusions.

—— Certaine Englishe Verses, presented vnto the Queenes most excellent Maiestie, by a Courtier: In ioy of the most happie disclosing, of the most dangerous conspiracies pretended by the late executed Traitours, against her royall person, and the whole Estate. . . . 1586. The verses, although clearly a complimentary gift, lack a formal dedication.

—— Regum gemmae Sacris Biblijs desumpta per Ludouicum Lloid ad Arma Inseruientem. . . . [1600?]. The Latin dedication (sigs. A2–A2ᵛ) follows an engraving of a prince kneeling in prayer (verso of the title-page). The dedication is followed by an "Oratio Reginæ" (sigs. A3–A4), an "Oratio Esther Reginæ pro liberatione populi sui" (sigs. A4–A5), an "Oratio Iudeth cilicio indutæ & cinere conspersæ ad Deum contra Holofernum" (sigs. A5–A6), and an "Oratio Susannæ cum ad supplicium duceretur" (sig. A6).

—— The Triplicitie of Triumphs. Containing, The order, solmpnitie and pompe, of the Feastes, Sacrifices, Vowes, Games, and Triumphes: vsed vpon the Natiuities of Emperours, Kinges, Princes, Dukes, Popes, and Consuls, with the custome, order and maners of their Inaugurations, Coronations and annointing. Wherein is also mentioned, the three most happy, ioynfull [sic] and triumphant daies, in September, Nouember and Ianuary, by the name of, Triplica Festa. . . . 1591. The dedication (sig. A2) declares that a desire to glorify Elizabeth's birthday, accession day, and coronation day inspires the work. Those "three most happy, ioyful & triumphant daies" eclipse in their celebrations all ancient nativities and triumphs.

Lok, Henry. Ecclesiastes, othervvise called the preacher. . . . 1597. In the dedication (sigs. A2–A4) of his verse paraphrase of Ecclesiastes Lok lauds Elizabeth's prosperity and peace, her services to religion and learning, and her trade and expansion of empire. Prefatory poems include (sig. A5ᵛ) Latin verses by John Lyly (see Bond's *Works*, I, 67) in honor of the queen. English verses to her appear on sig. A6ᵛ.

—— Sundry Christian passions, contained in two hundred Sonnets. . . . 1597 (bound with *Ecclesiastes*, sigs. I5–Y5ᵛ). A Shakespearean sonnet (sig. I6) dedicates the work.

Lupton, Thomas. A Persuasion from Papistrie: VVrytten chiefly to the obstinate, determined, and dysobedient English Papists, who are herein named & proued English enimies and extreme Enimies to Englande. . . . 1581. Although the dedication (sigs. a2–a2ᵛ) does not contain notable praise, the text is full of tributes to Elizabeth's mercy in dealing with papists, who, loyal to the pope, are necessarily disloyal to their queen.

Lupton, Thomas. [A detailed scheme devised by Thomas Lupton for a general collection towards repairing sea-banks and damages by floods in Lincolnshire, helping the poor in Lincoln, York, Canterbury, and London, and poor scholars at Oxford and Cambridge, . . . n. d.] Bodleian Library MS. Jones 17. On fol. 5 Lupton in twelve four-verse stanzas presents his queen this "good and semely gifte," confident of a gracious reception for the humblest offering.

Lyte, Henry. The light of Britayne. A Recorde of the honorable Originall & Antiquitie of Britaine. . . . 1588. The dedication (reprint in 1814; no pagination), which follows an engraving of Elizabeth, hails her as the "*bright Britona of Britayne: euen Britomartis President of Britaine.*"

M., D. F. R. de. Respuesta y desengano contra las falsedades . . . en bituperio de la Armada Inglesa, . . . Dirigida a la Sacra Chatolica y real Magestad de la Reyna Doña Isabel nuestra Señora, Por la gratia de Dios Reyna de Ingalaterra, . . . 1589. Beneath the queen's arms on the verso of the title-page are verses, "Bretaña a su Reyna y Señora." The dedication (sigs. A2–A3) lauds Elizabeth's prudence, justice, fortitude, and temperance. Praise of her appears throughout the volume. In the same year this work was translated into English by J. Lea, who at the end inserted some verses of his own in honor of the Armada victory and Elizabeth's peace.

Machiavelli, Niccolò. The Arte of warre, written first in Italiã . . . and set forthe in Englishe by Peter Whitehorne, . . . M.D.LX.[–1562; 2 pts.]. Whitehorne's dedication (sigs. a2–a4) offers the queen the "first fruictes of a poore souldiours studie."

Margaret, *of Angoulême.* A Godly Medytacyon of the christen sowle, concerninge a loue towardes God and hys Christe, compyled in frenche by lady Margarete quene of Nauerre, and aptly translated into Englysh by the ryght vertuouse lady Elyzabeth doughter to our late souerayne Kynge Henri the viij. . . . 1548. John Bale, who signs the dedication (sigs. A2–B1ᵛ), praises highly the learning of the young princess. The edition of this work which the *Short-title Catalogue* dates

[1568?] has a new dedication (sigs. A2–A5) to Elizabeth signed by James Cancellar.

Marianus, *Scotus*. Mariani Scoti, . . . chronica: ad Euangelij ueritatem, post Hebraicæ sacro sanctę scripturę & Septuaginta interpretum uariationem, magno iudicio discussam & correctam, certa enumeratione temporum conscripta. . . . Basileæ, [n.d.]. The English "noblissima Virgo" receives in the dedication (sigs. α2–α6ᵛ) an elaborate tribute to her learning and her wise avoidance of innovations in religion upon her accession. This dedication, signed by John Herold of Basel, the editor, is dated "M. D. LIX Anno, Cal. Februarij."

Marten, Anthony. A reconciliation of all the Pastors and Cleargy of this Church of England. . . . 1590. The author, "Sewer of her Maiesties most honorable Chamber," no doubt pleased his mistress by declaring in his dedication (sigs. A3–A4) his aim to be "to *Reconcile* all your Cleargie, and pastors of this Church, to a perfect vnitie in gouernement, and to perswade your people to geue eare to no other voyces then your Maiesty, and lawes of the Church haue commaunded."

—— A second Sound, or Warning of the Trumpet vnto Iudgement. Wherein is proued, that all the tokens of the Latter day, are not onlie come, but welneere finished. . . . 1589. The dedication (sigs. A2–A3) of this work likens the several blasts that will warn of Christ's second coming to those trumpet flourishes which announce that the queen begins a summer progress.

Martiall, John. A treatyse of the crosse gathered out of the Scriptures, Councelles, and auncient Fathers of the primitiue church, by Iohn Martiall Bachiler of Lavve and Studient in diuinitie. . . . Antwerp . . . 1564. The dedication (sigs. A2–A4) praises the queen for having always kept the cross "reuerently in youre chappel, notwithstanding many measures haue bene made to the contrary." In the next year appeared James Calfhill's *An aunswere to the treatise of the Crosse*, prefaced by an epistle to Martiall that abused him for presumptiously dedicating his book to the queen of Protestants who scorn popish idols.

Maunsell, Andrew. First part of the Catalogue of English printed Bookes: Which concerneth such matters of Diuinitie, as haue bin either written in our owne Tongue, or translated out of anie other language: And haue bin published, to the glory of God, and edification of the Church of Christ in England. . . . 1595. The dedication (sigs. *2–*2ᵛ) expresses gratitude that "these diuine bookes are so mightily increased since your MA. blessed raigne."

Melissus, Paulus. Melissi Schediasmata Poetica. Secundo edita multa auctiora. . . . Lutetiæ Parisiorum. . . . CIƆ IƆ LXXXVI. The Latin prose dedication (sigs. ā2–ā3) praises Elizabeth's erudition and unfailing encouragement to scholars of all countries. Dedicatory verses follow on sig. ā3ᵛ. Each of the nine books of the first part of this extensive volume has dedicatory verse to Elizabeth preceding it, and there is scattered verse lauding her. The second part of Melissus's poems is also dedicated (sigs. Aaa2–Aaa2ᵛ) to Elizabeth. Melissus explains that he again attempts the impossible ("quod ἀδύνατόν") in seeking to praise adequately Elizabeth's virtues as a ruler and her erudition as a scholar. Part II has dedicatory verse to Elizabeth at the beginning of its "Epica" and of each book of the "Elegiæ"; and praise of her appears in various other poems.

—— Ode Pindarica ad serenissimam potentissimamq. dominam Elisabetham . . . Augustæ Vindelicorum, A. M D XIIXC. The British Museum copy of this work (11408.c.41) has manuscript additions by the author on the two fly-leaves preceding the text, which consists of four laudatory Pindarics. A Latin prose dedication is on the verso of the title-page, and Melissus's portrait and coat of arms appear on the two final leaves.

Merbury, Charles. A briefe discourse of royall monarchie, as of the best common weale: VVherin the subiect may beholde the Sacred Maiestie of the Princes most Royall Estate. VVritten by Charles Merbury Gentlemen in duetifull Reuerence of her Maiesties most Princely Highnesse. . . . 1581. This book exalting monarchy above all other kinds of government is dedicated to Elizabeth in Italian prose (sig. *2).

Moffett, Thomas. Insectorum Siue minimorum animalium theatrum olim à Conrado Gesnero Thomaque Pennio inchoatum nunc Tho. Moufeti Londinatis operâ sumptibusq max. concinnatum auctum perfectum & Spirantibus ferè Iconibus illustratum, [n. d.]. British Museum MS. Sloane 4014 (=741). This work, which was printed in folio in 1634, has (fols. 5–6) a Latin prose dedication by Moffett in which "Diuæ Elizabethæ" has been changed to read "Diuo Iacobo" throughout.

Monacius, Janus Julius. Tres Excellente, & nouelle description contre la peste, & vn remede tres singulier, avec souueraine preseruation contre la contagion dicelle. Dedie A Tre-Illustre & Magnanime Princesse, Elizabeth Roine d'Angleterre. Par M. Ianus Jullius Monacius, Gentilhome Francois. . . . Premierement, Vn Poeme nouueau, fait sur l'Origine de la Roine, auec quelques autres euures Poetiques, tres magnifiques, faites a la gloire et louange d'icelle, par ledit Autheur. . . . [1560?]. The laudatory Latin dedication is on sigs. A2–A3ᵛ. Latin verses on sigs. A4–A8 contain interesting sea trope. Several French poems to "la rose et vray tronce de vertu magnifique" appear on sigs. B1–D4.

Morata, Olympia Fulvia. Olympiæ Fuluiæ Moratæ Foeminæ doctissimæ ac plane diuiniæ orationes, Dialogi, Epistolæ, Carmina, tam Latina quàm Græca: cum eruditorũ de ea testimonijs & laudibus. Hippolytæ Taurellæ elegia elegantissima. Ad sereniss. Angliæ reginam D. Elisabetam. . . . Basileæ M. D. LXII. The dedication (sigs. *2–*7), full of elaborate praise of Elizabeth's virtues, is signed by the editor of the learned Olympia's works, Cœlius Secundus Curio.

More, Sir George. A demonstration of God in his workes. . . . 1597. The dedication (sigs. A2–A4) expresses gratitude for the unequaled blessings of Elizabeth's reign. Striking tributes to the queen as miraculously preserved by God to be a "careful nurse of his church, and tender mother of his children," appear on sigs. B1ᵛ, B3–B4, C3, C4ᵛ–D1, O1–O3ᵛ, P4–P4ᵛ.

Morel, Jean. De ecclesia ab Antichristo per eius excidium liberanda, eaque ex Dei promissis beatissimè reparanda Tractatus: . . . Ad Serenissimam . . . Reginam: Nec non ad cæteros pios Reges, & Principes verè Christianos, quos Deus ab Antichristi servitute retraxit; de Sacrosancto Fœdere ex Dei mandato inter ipsos ineundo. . . . 1589. The dedication (sigs. ¶2–¶4ᵛ) lauds Elizabeth for her victories over all enemies through God's special guidance.

Morton, Thomas, *Bishop*. Salomon or a treatise declaring the state of the kingdome of Israel, as it was in the daies of Salomom. . . . 1596. The dedicatory material (sigs. A2–A2ᵛ) includes Latin verses lauding Elizabeth as a Solomon.

Motthe, Georges de la. Hymne. A tres-haute tres-puissante tres-vertueuse et tres-magnanime princesse, Elizabeth royne d'Angleterre, France, et Irelande. &c. Presentee a sa maiesté par . . . Georges de la Motthe, gentilhomme Francoys. 1586. Bodleian Library MS. Fr.e.1. This poem, presented to Elizabeth by a French refugee, is very richly decorated by him with miniature portraits of her, with birds, animals, flowers, emblematic devices, and the like. The dedication is on fols. 5–6ᵛ. On the verso of the portrait of Elizabeth (fol. 7), which I have reproduced as a frontispiece, is a French sonnet to her. The extravagant praise in the *Hymne* does not obscure the author's desire for patronage.

Mulcaster, Richard. Positions vvherin those primitiue circumstances be examined, which are necessarie for the training vp of children, . . . 1581. The dedication (sigs. *2–*4ᵛ) compliments Elizabeth's judgment for recognizing good and useful books. The epistle that dedicates Mulcaster's *The first part of the elementarie* (1582) to Leicester refers (sigs. *2–*2ᵛ) to this offering of his first work to the queen who rightly as "our parent" deserved it.

Munday, Anthony. A VVatch-vvoord to Englande To beware of traytours and tretcherous practises, which haue beene the ouerthrowe of many famous Kingdomes and common weales. . . . 1584. Latin verses to Elizabeth precede the dedication (sigs. *4–*4ᵛ). See above, p. 218.

Nazianzen, Gregory. [Gregorii Nazianzeni in Theophania siue de Natali Seruatoris oratio. Translated into Latin by (Sir) Anthony Cooke.] British Museum MS. Royal 5 E. XVII. The English dedication (fols. 1ᵛ–2ᵛ) to Elizabeth, to whom the work was offered as a new year's gift, is dated the "vijth of January 1560." Cooke suggests that the queen herself do Nazianzen "either in better latyne or goode Englishe, whiche if ye haue leysour none can doe better than yourselfe."

Nichols, John. Iohn Niccols Pilgrimage, whrein is displaied the liues of the proude Popes, ambitious Cardinals, lecherous Bishops, fat bellied Monkes, and hypocriticall Iesuites. . . . 1581. The dedication is on sigs. *2–*4.

—— The Oration and Sermon made at Rome, by commaundement of the foure Cardinalles, and the Dominican Inquisitour, vpon paine of death. By Iohn Nichols, latelie the Popes Scholler. . . . 1581. On the verso of the title-page are the queen's arms; thereafter (sigs. ¶2- ¶8ᵛ), an elaborate Latin dedication in which Elizabeth is a "florentissima Virgo," God's elect protector "veræ religionis."

Nichols, Philip, see Drake, Sir Francis.

Noot, Jan van der. Le theatre auquel sont exposés & monstrés les inconueniens & miseres qui suiuent les mondains & vicieux, ensemble les plaisirs & contentements dont les fideles ioüissent. . . . 1568. In the dedication (sigs. A4–A8ᵛ) a fugitive from the Low Countries lauds Elizabeth's godly and beneficent rule. An English translation of this work by T. Roest appeared in 1569.

Norden, John. A Chorographicall discription of the seuerall Shires and Islands of Middlesex. Essex. Surrey. Sussex. Hamshire Weighte Garnesey & Iarsey performed by the traueyle and uiew of Iohn Norden 1595. British Museum Additional MS. 31853. The dedication (fol. 2) is to the "MOST COMFORTABLE NVRSING MOTHER" of the "Israel of GOD IN THE BRITISH ISLES."

—— A Christian familiar comfort and incouragement vnto all English Subiects, not to dismaie at the Spanish threats. . . . With requisite praiers to almightie God for the preseruation of our Queene and Countrie. . . . 1596. The dedication is on sigs. A3–A3ᵛ. Praise of Elizabeth as led by God appears throughout the text.

Norden, John. A mirror for The Multitude, or glasse, Wherein maie be seene, the violence, the error, the weaknesse, and rash consent, of the multitude, and the daungerous resolution of such, as without regard for truth, endeuour to runne and ioyne themselues with the multitude: . . . 1586. Verses to Elizabeth are on the verso of the title-page beneath her arms. The dedication (sigs. *2–*3ᵛ) of this anti-papal work sees God as using Elizabeth to "cut off the aspiringe heade, and to breake the greedy iawes of that fierce *Holophernes* of Rome."

—— A progresse of Pietie. Or The harbour of Heauenly harts ease, to recreate the afflicted Soules of all such as are shut vp in anye inward or outward affliction. . . . 1596. The dedication (sigs. A3–A5ᵛ) is to a "most deare Queene, . . . [who] affordeth acceptance vnto the least showe of loyall loue." Throughout the text there are tributes to her, and prayers for her. On sigs. B3ᵛ–B4 twenty-eight verses laud her "most gracious gouernment."

—— Speculi Britaniæ pars The description of Hartfordshire, 1598. The formal printed dedication of this book is to Baron Beauchamp, Count of Hertford; but some manuscript verses in Norden's autograph opposite the title-page present the British Museum copy (G.3685) to Elizabeth, and plead for funds sorely needed for the completion of *Speculum Britanniæ*.

—— Speculum Britanniæ. The first parte An historicall, & chorographicall discription of Middlesex. . . . 1593. The dedication (sig. A2) anticipates the phrasing of that in Additional MS. 31853.

Ochino, Bernardino. Labyrinthi, hoc est, de libero aut seruo arbitrio, de diuina Prænotione, Destinatione, & Libertate Disputatio. . . . Basileæ . . . [n.d.]. The Latin dedication (sigs. A2–A2ᵛ) compliments the skill of the princess in discussing obscure points in the doctrine of predestination with the author ten years before he writes.

Ocland, Christopher. Anglorum prælia, Ab Anno Domini. 1327. Anno nimirùm primo inclytiss. Principis Eduardi eius nominis tertij, vsque ad annum Do. 1558. . . . 1580. For the dedication (sig. A2), see above, pp. 322–323.

Oxford Scholars. [Complimentary addresses to Elizabeth, in
Latin and Greek prose and verse, on her visit to Woodstock
and Oxford (1566), by members of the university.] British
Museum MS. Royal 12 A. XLVII. Prefatory verses and
decorative devices seem to constitute a presentation of this
manuscript (printed in Nichols, *The Progresses and Public
Processions of Queen Elizabeth*, 1788, I, under the year 1566).

Paget, Nicolaus (?). Breve Commentarium temporum sub
regno auspicatissimo Reginæ Elizabethæ omnibus numeris
beatissimæ & memoriæ perquam sacræ, [n.d.]. British Museum MS. Harleian 6353, fols. 177–194. This encomium on
Queen Elizabeth, which is addressed to her though dead, is
headed (fol. 178) "To the eternall honor of the Mirror of
Princes Queene Elizabeth of most famous Memorye." At the
head of the manuscript is a name, crossed out with a pen, and
now largely illegible. Nichols (*The Progresses, Processions, and
Magnificent Festivities of King James the First*, 1828, II,
213 n.) reads it as "Nicolaus Paget."

Palfreyman, Thomas. A myrrour or cleare glasse, for all estates,
to looke in, conteinyng briefly in it the true knovvlege and
loue of god, and the charitie of a faithfull christian tovvardes
his neyghbour. . . . M.D. LX. In the copy of this work in
the Cambridge University Library (Syn.8.56.40; the only
copy noted in the *Short-title Catalogue*) sigs. A2–A8 are missing, but on sig. B1 is a fragment of what the running title
indicates was a dedication "to the Quenes maiesty." Under
"Faultes escaped in pryntyng" at the end of the volume
(sig. Q5ᵛ) is the following note: "In the leaf of A. the. xii.
page, the xi. lyne, of the Queenes epistle, for into, reade vnto."

Parsons, Robert. A brief discours contayning certayne reasons
why Catholiques refuse to goe to Church. Written by a
learned and vertuous man, to a frend of his in England. And
Dedicated by I. H. to the Queenes most excellent Maiestie.
. . . Doway . . . 1580. "I. Howlet" (= Robert Parsons)
speaks for persecuted Catholics in his dedication (sigs. ‡2–
‡‡8ᵛ) by asking: "Whether then should children rōne in their
afflictions, but vnto the loue and tender care of their deare

mother, especiallye she being such a mother, as her power is sufficient to reléeue them in all poyntes, her good will testifyed by infinit benefites, and her noble and mercifull disposition knowen and renouned thorough out the world?" The dedicating of this work to the queen drew indignant protests from Protestants like Perceval Wilburn and William Fulke.

Paulet, William, *Marquis of Winchester*. The lord marques idlenes: Conteining manifold matters of acceptable deuise; as sage sentences, prudent precepts, morall examples, sweete similitudes, proper comparisons, and other remembrances of speciall choise. . . . 1586. Latin verses to Elizabeth are on the verso of the title-page beneath her arms, and precede the dedication (sigs. *3–A2).

Pembridge, Thomas. [Complimentary Latin verses to Elizabeth, n.d.] British Museum MS. Royal 12 A. XXXI. The verses, about two hundred and fifty elegiac couplets ending with a request for donations, are presented (fol. 1) "angliæ tutelæ ac spei vnicæ veræ ac Christianæ religionis nutrici."

Pena, Petrus, *and* L'Obel, Matthias de. Stirpium aduersaria noua, perfacilis vestigatio, suculentaque accessio ad Priscorum, prǫsertim dioscoridis & Recentiorum, Materiam Medicam. . . . 1570 [col. 1571]. The Latin dedication (sigs. A1–A2ᵛ) praises Elizabeth's peace.

Plato. Πλάτωνος ἄπαντα τὰ σωζόμενα. Platonis opera quæ extant omnia. Ex noua Ioannis Serrani interpretatione, . . . [Paris] . . . 1578. The elaborate Latin dedication of the first part (sigs. *2–*4), is signed by Joh. Serranus, the editor, and dated from Lausanne, "Anno vltimæ Dei patientiæ, M. D. LXXVII. CAL. OCTOBR." It lauds Elizabeth for her services to the surest philosophy, Christian truth, and to Frenchmen, the editor's countrymen.

Plutarch. [De capienda ex inimicis utilitate, translated into Latin by Johannes Rainoldus (probably the John Raynolds who was B. C. L. at Oxford in 1560), 1574.] British Museum MS. Royal 15 A. III. In the Latin prose dedication (fols. 1–7) Raynolds states that he had addressed verses to Elizabeth eight years before upon her visit to Oxford, and that gratitude

for the aid she then gave him evokes the presentation of his work. Latin and Greek epigrams lauding her are on fols. 7–8, one piece being praise of her name in its Hebrew meanings.

—— The Liues of Epaminondas, of Philip of Macedon, of Dionysius the elder, and of Octauius Cæsar Augustus: collected out of good authors. Also the liues of nine excellent chieftaines of warre, taken out of Latine from Emylius Probus by S. G. S. By whom also are added the liues of Plutarch and of Seneca: . . . And now translated into English by Sir Thomas North . . . 1602. This book, reissued in 1603 as the second part of the *Liues of the noble Grecians and Romanes*, is dedicated on sigs. a2–a2ᵛ.

—— The lives of the noble Grecians and Romanes, compared together by that graue learned philosopher and historiographer, Plutarke of Chæronea: translated out of Greeke into French by Iames Amyot . . . and out of French into Englishe, by Thomas North. . . . 1579. The dedication by Sir Thomas North (sigs. *2–*2ᵛ) declares that reading the lives of ancients who lived nobly for heathen princes cannot but kindle nobler service in the loyal subjects of a Christian princess.

—— Three moral treatises, no lesse pleasant than necessarie for all men to reade, VVhereof the first is called, The Learned Prince: The second, The Fruites of Foes: The third, The Port of Rest. Set foorth by Tho. Blundeuille . . . 1580. Verses (sig. A2) dedicate the first treatise "To the Queenes Highnes." A Shakespearean sonnet (sig. B5ᵛ) dedicates the second treatise to her; the third is addressed to "Iohn Asteley" and "Iohn Harington." "The Learned Prince" is probably identical with British Museum MS. Royal 18 A. XLIII.

Puttenham, George. The arte of English poesie. . . . 1589. This work, the authorship of which has been in dispute, is attributed to George Puttenham by its latest editors (Gladys D. Willcock and Alice Walker, Cambridge, 1936). It carries a woodcut portrait of Elizabeth which, as these editors (in a note opposite p. 1) observe, "from its original position (facing the opening of Book I), seems to have constituted Puttenham's dedication to the *Arte*." The woodcut breaks the fol-

lowing phrase: "*A colei Che se stessa rassomiglia & non altrui.*"
See above, p. 262. In the *Arte* (ed. Willcock and Walker,
p. 237) the author speaks of "an hympne written by vs to the
Queenes Maiestie entitled (*Minerua*)."

Puttenham, George. Partheniades. Printed from British Museum
MS. Cotton Vesp. E. viii in *Ballads from Manuscripts*, ed.
F. J. Furnivall and W. R. Morfill, II [1873], 72–91. The opening poem of the collection lauding Elizabeth is headed: "The
principall addresse in nature of a New yeares gifte"; and the
editors think that the work was "probably presented to the
Queen on New Year's Day, 1579."

Reniger, Michel. De Pii quinti et Gregorii decimi tertii Roman-
orum pontificum furoribus. Contra potentissimam principem
Elizabetham. . . . 1582. The controversial dedication occupies sigs. ¶2–¶¶¶6ᵛ.

—— A Treatise conteining two parts. 1 An Exhortation to
true loue, loyaltie, and fidelitie to her Maiestie. 2 A Treatise
against Treasons, Rebellions, and such disloyalties . . . 1587.
The dedication (sigs. A2–A2ᵛ) is not especially notable, but
several passages in the text are. After an account of the wild
rejoicings for Elizabeth's preservation, the author (sig. A5ᵛ)
declares: "But one thing passeth all that wee haue seene: the
louing affections of faithful subiectes to her Maiestie, which
as a fier burned inwardly in their heartes and bowels, as
outwardlie the fiers did in the streetes. And these in true
valewe and estimation passe all triumphes." Again (sig. T2):
"Touching her compassion to her poore people, she hath
heard their cry, and her motherly heart hath melted with
compassion ouer them," and "she traueyleth in continuall
daungers for vs."

Rich, Barnaby. A path-way to Military practise. . . . 1587.
The dedication (sigs. A2–A3ᵛ) refers to "*manie gratious
wordes for other of his writinges*" and thanks God for the many
blessings of Elizabeth's peaceful government.

Ripley, George. The compound of alchymy. . . . First written
by . . . George Ripley . . . & Dedicated to K. Eduuard the
4. . . . Set Foorth by Raph Rabbards . . . 1591. The dedi-

cation (sigs. A2-A4^v) declares that God's care has caused Elizabeth to flourish "*mauger the Diuell, the Pope, & the King of Spaine.*"

Robinson, Richard, *citizen of London*. [Eupolemia, Archippus, and Panoplia.] British Museum MS. Royal 18 A. LXVI. This curious medley, although addressed to James I, was originally begun in 1602 for Elizabeth. A "Carmen dedicatorium" to her is on fols. 3–3^v. (Professor C. B. Millican [*Spenser and the Table Round*, Cambridge, Mass., 1932, p. 61] has presented Robinson's *The auncient Order* [1583; "*Translated and Collected*" by Robinson] as dedicated to Elizabeth; but I should not take as a dedication a few verses praising Elizabeth [sig. B1] which he reproduces as "showing the Dedication to Elizabeth" inasmuch as sigs. *₊*1–*₊*3 of the volume are occupied by "The Epistle Dedicatory" [so designated in its running title] addressed to "*M. Thomas Smith* Esquier.")

Rogers, Thomas. A Golden Chaine, taken out of the rich Treasurehouse the Psalmes of King Dauid: also, The pretious Pearles of King Salomon; . . . 1579. The dedication (sigs. A2–A6) is to Elizabeth as the parent of her people. Her deeds resemble those of great Biblical kings.

Rushe, Anthony. A president for a Prince. Wherein is to be seene by the testimonie of auncient Writers, the duetie of Kings, Princes, and Gouernours. Collected and gathered by Anthonie Russhe, . . . 1566. The dedication (sigs. A1–B2^v) exhorts Elizabeth to emulate Biblical heroes and famed ancients, to be "cleaped a Mother of Religion, . . . a Nursse of Gods territorie and Church" that she may be "renowmed and accompted of vs your most louing and obedient children, our Mother the Queene."

Salterne, George. Tomumbeius siue Sultanici in Ægypto Imperij Euersio Tragœdia noua Sultanici . . . [not later than 1603]. Bodleian Library MS. Rawlinson Poet. 75. This manuscript play is dedicated (fol. 3) in Latin verses. See above, p. 106.

Saluste du Bartas, Guillaume de. Guilielmi Salustii Bartassii Hebdomas a Gabriele Lermæo latinitate donata. Ad serenissimam, atque illustrissimam Elizabetham, . . . 1591. The complimentary dedication is on sigs. A2–A4ᵛ.

Sandford, James. Certayne poemes dedicated to the Queenes moste excellent Maiestie, at the end of Sandford's translation from Ludovico Guicciardini, *Houres of recreation,* . . . 1576. The dedication is on sigs. Q1–Q2. The poems, in Latin, Greek, Italian, French, and English, are very laudatory. *Houres of recreation* is dedicated (sigs. A2–A8) to Sir Christopher Hatton. The dedication is a good example of dedications which, though not addressed to Elizabeth, yet render her striking homage. In an impressive tribute Sandford writes of a "peerelesse virgin" that lives and reigns "in greate quietnesse," and preserves "a greate multitude, as Christe saued all by his death and passion." See above, p. 325.

Sansovino, Francesco. Cento nouelle scelte da i piu nobili scrittori, . . . Venetia . . . M D LXI. The very laudatory dedication (sigs. *2–*3ᵛ) is dated "Di Venetia alli XXVI. di Settembre. MDLX."

Savile, Sir Henry. Rerum Anglicarum scriptores post Bedam praecipui, ex vetustissimis codicibus manuscriptis nunc primum in lucem editi. . . . CIↃ IↃ XCVI. The Latin dedication (sigs. ¶2–¶2ᵛ) pays tribute to Elizabeth's peace.

Segar, William. Honor Military, and Ciuill, contained in foure Bookes. . . . 1602. For the dedication (sig. *2), see above, pp. 175–176.

Seneca, Lucius Annæus. The sixt tragedie of . . . Seneca, entituled Troas, . . . Newly set forth in Englishe by Iasper Heywood . . . 1559. For a quotation from the dedication (sigs. A2–A3), see above, p. 123.

Shute, John. The first and chief groundes of architecture vsed in all the auncient and famous monymentes: . . . 1563. Shute dedicates his book (sig. A2) to his "*soueraigne lady (the perfect & natural head next vnto God of this our common weale,)*" encouraged by her "*delight in all kynd of good learning, and parfect skill in the tonges and sciences.*"

Smyth, William. Gemma fabri: Qua sacri Biblij margaritæ, non sigillatim, sed summatim fere omnes continentur, . . . 1598. This book, issued without Smyth's name, is dedicated (sig. A3–A3ᵛ) to Elizabeth as the nurse of the church.

Spenser, Edmund. The faerie queene. . . . 1590. For the dedication of the 1596 edition (sig. A1ᵛ), see above, p. 331.

Stafford, William. A compendious or briefe examination of certayne ordinary complaints, of diuers of our country men in these our dayes: . . . 1581. The dedication (sigs. **2–**2ᵛ) gratefully acknowledges the queen's pardon for some "vndutifull misdemeanour," and seeks to put under her protection a discussion of various industrial problems and abuses.

Strigelius, Victorinus. A third proceeding in the harmonie of King Dauids harp . . . Done in Latine by the learned Reuerend Doctor Victorinus Strigelius, . . . 1562. Translated into English by Richard Robinson . . . 1595. Latin verses on the verso of the title-page appear beneath the queen's arms, and Robinson's dedication (sigs. A3–A4) lauds Elizabeth as the "elect nursing Mother of Gods Israel." For Robinson's account of his unrewarded presentation of this work, see G. M. Vogt, "Richard Robinson's *Eupolemia*" (*Studies in Philology*, XXI [1924], 629-648). Elizabeth had her needy soldiers to look to, as she said. She could not give cash to every literary man who dedicated to her.

Sturm, John. Libri duo Ioannis Sturmii de periodis vnus. . . . Argentorati . . . M. D. L. Sturm addresses his book (sigs. A2–A3ᵛ) to the princess because his friend Ascham testifies to her great worth as a student.

Tacitus, Publius Cornelius. The ende of Nero and beginning of Galba. Fower bookes of the histories of Cornelius Tacitus. The life of Agricola. M. D. LXXXXI. The translator, Sir Henry Savile, signs the dedication (sigs. ¶2–¶2ᵛ). He declares the principal cause of his translating is to "*incite your Maiesty by this as by a foile to communicate to the world, if not those admirable cõpositions of your owne, yet at the least those most rare and excellent translations of Histories*" which Elizabeth has made.

Tallis, Thomas, *and* Byrd, William. Discantus cantiones, quae ab argumento sacrae vocantur, quinque et sex partium, . . . Serenissimæ Regineæ Maiestati à priuato Sacello gererosis, & Organistis. . . . 1575. Latin verses on the verso of the title-page and the dedication (sig. A2) testify to Elizabeth's patronage of music.

Tanner, Robert. A briefe Treatise for the ready vse of the Sphere: Lately made and finished in most ample large manner. . . . 1592. The dedication (sigs. ∴3–∴7) shows an humble subject's admiration for a queen whose knowledge and catholic taste make her appreciate any work offered her.

Tasso, Torquato. Godfrey of Bulloigne, or The Recouerie of Ierusalem. Done into English Heroicall verse, by Edward Fairefax . . . 1600. For a quotation from Fairfax's dedication in four six-line stanzas (sig. A2), see above, p. 359.

—— Scipii Gentilis Solymeidos libri duo priores de Torquati Tassi Italicis expressi. . . . 1584. The copies of this work which are in the Cambridge University Library and the John Rylands Library are dedicated (sigs. *1–*2) to Elizabeth, but the British Museum copy (11403.bb.32[5]) lacks the dedication to her.

—— Torquati Tassi Solymeidos, liber primus Latinis numeris expressus . . . a Scipio Gentili . . . 1584. The dedication lauding Elizabeth in Latin verses is on sigs. A2–A2ᵛ.

Tedder, William. The Recantations as they were seuerallie pronounced by VVylliam Tedder and Anthony Tyrrell: (sometime two Seminarie Priests of the English Colledge in Rome, and nowe by the great mercie of almightie God conuerted, vnto the profession of the Gospell of Iesus Christ) at Paules Crosse, . . . VVith an Epistle dedicatorie vnto her Maiestie, . . . M. D. LXXXVIII. On the verso of the title-page is an engraving of Elizabeth with six Latin verses to her beneath it. The book is dedicated (sigs. *2–*2ᵛ) as a new year's gift—"*the first fruites of our repentaunce.*"

Teshe, William. A booke contaning [*sic*] diuers sortes of hands, . . . Set forthe by Wyllyam Teshe of the Citye of yorke gentleman . . . 1580. British Museum MS. Sloane 1832. The dedication is on fol. 2; on fols. 7ᵛ–8 is a colored drawing of Elizabeth in a triumphal carriage with Fame announcing her and Teshe kneeling and presenting his book.

Tilney, Edmund. A brief and pleasaunt discourse of duties in Mariage, called the Flower of Friendshippe. . . . 1568. The dedication (sigs. A2–A3) associates the queen with various virtues.

Tolmer, Joannes. Naumachiæ, seu naualia prælia, inter omnium, quotquot vnquam fuere, potentissimas Classes, Hispanicam, & Anglicanam, anno 1588, Iulio, Augusto, & Semptembri mensibus, diuersis diebus, & locis inita, auspiciis augustissimæ Anglorum reginæ Elisabethæ, contra potentissimum Hispaniarum Regem Philippum. . . . Neapoli . . . M. D. LXXXIIX. The dedication (sig. A2) of this extended Latin poem is in highly complimentary verse.

Tooker, William. Charisma siue donum sanationis. . . . 1597. The dedication (sigs. *2–¶3ᵛ) celebrates the healing power of the queen's royal hands; see above, p. 217.

Turner, William. The first and seconde partes of the Herbal of William Turner Doctor in Phisick lately ouersene, corrected and enlarged . . . M. D. LXVIII. The dedication (sigs. *2–*3ᵛ) lauds Elizabeth's skill in Latin and other languages.

Twist, Robert. In Auspicatissimum diem Augustissimæ, Serenissimæ, & potentissimæ Principis, Diuæ Elizabethæ, . . . Carmina . . . conscripta 1597. British Museum MS. Royal 12 A. VIII. These Accession Day verses in Latin and Greek by an alumnus of Westminster School conclude (fol. 12ᵛ) with a request that the queen receive them, however humble their quality.

Ubaldini, Petruccio. Militia del Gran Duca Thoscana. . . . 1597. Ubaldini, an Italian illuminator and scholar who had served Tudor sovereigns as early as 1545, dedicates (sigs. A2–A4) to the last of them this work on the military system of Tuscany.

—— [La vera forma e regola dell' eleggere e coronare in imperadori.] British Museum MS. Royal 14 A. VIII. The work, dedicated (fols. 1–2) to Elizabeth as a new year's gift, is dated "di Corte," January 1, 1564.

Ubaldini, Petruccio. Le vite delle donne illustri del regno d' Inghilterra, & del Regno di Scotia, . . . 1591. The dedication (sigs. ¶2–¶4ᵛ) pays high compliment to the most illustrious lady of England.

—— [Le Vite e i Fatti di sei Donne Illustri.] British Museum MS. Royal 14 A. XIX. This work is dedicated (fols. 2–2ᵛ) as a new year's gift, 1577.

Vennar, Richard. The right way to heaven: And the true testimonie of a faithfull and loyall subiect: . . . 1601. The dedication (sig. A1) offers the queen "this little handfull of my hart's labour," which contains much laudatory verse to her.

Vermigli, Pietro Martire. The Common Places of the most famous and renowmed Diuine Doctor Peter Martyr, diuided into foure principall parts . . . Translated and partlie gathered by Anthonie Marten, one of the Sewers of hir Maiesties most Honourable Chamber. . . . 1583. The translator in his dedication (sigs. a3–a5ᵛ) blesses the day when Elizabeth, peer of great Biblical heroes, came to restore the decayed church and cleanse it of foul poperie.

Veron, Jean. A fruteful treatise of predestination and of the diuine prouidence of god, with an apology of the same, against the swynyshe gruntinge of the Epicures and Atheystes of oure time. . . . [1561]. The dedication (sigs. ❡ 2–❡ 8ᵛ) is to the "supreme gouernor of this realme, aswel in causes Ecclesiastical, as temporal."

Villiers, Ubert Philippe de. Hymnes de la Deîté du Pére du Filz, et du Saint Esprit dediées a tres vertueuse et tres inuincible royne Elizabeth royne d'Angleterre de France & d'Yrlande. British Museum MS. Royal 19 B. II. The author, secretary to the Prince of Condé, dates his dedication (fols. 2–3) "De LONDRES, ce premier d'Octobre *1568*."

Wateson, George. The cures of the Diseased, in remote Regions. Preventing mortalitie, incident in Forraine Attempts, of the English Nation. . . . 1598. In the dedication (sigs. A3–A3ᵛ) the author, cured of *"the* Tabardilla *Pestilence"* when a prisoner in Spain, offers his remedy to his queen and her people.

Webbe, Edward. The Rare and most wonderfull things which Edw. Webbe an Englishman borne, hath seene and passed in his troublesome trauailes, in the Cities of Ierusalem, Damasko, Bethlehem and Galely: and in the landes of Iewrie, Egypt, Grecia, Russia, and Prester Iohn. . . . 1590. After the dedication (sigs. A2–A2ᵛ) there are (sig. A3ᵛ) "Verses written vpon the Alphabet of the Queenes Maiesties name," which rejoice in God's guidance for "*our strength and stay.*"

Weever, John. An Agnus Dei. . . . 1601. This miniature book, a survey of the birth, life, and death of Christ, is dedicated (sig. A2) "*To Her High Maiestie.*"

Westminster Scholars. Ad Augustissimam, Serenissimam & potentissimam Diuam Elizabetham . . . Carmina ab eius Scholæ Westmonasteriensis alumnis Maiestati eius deuotissimis conscripta 1597. British Museum MS. Royal 12 A. XLI. Twenty-one Westminster boys strike familiar themes in these complimentary verses.

Whetstone, George. The English Myrror. . . . 1586. The dedication (sigs. ¶2–¶2ᵛ) follows laudatory acrostic verses on the verso of the title-page. See above, pp. 321–322.

Willet, Andrew. Synopsis papismi, that is, a generall viewe of papistry: wherein the whole mysterie of iniquitie, and summe of Antichristian doctrine is set downe, which is maintained this day by the Synagogue of Rome, against the Church of Christ, . . . Collected by Andrew Willet . . . 1592. The dedication (sigs. A2–A3ᵛ) is to Elizabeth as "the mother of Israel, a nurse to the people of God," who has "bene wont to accept with great fauour and regard, the meanest gifts of your subiects, yea hath not refused to receiue posies and nosegaies at their hands."

William of Newburgh. Rerum Anglicarum libri quinque, Recens ceu è tenebris eruti, & in studiosorum gratiam in lucem dati: . . . Antuerpiæ, . . . M. D. LXVII. Gulielmus Silvius signs the laudatory dedication (sigs. A2–A3) and dates it "Antuerpiæ IIII. Idus Mart. M. D. LXVII."

Wollaye, Edward. An admonysyone to evarye degrye, showing the right waye to joye and parfyte reste . . . [n.d.]. British

Museum MS. Royal 17. A. XIX. This series of poems on the duties of all classes of society, with warnings to evil-doers, is preceded by a "Preface to the queene" (fols. 3^v–9^v), and a "Memoryall to the queene" (fols. 11–16^v) in four-verse stanzas. A few verses presenting the manuscript are on fol. 1^v.

Wykehamists. [Carmina Scholæ Wichamicæ ad Elisabetham reginam, *ca.* 1573.] Bodleian MS. Rawlinson poet. 187. These forty-eight poems, all in Latin except three in Greek, are inscribed (fol. 4): "Serenissimæ atq illustrissimæ principi Elizabethæ Angliæ Franciæ & Hyberniæ reginæ Scholares Wichamici."

INDEX

INDEX